Introduction To COMPUTER SCIENCE

RAMON A. MATA-TOLEDO, Ph.D.

Associate Professor of Computer Science
James Madison University

PAULINE K. CUSHMAN

Associate Professor of Integrated Science and Technology and Computer Science
James Madison University

Schaum's Outline Series

McGRAW-HILL

New York San Francisco Washington, D.C. Auckland Bogotá Caracas
Lisbon London Madrid Mexico City Milan Montreal New Delhi
San Juan Singapore Sydney Tokyo Toronto

Dr. RAMON A. MATA-TOLEDO is a tenured Associate Professor of Computer Science at James Madison University. He holds a Ph.D. from Kansas State University in Computer Science. He earned his M.S. and M.B.A. from the Florida Institute of Technology. His bachelor degree with a double major in Mathematics and Physics is from the Instituto Pedagogico de Caracas (Venezuela). Dr. Mata-Toledo's main areas of interest are databases, natural language processing, and applied mathematics. He is the author of numerous papers in professional magazines, national and international congresses. He is also a coauthor of *Schaum's Outline of Basic Mathematics with Applications to Science and Technology.* Dr. Mata-Toledo can be reached at mata1ra@jmu.edu

Dr. PAULINE K. CUSHMAN is an Assistant Professor of Integrated Science and Technology and Computer Science at James Madison University. She holds a Ph.D. from the University of Louisville in Computer Science and Engineering. She earned an M.A. in Reading Education from West Virginia University and an M.S. in Information Systems from the West Virginia College of Graduate Studies. Her bachelor degree with a major in Elementary Education is from Davis and Elkins College. Dr. Cushman's main areas of interest are intelligent systems, multimedia, and web design. Dr. Cushman can be reached at cushmapk@jmu.edu

Schaum's Outline of Theory and Problems of
INTRODUCTION TO COMPUTER SCIENCE

2 3 4 5 6 7 8 9 10 11 12 13 14 15 16 PRS PRS 9 0 9 8 7 6 5 4 3 2

ISBN 0-07-134554-X

Sponsoring Editor: Barbara Gilson
Production Supervisor: Tina Cameron
Editing Liaison: Maureen B. Walker
Project Supervision: Keyword Publishing Services

Library of Congress Cataloging-in-Publication Data

McGraw-Hill

A Division of The ***McGraw-Hill*** *Companies*

DEDICATION

Dedicated to my wife Anahis for a wonderful marriage and her continuous love and encouragement throughout the years. To my children Harold, Lys, and Hayley for the inspiration they provide. To Mami Nina and Lis Violeta for their prayers, love, and constant dedication. Two women without whom my world would have beeen totally different. Finally I thank my Lord and Savior, the salvation of Israel, for His blessing and unfailing love.

RAMT

Dedicated to my husband Jim for his love and support, to my children, Chuck, Jeni, and Cindy, for their friendship, and to all my students throughout the years who have prodded me to explain programming concepts using the simplest terms possible.

PKC

PREFACE

This book was written for those individuals who want a general introduction to computer science concepts and a clear understanding of the applicability of these concepts in different languages. The purpose of this book is to present the material without extensively examining the complexities of any particular language. Our examples make use of Visual Basic, C, C++, and Java constructs. By exposing the reader to these languages, we hope that, in spite of their diversity of implementation, the reader will capture the uniformity of the basic computer science concepts.

The material has been divided into nine chapters, which cover basic programming concepts and provide students with pertinent definitions and principles as they are applied in computer science. The examples and solved problems allow the students to apply their knowledge and amplify the theory, as well as provide the repetition of basic principles so vital to effective learning. Students are encouraged to try the examples and do the programming activities in the appropriate environments.

We would like to thank the staff of the Schaum's Outline Series, and our many friends and colleagues, who have encouraged us to pursue this endeavor. If the readers enjoy this book and find it helpful in increasing their computer expertise, we will feel richly rewarded.

RAMON A. MATA-TOLEDO
PAULINE K. CUSHMAN

CONTENTS

CHAPTER 1 **Basic Concepts of Computers** 1

1.1 Computer Structures 1
1.2 Bus Structure 5
1.3 Basic Operation of the Computer 5
1.4 Representation of Data in Memory 7
1.5 Conversion Between the Binary, Octal, and Hexadecimal Systems 10
1.6 Rules for Forming Numbers in Any System 12
1.7 Arithmetic Operations in the Binary, Octal, and Hexadecimal Systems 13
1.8 Representing Numbers in a Computer 17

CHAPTER 2 **Program Planning and Design** 46

2.1 Programming 46
2.2 Problem Solving 46
2.3 Algorithms 47

CHAPTER 3 **Program Coding and Simple Input/Output** 63

3.1 Programming Languages 63
3.2 Variables and Constants 65
3.3 Assignment Statements 67
3.4 Arithmetic Expressions and Operator Precedence 68
3.5 Comment Statements 70
3.6 Simple Input/Output 70
3.7 Writing a Complete Program 79

CHAPTER 4 **Control Structures and Program Writing** 89

4.1 Boolean Expressions 89
4.2 Control Structures—Definitions 94
4.3 Selection 94
4.4 Repetition 100

CHAPTER 5 **Functions and Subroutines** 117

5.1 Functions 117
5.2 Subroutines 122
5.3 Scope and Lifetime of Identifiers 123
5.4 Parameter-Passing Mechanisms 129

CHAPTER 6 **Arrays and Strings** **155**

6.1 Introduction to Arrays 155
6.2 Arrays in Visual Basic 158
6.3 Arrays in C/C++ and Java 162
6.4 Searching 171
6.5 Sorting 174

CHAPTER 7 **Data Files** **193**

7.1 Introduction 193
7.2 Data Terminology 194
7.3 File Organization 195
7.4 Text and Binary Files 195
7.5 Opening and Closing Files 195

CHAPTER 8 **Object-Oriented Programming** **228**

8.1 Introduction to Object-Oriented Programming 228
8.2 Inheritance and Data Abstraction 231
8.3 Advantages of Object-Oriented Programming 231
8.4 Object-Oriented Environment in Visual Basic 232
8.5 Classes and Inheritance in C++ 233
8.6 Classes and Inheritance in Java 240

CHAPTER 9 **Data Structures** **261**

9.1 Introduction to Data Structures 261
9.2 Linked Lists 261
9.3 Stacks 271
9.4 Queues 274

Appendix A **The Translation Process** **290**

Index **295**

Basic Concepts of Computers

A **computer** is a device which, under the direction of a program, can process data, alter its own program instructions, and perform computations and logical operations without human intervention. The term **program** refers to a specific set of instructions given to the computer to accomplish a specific task. A **programmer** is a person or group of persons who write instructions to the computer. Programs, in general, are referred to as "***software***."

A computer can be considered at two different levels: its architecture and its implementation. The architecture consists of the user-visible interface as seen by the programmer. That is, the structure and operation of the computer from the programmer's point of view. The implementation of the computer is the construction of that interface using specific hardware (and possible software components). In this book we will refer to computer components such as monitors, printers, keyboards, and some other of its electronics as "***hardware***."

1.1 COMPUTER STRUCTURES

Most computer systems generally consist of three basic structures or subsystems: the high-speed memory unit, the central processing unit, and the peripheral devices that comprise the I/O subsystem (see Fig. 1-1).

1.1.1 The Memory Unit

The memory unit of the computer, also called **main memory** or **physical memory**, stores all the instructions and data that the central processing unit can directly access and execute. The memory of the majority of computers consists of chips made of metal oxide on silicon. This type of memory is also called ***Random Access Memory*** or RAM.

The memory of the computer is generally divided into logical units of the same size. The most common unit is called a ***byte***. Each byte is made up of 8 consecutive ***bits*** or ***binary digits*** (see Fig. 1-2). Each individual bit can be magnetized to one of two different states, hence the name of binary. One state is said to represent 1; the other represents 0. Sometimes, these two states are referred to as "On" and "Off" respectively.

Each byte has associated with it a unique address. According to the convention used, addresses can increase from right to left or left to right (see Fig. 1-3). In this book we will assume that addresses

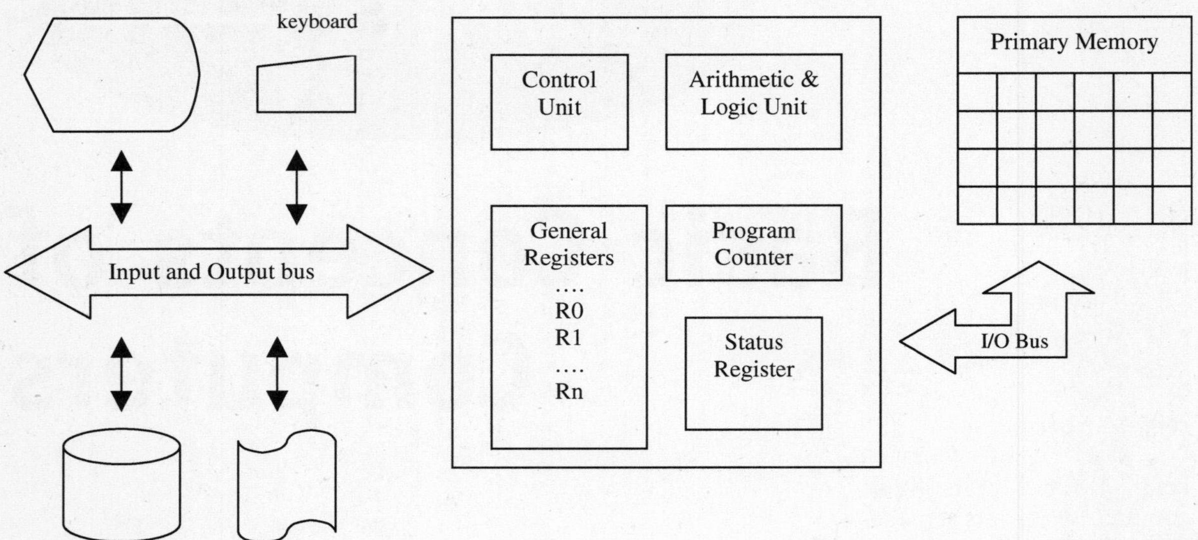

Fig. 1-1 Basic computer structure.

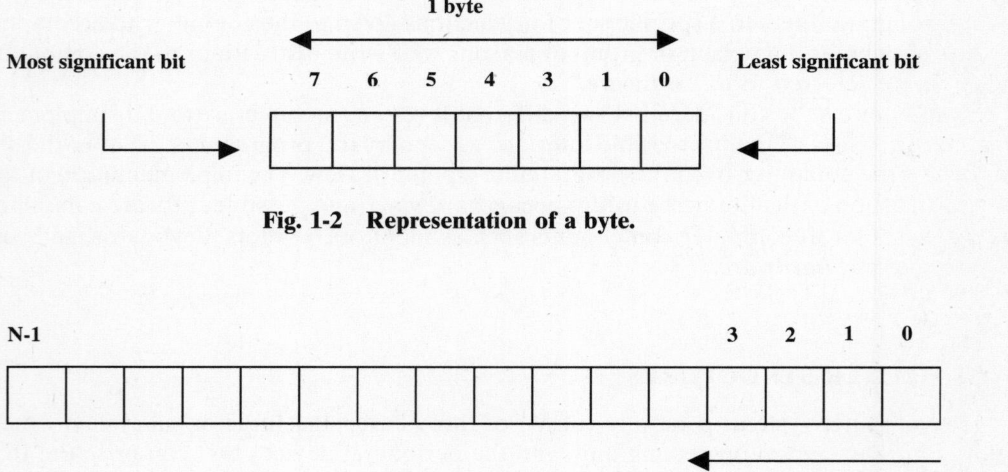

Fig. 1-2 Representation of a byte.

Fig. 1-3 Increasing addresses.

increase from right to left unless we specify otherwise. The ***address space*** is the set of all unique addresses that a program can reference. The number of bits used to represent an address determines the size of the address space. The size of this space can be calculated by 2^N where N is the number of bits used to represent the address. It is important to observe that there is a difference between the address of a memory unit and the content of that unit. The address of a byte is fixed whereas its content may vary.

Bytes are also grouped into larger units. Depending on the convention used by the manufacturers, these larger units can be called by different names. Table 1-1 shows the common names of some of the smaller and larger units.

Table 1-1

1 nibble	4 consecutive bits
1 byte	8 consecutive bits
1 word	2 consecutive bytes
1 longword	4 consecutive bytes
1 quadword	8 consecutive bytes
1 octaword	16 consecutive bytes

As shown in Fig. 1-2, the bits of a byte are generally numbered from right to left beginning with 0. The rightmost bit is called the ***least significant bit*** (lsb). Likewise, the leftmost bit is called the ***most significant bit*** (msb).

Since each bit of a byte can only store one of two values, either a zero or one, there are 2^8 different configurations of bits within a byte. Each combination represents a unique value. The value that each combination of bits represents in a byte depends on the convention used to interpret these values (see Example 1.5). Assuming that the bits are unsigned, the decimal value represented by the bits of a byte can be calculated as follows:

(1) Number the bits beginning on the rightmost bit position using superscripts. The superscript of the rightmost position is zero. The superscript of the next bit to its left is 1, the superscript of the next bit to the left is two and so on.
(2) Use each superscript as the exponent of a power of 2.
(3) Multiply the value of each bit by its corresponding power of 2.
(4) Add the products obtained in the previous step.

EXAMPLE 1.1 What is the decimal value of the unsigned binary configuration 11001101?

(1) Number the bits beginning on the rightmost bit position using superscripts as shown below.

$$1^7 1^6 0^5 0^4 1^3 1^2 0^1 1^0$$

(2) Use each superscript as the exponent of a power of 2.

$$(1*2^7) + (1*2^6) + (0*2^5) + (0*2^4) + (1*2^3) + (1*2^2) + (0*2^1) + (1*2^0)$$

(3) Multiply the value of each bit by its corresponding power and add the results

$$(1*128) + (1*64) + (0*32) + (0*16) + (1*8) + (1*4) + (0*2) + (1*1) = 205$$

Therefore, the decimal value of the unsigned binary configuration 11001101 is 205. Remember that 2^0, by definition, is equal to 1. Another method to calculate the value of an unsigned binary number is explained in solved problem 1.19.

The size of the memory of a computer, as indicated before, is measured in bytes. However, the size of the memory is generally expressed in larger units. One of the most common units is the Kilobyte or Kbyte or simply K. In computer lingo, 1 K is equal to 1024 bytes. Whenever a rough approximation is required, 1K can be considered as being equivalent to 1000 bytes. Table 1-2 shows some of the other units currently used to measure primary memory. As of the writing of this book, the Megabyte or MB ($\approx 10^6$ bytes) is the most commonly used unit to express the size of the primary memory; however, it is expected that some of the larger units will be used more frequently in the near future. The symbol $\approx$ should be read as "approximately equal to."

Table 1-2

1 Kilobyte	=1024 bytes
1 Megabyte	$\approx 10^6$ bytes
1 Gigabyte	$\approx 10^9$ bytes
1 Terabyte	$\approx 10^{12}$ bytes
1 Petabyte	$\approx 10^{15}$ bytes
1 Exabyte	$\approx 10^{18}$ bytes

EXAMPLE 1.2 A computer is advertised as having a primary memory of 32 Megabytes or "Megs." What is the true size of the memory in bytes?

$$32 \text{ Mbytes} = 32{*}10^3 \text{ Kbytes} = 32{*}10^3{*}1024 \text{ bytes} = 32{,}768{,}000 \text{ bytes}$$

1.1.2 The Central Processing Unit

The ***Central Processing Unit*** (CPU) or processor is the "brain of the computer." It is in the CPU where most of the activity that occurs inside the computer takes place. The CPU is generally subdivided into two basic subunits: the ***Arithmetic-Logic Unit*** (ALU), and the ***Control Unit*** (CU).

The main activity of the CPU consists of retrieving (fetching) instructions from memory and executing these instructions. As the instructions are fetched from memory they are decoded. Decoding an instruction means interpreting what the instruction is all about and what are its operands, if any. Executing means doing what the instruction is meant to do.

The ALU or the Arithmetic-Logic Unit of the CPU, as its name implies, is where the arithmetic operations (addition, subtraction, etc.) are performed. Similarly, other operations such as the comparison of two numbers are also carried out in the ALU. Internal to the CPU there are a number of "general" registers that provide local, high-speed storage for the processor. Consider a typical situation where two numbers located in main memory are to be added. This operation may be executed as follows: first, the numbers, located in main memory, are fetched into the internal registers of the ALU where the addition is carried out. The sum, if necessary, may be stored back into some particular memory location.

In addition to these high-speed internal registers, the CPU contains one or more "status registers" that provide information about the state of the processor, the instruction being processed, any other special condition that may have occurred, and the actions that need to be taken to handle these special conditions.

The Control Unit in the CPU manages the movement of data within the processor. For example, to add the numbers of the previous example, the operands had to be moved from memory to the ALU. It is the responsibility of the control unit to manage this movement of data. If the result of the addition is to be stored back in memory the control unit will manage this task too. Incorporated within the control unit is a decoder which determines the operation that the computer needs to carry out.

1.1.3 The Input and Output Unit

Computers accept information via input devices. Input devices are employed by the user to send information to the computer. Two of the most common input devices are the keyboard and the mouse. Output devices are used to send information to the user. The most common output devices are the monitor and the printer. Other devices such as some of the external storage units (hard disks, tapes, jazz or zip drives) may serve a dual purpose. Input and output are among the most complex operations carried out by the CPU. Details about the physical characteristics of the I/O devices and the data format that they require are handled by system programs that are invisible to the user. A discussion of the issues involved in I/O processing is beyond the scope of this book.

1.2 BUS STRUCTURE

To transfer data within its different components the computer uses a collection of wires called a **bus**. A computer system typically has three such buses: the address bus, the data bus, and the control bus. The data bus is used for transmission of data. A data bus must have as many wires as there are bits in the memory unit selected for a particular computer. To access data in memory it is necessary to issue an address to indicate its location. The CPU sends address bits to memory via the address bus.

Figure 1-4 shows a two-bus structure computer. The CPU interacts with memory via the memory bus. Input and Output functions are conducted via the I/O bus. Other configurations are also used. Figure 1-5 shows a single-bus structure used in some small computers.

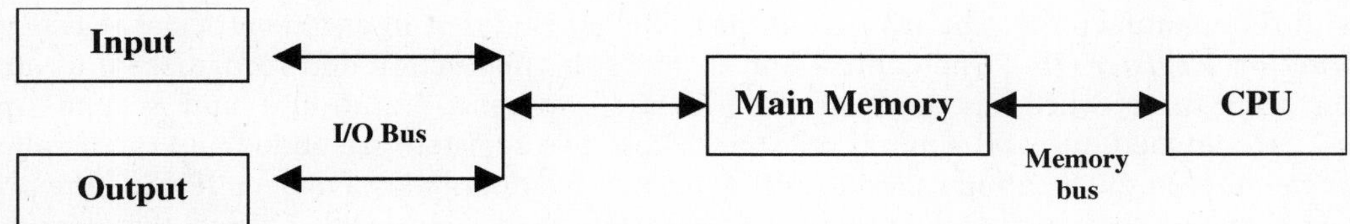

Fig. 1-4 A two-bus structure.

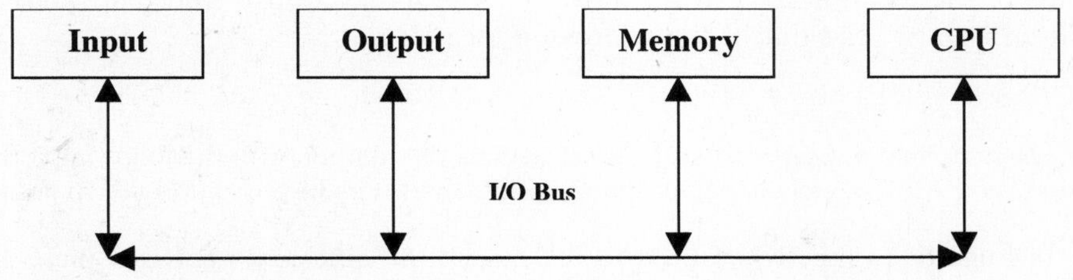

Fig. 1-5 Single bus structure.

EXAMPLE 1.3 Assuming that the basic unit of a computer is a word, how many bits can be transferred by the data bus at any one time?

The answer depends on the number of bits that are in a word. Using Table1-1 the number of bits that needs to be transferred is at least 16 bits. We say at least since some additional control information may be carried on the data bus.

1.3 BASIC OPERATION OF THE COMPUTER

As previously indicated, the operation of the computer is controlled by the instructions of a program. The CPU fetches the individual instructions directly from memory before executing them; however, before executing the instructions, how does the computer know what each instruction means? The answer to this question is easy. The computer decodes each instruction according to a predefined format. The general format of an instruction may look like this:

operator [operand1], [operand2], [operand3]

where the operator indicates the type of action to be performed (ADD, SUBTRACT, MULTIPLY, etc.) and the operands are the "pieces" of information on which the action indicated by the operator is going to be performed. The square brackets around the operands indicate that the operands are optional. According to this general format, an instruction may have zero, one, two, or three operands.

The reader should be aware that the computer only sees a sequence of 0's and 1's. It does not see an operator like "ADD" or "SUBTRACT"; instead it sees their predefined equivalent numerical code such as 10000001 for ADD or 10000110 for MULTIPLY.

The format of a typical instruction may look something like this:

ADDW3 location1, location2, result

This particular instruction adds the contents of the words at the addresses called location1 and location2 and stores the sum at the address called result. The "W" indicates that the operands are words whereas the suffix "3" indicates that there are three operands in this instruction.

This instruction requires several steps to be carried out. First, the instruction is transferred from memory into the CPU. The location of the instruction currently being executed is kept in one of the CPU special registers called the ***instruction counter*** (IC) or ***program counter*** (PC)—the terminology varies with the manufacturer. The instruction just fetched is stored in another special register called the ***Instruction Register*** (IR). The control unit decodes the instruction and recognizes it as an ADD operation with three word operands. Then, the first operand (location1) and second operand (location2) are fetched into two general registers. These two registers are added and the result stored back into memory in the location called result. After the two operands have been fetched the program counter is updated so it points to the next instruction to be executed. During this process, two additional registers facilitate the communication between the CPU and main memory. These registers are the ***memory address register*** (MAR) and the ***memory data register*** (MDR). The MAR is used to hold the address of the location to or from which data are being transferred. The MDR contains the data to be written into or read out of the addressed location.

EXAMPLE 1.4 Assume that a computer has two instructions for addition with the following formats: ADDW2 location1, location2 and ADDW3 location1, location2, result. Does it make any difference to use one instruction over the other?

To answer this question properly we need to understand the differences between these two instruction formats. The first ADD instruction contains two word operands. Hence, the name ADDW2. Let us assume that in this type of instruction the result of the operation, as defined by the computer manufacturer, is stored into the second operand. This type of ADD operation is called a destructive add instruction since the value of location2 will be replaced by the result of the addition (see Fig. 1-6).

The second instruction contains three word operands, hence the name ADDW3. In this type of ADD instruction the result of the addition of the first two operands is stored into the location specified by the third operand. This type of instruction is called a non-destructive add since the values of the operands remain intact after the instruction is executed (see Fig. 1-7).

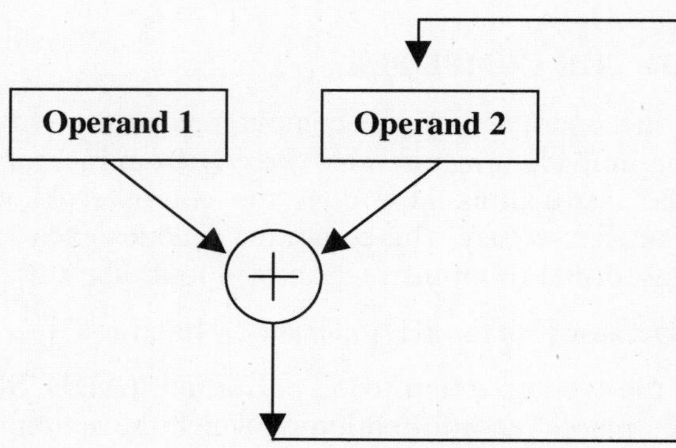

Fig. 1-6 Destructive add.

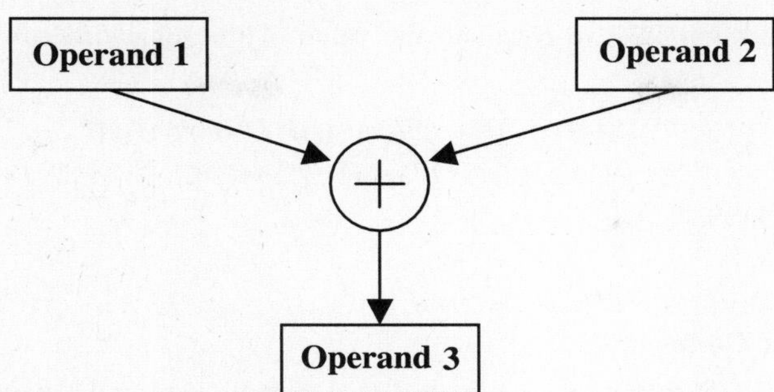

Fig. 1-7 Non-destructive add.

1.4 REPRESENTATION OF DATA IN MEMORY

If we could look at the content of the memory of a computer we would find that all types of data and instructions are represented using only 0's and 1's. Therefore, an obvious question is how can the computer tell the type of information that is stored on a particular location? The answer is simple; the computer knows the type of data stored in a particular location from the context in which the data are being used. This allows the computer to interpret it properly. Example 1.5 shows that a string of data may have different interpretations.

EXAMPLE 1.5 Given the sequence of 4 bytes shown below, what would be the values of this sequence if we consider it as being formed by (*a*) four individual bytes? (*b*) two-word integers with two bytes per word? (*c*) a longword integer with four bytes per longword?

01100011	01100101	01000100	01000000

← increasing addresses

The value of each individual byte can be calculated using the procedure indicated in Section 1.1.1. The subscript indicated in parenthesis at the right-hand corner of a number indicates if the number is binary $_{(2}$ or decimal $_{(10}$. This number, as we will see later, is called the base or radix of the number.

(*a*) Considering the bytes from right to left, we have

$01000000_{(2} = 0^7 1^6 0^5 0^4 0^3 0^2 0^1 0^0 = (1*2^6) = 64_{(10}$

$01000100_{(2} = 0^7 1^6 0^5 0^4 0^3 1^2 0^1 0^0 = (1*2^6) + (1*2^2) = 64 + 4 = 68_{(10}$

$01100101_{(2} = 0^7 1^6 1^5 0^4 0^3 1^2 0^1 1^0 = (1*2^6) + (1*2^5) + (1*2^2) + (1*2^0) = 64 + 32 + 4 + 1 = 101_{(10}$

$01100011_{(2} = 0^7 1^6 1^5 0^4 0^3 0^2 1^1 1^0 = (1*2^6) + (1*2^5) + (1*2^1) + (1*2^0) = 64 + 32 + 2 + 1 = 99_{(10}$

(*b*) The first two-byte word consists of the two rightmost bytes; using the procedure of Section 1.1.1 we have that

$$\begin{aligned} 0100010001000000_{(2} &= 0^{15} 1^{14} 0^{13} 0^{12} 0^{11} 1^{10} 0^9 0^8 0^7 1^6 0^5 0^4 0^3 0^2 0^1 0^0 \\ &= (1*2^{14}) + (1*2^{10}) + (1*2^6) \\ &= 17{,}472_{(10} \end{aligned}$$

The next two-byte word is 0110001101100101. Using the procedure of Section 1.2.1, we have that

$$\begin{aligned} 0110001101100101_{(2} &= 0^{15} 1^{14} 1^{13} 0^{12} 0^{11} 0^{10} 1^9 1^8 0^7 1^6 1^5 0^4 0^3 1^2 0^1 1^0 \\ &= (1*2^{14}) + (1*2^{13}) + (1*2^9) + (1*2^8) + (1*2^6) + (1*2^5) + (1*2^2) + (1*2^0) \\ &= 24{,}445 \end{aligned}$$

(*c*) Using the procedure of Section 1.2.1 to calculate the value of the longword consisting of four bytes we have that

$0^{31}1^{30}1^{29}0^{28}0^{27}0^{26}1^{25}1^{24}0^{23}1^{22}1^{21}0^{20}0^{19}1^{18}0^{17}1^{16}0^{15}1^{14}0^{13}0^{12}0^{11}1^{10}0^{9}0^{8}0^{7}1^{6}0^{5}0^{4}0^{3}0^{2}0^{1}0^{0}{}_{(2} =$
$(1*2^{30}) + (1*2^{29}) + (1*2^{25}) + (1*2^{24}) + (1*2^{22}) + (1*2^{21}) + (1*2^{18}) + (1*2^{16}) + (1*2^{14}) +$
$(1*2^{10}) + (1*2^{6}) = 1{,}667{,}580{,}992_{(10}$

1.4.1 Number Systems and Codes

The most commonly used numbering system is the decimal system. However, due to the binary nature of its electronic devices, the use of the decimal system by the computer is limited. Most of the data representation and arithmetic operations are carried out in the binary system or some of its "shorthand" notation such as the octal or hexadecimal systems. However, before considering the binary, octal, or hexadecimal systems, let us review some of the characteristics of the decimal system.

The decimal system, as its name indicates, is based on the number 10. The number 10 itself is called the ***basis*** or ***radix*** of the system. In any numerical system, the basis tells us how many different symbols there are in the system. In the decimal system these symbols are called digits. They are the familiar 0, 1, 2, 3, 4, 5, 6, 7, 8, and 9. Notice that they range in value from 0 to 9. This is a particular case of a more general rule that can be stated as follows:

"Given any positive integer basis or radix N, there are N different individual symbols that can be used to write numbers in the system. The value of these symbols ranges from 0 to N − 1."

In addition to the binary system, the computer and telecommunication fields make extensive use of some other numerical systems. They are the octal (its basis is 8) and the hexadecimal (its basis is 16) systems. Example 1.6 explains the basic elements of these systems.

EXAMPLE 1.6 How many different symbols are there in the octal and hexadecimal systems? What are the ranges of these symbols?

The basis of the octal system is 8. That is, N = 8. Therefore, there are 8 different symbols. The range of these values varies from 0 to (8 − 1). That is, from 0 to 7. These symbols are: 0, 1, 2, 3, 4, 5, 6, and 7. We call all of these symbols by their decimal names: one, two, three, and so on.

The basis of the hexadecimal system is 16. That is, N = 16. Therefore, there are 16 different symbols. The values of these symbols range from 0 to (16 − 1) or from 0 to 15. These symbols are 0, 1, 2, 3, 4, 5, 6, 7, 8, 9, A, B, C, D, E, and F. Notice that after 9, the symbols are the letters A through F. In this system, the letter A stands for 10, the B for 11, the C for 12, the D for 13, the E for 14, and the F for 15. The reason for choosing letters instead of combination of numerical symbols to represent symbols higher than 9 is to keep all symbols single characters.

To indicate the basis on which a given number is written, we will use a subscript at the lower right side of the number. As indicated in Section 1.4, the notation $0101_{(2}$ indicates that the number is binary. Likewise, the notation $01256_{(8}$ will indicate that the number is written in base 8. When referring to numbers of the decimal system, the subscript is generally omitted. However, we will use it whenever it is necessary to clarify the text. Although the word digit generally refers to the individual symbols of the decimal system, it is also common to call the individual symbols of the other numerical systems by this name.

1.4.2 Positional Systems

All the numerical systems that we have considered so far, including the decimal system, are ***positional systems***. That is, the value represented by a symbol in the numerical representation of a number depends on its position in the number. For example, in the decimal system, the 4 in the number

478 represents 400 units; the 4 in the number 547 represents 40 units. This fact can be seen more clearly if we decompose the number as follows:

$$\mathbf{4}78 = \mathbf{400} + 70 + 8$$
$$5\mathbf{4}7 = 500 + \mathbf{40} + 7$$

In any positional system, the value of any digit in the representation of a number can be calculated using the following steps: (1) Number the digits from right to left using superscripts. Begin with zero, as the superscript of the rightmost digit, and increase the superscripts by 1 as you move from left to right. (2) Use each superscript to form a power of the basis. (3) Multiply the digit's own value, in decimal, by its corresponding power of the basis.

To calculate the decimal equivalent of the entire number, sum all the products obtained in step 2.

EXAMPLE 1.7 What is the value of each digit in the number $1228_{(10}$?

The basis is 10 since the number is a decimal number. To calculate the value of each digit follow the steps indicated below.

(1) Number the digits using superscripts. Begin with 0 in the rightmost position and increase the superscripts as you move from right to left. The number should look like this:

$$1^3 2^2 2^1 8^0$$

(2–3) Use the superscripts to form powers of the basis and multiply the digit's own value, in decimal, by its corresponding power:

The value of 1 in **1**228 is equal to $1*10^3 = 1*1000 = 1000$.

The value of the first 2 (from left to right) in 1**2**28 is equal to $2*10^2 = 2*100 = 200$

The value of the second 2 (from left to right) in 12**2**8 is equal to $2*10^1 = 2*10 = 20$

The value of 8 in 122**8** is equal to $8*10^0 = 8*1 = 8$.

EXAMPLE 1.8 What is the value of each digit in the number $1253_{(8}$? What is the decimal equivalent of the number?

The basis is 8 since the number is written in the octal system. Using a procedure similar to the one in the previous example, we can use superscripts and write the number as $1^3 2^2 5^1 3^0$. Using these superscripts as the power of the basis we have:

The value of 1 in 1253 is equal to $1*8^3 = 1*512 = 512$

The value of 2 in 1253 is equal to $2*8^2 = 2*64 = 128$

The value of 5 in 1253 is equal to $5*8^1 = 5*8 = 40$

The value of 3 in 1253 is equal to $3*8^0 = 3*1 = 3$

The decimal equivalent of the number is obtained by adding all the previous products.

$$\begin{aligned} 1253_{(8} &= (1*8^3) + (2*8^2) + (5*8^1) + (3*8^0) \\ &= (1*512) + (2*64) + (5*8) + (3*1) \\ &= 512 + 128 + 40 + 3 \\ &= 683 \end{aligned}$$

Notice that whenever we find the decimal equivalent of number, we also determine the individual value of each digit. We will use this combined method from now on.

EXAMPLE 1.9 What is the value of each digit in the number $1A5F_{(16}$? What is the decimal equivalent of the number?

The basis is 16 since the number is written in the hexadecimal system. Using superscripts we can write the number as $1^3 A^2 5^1 F^0$. To calculate the decimal equivalent of this hexadecimal number, substitute the symbols A and F by their respective decimal equivalents of 10 and 15. The decimal equivalent of the number is obtained by adding all the previous powers.

$$\begin{aligned} 1A5F_{(16} &= (1*16^3) + (10*16^2) + (5*16^1) + (15*16^0) \\ &= (1*4096) + (10*256) + (5*16) + (15*1) \\ &= 4096 + 2560 + 80 + 15 \\ &= 6751 \end{aligned}$$

The value of 1 in 1A5F is equal to $1*16^3 = 1*4096 = 4096$

The value of A in 1A5F is equal to $10*16^2 = 2*256 = 2560$

The value of 5 in 1A5F is equal to $5*16^1 = 5*8 = 80$

The value of F in 1A5F is equal to $15*16^0 = 3*1 = 15$

1.5 CONVERSION BETWEEN THE BINARY, OCTAL, AND HEXADECIMAL SYSTEMS

Table 1-3 shows the representation of the first fifteen decimal numbers in the binary, octal, and hexadecimal systems. Notice that each unique binary sequence is equivalent to one and only one symbol in each of these systems. We can use this equivalence between the binary, octal, and hexadecimal systems as a shorthand notation to convert values between any of these bases.

Table 1-3 Binary, Octal, Hexadecimal, and Decimal Equivalents.

Binary	Octal	Hexadecimal	Decimal
0001	1	1	1
0010	2	2	2
0011	3	3	3
0100	4	4	4
0101	5	5	5
0110	6	6	6
0111	7	7	7
1000	10	8	8
1001	11	9	9
1010	13	A	10
1011	14	B	11
1100	14	C	12
1101	15	D	13
1110	16	E	14
1111	17	F	15

1.5.1 Conversion from Hexadecimal to Binary and Vice Versa

Given a hexadecimal number, we can find its binary equivalent by replacing each hexadecimal symbol by its corresponding binary configuration (see Table 1-3).

EXAMPLE 1.10 What is the binary equivalent of the hexadecimal number AF3B1?

Replacing each hexadecimal symbol by its corresponding binary sequence (see Table 1-3) we obtain

A F 3 B 1
1010 1111 0011 1011 0001

Notice that to facilitate the reading of the resulting binary number we have separated it into four-bit groups.

To convert binary numbers to their hexadecimal equivalents, we can follow a two-step procedure that is almost the reverse of the previous process.

Step 1. Form four-bit groups beginning from the rightmost bit of the binary number. If the last group (at the leftmost position) has less than four bits, add extra zeros to the left of the bits in this group to make it a four-bit group.

Step 2. Replace each four-bit group by its hexadecimal equivalent (see Table 1-3).

EXAMPLE 1.11 What is the hexadecimal equivalent of the binary number shown below?

011001111010101010100111

Step 1. Forming four-bit groups beginning from the rightmost bit we have

01 1001 1110 1010 1010 0111

Since the last group (the leftmost) has only two bits, it is necessary to add two extra zero bits to the left of these bits to make it a four-bit group. The number should look like this:

0001 1001 1110 1010 1010 0111

Step 2. Replacing each group by its hexadecimal equivalent (see Table 1-3) we obtain

$19EAA7_{(16}$

1.5.2 Converting Decimal to Other Bases

The conversion of a given decimal number to another integer basis **r** $(r > 0)$ is carried out by initially dividing the number by r, and then successively dividing the quotients by r until a zero quotient is obtained. The decimal equivalent is obtained by writing the remainders of the successive divisions in the opposite order to that in which they were obtained. Example 1.12 illustrates this method.

EXAMPLE 1.12 What is the binary equivalent of decimal 41?

Since we want to convert decimal 41 to binary, we need to divide by the binary basis, that is, r = 2.

The initial number (41) is divided by 2 to obtain a quotient of 20 and a remainder of 1. The previous quotient of 20 is then divided by 2; this gives us a quotient of 10 and a remainder of 0. This new quotient of 10 is again divided by 2 to obtain 5 as the quotient and 0 as the remainder. The quotient of 5 is now divided by 2 to obtain a quotient of 2 and a remainder of 1. The new quotient is again divided by 2 to obtain a new quotient of 1 and a remainder of 0. This last quotient of 1 is divided by 2 again to obtain a quotient of 0 and a remainder of 1. Since we obtained a zero quotient the process stops. To form the binary number we write the remainders in the opposite order to that in which they were obtained, beginning with the last remainder. This process is shown below.

Number	Quotient When Dividing by 2	Remainder
41	20	**1**
20	10	**0**
10	5	**0**
5	2	**1**
2	1	**0**
1	0	**1**

The binary equivalent of decimal 41 is 101001. That is, $41_{(10} = 101001_{(2}$.

We can verify this result by converting 101101 to its decimal equivalent according to the procedure of Section 1.4.

$$
\begin{aligned}
1^5 0^4 1^3 0^2 0^1 1^0 &= (1*2^5) + (0*2^4) + (1*2^3) + (0*2^2) + (0*2^1) + (1*2^0) \\
&= 32 + 0 + 8 + 0 + 0 + 1 \\
&= 41
\end{aligned}
$$

EXAMPLE 1.13 What is the octal representation of decimal 41?

In this case we want to convert a decimal value to octal. Therefore, we need to divide by the octal basis, that is, by 8. Using the abbreviated method of the previous example we have that

Number	Quotient When Dividing by 8	Remainder
41	5	**1**
5	0	**5**

↑

Therefore, $41_{(10} = 51_{(8}$.

We can verify this result by noting that

$$
\begin{aligned}
51_{(8} &= (5*8^1) + (1*8^0) \\
&= (40) + (1) \\
&= 41_{(10}
\end{aligned}
$$

1.6 RULES FOR FORMING NUMBERS IN ANY SYSTEM

Table 1-3 shows the equivalent of some numbers in binary, octal, and hexadecimal. In any of these systems, how do we form consecutive numbers higher than that represented by their largest individual symbol? In the decimal system, with a single digit, the largest number that we can form is nine. To represent numbers exceeding nine we use more than one digit as indicated below:

0 1 2 3 4 5 6 7 8 9 **10 11 12 13 14 15 16 17 18 19 20 21 22 23 24 25 26 27 28 29 30 31 32 33 34 35 36 37 38 39** . . . **90 91 92 93 94 95 96 97 98 99 100 101 102 103 104 105 106 107 108 109 110 111 112 113 114 115 116 117 118 119 120** . . .

After writing all single digits, we form all two-digit combinations beginning with 1. Then we form all two-digit combinations beginning with 2 and so on until we reach 99. After exhausting all two-digit combinations we start forming three-digit combinations; then we continue with all four-digits combinations and so on. This process can be continued forever. A similar procedure can be applied to other numerical systems. To form numbers higher than 7 in the octal system we use a similar formation rule as shown in Table 1-3.

EXAMPLE 1.14 In the hexadecimal system, how are the numbers greater than F formed?

0 1 2 3 4 5 6 7 8 9 A B C D E F 10 11 12 13 14 15 16 17 18 19 1A 1B 1C 1D 1E 1F 20 21 22 23 24 25 26 27 28 29 2A 2B 2C 2D 2E 2F 30 31 32 33 34 35 36 37 38 39 3A 3B 3C 3D 3E 3F . . . **F0 F1 F2 F3 F4 F5 F6 F7 F8 F9 FA FB FC FD FE FF 100 101** . . . and so on.

Notice that, after writing all the single digits (shown in italics), it is necessary to form all possible two-digit combinations of the single digits, beginning with 1. Once this sequence has been exhausted, the two-digit combinations beginning with 2 are formed. This process is repeated until all two-digit combinations beginning with F are completed. At this moment, it is necessary to form all three-digit combinations, beginning with **100** and ending with **FFF**. The process is then repeated for all four-digit combinations and so on.

1.7 ARITHMETIC OPERATIONS IN THE BINARY, OCTAL, AND HEXADECIMAL SYSTEMS

Arithmetic operations on the binary, octal, and hexadecimal systems follow similar rules to that of the decimal system. To facilitate the explanation of arithmetic operations in any of these systems, let us review how these operations are carried out in the decimal system. Remember that in a + b, a is called the ***augend*** and b is the ***addend***. Likewise in c − d, c is called the ***minuend*** and b is the ***subtrahend***.

EXAMPLE 1.15 In the decimal system the result of adding 452 and 385 is 837. How do we obtain this result?

```
452 +
385
———
  7 ← Two plus five is seven. There is a single symbol for the number seven.
```

```
452 +
385
———
 37 ← Five plus eight is thirteen. There is no single symbol for the number thirteen. Since 13 = 1*10 + 3 we write 3 and carry 1.
```

Notice that since thirteen is greater than nine we need more than one digit to represent thirteen. The rule for forming numbers (see Section 1.6) shows that, for number thirteen, 3 "accompanies" the number "one" that is carried.

```
1    ← carry
452 +
385
———
837 ← One plus four is five. This five plus three is eight. There is a single symbol for eight.
```

EXAMPLE 1.16 When we subtract decimal 23 from decimal 4005 we obtain 3033. How do we obtain this result?

```
 4015
 −982
 ———
    3 ← Five minus two is three. Therefore, write the symbol for three.
```

```
   11
 4015
 −982
 ———
   33 ← Since one is less than eight we "borrow" one unit from the digit to the left of the one. The borrowed unit is equivalent to
        "borrowing" 10. This 10 plus 1 is equal to 11. Therefore, write 3 since 11 − 8 = 3.
```

```
  9
 4015
 −982
 ———
  033 ← The zero to the left of the one became a 9 (the basis of the decimal system minus 1). Write 0 since 9 − 9 = 0.
```

```
 3
 4015
 −982
 ———
 3033 ← The 4 to the left of the 0 "paid" the 10 that was previously "borrowed" by the 1. The 4 decreases to 3.
```

1.7.1 Addition of Binary Numbers

The rules for adding or subtracting binary numbers are very similar to the ones used in the decimal system. The major difference is that we are limited to only two digits. Table 1-4 shows the rules of binary addition. To carry out these arithmetic operations properly it is necessary to align the numbers in their rightmost digit as we do in decimal arithmetic.

Table 1-4 Addition of Binary Numbers.

0 + 0 = 0
0 + 1 = 1
1 + 0 = 1
1 + 1 = 0 with a carry of 1

EXAMPLE 1.17 What is the result of adding binary numbers 10111100 and 11001111?

```
10111100 +
11001111
________

       1 ← 0 plus 1 is 1. There is a symbol for 1.
10111100 +
11001111
________

      11 ← 0 plus 1 is 1. There is a symbol for 1.
     1   ← carry
10111100 +
11001111
________

     011 ← 1 plus 1 is 0 with a carry of 1.
    1
10111100 +
11001111
________

    1011 ← 1 (the carry) plus 1 is 0 with a carry of 1. This 0 plus 1 is 1. Therefore, write 1 and carry 1.
   1
10111100 +
11001111
________

   01011 ← 1 (the carry) plus 1 is 0 with a carry of 1. This 0 plus 0 is 0. Therefore, write 0 and carry 1.
  1
10111100 +
11001111
________

  001011 ← 1 (the carry) plus 1 is 0 with a carry of 1. This 0 plus 0 is 0. Therefore, write 0 and carry 1.
 1
10111100 +
11001111
________

 0001011 ← 1 (the carry) plus 0 is 1. This 1 plus 1 is 0 with a carry of one. Therefore, write 0 and carry 1.
```

```
 1
 10111100 +
 11001111
 ---------
 110001011 ← 1 (the carry) plus 1 is 0 with a carry of 1. This 0 plus 1 is 1. Therefore, write 1 and carry 1. Since there are no more
             digits to add we write the carry (in bold) as the leftmost digit.
```

The process of subtracting binary numbers is very similar to that of the decimal system. The main difference is that instead of "borrowing ten" we "borrow two" from the high-order digits (those to the left of a particular digit).

EXAMPLE 1.18 Subtract 11 from 1001 in binary.

```
 1001
  -11
 ----
    0 ← 1 minus 1 is 0.

 1001
  -11
 ----
   10 ← 0 is less than 1. It is necessary to borrow "two" units from the higher unit. This two plus zero is two. Two minus one is
        one. Therefore, write 1.

  1
 1001
  -11
 ----
  110 ← The zero to the left became a 1 (the basis minus 1). This 1 minus the zero of the subtrahend (not shown here but
        assumed) is 1. Therefore, write 1.

 0
 1001
  -11
 ----
 0110 ← The leftmost 1 paid the "two" previously borrowed by the zero. This 1 becomes a zero. This zero minus the zero of
        the subtrahend (not shown here but assumed) is 0. Since this zero is the leftmost digit it is not generally written;
        however, we write it here for the sake of explanation.
```

1.7.2 Addition and Subtraction of Hexadecimal Numbers

Carrying out arithmetic operations in the binary system is an error-prone task since it is easy to get confused with so many ones and zeros. For this reason it is preferable to carry out arithmetic operations in the hexadecimal system and then transform the results back to binary if necessary. The rules for adding and subtracting numbers in the hexadecimal system are similar to the ones used for the decimal system. However, we need to keep in mind that when performing additions there will be a carry whenever we exceed the value F. Likewise, when performing subtractions, if we need to "borrow" we always "borrow sixteen" instead of "borrowing ten" as we do in the decimal system. To simplify the process of doing arithmetic operations in the hexadecimal system it is convenient to think "in decimal" and then translate the results back to hexadecimal. The following example illustrates this process.

EXAMPLE 1.19 What is the result of adding the hexadecimal numbers 1A23 and 7C28?

```
1A23 +
7C28
-----
   B ← Three plus eight is eleven. There is a symbol for eleven. Therefore, write B.

1A23 +
7C28
-----
  4B ← Two plus two is four. There is a symbol for four. Therefore, write 4.

1A23 +
7C28
-----
 64B ← Thinking "in decimal" we have that ten plus twelve is twenty-two. Since 22 = 16*1 + 6, write 6 and carry 1.

1
1A23 +
7C28
-----
964B ← One (the carry) plus one is two. This two plus seven is nine. There is a symbol for nine. Therefore, write 9.
```

EXAMPLE 1.20 What is the result of subtracting in the hexadecimal system B2 from 1F00A?

```
1F00A
  -B2
-----
    8 ← Ten minus two is eight. There is a symbol for eight. Therefore, write 8.

1F00A
  -B2
-----
   58 ← Zero is less than eleven. Therefore, borrow "16" from the higher unit. This sixteen plus zero is sixteen. This sixteen minus
        eleven is five. Thus, write 5.

  F
1F00A
  -B2
-----
  F58 ← This zero became F (the basis minus 1). This F minus the zero of the subtrahend (not shown but understood) is F.
        Therefore, write F.

 E
1F00A
  -B2
-----
 EF58 ← The F "paid" the 16 that was "borrowed" by the leftmost zero. The F became an E. This E minus the zero of the
        subtrahend (not shown but understood) is E. Therefore, write E.

1F00A
  -B2
-----
1EF58 ← One minus the zero of the subtrahend (not shown but understood) is 1. Therefore, write 1.
```

1.8 REPRESENTING NUMBERS IN A COMPUTER

All numerical data are represented inside the computer as a sequence of zeros and ones. The arithmetic operations, particularly the subtraction, raise the possibility that the result might be negative. How does the computer know whether a particular number represents a negative quantity or not? The answer to this question depends on the convention used to represent the numbers. In addition to the unsigned representation of a numerical quantity already discussed (see Section 1.1.1), there are some other conventions to represent both negative and positive numbers inside the computer. In this section we will discuss only two of these conventions (the sign-magnitude and the two's complement). An additional convention (one's complement) will be discussed later in the chapter (see solved problem 1.21). Any numerical convention needs to differentiate two basic elements of any given number: its sign (positive or negative) and the numerical value itself without the sign (the magnitude).

When representing numbers in any of these conventions the notion of "basic unit" needs to be stated explicitly since it may vary from manufacturer to manufacturer. In addition, it is necessary to choose one of the bits of the basic unit as the "sign bit." The leftmost bit is generally selected for this purpose. As any other bit, this bit can be 1 or 0. Computer manufacturers have agreed to use 0 as the "positive" sign and 1 as the "negative" sign.

1.8.1 The Sign-magnitude Convention

In this convention, given a basic unit of n bits, the leftmost bit is used exclusively to represent the sign. The remaining (n − 1) bits are used for the magnitude. Figure 1-2 shows that bit number 7 is considered the sign bit. The remaining digits (0 through 6) are used to represent the magnitude. The range of numbers that can be represented in this convention varies from $-2^{n+1} + 2^{n-1} - 1$.

EXAMPLE 1.21 What is the sign-magnitude representation of the decimal numbers −41 and +41 if the basic unit is a byte?

Since the number +41 is positive we have to set the sign bit to 0. The remaining 7 bits will be used to represent the magnitude.

The binary representation of decimal 41 is given by the following binary sequence 0101001. That is, $41_{(10} = 0101001_{(2}$.

The sign-magnitude representation of the number is $00101001_{(2}$.

To represent the sign-magnitude of −41 we only need to change the sign bit from zero to 1. Since the binary representation of its magnitude is the same, we have that the sign-magnitude of −41 is $10101001_{(2}$.

EXAMPLE 1.22 What is the decimal equivalent value of the sign-magnitude binary sequence 10110111?

The number is negative since its sign (the leftmost bit) is 1.

The magnitude of the number is given by the sequence of bits 0110111. Using the procedure of Section 1.1.1 we find that

$$\begin{aligned} 0110111_{(2} &= (1*2^5) + (1*2^4) + (1*2^2) + (1*2^1) + (1*2^0) \\ &= 32 + 16 + 4 + 2 + 1 \\ &= 55 \end{aligned}$$

Therefore, the decimal equivalent of the number 10110111 represented in sign-magnitude is −55.

Addition of two numbers in sign-magnitude is carried out using the usual conventions of binary arithmetic. However, if both numbers have the same sign, we add their magnitude and copy the same sign. If the signs are different, we determine which number has the larger magnitude and subtract the other from it. The sign of the result is the sign of the operand with the larger magnitude.

As indicated before, given n bits, in sign-magnitude representation, the range of numbers that can be represented varies from $-2^{n+1} + 2^{n-1} - 1$. Therefore, if the result of an arithmetic operation falls outside that range, we will say that the operation causes an **overflow**.

EXAMPLE 1.23 What is the decimal value of the sum of the binary numbers 10100011 and 00010110 if they are represented in sign-magnitude? Assume that the basic unit is the byte.

Notice that the numbers have different signs: 10100011 is negative and 00010110 is positive. To calculate their sum, it is necessary to find out which of these two numbers has the larger magnitude. Using the procedure of Section 1.1.1 we have that:

Number: 10100011
Sign: 1 (negative)
Magnitude: 0100011 $= (1*2^5) + (1*2^1) + (1*2^0)$
$= 32 + 2 + 1$
$= 35$
Decimal value: -35

Number: 00010110
Sign: 0 (positive)
Magnitude: 0010110 $= (1*2^4) + (1*2^2) + (1*2^1)$
$= 16 + 4 + 2$
$= 22$
Decimal value: $+22$

Value with the largest magnitude: 35 since $35 > 22$.
Sign of the difference: negative (sign of the number with the larger numerical value)
Numerical value of the difference: $13(35 - 22 = 13)$
Therefore, the decimal value of the sum is -13.

1.8.2 The Two's Complement Convention

The **two's complement convention** or **2's complement** is the most popular among computer manufacturers since it does not present any of the problems of the sign-magnitude or one's complement (see solved problems 1.21 and 1.22). Positive numbers are represented using a similar procedure to that of the sign-magnitude. Given n bits, the range of numbers that can be represented in two's complement is -2^{n-1} to $2^{n-1} - 1$. Notice that the range of negative numbers is one larger than the range of the positive values.

To represent a negative number in this convention, follow the three-step process shown below:

Step 1. Express the absolute value of the number in binary.

Step 2. Change all zeros to ones and all ones to zeros in the binary number obtained in the previous step. This process is called "***complementing the bits.***"

Step 3. Add one to the binary number of step 2.

In the two's complement convention, given a negative number, to find its positive counterpart we exercise steps 2 and 3 of the previous process.

EXAMPLE 1.24 What is the two's complement representation of -31?

Step 1. The absolute value of the number is 31. Using the procedure of Section 1.5.2, we have that the binary representation is $00011111_{(2}$. That is, $31_{(10} = 00011111_{(2}$.

Step 2. Changing all zeros to ones and vice versa, we have that the number looks like 11100000.

Step 3. Adding 1 we have that

$$\begin{array}{r} 11100000 + \\ 1 \\ \hline 11100001 \end{array}$$

Therefore, the two's complement representation of -31 is 11100001. Notice that the sign of the result is 1 as it should be.

EXAMPLE 1.25 What is the decimal positive value of the two's complement number 11100100?

Follow steps 2 and 3 of the procedure indicated above since the number is negative.

Step 2. Complement all bits of the given number. That is, change 11100100 to 00011011.

Step 3. Add 1 to the previous result and we have

```
00011011 +
       1
--------
00011100
```

Therefore, the positive counterpart of 11100100 is 00011100. The value of the latter number can be calculated using the procedure of Section 1.1.1. Thus, the decimal positive counterpart of the given number is 28.

1.8.2.1 Arithmetic Operations in Two's Complement

To add numbers represented in two's complement treat the numbers as unsigned integers. That is, treat the sign bit as any other bit of the number. Ignore any carry out of the leftmost position if there is one. To subtract two's complement numbers, treat the numbers as unsigned integers. If a borrow is needed in the leftmost place, borrow as if there were another bit to the left of the minuend.

EXAMPLE 1.26 What is the result of the addition of the numbers 11000111 and 11011101 if both numbers are represented in two's complement notation? What is the decimal value of the result?

```
11000111 +
11011101
--------
       0 ← 1 + 1 = 0 with a carry of 1. Write 0 and carry 1.
```

```
      1
11000111 +
11011101
--------
      00 ← The carry plus one is zero with a carry of 1. This zero plus zero is zero. Write 0 and carry 1.
```

```
      1
11000111 +
11011101
--------
     100 ← The carry plus one is zero with a carry of 1. The zero plus one is one. Therefore write one and carry 1.
```

```
    1
11000111 +
11011101
--------
    0100 ← The carry plus zero is one. This one plus one is zero with a carry of one. Therefore, write zero and carry one.
```

```
   1
11000111 +
11011101
--------
   00100 ← The carry plus zero is one. This one plus one is zero with a carry of one. Write 0 and carry 1.
```

```
  1
11000111 +
11011101
--------
  100100 ← The carry plus zero is one. This one plus zero is one. Therefore, write 1.
```

11000111 +
11011101

0100100 ← One plus one is zero with a carry of one. Therefore, write zero and carry one.

1
11000111 +
11011101

10100100 ← The carry plus one is zero with a carry of one. This zero plus one is one. Therefore, write 1 and ignore the carry.

The decimal value of the result is −92. Note that −92 = −57 −35. Observe that 10100100 = −92, 11000111 = −57 and 11000111 = −35.

EXAMPLE 1.27 What is the result of subtracting 11011101 from 00111001? Assume that both numbers are represented in two's complement notation.

00111001
−11011101

---

0 ← One minus one is zero. Therefore, write zero.

00111001
−11011101

---

00 ← Zero minus zero is zero. Therefore, write zero.

00111001
−11011101

---

00 ← Zero is less than one. Borrow "two" from higher unit. Since two minus one is one, write one.

0
00111001
−11011101

1100 ← The one (shown in bold and strikethrough) "paid" the unit that was borrowed by the zero. The one became a zero. Since this zero is less than one, borrow "two" from the higher unit. Therefore, write one since two minus one is one.

0
00111001
−11011101

11100 ← The one (shown in bold and strikethrough) "paid" the unit borrowed in the previous step. The one became a zero. Since zero is less than one, follow a process similar to the one described in the previous step. Therefore, write one.

0
00111001
−11011101

011100 ← The one (shown in bold and strikethrough) "paid" the unit borrowed in the previous step. The one became a zero. Since zero minus is zero. Therefore, write zero.

00111001
−11011101

1011100 ← Zero is less than one. Borrow a "two" and write one since two minus one is one.

1
00111001
−11011101

01011100 ← The zero became a one. Write zero since one minus one is zero.

Notice that the previous operation assumes that there is an "invisible" one-bit to the left of the minuend. This "invisible" bit paid the 2's borrowed by the leftmost zeros.

1.8.2.2 Overflow Conditions in Two's Complement

As indicated before, given n bits, the range of numbers that can be represented in two's complement is -2^{n-1} to $2^{n-1}-1$. Whenever the result of an operation falls outside that range an overflow condition occurs. We will notice that in all overflow conditions, the sign of the result of the operation (addition or subtraction) is different than that of the operands. That is, if the operands are both positive, the result is negative or if the operands are both negative the result is positive. Solved problems 1.15 and 1.16 illustrate another method to detect if an overflow has occurred.

EXAMPLE 1.28 What is the result of adding the following two's complement numbers 11000111 and 10100100?

11000111 +
10100100

---

1 ← Write one since one plus zero is one.

11000111 +
10100100

---

11 ← Write one since one plus zero is one.

11000111 +
10100100

---

011 ← Write zero since one plus one is zero with a carry of one.

1
11000111 +
10100100

1011 ← The carry plus zero is one. This one plus zero is one. Therefore, write one.

11000111 +
10100100

01011 ← Zero plus zero is zero. Therefore, write zero.

11000111 +
10100100

101011 ← Zero plus one is one. Therefore, write one.

11000111 +
10100100

1101011 ← One plus zero is one. Therefore, write one.

```
              11000111 +
              10100100
              ________
Overflow →    01101011 ← One plus one is zero with a carry of one. Therefore, write one and ignore the carry.
```

Notice that an overflow condition has occurred since the result of the addition is positive while the operands are both negative. A closer look at this result reveals that its numerical value falls outside the range of the values allowed for a byte in two's complement. In fact, with 8 bits the range varies from -2^7 to $2^7 - 1$ or from -128 to 127 (see Section 1.8.2). The decimal value of the sum obtained above is -149. This value is well outside the range -128 to 127.

1.8.3 Binary and Alphanumeric Codes

Humans are more comfortable working with decimal numbers than working with long strings of 0's and 1's. Computers, on the other hand, operate much faster when working with binary data. To bridge this communication gap between the human and the machine, several numerical codes have been devised so that the decimal digits are represented by sequences of binary digits. This way, the computer can perform all its operations in binary and then convert the results back to decimal form for human consumption. In this section we will consider some of the numerical "weighted codes" (BCD and Hamming) and the alphanumeric ASCII code.

A ***binary code*** is a group of n bits that assume up to 2^n distinct combinations of 0's and 1's with each combination representing one element of the set that is being coded. For example, with a group of two bits we can form a set of four different elements. That is, we can represent up to four different elements of a set. The 2^2 different combinations that we can form with two bits are: 00, 01, 10, and 11. We can associate each of these combinations with a unique element of another set. We say then that each combination "represents" one element of the set. To represent a set of eight elements we only need three bits; to represent sixteen elements we only need four bits. Notice that if the number of elements that needs to be represented is not a power of two, the binary code will have some unassigned bit combinations. The following problem illustrates this fact.

EXAMPLE 1.29 How many bits are necessary to represent the first 10 decimal digits?

Since $2^3 < 10 < 2^4$ the minimum number of bits to represent the first 10 decimal digits is $n = 4$. However, since $2^4 = 16$, there will be 6 $(=16 - 10)$ combinations of these four bits that cannot be assigned to a unique single decimal digit.

1.8.3.1 Weighted Codes

To represent decimal digits using four bits some of the most popular codes are the **weighted codes**. In this type of code each bit is assigned a "weight." The value of the decimal digit represented by each combination of bits is obtained by multiplying each bit by its weight and adding up these individual products. If w_1, w_2, w_3, and w_4 are the respective weights of bits b_1, b_2, b_3, and b_4 then the decimal number N that they represent is

$$N = w_1 b_1 + w_2 b_2 + w_3 b_3 + w_4 b_4$$

A sequence of binary digits representing a decimal digit is called a ***code word***. Table 1-5 shows two binary codes. The code with weights 8, 4, 2, and 1 is known as the BCD (***Binary-Coded-Decimal***) code. Each code word in BCD is the binary equivalent of the digit that it represents.

Table 1-5 Decimal Representation of Digits 0–9 in Two Different Weighted Codes.

Decimal Digit	Weight 8-2-4-1	Weight 2-4-1-2
0	0 0 0 0	0 0 0 0
1	0 0 0 1	0 0 0 1
2	0 0 1 0	0 0 1 0
3	0 0 1 1	0 0 1 1
4	0 1 0 0	0 1 0 0
5	0 1 0 1	1 0 1 1
6	0 1 1 0	1 1 0 0
7	0 1 1 1	1 1 0 1
8	1 0 0 0	1 1 1 0
9	1 0 0 1	1 1 1 1

EXAMPLE 1.30 In the 2-4-2-1 code, the representation of decimal 9 is given as 1111. Notice that

$$1*\mathbf{2} + 1*\mathbf{4} + 1*\mathbf{2} + 1*\mathbf{1} = 9$$

It is interesting to observe that in some codes the representation of some decimal numbers may not be unique. Consider the code 2-4-2-1 where we can represent decimal 7 in two different ways:

$$1*\mathbf{2} + 1*\mathbf{4} + 0*\mathbf{2} + 1*\mathbf{1} = 7 \qquad \text{and} \qquad 0*\mathbf{2} + 1*\mathbf{4} + 1*\mathbf{2} + 1*\mathbf{1} = 7$$

Two questions need to be answered concerning the dual representation of a digit. First, how does the computer know which one is the correct code? Second, can both be used interchangeably? The answer to the latter question is no. Only one code word can be used. However, this does not answer which of the two code words is the correct one. To answer this question satisfactorily we need to define the notion of a ***self-complementing code***. A code is said to be self-complementing if, given any decimal digit N and its corresponding code word $X_1X_2X_3X_4$, the value of $9 - N$ (the 9's complement of the decimal) can be obtained by complementing the bits of the code word. We will use the notation $\bar{X}$ to indicate the complement of a bit X.

EXAMPLE 1.31 The code 2-4-2-1 is self-complementing. Notice that in this code the 9's complement of any decimal can be obtained by complementing the bits of its corresponding code word.

Decimal (N)	2-4-2-1	9 − N	Representation of 9 − N in 2-4-2-1
0	0 0 0 0	9	1 1 1 1
1	0 0 0 1	8	1 1 1 0
2	0 0 1 0	7	1 1 0 1
3	0 0 1 1	6	1 1 0 0
4	0 1 0 0	5	1 0 1 1
5	1 0 1 1	4	0 1 0 0
6	1 1 0 0	3	0 0 1 1
7	1 1 0 1	2	0 0 1 0
8	1 1 1 0	1	0 0 0 1
9	1 1 1 1	9	0 0 0 0

1.8.3.2 American Standard Code for Information Interchange

Computers are also used extensively to process alphanumeric information. To carry out this task the most common approach is to encode the individual characters that need to be manipulated. On a typical English computer keyboard there are at least 128 different characters:

Digits:	10
Letter (upper and lower):	52
Special symbols:	33 includes !, @, #, $, %, ^, &,*, (,) etc.
Control characters:	33 includes Enter, space, backspace, etc.
	128

The minimum number of bits necessary to represent these many characters is 7 since $2^7 = 128$ (see Section 1.8.3). The most common code in the computer industry is the 7-bit code known as the American Standard Code for Information Interchange or ASCII for short. However, since the basic unit of storage is the byte, all ASCII codes are represented using eight bits. This leaves the most significant bit as zero. Another code used extensively by the International Business Machines Corporation is the Extended Binary Coded Decimal Interchange Code or EBCDIC for short. In this book we only consider the ASCII code. The set of ASCII characters is shown in Chapter 3. The ASCII code was developed by the American National Standards Institute (ANSI) to allow information exchanges between equipment created by different manufacturers.

EXAMPLE 1.32 What is the ASCII representation of the message "Hello World"? Assume that addresses increase from left to right.

A sequence of characters is represented in memory as a series of consecutive bytes. Each byte holds one ASCII character code. Using the chart in Chapter 3 (see page 64) and the hexadecimal equivalent of each character the message representation is

H	e	l	l	o		W	o	r	l	d
48	65	6C	6C	6F	20	57	6F	72	6C	64

Observe that the space character (hex 20 or decimal 32) is a character like any other. However, the authors recognize that it is an elusive character that is very difficult to see. We have also assumed that the addresses increase from left to right to facilitate the reading of the characters.

1.8.4 Error Detection

When binary data are transmitted over any type of communication line, the possibility of an error in the transmission always exists due to equipment failure or the presence of "noise." When an error occurs it is possible that one or more bits of a byte could change from 0 to 1 or vice versa. Whenever this happens a code word can be changed into an incorrect but valid code or to a sequence of bits which do not represent anything. In this book we will only consider the detection and correction of single errors. That is, errors where only one single bit changes.

The numbers of bits that have to change within a byte before the byte is converted into an invalid code is sometimes used as a criterion for classifying codes. If only one bit of a byte needs to change, the code is said to be a ***single-error-detecting code***. If only two bits need to change then the code is said to be a ***two-error-detecting code***. To detect single errors we use an extra ***parity check*** bit. A parity bit is used to ensure that each code word, including the parity bit, has an even numbers of 1's (even parity) or an odd number of 1's (odd parity). Table 1-6 shows the even parity bit for the error-detecting code 8-2-4-1.

Table 1-6

Decimal Digit	Weight 8-2-4-1	Parity Bit (even parity)
0	0 0 0 0	0
1	0 0 0 1	1
2	0 0 1 0	1
3	0 0 1 1	0
4	0 1 0 0	1
5	0 1 0 1	0
6	0 1 1 0	0
7	0 1 1 1	1
8	1 0 0 0	1
9	1 0 0 1	0

One of the most common tasks encountered in any computer system is that of transmitting information from one computer to another. The computer that sends the information is called the ***source***; the computer that receives the information is called the ***destination***. Both sender and receiver follow international standards to accomplish this task. It is assumed that the transmitted signal is divided into a series of one-bit intervals of length T. During each of these intervals the source will send either a 0 or a 1 (shown in Fig. 1-8 as high and lows).

To communicate among themselves, computers may follow a convention like the one illustrated in Fig. 1-9. It is the responsibility of the destination to detect the value and correctness of the received signal.

The process that two computers may use to communicate with each other can be described as indicated below. We will use Fig. 1-9 as a reference.

(1) If the source is not sending any message, it continuously transmits a sequence of 1's.

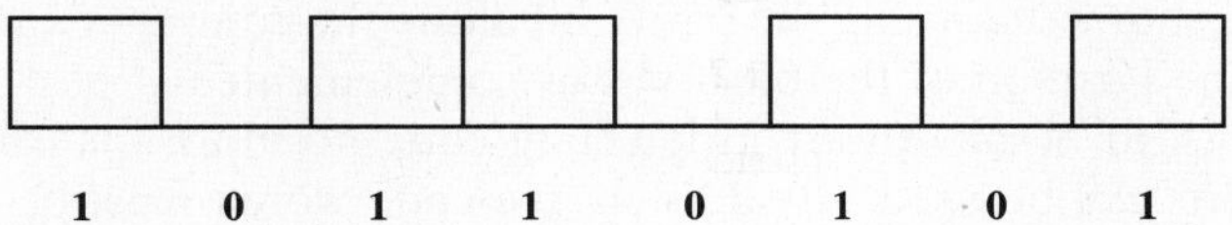

Fig. 1-8 Representation of 1 and 0 as high and lows.

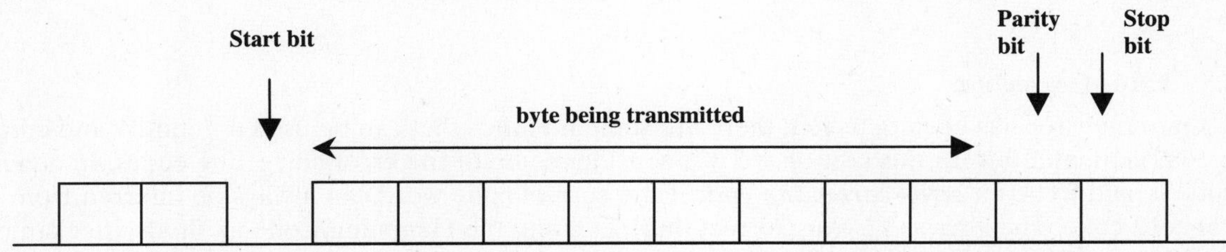

Fig. 1-9 Typical byte format for data transmission.

(2) A 0-bit indicates the beginning of the message. This first 0-bit is called the **start bit**. It is assumed that the bytes making up the message follow the start bit.
(3) The parity check bit is set according to the parity convention being used (even or odd).
(4) After the parity check bit another 1-bit (the **stop bit**) is transmitted to indicate that the transmission of the entire byte has been completed.
(5) At this point the source may continue transmitting the next byte or it may start transmitting a continuous sequence of 1's indicating that there are no more messages for the time being.

EXAMPLE 1.33 Two computers are communicating with each other using the data format convention of Fig. 1-9, the ASCII character set and even parity. The message shown below has a parity error. How does the computer recognize that an error has occurred? Can the computer tell the position of the complemented bit? Assume that the start bit is not shown. The arrow indicates the direction in which the characters need to be considered.

⟶

0101011001 0110100101 0110111101 0110110001 0110010101 0110010001
0111001111 0010000011 0110000111 0111001001 0110010101 0010000011
0110001011 0110110001 0111010111 0110010101 0010111001

Using the format of Fig. 1-9 each sequence of ten bits (one 8-bit byte, one parity check bit and one stop bit) can be considered as the representation of a single character of the message. Working with each group of bits separately and dropping the stop bit we can check the rightmost bit, the parity bit (shown in bold below).

1. 01010110**0** ✔	2. 01101001**0** ✔	3. 01101111**0** ✔	4. 01101100**0** ✔
5. 01100101**0** ✔	6. 01100100**0** ✘	7. 01110011**1** ✔	8. 00100000**1** ✔
9. 01100001**1** ✔	10. 01110010**0** ✔	11. 01100101**0** ✔	12. 00100000**1** ✔
13. 01100010**1** ✔	14. 01101100**0** ✔	15. 01110101**1** ✔	16. 01100101**0** ✔
17. 00101110**0** ✔			

The parity check bit of group No. 6 should be one instead of zero since we are working with even parity. Observe that the computer cannot tell the position of the erroneous complemented bit. Use the chart in Chapter 3 to decode the message. Can you guess the word that was changed? Can you tell the bit that was complemented? We leave these questions as an exercise for the reader.

The previous example shows that using the parity bit alone the computer can tell that an error has occurred but cannot tell the position of the bit that was complemented.

In general, given n bits, to obtain an error-detecting code no more than half of the 2^n possible combinations of these n bits can be used. In addition, the code words must be chosen in such a way that, for any code word to produce another valid word, at least two bits must be complemented. The minimum number of bits that need to change in a code word to produce another valid coded word is called the ***minimum distance*** of the code. Therefore, we can rephrase the previous statement by saying that given n bits, to obtain an error-detecting code its minimum distance must be two or more. The even parity 8-4-2-1 code shown in Table 1-6 has a minimum distance of two.

1.8.5 Error Correction

Once an error has been detected, there are some methods that can be used to identify and correct the complemented bit. In this section we will consider some of the error-correcting codes. In general, a code is said to be an ***error-correcting code*** if the correct code word can always be inferred from the erroneous code. The Forward Error Correction (FEC) and the Hamming Code methods are examples of this type of code. Both methods require additional redundant bits to identify and correct the errors.

1.8.5.1 Forward Error Correction

In this correction schema, a **parity block** complements the parity bit of each byte after a predetermined number of n bytes. Each bit of the parity block checks the parity of the preceding n bits that occupy the same position in the preceding n bytes. Using both pieces of information it is possible to find and correct the bit in error. Example 1.34 illustrates this method and the use of the msb of an ASCII code as a parity bit.

EXAMPLE 1.34 Assume that two computers communicate with each other using ASCII code and that a parity block is transmitted every four bytes. In addition, consider that even parity is used at both the byte level and the block level. Parity bits are shown in italics and the parity block is shown in bold.

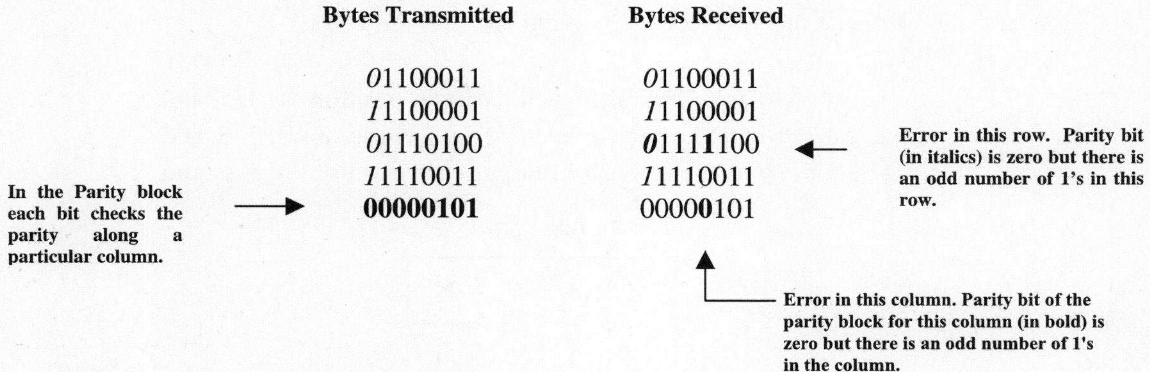

It is the responsibility of the receiving computer to check the parity of every column and every row. Whenever the computer identifies the bit in error in a particular byte it complements the bit to recover from the error.

1.8.5.2 Hamming Code

This method can be used to provide multiple-error detection. The fundamental principles in constructing this code for **m** given bits are as follows:

(1) Add **k** additional ***parity checking bits*** denoted by p_1, p_2, ... p_k to the m given bits. The resulting code will have code words of (m + k) bits. Choose the value of k so that it satisfies the inequality

$$2^k \geq m + k + 1$$

For example, if we want to transmit four data bits (m = 4), the value of k must be 3 since

$$2^3 \geq 4 + 3 + 1$$

This result implies that we need to add three parity checking bits denoted by p_1, p_2, and p_3.

(2) Number the (m + k) bits 1 through m + k; start by assigning 1 to the most significant bit and continue until you assign the value m + k to the least significant bit. Consider these numbers as the positions of the bits in a code word.

(3) Place the checking bits in positions 1, 2, 4 ... 2^{k-1} of the code word.

When k = 3, the checking bits are placed in positions 1, 2, and 2^{3-1}. That is, in positions 1, 2, and 4.

The position of the bits b_1, b_2, b_3, and b_4 and the checking bits p_1, p_2, and p_3 in the encoded word is as follows:

Position →	1	2	3	4	5	6	7
	p_1	p_2	b_1	p_3	b_2	b_3	b_4

(4) Form k sets, $P_1, P_2 \ldots P_k$ of binary numbers. The binary numbers in set P_j should be such that their representation has k or fewer bits and has 1 in the j_{th} position. Select p_j in such a way that it has even parity in the positions indicated by the elements of the set P_j.

For k = 3 form sets P_1, P_2, and P_3. The elements of each of these sets should have 3 or fewer bits in their representation. Table 1-7 shows the seven possible combinations that we can form with 3 bits that satisfy the condition of step 4. According to this table the sets and their elements are:

$$P_1 = \{1,3,5,7\} \qquad P_2 = \{2,3,6,7\} \qquad P_3 = \{4,5,6,7\}$$

Notice that the elements of P_1 have 1's in column 1, the elements of P_2 have 1's in column 2, and the elements of P_3 have 1's in column 3.

Therefore,

select p_1 so as to establish even parity in positions 1, 3, 5, and 7.
select p_2 so as to establish even parity in positions 2, 3, 6, and 7.
select p_3 so as to establish even parity in positions 4, 5, 6, and 7.

Table 1-7

	P_3	P_2	P_1
1.	0	0	1
2.	0	1	0
3.	0	1	1
4.	1	0	0
5.	1	0	1
6.	1	1	0
7.	1	1	1

(5) Form the code word to be transmitted by adding the appropriate checking digits so that the parity condition of the previous step is satisfied.

EXAMPLE 1.35 If the sequence 1101 (data) is to be transmitted, what is the code word if Hamming Code is used?

Position	1	2	3	4	5	6	7
	p_1	p_2	b_1	p_3	b_2	b_3	b_4
Transmitted data			1		1	0	1
Even parity in positions 1, 3, 5, 7 requires that $p_1 = 1$	**1**		**1**		**1**	0	**1**
Even parity in positions 2, 3, 6, 7 requires that $p_2 = 0$	1	**0**	**1**		1	**0**	**1**
Even parity in positions 4, 5, 6, 7 requires that $p_3 = 0$	1	0	1	**0**	**1**	**0**	**1**

The code word is formed by concatenating the value of the bits in positions 1 through 7. In this case the actual word being transmitted is 1010101.

Note: The reader should be aware that depending on how the bits are numbered we may obtain a different value. In this section, as indicated in step 2, we assign the value 1 to the most significant bit and the value 7 to the least significant bit. The code will work with either convention as long as the reader is consistent in using the numbering scheme.

To locate and correct the error use the following steps:

(1) Perform k parity checks on selected digits of each code word. The result of each of these parity checks is either 0 if no error has occurred or 1 if an error has been detected.

(2) Using the results of the parity tests, form a binary number $r_k r_2 \ldots r_1$. The decimal value of this number gives the position of the erroneous digit.

EXAMPLE 1.36 Assume that the word sent is 1010101. If the word received is 1011101, find the position of the bit in error using the procedure indicated above.

(1) Since three checking digits were added, three parity checks need to be performed.

Position	1	2	3	4	5	6	7	
	p_1	p_2	b_1	p_3	b_2	b_3	b_4	
Data	1	0	1	1	1	0	1	
parity check for p_1 =	1		1		1		1	r1 = 0 since parity is even
parity check for p_2 =		0	1			0	1	r2 = 0 since parity is even
parity check for p_3 =				1	1	0	1	r3 = 1 since parity is odd

The position of the erroneous bit is $r_3 r_2 r_1 = 100$. The decimal value of this number is $1^2 0^1 0^0 = 1*2^2 = 4$. This result indicates that the erroneous bit occupies position 4 on the received byte as we have already assumed. The bit on the 4th position is then complemented to form the correct message.

Solved Problems

1.1 Early "minicomputers" had 16-bit addresses. How many different addresses did the address space have?

Since the addresses are 16 bits long, there are 2^{16} or 65,536 addresses.

1.2 Modern computers use 32-bit addresses. How many different addresses does the address space have?

Since the addresses are 32 bits long, there are 2^{32} or 4,294,967,296 unique different addresses.

1.3 Assume that a program with 4,294,836,224 bytes of instructions and data is to reside in the memory of a computer of brand XYZ. What is the minimum size (in bits) of the addresses of this computer if the program is to run successfully?

The size of the address space is given by 2^N where N is the number of bits used to represent an address. Since $2^{16} < 4{,}294{,}836{,}224 < 2^{32}$, the minimum number of bits necessary to represent addresses is 32.

1.4 The ASCII representation (in hexadecimal) of the character string "HI THERE!" is shown below. If the H is stored in byte 5C1B, what is the address of the byte that contains the letter R? Would the address of the byte that contains the letter R be different if all the letters were lowercase? To facilitate the reading of the string we will assume that the addresses increase toward the right.

H	I		T	H	E	R	E	!
48	49	20	54	48	65	52	65	21

5C1B ⟶

The byte that contains the letter R is 6 bytes away, therefore, its address is

$$\begin{array}{r} 5C1B + \\ 6 \\ \hline 5C21 \end{array}$$

The address of this byte remains the same regardless of its contents.

1.5 The hard disk of a computer has a capacity of 4 Gigabytes; how many bytes does it really have?

4 Gigabytes = $4*10^6$ Kilobytes = $4*10^6*1024$ bytes = 4,096,000,000 bytes

1.6 Some instructions like the one shown below explicitly state the size of their operands. In this case the instruction "moves" (copies) the content of the word beginning at location ALPHA to the word beginning at location ALPHA + 6. Using the instruction indicated below, show the contents of these memory locations after the instruction gets executed. Assume that a word occupies two bytes.

MOVW ALPHA, ALPHA + 6

Content of memory before the instruction gets executed (shown in hexadecimal).

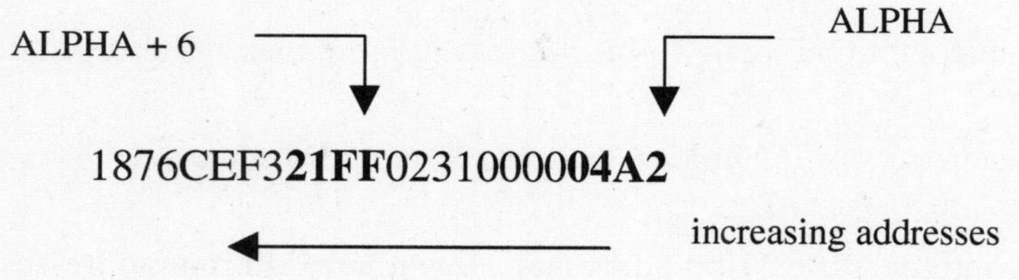

ALPHA + 6 ↓ ALPHA ↓

1876CEF3**21FF**0231000**04A2**

⟵ increasing addresses

ALPHA is a named memory location or a symbolic address. The address ALPHA + 6 is six bytes away from ALPHA in the direction in which the addresses increase. Since a word occupies two bytes, the word beginning at ALPHA has A242 as its content. These two bytes are copied into position ALPHA + 6, therefore, the contents of these memory locations after the instruction is executed looks like this:

1876CEF3**04A2**0231000004A2

Notice that the content of location ALPHA has not changed.

1.7 Show the contents of locations ALPHA and BETA after executing the instruction indicated below. Assume that the initial contents of the operands at locations ALPHA and BETA are 01100101 and 01010001 respectively. Do all operations in two's complement arithmetic.

ADD2B ALPHA, BETA

In this case the instruction calls for adding the bytes at location ALPHA and BETA. This situation is pictured below with the operands shown in bold before and after the execution of the operation.

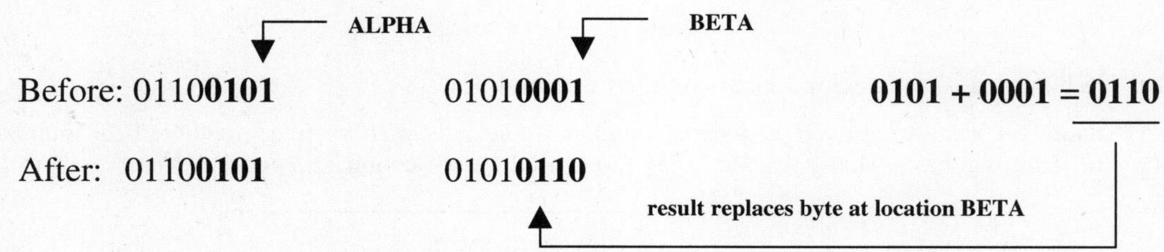

As already mentioned, the operator calls for adding two bytes. The symbolic addresses of these two bytes are ALPHA and BETA respectively. Since there are two operands the addition is destructive (see Example 1.4). Therefore, the byte at location BETA will be replaced by the result of the operation. This example also illustrates that the address of any memory location is the address of its first byte in the direction in which the addresses increase.

1.8 Given the sequence $10001100_{(2}$, show its decimal equivalent if it is considered (*a*) an unsigned binary number, (*b*) a sign-magnitude number, (*c*) a two's complement number.

(*a*) If this sequence is considered as an unsigned binary number its decimal equivalent is

$$1^7 0^6 0^5 0^4 1^3 1^2 0^1 0^0 = (1*2^7) + (1*2^3) + (1*2^2) = 128 + 8 + 4 = 140$$

(*b*) If this sequence is considered as a sign-magnitude number we have that

Sign bit = 1. Therefore, the number is negative.

Magnitude: $0^6 0^5 0^4 1^3 1^2 0^1 0^0 = (1*2^3) + (1*2^2) = 8 + 4 = 12$

Therefore, the decimal equivalent of this number is -12.

(*c*) If this sequence is considered as a two's complement number we have that

Sign bit = 1. Therefore, the number is negative.

Using the procedure described in Section 1.8.2 we need to

(1) complement of the number: 10001100 — Change 0's to 1's and 1's to 0's

↓

01110011

(2) add one to the complemented number

```
01110011 +
       1
--------
01110100
```

The decimal equivalent of this last sequence is $0^7 1^6 1^5 1^4 0^3 1^2 0^1 0^0 = (1*2^6) + (1*2^5) + (1*2^4) + (1*2^2) = 116$. Therefore, the decimal equivalent of the number is -116.

1.9 What is the decimal equivalent of $CA14_{(16}$?

Using the procedure of Section 1.4.2 we have that

$$CA14_{(16} = C*16^3 + A*16^2 + 1*16^1 + 4*16^0$$

Replacing C for 12 and A for 10, their respective decimal equivalents, we obtain

$$\begin{aligned} CA14_{(16} &= (12*4096) + (10*256) + (1*16) + (4*1) \\ &= 51{,}732 \end{aligned}$$

1.10 What is the hexadecimal equivalent of decimal 331?

Since we want to convert a decimal number to hexadecimal we need to divide the number by the hexadecimal basis. That is, by 16. Using the procedure of Section 1.5.2 we have that

Number	Quotient When Dividing by 16	Remainder
331	20	11 (=B)
20	1	4
1	0	1

The hexadecimal equivalent of decimal 331 is $14B_{(16}$.

We can verify that this is the correct result as follows:

$$14B_{(16} = (1*16^2) + (4*16^1) + (B*16^0)$$

Replacing B by its decimal equivalent we have that

$$\begin{aligned} 14B_{(16} &= (1*256) + (4*16) + (11*1) \\ &= 256 + 64 + 11 \\ &= 331 \end{aligned}$$

1.11 What is the binary equivalent of decimal 115?

Since we want to convert a decimal number to binary we need to divide the number by the binary basis. That is, by 2. To obtain the binary equivalent follow the procedure of Section 1.5.2.

Number	Quotient When Dividing by 2	Remainder
115	57	1
57	28	1
28	14	0
14	7	0
7	3	1
3	1	1
1	0	1

The binary equivalent of decimal 115 is $1110011_{(2}$.

We can verify that the result is correct by noting that

$$\begin{aligned}1^6 1^5 1^4 0^3 0^2 1^1 1^0{}_{(2} &= (1*2^6) + (1*2^5) + (1*2^4) + (0*2^3) + (0*2^2) + (1*2^1) + (1*2^0)\\ &= (1*64) + (1*32) + (1*16) + (1*2) + (1*1)\\ &= 64 + 32 + 16 + 2 + 1 = 115\end{aligned}$$

Another way of obtaining the binary equivalent of the decimal number is to convert this value to its hexadecimal or octal equivalent and then express it in binary. This is illustrated below.

Number	Quotient When Dividing by 16	Remainder
115	7	3
7	0	7

The equivalent hexadecimal number of decimal 115 is $73_{(16}$. Expressing this hexadecimal number in binary according to the procedure of Section 1.5.1 we have that

$$73_{(16} = 01110011_{(2}$$

1.12 What is the octal equivalent of decimal 1144?

Since we want to convert a decimal number to an octal we need to divide the number by the octal basis. That is, by 8. Using the procedure of Section 1.5.2 we have that

Number	Quotient When Dividing by 8	Remainder
1144	143	0
143	17	7
17	2	1
2	0	2

The octal equivalent of decimal 1144 is $2170_{(8}$. We can verify this result as follows:

$$\begin{aligned}2170_{(8} &= (2*8^3) + (1*8^2) + (7*8^1) + (0*8^0)\\ &= (2*512) + (1*64) + (56) + (0*1)\\ &= 1024 + 64 + 56\\ &= 1144\end{aligned}$$

1.13 What is the octal equivalent of $101001110101_{(2}$?

Since $2^3 = 8$ we can write each individual octal number using only three bits. We can use a procedure similar to the one used for converting binary numbers to their hexadecimal equivalents (see Section 1.5.1). However, instead of forming groups of four bits we form groups of three bits. Therefore,

$$101001110101_{(2} = 101\ 001\ 110\ 101 = 5165_{(8}$$

1.14 What is the hexadecimal equivalent of $111101001_{(2}$?

Forming groups of four bits beginning from the rightmost bit according to the procedure of Section 1.5.1 we have that

$$111101001_{(2} = 1\ 1110\ 1001 = \mathbf{000}1\ 1110\ 1001$$

Notice that it was necessary to add three bits (shown in bold) to the left of the single bit of the leftmost group to make it a four-bit group.

Using Table 1-3, the hexadecimal equivalent of the given binary number is

$$111101001_{(2} = 1\ 1110\ 1001 = \mathbf{000}1\ 1110\ 1001 = 1E9_{(16}$$

1.15 What is the result of adding the two's complement numbers 01100100 and 00011100? If an overflow occurs explain why.

```
01100100 +
00011100
________
      00 ← Zero plus zero is zero. Therefore, write zero.

01100100 +
00011100
________
     000 ← One plus one is zero with a carry of one. Therefore, write zero and carry one.

    1
01100100 +
00011100
________
    0000 ← One (the carry) plus zero is one. This one plus one is zero with a carry of one. Therefore, write zero
           and carry one.

   1
01100100 +
00011100
________
  000000 ← One (the carry) plus one is zero with a carry of one. This zero plus zero is zero. Therefore, write zero
           and carry one.

  1
01100100 +
00011100
________
 0000000 ← One (the carry) plus one is zero with a carry of one. This zero plus zero is zero. Therefore, write zero
           and carry one.

 1
01100100 +
00011100
________
10000000 ← One (the carry) plus zero is one. This one plus zero is one. Therefore, write one.
```

Notice that both operands are positive but the result is negative. Therefore, the result overflows.

The result of this addition illustrates another way of determining if an overflow has occurred. Notice that there was a carry into the sign bit but there was no carry out of it.

1.16 What is the result of adding the two's complement numbers 10011011 and 11100011? If an overflow occurs explain why.

```
            10011011 +
            11100011
            ________
                   0 ← One plus one is zero with a carry of one. Therefore, write zero and carry one.
                  1
            10011011 +
            11100011
            ________
                  10 ← One (the carry) plus one is zero with a carry of one. This zero plus one is one. Therefore, write one
                       and carry one.
                 1
            10011011 +
            11100011
            ________
                 110 ← One (the carry) plus zero is one. This one plus zero is one. Therefore, write one.
            10011011 +
            11100011
            ________
                1110 ← One plus zero is one. Therefore, write one.
            10011011 +
            11100011
            ________
               11110 ← One plus zero is one. Therefore, write one.
            10011011 +
            11100011
            ________
              111110 ← Zero plus one is one. Therefore, write one.
            10011011 +
            11100011
            ________
             1111110 ← Zero plus one is one. Therefore, write one.
Carry out → 1 10011011 +
            11100011
            ________
            01111110 ← One plus one is zero with a carry of one. Therefore, write zero and carry one.
```

The addition overflows since the operands are both negative and the result is positive. This result illustrates another condition for detecting an overflow. Notice that there is a carry out of the sign bit but there is no carry into it.

This condition and the one already mentioned in solved problem 1.15 allows us to detect when an overflow has occurred. Therefore, we can say that when performing additions in two's complement an overflow occurs if

(*a*) there is a carry into the sign bit and no carry out of the sign bit

or

(*b*) there is a carry out of the sign bit and no carry into the sign bit.

1.17 What is the result of adding the hexadecimal numbers 143AF and 215B7?

```
 143AF +
 215B7
 ------
      6 ← "Thinking in decimal" we have that 15 plus 7 is 22. Since 22 = 1*16 + 6, write 6 and carry 1.

    1
 143AF +
 215B7
 ------
     66 ← 1 (the carry) plus ten is eleven. 11 plus 11 is 22. Since 22 = 1*16 + 6, write 6 and carry 1.

    1
 143AF +
 215B7
 ------
    966 ← 1 (the carry) plus three is four. 4 plus 5 is 9. Therefore write 9.

 143AF +
 215B7
 ------
   5966 ← Four plus one is five. Therefore write 5.

 143AF +
 215B7
 ------
  35966 ← One plus two is three. Therefore write 3.
```

1.18 What is the result of multiplying 00001101 by 00000101?

Multiplication in binary can be carried out the same way we multiply in decimal. The major difference is that we are restricted to the use of the symbols 0 and 1. In this case $1101_{(2} = 13$ and $101_{(2} = 5$.

```
    1101 ×
     101
    -----
    1101 +
   0000
  1101
  -------
 1000001
```

Notice that $1000001_{(2} = 65$. This is the same result that we would have obtained in the decimal system since 65 = 13*5.

1.19 What is the decimal equivalent of the unsigned binary number 11001001?

Using the procedure indicated in Section 1.1.1 we have that

$$\begin{aligned} 11001001_{(2} &= 1^7 1^6 0^5 0^4 1^3 0^2 0^1 1^0 \\ &= (1*2^7) + (1*2^6) + (1*2^3) + (1*2^0) \\ &= 128 + 64 + 8 + 1 \\ &= 201 \end{aligned}$$

Another method that is widely used for calculating the decimal equivalent of a binary number is **Horner's method**. This procedure, which works for any base, is as follows:

"Start with the first digit on the left and multiply it by the base. Then add the next digit and multiply the sum by the base. Continue this process until you add the last digit."

In this particular case we have to multiply by 2 since the number is binary.

$11001001_{(2} \rightarrow 1*2 = 2$
$2 + 1 = 3$ and $3*2 = 6$
$6 + 0 = 6$ and $6*2 = 12$
$12 + 0 = 12$ and $12*2 = 24$
$24 + 1 = 25$ and $25*2 = 50$
$50 + 0 = 50$ and $50*2 = 100$
$100 + 0 = 100$ and $100*2 = 200$
$200 + 1 = 201$

1.20 Use Horner's method to calculate the decimal equivalent of the number $2341_{(8}$.

Since the number is octal we need to multiply by 8.

$231_{(8} \rightarrow 2*8 = 16$
$16 + 3 = 19$ and $19*8 = 152$
$152 + 4 = 156$ and $156*8 = 1248$
$1248 + 1 = 1249$.

Therefore, $2341_{(8} = 1249$

1.21 Another convention for representing both positive and negative numbers in a computer is the **one's complement notation or 1's complement**. This convention was devised to make the addition of two numbers with different signs the same as for two numbers with the same sign. In this convention, positive numbers are represented in the usual way. To represent a negative number start with the binary representation of the absolute value of the number and complement all its bits. To carry out arithmetic operations treat the sign bit as any other bit. However, when performing an addition, if there is a carry out of the most significant bit add this bit to the rightmost bit. This is known as the ***end-around carry***.

Overflows are detected following similar conventions to those of the 2's complement (see Section 1.8.2.2 and solved problems 1.15 and 1.16). The range of values that can be represented in this convention using n bits is -2^{n-1} to $+2^{n-1} - 1$.

What is the 1's complement representation of decimal −35? Use a byte to represent the number.

(1) Start with the binary representation of the absolute value of the number. In this case,

$$35 = 00100011_{(2}$$

(2) Complement all the bits of the binary number obtained in the previous step.

00100011
↓ Changing 0's to 1's and vice versa.
11011100

The 1's complement of decimal −35 is 11011100.

1.22 Given the bit patterns shown below, find their equivalent values in the conventions indicated below.

Bit Pattern	Sign-magnitude	1's Complement	2's Complement	Unsigned
000	0	0	0	0
001	1	1	1	1
010	2	2	2	2
011	3	3	3	3
100	−0	−3	−4	4
101	−1	−2	−3	5
110	−2	−1	−2	6
111	−3	−0	−1	7

This example shows that in order to interpret the content of any memory location correctly it is necessary to know the convention being used. Notice that the positive values have the same representation in all conventions. The zero value has two different representations in sign-magnitude and 1's complement. This complicates the logic of the ALU.

1.23 What is the result of adding the 1's complement numbers 00100001 and 11101010?

0010000**1** +
1110101**0**
____
0000101**1** ← One plus zero is one.

001000**0**1 +
111010**1**0
____
000010**1**1 ← Zero plus one is one.

00100**0**01 +
11101**0**10
____
00001**0**11 ← Zero plus zero is zero.

0010**0**001 +
1110**1**010
____
0000**1**011 ← Zero plus one is one.

001**0**0001 +
111**0**1010
____
000**0**1011 ← Zero plus zero is zero.

00**1**00001 +
11**1**01010
____
00**0**01011 ← One plus one is zero with a carry of one.

```
 1
 00100001 +
 11101010
 ---------
 00001011 ← One (the carry) plus zero is one. This one plus one is zero with a carry of one.
 1
 00100001 +
 11101010
 ---------
1 00001011 ← One (the carry) plus zero is one. This one plus one is zero with a carry of one.
        1 +
 ---------
 00001100 ← One (the carry) plus zero is one. This one plus one is zero with a carry of one.
```

1.24 What is the result of 10001011 − 10101 in two's complement?

```
10001011 −
   10101
---------
       0 ← One minus one is zero.
10001011 −
   10101
---------
      10 ← One minus zero is one.
10001011 −
   10101
---------
     110 ← Zero is less than one. Borrow "two" from higher unit. Two plus zero is two. Two minus one is one.
    0
10001011 −
   10101
---------
    0110 ← The one (in bold) became zero since it "paid" the "borrowed" two. Zero minus zero is zero.
10001011 −
   10101
---------
   10110 ← Zero is less than one. Borrow "two" from higher unit. Two plus zero is two. Two minus one is one.
  1
10001011 −
   10101
---------
  110110 ← Zero became one (basis minus one). One minus zero (not shown) is one.
 1
10001011 −
   10101
---------
 1110110 ← Zero became one (basis minus one). One minus zero (not shown) is one.
```

0
~~1~~0001011 –
10101

01110110← Zero became one (basis minus one). Zero minus zero (not shown) is zero.

1.25 What is the result of the following hexadecimal operation: 9A8C7B – BD35?

9A8C7**B** –
BD3**5**

99CF4**6**← Eleven minus five is six.

9A8C**7**B –
BD**3**5

99CF**4**6← Seven minus three is four.

9A8**C**7B –
B**D**35

99C**F**46← Twelve is less than thirteen. Borrow "16" from higher unit. Sixteen plus twelve is twenty-eight. Twenty-eight minus thirteen is fifteen. Therefore, write F.

7
9A**8**C7B –
BD35

99**C**F46← Eight became seven since it paid the "borrowed" sixteen. Seven is less than eleven. Borrow sixteen from higher unit. Seven plus sixteen is twenty-three. Twenty-three minus eleven is twelve.

9
9~~**A**~~8C7B –
BD35

9**9**CF46← The A (ten) became nine since it paid the "borrowed" sixteen. Nine minus zero (not shown) is nine.

9A8C7B –
BD35

99CF46← Nine minus zero (not shown) is nine.

1.26 If n bits can represent 2^n different numbers, why is the largest unsigned number only $2^n - 1$ and not 2^n?

There are 2^n different numbers between 0 and $2^n - 1$. However, since the sequence begins with 0 the largest representation is 2^{n-1}.

1.27 The error detection code shown below is known as the "2-out-of-five" code since it consists of all possible combinations of two 1's in a five-bit coded word. What is the value of the parity check bit if even parity is assumed?

Decimal Value	Weight 0 1 2 4 7
0	0 0 0 1 1
1	1 1 0 0 0
2	1 0 1 0 0
3	0 1 1 0 0
4	1 0 0 1 0
5	0 1 0 1 0
6	0 0 1 1 0
7	1 0 0 0 1
8	0 1 0 0 1
9	0 0 1 0 1

The number of bits in every row is even, therefore the parity bit is zero in all rows.

Note: in this code, with the exception of the code word for decimal 0, all entries can be derived from the 1-2-4-7 code. This also shows that the assignment of code word to decimal digits does not necessarily follow a logical pattern.

1.28 Using the Forward Error Code of Section 1.8.5.1 find the bit in error for the sequence of bytes shown below. Assume that (*a*) a parity block is sent every five bytes and that even parity is being used at both the byte and the block level, (*b*) the leftmost bit of every byte is used as parity bit.

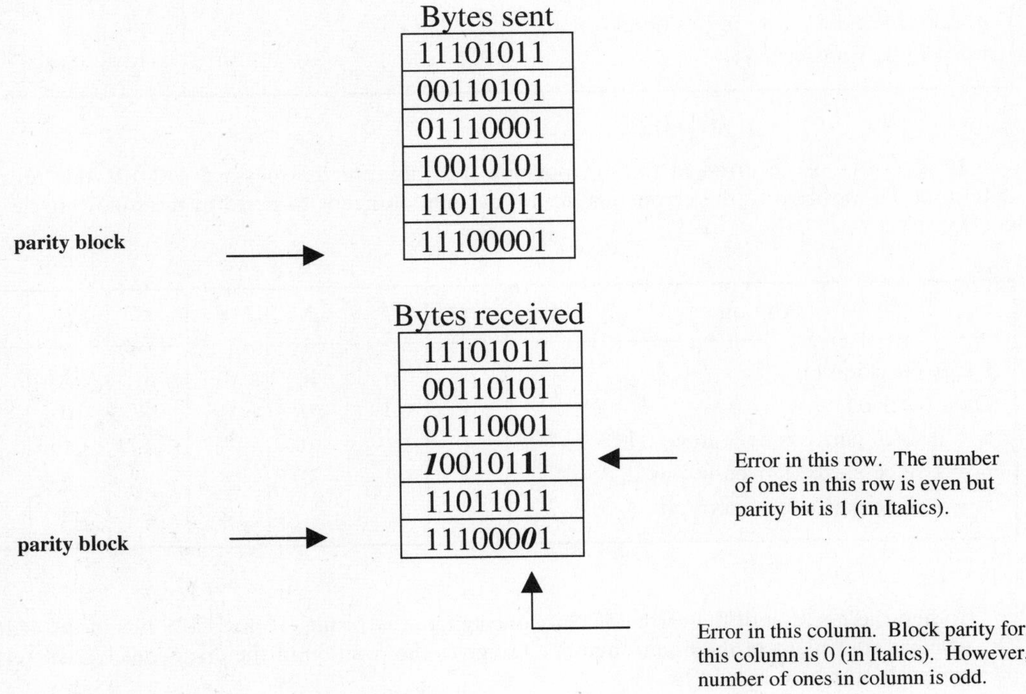

1.29 Use the format of Fig. 1-9 to find the error in the following sequence of bytes. Assume even parity.

1010111011 0110100101 0110111101 0110110001 0110010101 0110010001
0111001111 0010000011 0110000111 0111001001 0110010101 0010000011
0110001011 0110110001 0111010111 0110010101 0010111001

Working with each group separately and dropping the stop bit we can check the rightmost bit (shown here in bold).

1. 10101110**1** ✔	2. 01101001**0** ✔	3. 01101111**0** ✔	4. 01101100**0** ✔
5. 01100101**0** ✔	6. 01100100**1** ✔	7. 01110011**1** ✔	8. 00100000**1** ✔
9. 01100001**1** ✔	10. 01110010**0** ✔	11. 01100101**0** ✔	12. 00100000**1** ✔
13. 01100010**1** ✔	14. 01101100**0** ✔	15. 01110101**1** ✔	16. 01100101**1** ✘
17. 00101110**0** ✔			

The parity bit of group No. 16 should be zero instead of one.

1.30 Using the Hamming code method of Section 1.8.5.2 and four-bit data, what are the values of the checking bits if the message to be sent is 0110? Show the procedure to determine that an error has occurred in the 6th position of the received message.

Position	1	2	3	4	5	6	7
Parity checking bits	p_1	p_2	b_1	p_3	b_2	b_3	b_4
Data			0		1	1	0
p_1 requires even parity in positions 1, 3, 5, 7	1		0		1		0
p_2 requires even parity in positions 2, 3, 6, 7		1	0			1	0
p_3 requires even parity in positions 4, 5, 6, 7				0	1	1	0
word to be transmitted	1	1	0	0	1	1	0

If an error has occurred in the 6th position it is because the message 1100101 was received. To determine the position of the erroneous bit the destination needs to perform the following three parity checks.

Position	1	2	3	4	5	6	7
Parity checking bits	p_1	p_2	b_1	p_3	b_2	b_3	b_4
Data received	1	1	0	0	1	0	0
$r_1 = 0$ since parity is even in pos. 1, 3, 5, 7	1		0		1		0
$r_2 = 1$ since parity is even in pos. 2, 3, 6, 7		1	0			0	0
$r_3 = 1$ since parity is even in pos. 4, 5, 6, 7				0	1	0	0

To find the position of the erroneous bit concatenate the results of the parity bits in the order $r_3r_2r_1$. The decimal equivalent of the binary number 110 gives the position of the erroneous bit. The erroneous bit is in position 6 as it should be.

Supplementary Problems

1.31 In Fig. 1-3 the last address is given as N − 1. Why is this? If a memory location (a byte) has an address of 100, how many bytes precede it?

1.32 If a machine has a 4-bit address, what is the size of the address space? What is the address of the last memory location?

1.33 A program and its data are 63,816 bytes long. What is the minimum number of bits that are needed to represent addresses if the program and its data are going to reside in memory simultaneously?

1.34 Assume that machine XYZ uses bytes operands in all its instructions and that machine WRT uses word operands in all its instructions. If both machines have 32-bit addresses, which of the two machines has the largest address space?

1.35 Show the contents of locations ALPHA and BETA after executing the instruction indicated below. Assume that the initial contents of the word operands at location ALPHA and BETA are 00101010 and 00001100 respectively. Do all operations in two's complement arithmetic.

ADD2W ALPHA, BETA

1.36 Show the contents of locations ALPHA and BETA after executing the instruction indicated below. Assume the initial contents of the word operands at locations ALPHA and BETA are 01100101 and 01010010 respectively. Do all operations in two's complement arithmetic.

ADD2B ALPHA, BETA

1.37 Given a binary number, how can we tell if its decimal equivalent is odd or even?

1.38 Assume that during transmission a byte has two of its bits complemented. If even parity is being used, can the computer detect that an error has occurred in that byte?

1.39 What ASCII hexadecimal numbers can also be interpreted as English words?

1.40 What is a 10? Hint: assume that 10 is written in binary, octal, and hexadecimal and then find its decimal equivalents.

1.41 How can we determine that an overflow has occurred when performing an addition with unsigned binary numbers? Assume that the operands are both n-bit numbers.

1.42 Two's complement is the most popular convention for representing both positive and negative numbers since it does not have any of the problems of 1's complement or sign-magnitude. What are the problems with these two conventions?

1.43 Complete the following table by converting the number shown in each row into the other bases.

Decimal	Binary (unsigned)	Octal	Hexadecimal
125			
	10001001		
		326	
			3A2F
1949			

1.44 What is the result of the following hexadecimal arithmetic operations?

(*a*) B214 + C27 (*b*) 21FE + 6ABC (*c*) ABDE − CAF (*d*) DCAF − CAFE

1.45 What is the decimal equivalent of the bit sequence 10101010 if it is represented in the conventions indicated below? Assume that the byte is the basic unit.

(*a*) unsigned (*b*) sign-magnitude (*c*) 1's complement (*d*) 2's complement

1.46 What is the result of adding the 2's complement number shown below? In each case indicate if an overflow has occurred.

(*a*) 01010010 + 11101101 (*b*) 11011101 + 11010111 (*c*) 11000111 + 11100011 (*d*) 10111100 + 00111101

1.47 What is the result of subtracting the following 2's complement numbers?

(*a*) 00111111 − 11101101 (*b*) 10111000 − 11011011 (*c*) 10101010 − 11100011 (*d*) 11111001 − 00111101

Answers to Supplementary Problems

1.31 Addresses begin with 0, therefore, the last address is always N − 1. There are 100 addresses between 0 and 99. If we include the 100th location, there are 101 memory locations.

1.32 The size of the address space is 2^4. The address of the last memory location is $2^4 - 1$.

1.33 The minimum address size is 2^{16} since $2^{15} < 63816 < 2^{16}$.

1.34 The address space of both machines is 2^{32} bytes long.

1.35 After executing the instruction, the content of location BETA is 00110110. Location ALPHA remains unchanged.

1.36 After executing the instruction, the content of location BETA is 0101**0111**. Notice that only the byte at location BETA was changed. Location ALPHA remains unchanged.

1.37 Any binary number with an odd decimal equivalent has its rightmost bit equal to 1. Likewise, any binary number with an even decimal equivalent has its rightmost bit equal to 0.

1.38 No, if two of the bits are complemented the number of 1-bits and 0-bits remains the same. Therefore, the computer cannot tell that an error has occurred.

1.39 All ASCII codes within the hexadecimal range 41 through 5A represent uppercase letters. Hexadecimal ASCII values 61 through 7A represent lowercase letters.

1.40 Regardless of the value of the basis r ($r > 0$), in all numerical positional systems, 10 always represents the value of the basis.

1.41 The result of the addition will have $n + 1$ bits.

1.42 Problems with sign-magnitude: arithmetic operations with numbers of different signs increase the complexity of the ALU. Adding two numbers with different signs requires that the sign and magnitude of the larger number be determined before the addition is carried out. This increases the overhead considerably, particularly if there are millions of operations to be performed.

Problems with 1's complement: there are two representations for zero that add unnecessary tests when performing arithmetic operations. The carry around bit increases the amount of work required to add two numbers.

1.43

Decimal	Binary (unsigned)	Octal	Hexadecimal
125	1111101	175	7D
137	10001001	211	89
214	11010110	326	D6
14895	11101000101111	35057	3A2F
1949	11110011101	3635	79D

1.44 (*a*) BE3B (*b*) 8CBA (*c*) 9F2F (*d*) 11B1

1.45 (*a*) 170 (unsigned) (*b*) −34 (sign-magnitude) (*c*) −85 (1's complement) (*d*) −86 (2's complement)

1.46 (*a*) 00111111 (*b*) 10111000 (*c*) 10101010 (*d*) 11111001

1.47 (*a*) 01010010 (*b*) 11011101 (*c*) 11000111 (*d*) 10111100

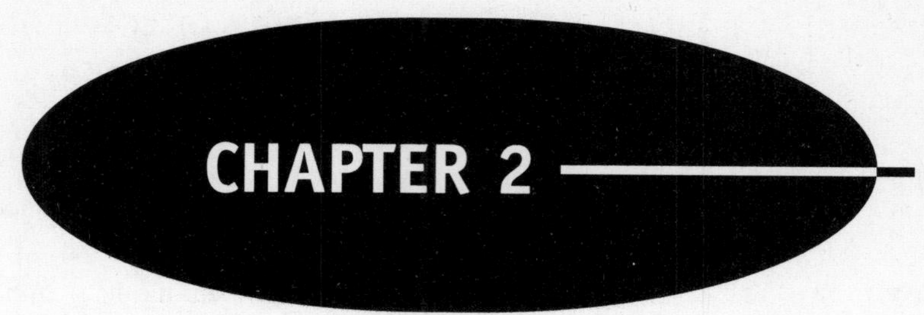

CHAPTER 2

Program Planning and Design

2.1 PROGRAMMING

The basic flow of computer processing, as shown in Fig. 2-1, is "Input, Process, Output." The art of ***programming*** involves writing instructions to tell the computer how to process specific information. Some kind of data is sent into the program, and then the processed data are sent out from the program. For example, in a payroll-processing program, the hours worked and hourly salary for a number of employees might be the input. The program would then calculate the gross pay, the various deductions to be subtracted, and the net pay. One output would be the actual paychecks. In order for the processing to be completed successfully, the program must execute the correct calculations in the correct order.

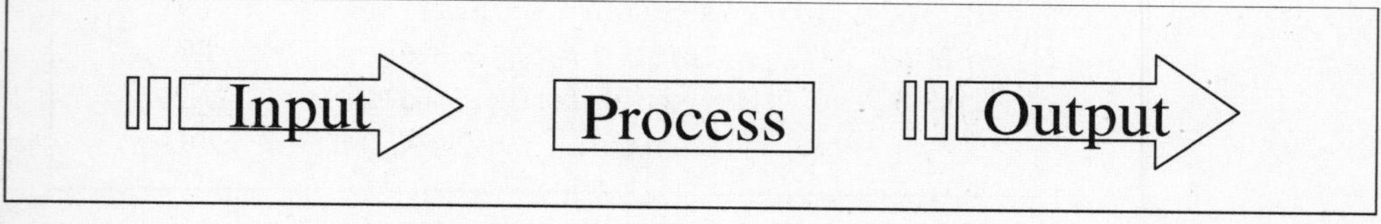

Fig. 2-1 Processing flow.

EXAMPLE 2.1 What would be the input, process, and output for a program to calculate a semester grade point average?

Input: Letter grades from all the courses in the semester, and the grading scale used (e.g. A = 4.0, B = 3.0, etc.)

Process: Add up the numerical values of all the course grades and divide by the number of courses

Output: The grade point average for the semester

2.2 PROBLEM SOLVING

Computer programs are written to solve problems. In English classes, writing a research paper is much easier if the outline is constructed first. The actual writing then follows the outline. In the same way, coding a computer program should not be started until all the plans are made. First, a solution is created, and then the program is coded in a computer language. The key is planning.

There are five basic steps to programming. Each step is essential in the process. Following the first two steps carefully will ultimately result in less time, energy, and frustration in the final steps.

Step 1. **Analyze the problem and develop the specifications.** The programmer must completely understand and be able to write a precise statement of the problem. In order to develop the exact specifications, there are several questions that must be asked.

- What are the inputs to the problem? What is known, what will be given, and in what form?
- What are the outputs desired? What kind of report, chart, or information is required?
- What would be the processing steps necessary to go from the given input to the desired output?

Step 2. **Design a solution.** A precise set of steps must be developed, that, when applied to the problem, will lead to the best solution. This is the outline from which the code will be written. The series of steps should be unambiguous, detailed and finite, able to be completed in a reasonable period of time. The solution must be complete and effective. It is helpful to test the solution by "walking through" the steps with data from Step 1 in order to be sure the solution designed is the best one possible.

Step 3. **Code the program in a programming language with documentation.** If the solution has been completely and carefully designed, translation into a programming language will be relatively straightforward. Usually, the programmer can write the code step by step exactly according to the solution. The more complete the solution, the less time and energy it takes to write the code. An integral part of the coding process, but one ignored by many programmers, is documentation. Each step of the code should be explained with comments, so the original (or a future) programmer will completely understand how the solution was reached. Both debugging during the programming process and changing the program later are greatly facilitated by good comments embedded within the code.

Step 4. **Test the program.** This step is an iterative process with the previous step. Many novice programmers write out the entire program before testing. Then, if it doesn't work, they have no idea which section of the code has a problem. Instead, as each part of the code is written, it should be tested. For example, in the payroll program, first the programmer can write the code to accept the hours worked and hourly salary, and then test to be sure the correct values have been received by the program. It would not help to write the processing section before the inputs have been received correctly.

Step 5. **Validate the program.** Once the program has been written in its entirety, and is working for a few test cases, it should be validated by extensive testing. Just because it works for one set of test inputs does not mean it will work in every case. A broad range of test values should be applied. This is also where the user interface is examined. Are the directions sufficient? How does it handle invalid input? What happens if the user enters character data instead of numeric? Extensive fine-tuning of the program in every situation is necessary before it can be considered complete.

These five steps are essential to the problem-solving and programming process. The heart of Step 2 is the design of the algorithm.

2.3 ALGORITHMS

The goal of the problem-solving process explained above is to develop an ***algorithm***, or set of steps to solve the problem. We use algorithms every day. Whenever we are doing a task, such as following a recipe or assembling a bookcase, the algorithm tells us each step in the proper order.

EXAMPLE 2.2 Write the algorithm to make a peanut butter and jelly sandwich.

1. Put the bread, peanut butter, jelly, knife, and plate onto the workspace.
2. Place two slices of bread on the plate.
3. Using the knife, spread peanut butter on one slice.
4. If you want jelly, using the knife, spread jelly on the other slice.
5. Slap the two slices together, sticky side in.
6. Repeat steps 2 through 5 for each sandwich needed.
7. Eat the sandwiches.

In the algorithm above, step 1 is the input, steps 2 through 6 explain the process, and step 7 is the output. It is clear from the algorithm that we should not do step 5 before step 3, or the sandwich would not be very interesting. Step 4 lets us make a choice whether to include jelly in the sandwich. Clearly, a number of other "if" statements could be included for choosing bananas, pickles, or any other ingredients. Also, step 6 allows us the flexibility to repeat the same process exactly several times.

To be correct, an algorithm has some specific characteristics. An algorithm:

- Has input, performs a process, and gives output.
- Must be clear and unambiguous.
- Must correctly solve the problem.
- Can be followed with paper and pencil.
- Must execute in a finite number of steps.

When writing algorithms for more complex numeric problems, usually all the input is obtained in the first few steps and the output is given in the last few steps. Many steps can be subdivided. For example, examine the algorithm in Example 2.3 below. Steps 1 through 3 are input, 4 and 5 are processing, and 6 is output. Steps 3 and 5 are subdivided into two parts for clarity.

EXAMPLE 2.3 Write the algorithm for a simple ATM machine.

1. Get the password from the user.
2. If the password is not valid, construct an error message and skip to step 6.
3. Get the inputs.
   - 3.1. Get the transaction type (deposit or withdrawal), and the amount from the user.
   - 3.2. Get the current balance from the bank.
4. If the transaction type is deposit, add the amount to the current balance.
5. If the transaction type is withdrawal, check the current balance.
   - 5.1. If amount is greater than the current balance, construct an error message and skip to step 6.
   - 5.2. If amount is equal to or less than the current balance, subtract the amount from the current balance.
6. Output the error message or the cash, and the current balance.
7. Ask the user whether to repeat steps 3 through 6 for another transaction.

2.3.1 Pseudocode and Flowcharting

The algorithms in the previous section have been written in a structured English method called ***pseudocode***. Notice that all the lines of pseudocode contain a specific verb. In pseudocode, the steps of the algorithm are numbered in such a way that one action is executed per line. If a line requires two steps, it is subdivided in outline form to the next level (e.g., 3.1, 3.2, etc.).

Pseudocode is usually a good way to begin to design a solution to the problem. It lists the steps of the algorithm. However, it is not always easy to begin coding the program from pseudocode,

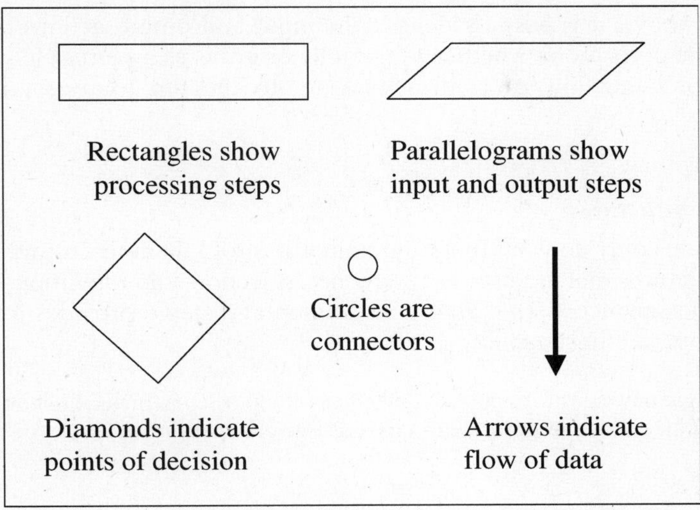

Fig. 2-2 Flowchart shapes.

because the program flow is not clear. The conditional statements and the statements to skip to another step do not provide enough of a picture of what should happen when.

In order to express the flow of processing in a much more lucid fashion, many programmers use a ***flowchart***, which is a structured picture map showing the steps of the algorithm. The shapes usually used for each part of the flowchart are described in Fig. 2-2.

EXAMPLE 2.4 A flowchart can be drawn for any algorithm. Draw a flowchart for the peanut butter sandwich algorithm shown in Example 2.2.

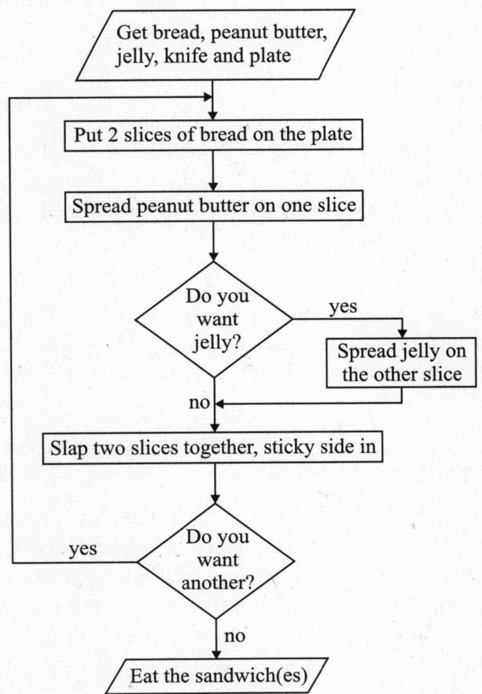

In the flowchart above, it is easy to identify the input and output actions because of the shapes used. The result of the decision on whether to use jelly or not is clear, either jelly is added or it is not. Also, the arrow shows the flow of control back up to the top to repeat the sandwich-making process.

2.3.2 Basic Control Structures

Computer programs only do what the programmer has told them to do, and in that specific order. The basic control structures that are used are sequence, selection, and repetition. In Example 2.4, most steps are executed in sequence. Step 4 allows a selection and step 6 provides for repetition.

Most programs operate in sequence.

EXAMPLE 2.5 A simple flowchart for two ATM machines could be constructed as shown in Fig. 2-3. Each step, input, process, and output, is done in order, with no decisions or repetitions.

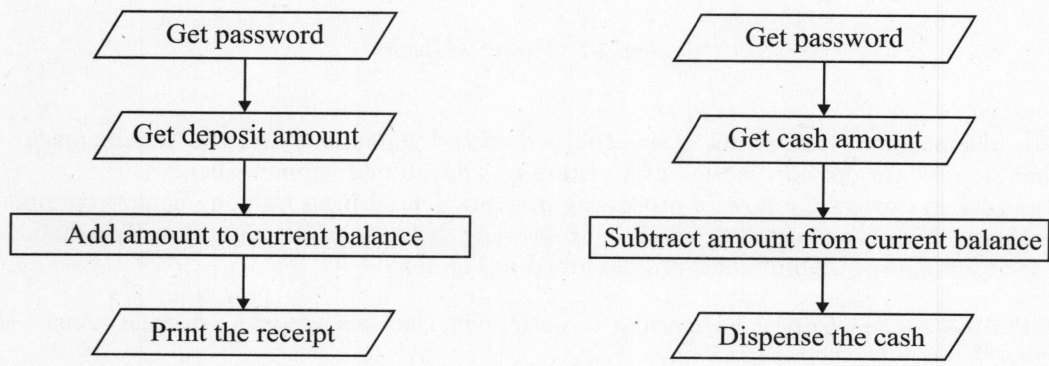

Fig. 2-3 Flowcharts for two simple ATM machines.

It is clear from the flowcharts that some decisions are necessary. The example describes two separate machines, one for withdrawal and one for deposit. Usually, you want one machine to handle both. Also, what if the password is not good? What if there is not enough money in the account for withdrawal? The flowchart needs to be constructed carefully, one section at a time.

EXAMPLE 2.6 Design one machine to determine if the transaction is a deposit or withdrawal. If the password is not good, nothing else should be done except an error message, and if there is not enough balance for the withdrawal, an error message should be given. A complete flowchart is shown in Fig. 2-4.

2.3.3 Top-down Design and Data Abstraction

The algorithms demonstrated in the previous sections are fairly simple. Most often problems cannot be solved in such a simple way. To attack more complex problems, ***top-down design*** is used. In top-down design, the overall problem is broken into the main tasks (usually input, process, output), and then each of these tasks is broken down into subtasks until a simple solution can be seen for each subtask. Usually ***hierarchy charts*** are used as a help in top-down design. Hierarchy charts differ from flowcharts in that they indicate *what* should be done, not *how* the job will be accomplished. Instead

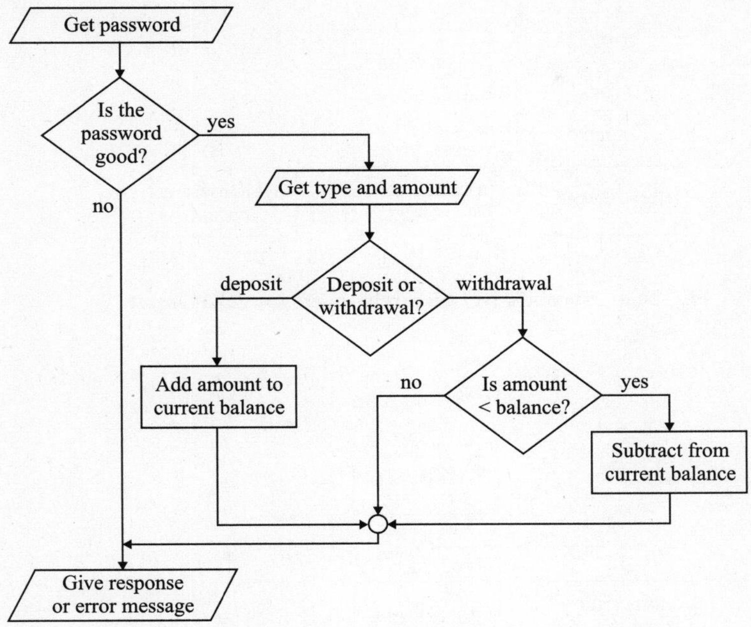

Fig. 2-4 Complete ATM machine flowchart.

of indicating the flow of data, they illustrate the tasks, or modules, for each part of the solution. The only flow of data important is what should go into and come out of each module.

EXAMPLE 2.7 Look back at the ATM program example. The overall task, or the module at the highest level, is to simulate an ATM machine. The main subtasks would be to get the inputs, to perform the calculations, and to give the outputs. The first draft of the hierarchy chart is illustrated in Fig. 2-5.

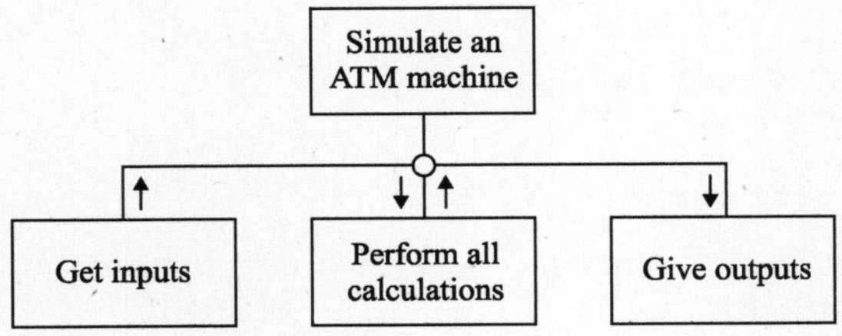

Fig. 2-5 First-level ATM hierarchy chart.

Each box represents a module of the solution. Notice, like pseudocode and flowcharts, each task begins with a verb to show the action that must be performed by that module. Arrows coming from a box indicate data coming out from that module, and arrows going into the box denote data needed by that module.

Now that the overall task and the main subtasks have been identified, each module can be subdivided even further into all the tasks that must be performed in that section. The next level for the inputs and outputs is fairly straightforward, as shown in Fig. 2-6.

The calculation module is a little more complex. There are two main subtasks, one to handle deposits and one to handle withdrawals. Each of these subtasks can be further broken down into other simpler tasks. Look at Fig. 2-7 to see the hierarchy chart for this task.

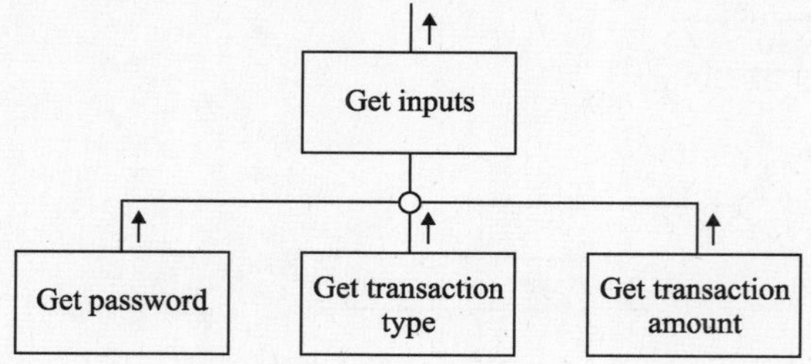

Fig. 2-6a Second-level hierarchy chart for ATM input.

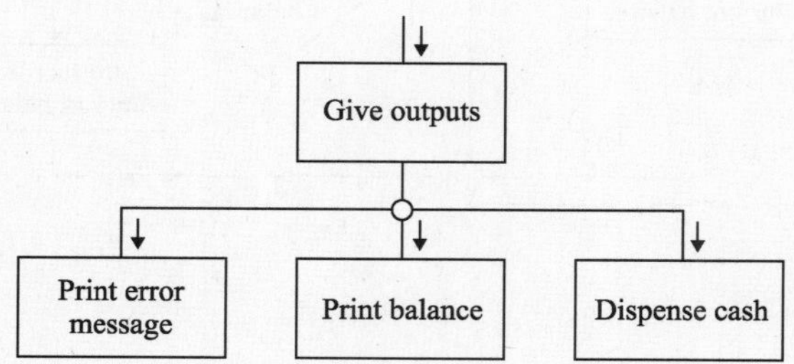

Fig. 2-6b Second-level hierarchy chart for ATM output.

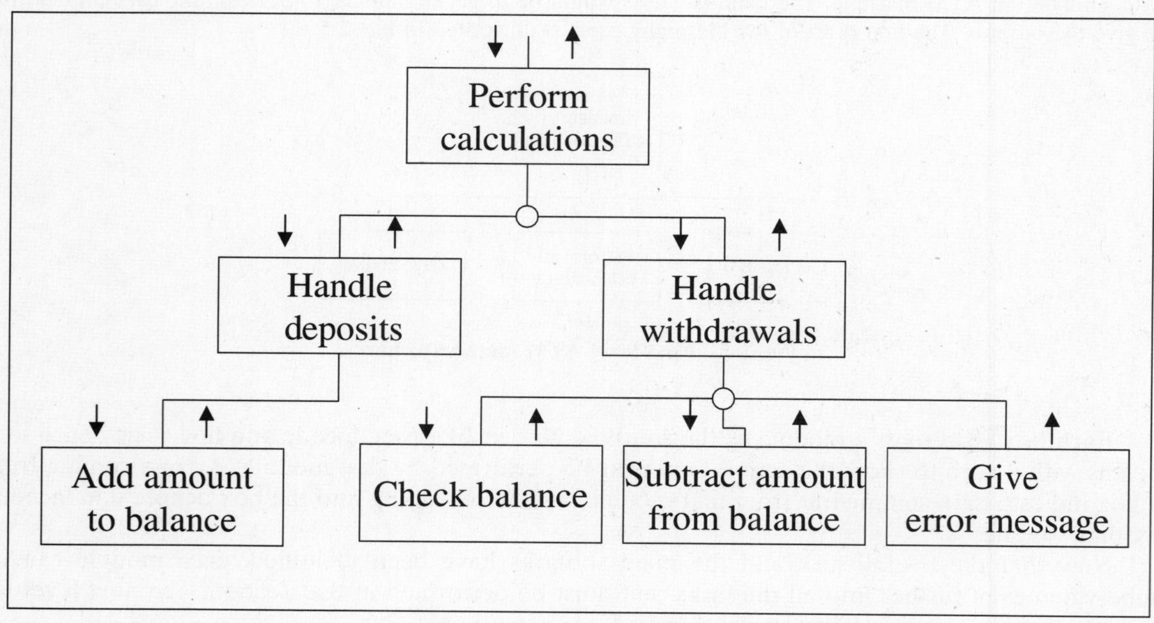

Fig. 2-7 Second- and third-level hierarchy chart for ATM calculations.

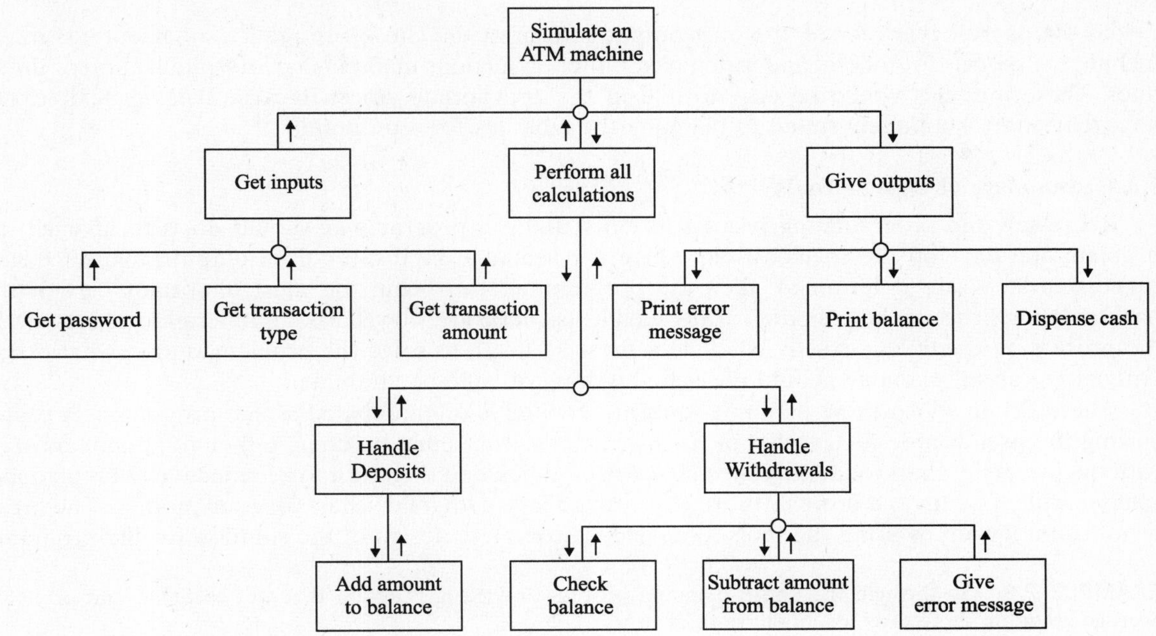

Fig. 2-8 Complete hierarchy chart for ATM machine.

The Handle withdrawals module must check the balance to see if there is enough money in the account before adjusting the balance. If there is not enough money, an error message is generated. An error message is also needed in the module that gets the password. A complete hierarchy chart is found in Fig. 2-8.

EXAMPLE 2.8 Draw the hierarchy chart for a payroll-processing program.

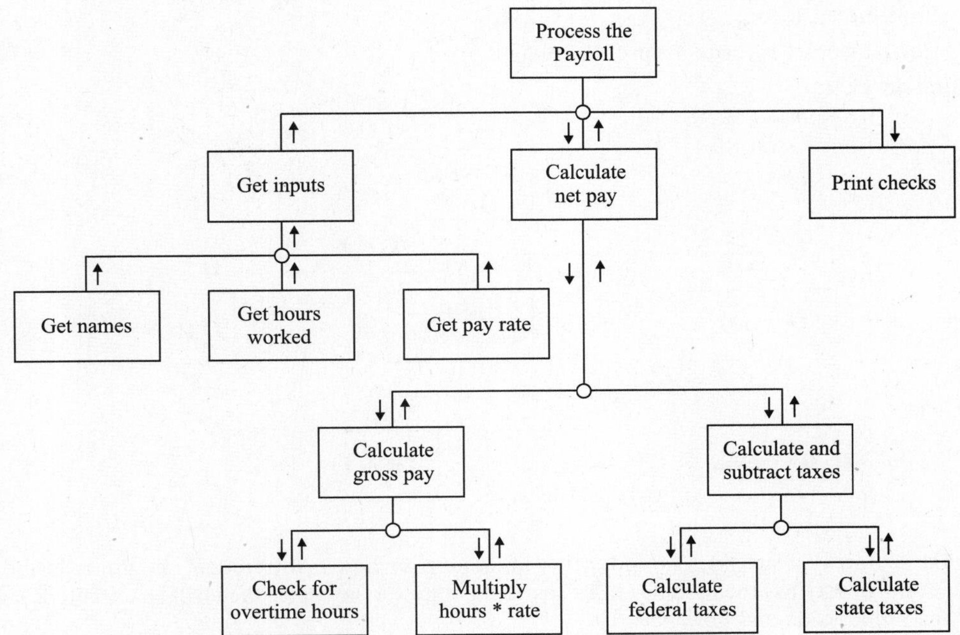

In the payroll chart above, the only output is to print the checks. In reality, other outputs might include the reports for federal and state taxes. Other deductions might include hospitalization or union dues. These modules would be easy to add in the appropriate place. Because it is so flexible, the hierarchy chart is uniquely suited to planning the modules for a program.

2.3.4 Summary of Design Tools

To review the programming process, the first thing a programmer should do is to analyze the problem and develop the specifications. Once the available inputs, required outputs, and necessary processing steps are determined, then the programmer can begin the most important part of the programming process, the planning. Tools such as pseudocode, flowcharts, and hierarchy charts aid in the process of identifying exactly what steps must be taken to solve the problem, and in what order. Only after careful planning should the actual writing of code be attempted.

The order in which these planning tools are created is often debated. Some programmers prefer writing the pseudocode first, to list in English exactly what must be done. Other programmers start with the hierarchy chart to identify the necessary modules, and then turn to pseudocode to break down each module. Usually the flowcharts are constructed last, with a flowchart for each module. The order is not as important as using the tools to develop a complete design of the solution for the program.

EXAMPLE 2.9 Go through the entire planning process to write a program that will calculate and print the average grade on three tests for an entire class.

Step 1. **Analyze the problem and develop the specifications.**

Input: 3 test scores for each student

Output: The student's average grade

Process: Add the 3 scores together and divide by 3

Step 2. **Design a solution.**

1. Pseudocode:
   1. Get the 3 test scores
   2. Add the scores together
   3. Divide the sum by 3
   4. Print the average
   5. Repeat steps 1 through 4 for each student
2. Hierarchy chart:

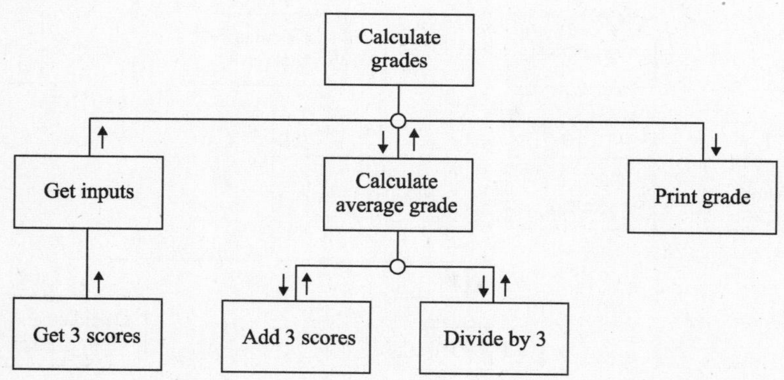

Notice that the hierarchy chart gives no indication of looping, or how many students might be in the class. The hierarchy chart only describes the modules to be written, not how many times they will be executed. The iteration is shown in the pseudocode and flowchart.

3. Flowchart:

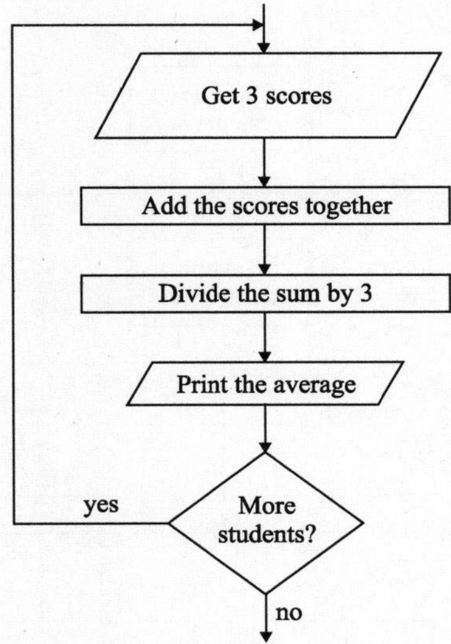

Solved Problems

2.1 What would be the input, process, and output for a program to change Fahrenheit temperatures into Celsius?

Input: Temperature in Fahrenheit

Output: Temperature in Celsius

Process: Apply the formula Celsius = 5/9 * (Fahrenheit – 32)

2.2 True or False. The first thing a good programmer does when asked to write a computer program is to sit down at the computer and begin typing in code.

False. Coding does not begin until the problem is examined, analyzed, and a complete solution is designed.

2.3 Write the algorithm in pseudocode for a simple calculator.

1. Get two numbers and the operation desired
2. Check the operation
   - 2.1. If the operation is addition, the result is the first + the second
   - 2.2. If the operation is subtraction, the result is the first – the second
   - 2.3. If the operation is multiplication, the result is the first * the second
   - 2.4. If the operation is division, check the second number

     If the second number is zero, construct an error message

     If the second number is not zero, the result is the first / the second
3. Print out the result or the error message

2.4 Draw the hierarchy chart for a simple calculator.

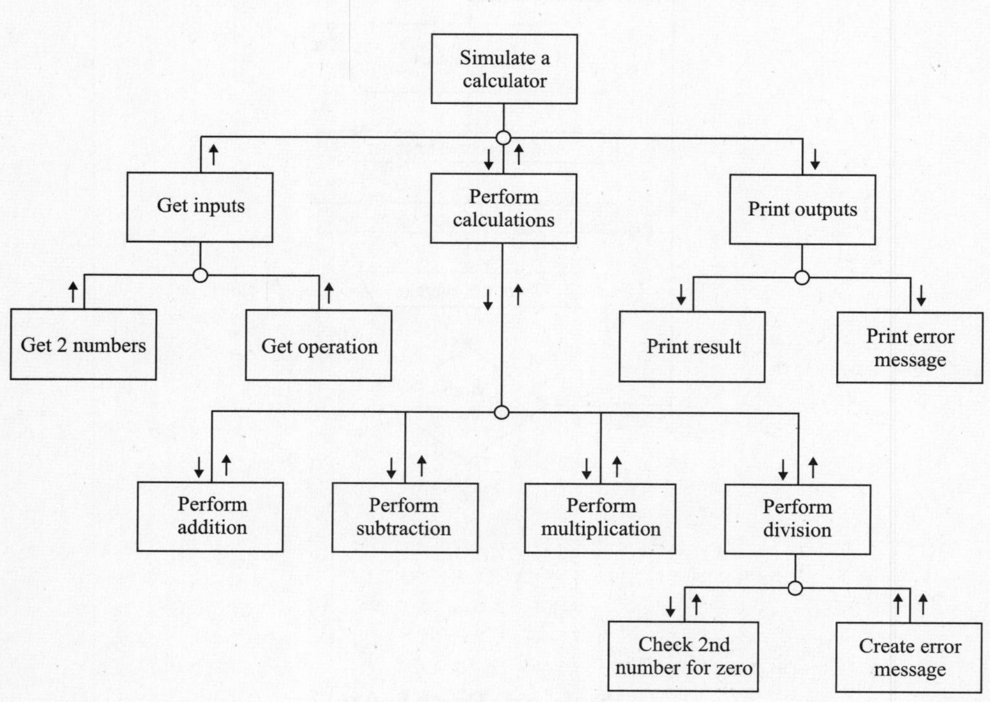

2.5 Go through the entire planning process to write a program that will handle the checkout for a hotel room. This hotel charges $55 for one person, $60 for two, and $65 for three or more.

Step 1. **Analyze the problem and develop the specifications.**

Input: Number of nights, number of people in the room, meal charges

Output: The printed bill, including tax

Process: Calculate the room charges, add the meal charges, and then add the tax

Step 2. **Design a solution.**

Pseudocode:

1. Get the number of nights and number of people in the room from the customer
2. Get the meal charges from the restaurant
3. Calculate bill
   - 3.1. Look up the room charge for that number of people
   - 3.2. Multiply by the number of nights
   - 3.3. Add the meal charges
   - 3.4. Calculate and add the tax
4. Print the bill

Hierarchy chart:

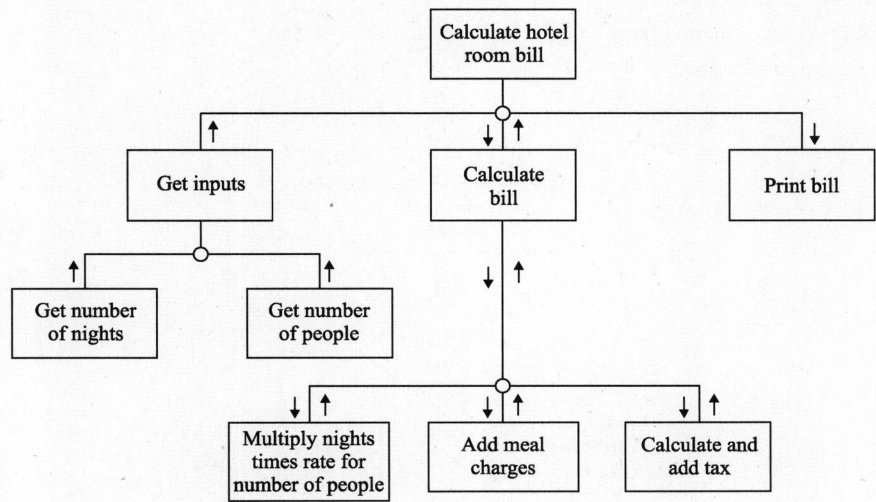

Flowchart:

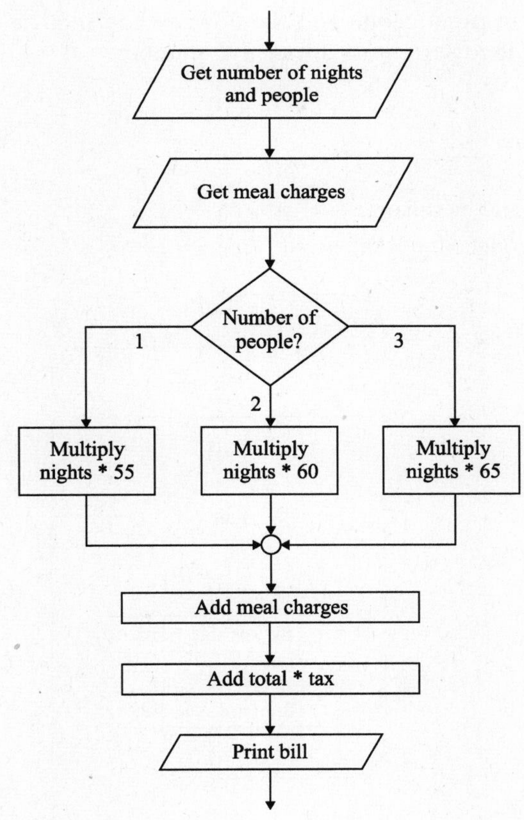

2.6 Draw a flowchart from the following pseudocode to input two numbers and print the larger.

1. Get number1 and number2
2. Compare to see which is larger
3. Print the larger number

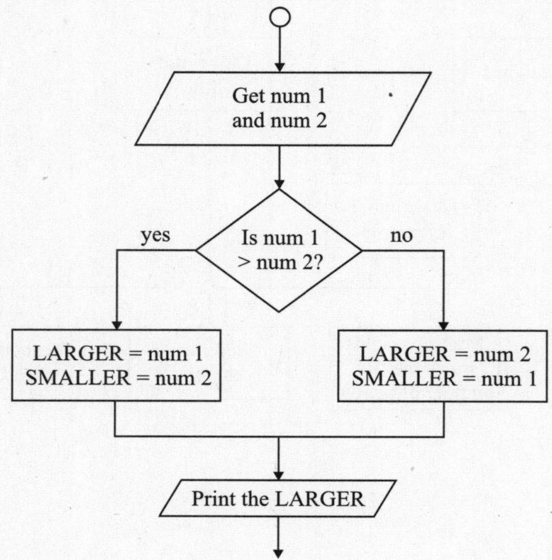

2.7 Write an algorithm in pseudocode and the flowchart to input a number and print the number and its square until the user enters a negative number.

Pseudocode:

1. Get the number
2. Calculate its square
3. Print the number and its square
4. Repeat steps 1 through 3 until the person enters −1

Flowchart:

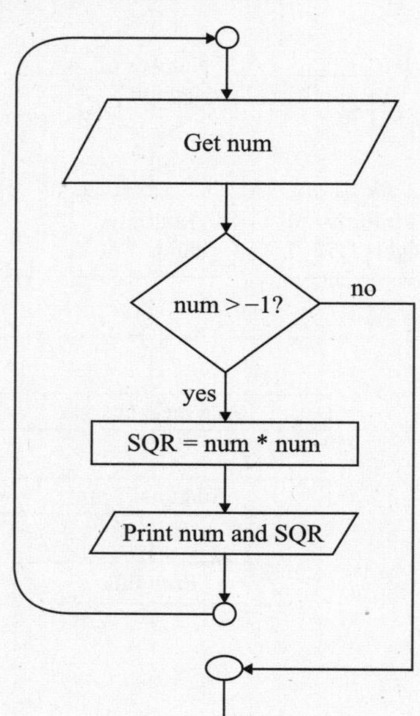

2.8 Write an algorithm in pseudocode and the flowchart to input a series of test scores until the user enters negative one (−1) and then print out the average score of all the numbers. You do not know how many numbers are coming into the program.

Pseudocode:

1. Get the score
2. Add it to the running sum
3. Add one to the count of scores
4. Repeat steps 1 through 3 until the person enters −1
5. Calculate average by dividing running sum by the count of scores
6. Print out the average

Flowchart:

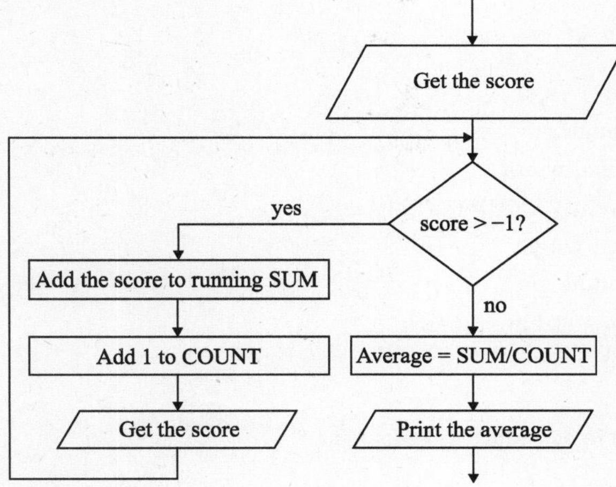

Supplementary Problems

2.9 What would be the input, process, and output for a program to calculate the miles per gallon for a specific vehicle?

2.10 What is the last step of the programming process? Why is it important?

2.11 Write the algorithm in pseudocode for a program to calculate the area of simple shapes.

2.12 Draw the hierarchy chart for a program to calculate the area of simple shapes.

2.13 The Bigg family is having a reunion. They want to know how many people will attend the reunion, and also the percentage of attendance broken into these age groups: preschool age (0 through 5), school age (6 through 12), teens (13 through 19), adults (20 through 64) and seniors (65 and up). Go through the entire planning process to write a program that will calculate the attendance by age groups.

2.14 Draw a flowchart from the following pseudocode to input three numbers and print out their sum and their average.

1. Get number1, number2, and number3.
2. Add them together for the sum.
3. Divide the sum by 3 for the average.
4. Print the sum and the average.

Answers to Supplementary Problems

2.9 Input: The distance traveled, and the number of gallons used by a specific vehicle

Process: Divide the distance by the number of gallons

Output: The miles per gallon for that vehicle

2.10 The last step is the validation of the program. Just because the program works with one set of data does not mean it performs correctly in every situation. The programmer cannot be confident that the program works well until a broad range of test cases have been examined.

2.11 The algorithm would be:

1. Get the shape desired
2. If the shape is a rectangle,
   2.1. Get the length and width
   2.2. Calculate the area as length * width
3. If the shape is a right triangle,
   3.1. Get the base and height
   3.2. Calculate the area as base * height / 2
4. If the shape is a circle
   4.1. Get the radius
   4.2. Calculate the area as radius * radius * 3.14
5. Print out the area

2.12 The hierarchy chart:

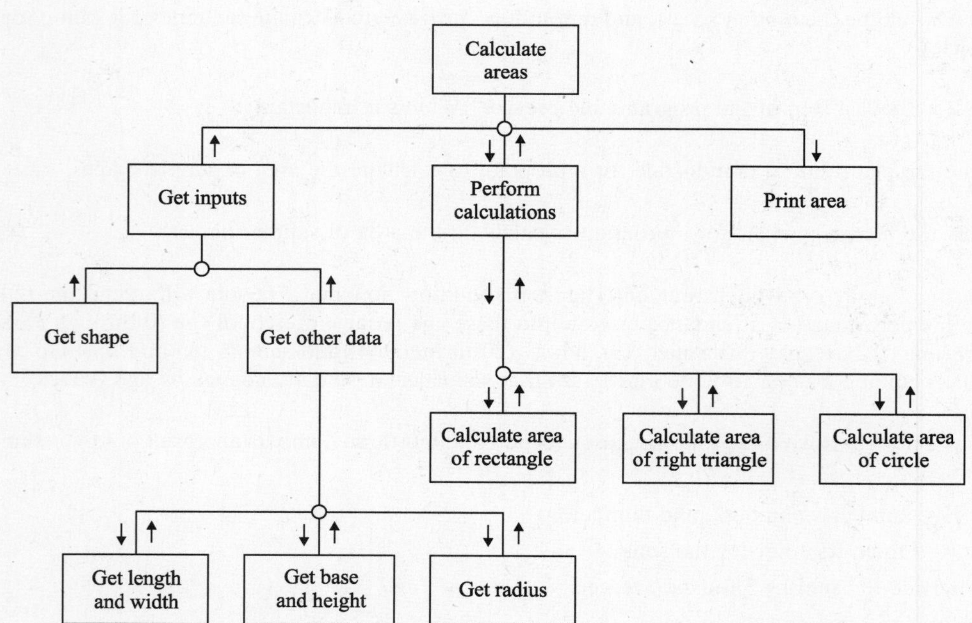

2.13 The program for the Bigg family:

Step 1. **Analyze the problem and develop the specifications.**

Input: Ages of each person attending

Output: The chart of people in each age group

Process: Add 1 to the age group for each person's age

Step 2. **Design a solution.**

Pseudocode:

1. Get the age of the person
2. Add it to the appropriate age group
3. Repeat steps 1 and 2 for each person coming
4. Calculate percentage for each age group
   4.1. Find the grand total for all age groups
   4.2. Divide each age group total by the grand total
5. Print the chart of attendance

Hierarchy chart:

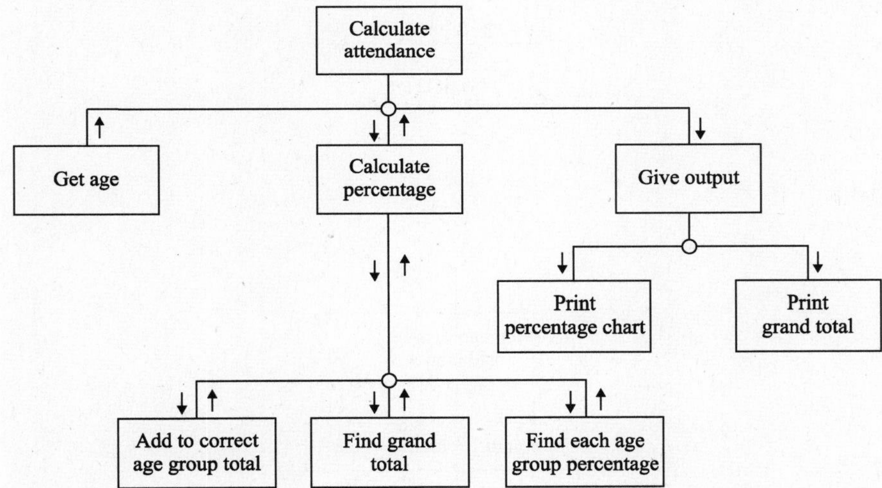

Flowchart:

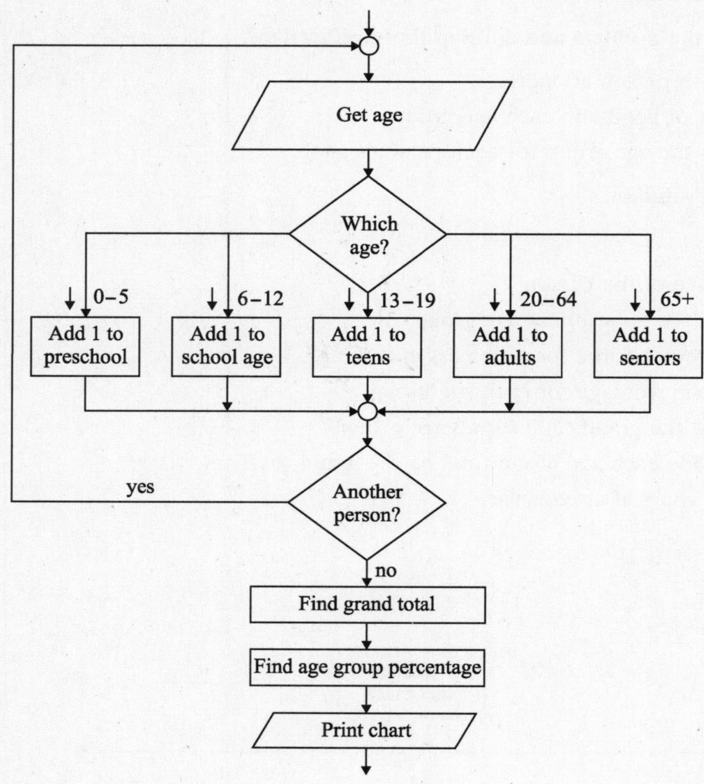

2.14 Flowchart.

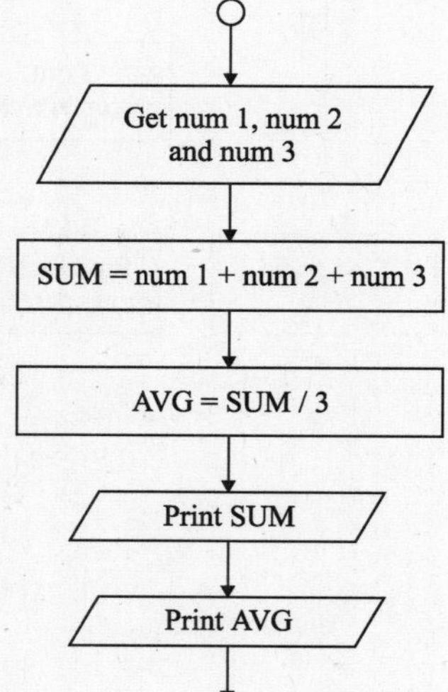

Program Coding and Simple Input/Output

3.1 PROGRAMMING LANGUAGES

Recall the steps of the programming process listed in Chapter 2:

- Step 1. Analyze the problem and develop the specifications.
- Step 2. Design a solution.
- Step 3. Code the program in a programming language with documentation.
- Step 4. Test the program.
- Step 5. Validate the program.

Once the problem is thoroughly analyzed and the algorithm is completely designed, then the third step, that of writing the program in code, is started. The algorithms and flowcharts help us human beings understand how to solve the problem. But the computer needs to have the program written in machine language that it can understand. Fortunately, we do not have to write all our programs in the machine's 1's and 0's. We write source code that a translating program changes into machine language.

There are two kinds of translating programs, compilers and interpreters. ***Compilers*** take the entire source code program and change it into machine language. Only after the source code is translated in its entirety can the computer execute the program. ***Interpreters*** translate and execute each line, one at a time. If an error is encountered, the program stops at that point. These translators, both compilers and interpreters, are very literal and specific. A more general explanation of the translation process is found in Appendix A.

Our source code must be exact to be understood by the computer. In order to make it equally clear for human beings, comments are embedded into the code that the computer ignores. This ***documentation*** of code will be explained later in the chapter.

The languages addressed in this and the following chapters are Visual Basic (Microsoft's structured dialect of the older Basic language), C, C++, and Java. These languages are very different. C and C++ source code is usually compiled and Visual Basic is interpreted. In both cases stand-alone programs (executables) can be created to run on computers that do not have a C/C++ compiler or a Visual Basic interpreter. However, the portability of the program is usually limited to the same operating system used in the original translating process.

On the other hand, Java is a language that is both compiled and interpreted. The source code is compiled, not into machine language, but into a bytecode that can be interpreted by many different kinds of operating systems. The interpreter on any other computer then translates the bytecode into the machine language needed by that system. Therefore, Java has the advantage of being more portable than other languages. Certain kinds of Java programs, called ***applets***, can even be embedded into pages sent over the World Wide Web and run by any Java-aware Internet browser.

All three of these languages use the same alphabet which includes any character found on the computer keyboard. Any of these characters must be translated into machine language. For instance, when you type the letter "t", or press the spacebar, your message must be represented in the computer's memory in some way. A standard code has been developed with a specific numeric representation of every character that can be used by programming languages. The American Standard Code for Information Interchange (ASCII) is consistently used by most computers and peripheral

Table 3-1 ASCII Character Set.

Decimal	Character	Decimal	Character	Decimal	Character	Decimal	Character
0	nul	32	space	64	@	96	‘
1	soh	33	!	65	A	97	a
2	stx	34	"	66	B	98	b
3	etx	35	#	67	C	99	c
4	eot	36	$	68	D	100	d
5	enq	37	%	69	E	101	e
6	ack	38	&	70	F	102	f
7	bel	39	’	71	G	103	g
8	bs	40	(	72	H	104	h
9	ht	41	)	73	I	105	i
10	nl	42	*	74	J	106	j
11	vt	43	+	75	K	107	k
12	ff	44	,	76	L	108	l
13	cr	45	-	77	M	109	m
14	soh	46	.	78	N	110	n
15	si	47	/	79	O	111	o
16	dle	48	0	80	P	112	p
17	dc1	49	1	81	Q	113	q
18	dc2	50	2	82	R	114	r
19	dc3	51	3	83	S	115	s
20	dc4	52	4	84	T	116	t
21	nak	53	5	85	U	117	u
22	syn	54	6	86	V	118	v
23	etb	55	7	87	W	119	w
24	can	56	8	88	X	120	x
25	em	57	9	89	Y	121	y
26	sub	58	:	90	Z	122	z
27	esc	59	;	91	[	123	{
28	fs	60	<	92	\	124	|
29	gs	61	=	93	]	125	}
30	rs	62	>	94	^	126	~
31	us	63	?	95	_	127	del

devices. The numbers from 0 to 255 represent each letter, number, space, punctuation mark, and other character available to the programming languages. The portion of the ASCII chart usually used is seen in Table 3-1. ASCII 0 through 31, and also 127, are unprintable characters representing various messages that can be sent. For example, 12 sends a form feed to the printer and 7 makes a beeping sound.

3.2 VARIABLES AND CONSTANTS

A ***variable*** is a memory location whose contents can be filled and changed during the execution of the program. A ***constant*** is a memory location whose contents stay the same during the execution of the program. The computer needs to know which locations will be accessed during the program, so all variables and constants must be declared in some way. Declaring variables or constants entails telling the computer not only whether they will change or stay the same, but also *how many* locations will be used, *what* they will be called in the program, and the *type* of data they will hold.

3.2.1 Simple Data Types

Remember that a memory location contains a series of 1's and 0's. That series, as explained in Section 1.4, can represent a variety of things: an integer, a real number (also called a floating-point number), an ASCII code for a character, or simply a 1-bit yes/no value. For example, the 2-byte word

[00000000 01000001]

could represent the number 65 if it is an integer, or the letter "A" if it is a character. Each programming language uses different conventions. The available simple data types and the amount of memory used by each are listed in Table 3-2 for Visual Basic, C, C++, and Java. Notice that Visual Basic has no type for an individual character. All character data are processed as Strings. See Chapter 6 for a complete explanation of the VB String type.

Table 3-2 Simple Data Types.

Type	Size and Name in Visual Basic	Size and Name in C/C++	Size and Name in Java
boolean	1 bit – Boolean	Only available in some compilers	1 bit – boolean
character	no character type	1 byte – char	2 bytes – char
short integer	no short type	2 bytes – short	2 bytes – short
integer	2 bytes – Integer	4 bytes – int	4 bytes – int
long integer	4 bytes – Long	4 or 8 bytes – long	8 bytes – long
floating point	4 bytes – Single	4 bytes – float	4 bytes – float
double precision	8 bytes – Double	8 bytes – double	8 bytes – double

Before using any memory location, the program must include a declaration specifying whether the memory location represents a variable or a constant, what type of data it will contain, and what it will be called in the program. The computer then finds a memory location and reserves that space for the whole time the program is running. The programmer only uses the name specified, not the actual address of the variable in memory. However, in C and C++ the actual memory location can be determined by use of the ***address*** operator, &. For example, if an integer variable *num1* is declared, its address in memory is *&num1*. Also, the number of bytes actually used can be accessed using the function ***sizeof(variable)***. See Exercise 3.4 at the end of the chapter for an example.

Declaring variables in Visual Basic makes use of the **Dim** operator, giving the ***Dimension*** of the variable. The actual syntax is:

```
Dim variablename As type
```

In C, C++ and Java the type name is listed first, and then the variable name. The syntax is:

type variablename;

In all four languages, a constant can be declared. C, C++, and Visual Basic use the reserved word **const** and Java uses the word **final**. Some examples of declarations are given in Table 3-3. Notice that any programming statement in C, C++, and Java is followed by a semicolon. C, C++, and Java are case-sensitive, and all data types are specified in lowercase. Although Visual Basic is not case-sensitive, the editor adjusts the Const, Dim and data type names to begin with uppercase letters.

Table 3-3 Declaring Variables and Constants.

Visual Basic	Java	C/C++	Explanation
Const NUM = 2	final int NUM = 2;	const int NUM = 2;	Declare a constant integer with the value 2.
Const PI = 3.14	final float PI = 3.14;	const float PI = 3.14;	Declare a constant floating-point number for π.
Dim sum As Integer	int sum;	int sum;	Declare an integer variable called sum. No value is yet assigned to it.
Dim myCh As String	char myCh;	char myCh;	Declare a variable that will contain only one character. In Visual Basic, even one character is called a String.
Dim interestRate As Single	float interestRate;	float interestRate;	Declare a variable that will contain a floating-point number with decimal values.

Choosing the identifier name for variables and constants is left to the programmer. A convention used by most programmers uses all uppercase letters for the names of constants (e.g., PI). Variable names generally begin with lowercase, but mixed case is often used for clarity (e.g., interestRate). Most languages have a few rules:

- No reserved words in the language can be used. (Reserved words are any words used to implement specific features.)
- Identifiers begin with a letter and may contain only letters, underscores, or digits.
- Identifiers are usually kept to under 30 characters in length.

The allowed length is different for each language and even sometimes for individual compilers of the same language. The general rule is that identifiers should be long enough to be meaningful, but not too long that mistakes would be made in typing. One-character variable names are not usually explicit enough to help the programmer. For example, the purpose of a variable called *sum* is more evident than a variable called *x*. Reading and debugging the program is much easier when variables and constants have meaningful names.

Constants are usually easy to name because they represent a specific value. Some good examples are PI, RATE, MAXNAMES. Variable names are often harder to choose. Here is a list of good variable names that are legal and also meaningful:

first_initial	num1	amtToDeposit
mpg	myList	newBalance
gallonsUsed	tempNum	side4

Remember that C, C++, and Java are case-sensitive. Therefore, *myList* would be a different variable from *mylist*. The programmer must be very careful to use consistent spelling and case for all identifiers.

3.3 ASSIGNMENT STATEMENTS

Once you have chosen a name and reserved the location for a variable, you must give it a value. There are three main methods of getting values into variables:

- Read in a value from a file
- Ask the user to type in a value
- Assign a value within the program

File input and output will be covered in Chapter 7. Reading in values from the keyboard will be covered later in this chapter. This section explains ***assignment*** statements, or statements that explicitly place values into memory locations. The syntax for an assignment statement is:

variable name = value

The assignment is always made from left to right. There are a few rules for assignment statements that must be followed in every language.

(1) Only one variable name can be on the left of the equal sign because it is the destination location that will be changed.

(2) Constants cannot be on the left, because they cannot be changed.

(3) The value on the right of the equal sign may be a constant, another variable, or a formula or arithmetic expression combining constants and variables.

(4) Anything on the right is not changed.

(5) The variable and value must be of the same data type.

EXAMPLE 3.1 Under the column **Statements** below, there is a series of C/C++ assignment statements that are to be executed in the order indicated. What is the content of each variable after each statement has been executed, knowing that *areaOfSquare* has been declared a floating-point variable, *initial* is a character, and *length* is an integer?

Statements	Contents of the Variables after the Statement		
	initial	*length*	*areaOfSquare*
a. before anything is done:	undefined	undefined	undefined
b. length = 5;	undefined	5	undefined
c. initial = ‘P’;	‘P’	5	undefined
d. areaOfSquare = length;	‘P’	5	5.0
e. areaOfSquare = initial;	‘P’	5	80.0
f. areaOfSquare = 37.5;	‘P’	5	37.5
g. length = areaOfSquare;	‘P’	37	37.5
h. initial = areaOfSquare;	‘%’	37	37.5

Lines b, c, and f are simple assignments placing constant values into the variables. Line d allows an integer value to be placed into a floating-point variable, and line e allows the ASCII value of the character "P" to be placed into the floating-point variable. Nothing is lost in either line. However, in lines g and h, a floating-point value was placed into a character and an integer variable. Although C/C++ gives no error messages, the floating-point constant will be truncated when placed into the integer variable. Likewise, the same integer part will be interpreted as an ASCII value when assigned to the character variable.

These statements would produce similar results in Java for lines b through f. However, Java would not allow lines g or h to compile. In that language it is illegal to assign a floating-point value to an integer or character variable.

EXAMPLE 3.2 Under the column **Statements** below, there is a series of Visual Basic assignment statements that are to be executed in the order indicated. What is the content of each variable after each statement has been executed, knowing *areaOfSquare* has been declared a single variable, *initial* as a string, and *length* as an integer?

Statements	Contents of the Variables after the Statement		
	initial	*length*	*areaOfSquare*
a. before anything is done:	space	0	0
b. length = 5	undefined	5	undefined
c. initial = "P"	"P"	5	undefined
d. areaOfSquare = length	"P"	5	5.0
e. areaOfSquare = initial	Gives an error message – type mismatch		
f. areaOfSquare = 37.5	"P"	5	37.5
g. length = areaOfSquare	"P"	38	37.5
h. initial = areaOfSquare	"37.5"	37	37.5

Notice that in Visual Basic, variables have default values before anything is assigned to them. In line g, assigning a floating-point number to an integer variable rounds the floating value to the nearest integer value rather than truncating. In line h, assigning a floating-point number into a string actually assigns the string value of the number. Also, C and C++ require single quotation marks around a single character. Visual Basic treats a single character as if it were a string of length 1, and requires double quotation marks.

Both these examples show that one must be very careful when writing assignment statements. Mixing data types on the left and right sides of assignment statements is very dangerous, and may produce unpredictable results. It is important always to follow the rule of explicitly assigning values of the same data type as the variable that appears on the left-hand side of an assignment statement.

3.4 ARITHMETIC EXPRESSIONS AND OPERATOR PRECEDENCE

The examples above placed only simple values, either constants or single variables, into the destination variables. The power of assignment statements is made possible through the use of formulas and arithmetic expressions. The expression on the right is computed and then the result is assigned to the destination variable on the left.

The arithmetic operators used in expressions are listed in Table 3-4. The order in which the operations are executed follows the rules of arithmetic, with items in parentheses executed first, then multiplication, division, and modulus, and finally addition and subtraction. Operations with the same order of precedence are always computed left to right.

C, C++, and Java do not have explicit exponentiation operators. Exponentiation must be computed explicitly, or through the use of library functions, which will be explained later.

Table 3-4 Order of Precedence of Arithmetic Operators.

Operators	Operation	Order of Precedence	Associativity
( )	Parentheses	1	Inside out
^ (VB only)	Exponentiation	2	
* /	Multiplication and division	3	Left to right
\ (VB only)	Integer division	5	Left to right
% (C, C++, Java) or MOD (VB)	Modulo arithmetic	5	Left to right
+ −	Addition and subtraction	6	Left to right

A special note is important regarding division. Programming languages treat integer division differently from floating-point division. Division performed with floating-point numbers as either the dividend or the divisor will behave as expected, resulting in quotients with fractional parts. If both are integers, then integer division is performed instead, and the quotient is truncated to only the integer part of the value. Here are a few C/C++ examples where *real1* and *real2* have been declared as floating-point numbers.

```
real1=5.6;
real2=real1/2;     //floating point divided by integer -- real2 contains 2.8
real2=25/2.0;      //integer divided by floating point -- real2 contains 12.5
real2=25/2;        //integer divided by integer -- real2 contains 12
```

In Visual Basic integer division is done explicitly by changing the integer division sign from "/" to "\", as shown below.

```
real1=5.6
real2=real1/2      ' single dimension divided by integer --- real2 contains 2.8
real2=25/2         ' integer divided by integer using regular division operator
                   ' /-- real2 contains 12.5
real2=25\2         ' integer divided by integer using integer division operator
                   ' \-- real2 contains 12
```

In integer division, the division results in the truncated quotient. To find the remainder, the MOD or % operator is used. Consider the examples in Fig. 3-1 where 26 divided by 3 results in a quotient of 8, with a remainder of 2.

```
  8 <= quotient
3)26
  24
   2 <=remainder
```

C++ example:

```
firstInt=26;
secondInt=firstInt/3;       //secondInt contains 8
thirdInt=firstInt % 3;      //thirdInt contains 2
```

VB example:

```
firstInt=26
secondInt=firstInt\3        ' secondInt contains 8
thirdInt=firstInt Mod 3     ' thirdInt contains 2
```

Fig. 3-1 Modulo arithmetic.

EXAMPLE 3.3 Write the C/C++ and Visual Basic assignment statements to calculate the miles per gallon of a vehicle. Assume *distance*, *gallonsUsed*, and *mpg* have been declared as floating-point numbers, and *distance* and *gallonsUsed* have values.

```
mpg=distance / gallonsUsed;     // C/C++ statement
mpg=distance / gallonsUsed      ' VB statement
```

EXAMPLE 3.4 Write the C/C++ and Visual Basic assignment statements to change a Fahrenheit temperature into Celsius. Assume *fahrenheit* and *celsius* have been declared as floating-point numbers, and *fahrenheit* has a value.

```
celsius=(5.0/9)*(fahrenheit-32);    //C/C++ -- notice either the dividend or
                                    //divisor MUST be floating point
celsius=(5/9)*(fahrenheit-32)       ' VB statement -/ is used to force
                                    ' floating-point response
```

3.5 COMMENT STATEMENTS

Programming languages provide a way for programmers to embed in the code explanatory statements, or comments, that are non-executable. These statements are ignored by the compiler, but provide explanation for the human beings who are reading or writing the code. This is called ***documentation***.

Comments are critical to the understanding of code, and should be used liberally. There are a few general rules for including comments in the code:

(1) Include comments at the beginning listing the program name, the programmer's name, and a complete explanation of what the program is supposed to do.

(2) Include comments explaining each separate part of the code.

(3) Include comments explaining formulas or complex expressions.

(4) Include comments anywhere else they might be of help.

The method of commenting is different for each language. Visual Basic uses the apostrophe and C, C++, and Java use the double slash. Both indicate that everything else on the line should be ignored by the compiler. See Examples 3.3 and 3.4 above.

C, C++, and Java also allow commenting multiple lines. Here is an example:

```
/*The slash and star begin this multiple line comment which can be
  used for long explanations. It will be ignored by the compiler
  until the final star and slash are found. */
... rest of program
```

Comments will frequently be used in this book for explanatory purposes. Many programmers feel that you can never use too many comments.

3.6 SIMPLE INPUT/OUTPUT

Recall that the basic flow of computer processing is *input, process, output*. Programs can read input from and write output to files on disks. Handling of file input/output will be covered in Chapter 7. For the purposes of the next few chapters, we will assume there is a user sitting at the computer to provide the input from the keyboard and wanting to see the output on the screen. The program itself is supposed to process the information given by the user and then display the output. There must be program statements to accomplish these tasks.

One of the biggest differences between computer languages is how they handle input and output. Therefore, each of these languages will be addressed separately. Also, within each language there may be a variety of methods for input and output. Only the simplest will be addressed here.

3.6.1 C++ I/O

C++ does not have any built-in input/output commands. All C++ compilers, however, contain a package of object-oriented classes, called the **iostream** classes. The compiler views everything going in and out as **streams** of data. The program must extract the information from the input stream object, and insert data into the output stream object. The streams are viewed as separate objects, and the package is called a **library** of functions to help the programmer with the extraction (istream) and insertion (ostream) processes. The programmer must specify that these functions will be used by giving the compiler a message to include the required library. The syntax to include this library is:

```
#include <iostream.h>
```

The command must be given first, before any other program statements, and the # must be in the first column of the line. The compiler then finds the header file (.h) that explains all the resources that can be used in the program. A few of these are listed with explanation in Table 3-5.

Table 3-5 Some iostream.h Library Resources.

Resource	Type	Explanation
cin	object	Controls extraction from standard stream of bytes coming from keyboard
>>	extraction operator	Gets bytes from an input stream object
cout	object	Controls insertion to the standard stream of bytes going out to the screen
<<	insertion operator	Inserts bytes into the standard output stream object
cerr	object	Controls immediate insertion of messages to the standard stream of bytes going out to the screen
endl or '\n'	constant manipulator	Inserts newline character into the output stream object – makes the cursor go to the next line

The function for input is **cin** (pronounced "see in" for Console**IN**put). The extraction operator is available for use with any built-in data type. Whatever is typed at the keyboard is examined to be sure it is the correct data type, and then placed into the specified variable. A character variable will take the ASCII value of whatever is typed. A numeric value will accept only a number. If anything else is typed, the program crashes with a run-time error of data type mismatch.

EXAMPLE 3.5 The following example illustrates the use of **cin**.

General Syntax:
```
cin>>variable;
```
Examples:
```
cin>>num1;          // if a number is typed its value is placed into num1
cin>>char2;         // whatever is typed its ASCII value is placed into char2
cin>>num1>>num2;    // two numbers must be typed, separated by a space
```

The function for output is **cout** (pronounced "see out" for Console**OUT**put). Often another command is used for error messages, **cerr** (pronounced "see err" for Console **ERR**or messages). These messages are also displayed on the screen. However, it is helpful for the programmer to distinguish regular output from specific error messages that must be given by the program as it is executing. The insertion operator can be used with any built-in data type. If the variable is a numeric value, it is first converted into its ASCII representation in order to be displayed on the screen. Any number of items may be inserted into the output stream object, including the constant **endl** which sends the cursor to the next line. A string of characters contained in quotation marks can also be displayed.

EXAMPLE 3.6 The following illustrates the use of **cout**.

General Syntax: cout<<*output*;
Where *output* is a variable, a constant, "a literal string", or an expression

Statements where num1 is 4 and char1 is 'p':	**Output:**
`cout<<num1;`	4
`cout<<"The number is "<<num1<<endl;`	The number is 4
`cout<<"Your initial is "<<char1<<endl;`	Your initial is p
`cout<<"line 1"<<endl<<"line 2"<<endl;`	line 1 line 2
`cout<<"The sum of 4 and 5 is "<<4+5<<endl;`	The sum of 4 and 5 is 9

The programmer often needs to combine output and input in order to give a message to the user as to what should be typed on the keyboard. Never assume the user knows what to type. For example, the C++ lines needed to ask the user to type a positive integer and then read it into the variable *posInt* would be:

```
cout<<"Enter a number greater than zero =>";
cin>>posInt;
```

This concept of offering prompts to the user is important in any language. Directions should be clear and specific in order to minimize run-time crashes of type mismatch. In reality, the program should always check the input and allow for giving messages regarding incorrect data.

3.6.2 Java I/O

As specified at the beginning of this chapter, a Java program can be a stand-alone application or an applet that is embedded in a Web page. Input and output are handled very differently for those two situations. This section will present only the simplest input and output needed for a regular Java application. The Java I/O library must be included, or imported, in order to accomplish this task. The syntax for this is shown below. The asterisk means that ALL the functions and objects available in the java.io library will be imported.

```
import java.io.*;
```

Java uses the **System** object to read and print the stream object. Table 3-6 shows the most common I/O functions used in Java.

Table 3-6 Java I/O Commands.

Command	Explanation
System.out.print(..)	Insertion of whatever is in the parentheses into the standard stream of bytes going out to the screen
System.out.println(..)	Insertion of whatever is in the parentheses into the standard stream of bytes going out to the screen, then inserts newline character
System.out.flush()	Forces whatever is in the buffer to be displayed before reading
System.in.read()	Controls extraction from standard stream of bytes coming from keyboard
System.in.skip(n)	Skips n characters of input stream – used to pass unwanted values such as Enter

Like C++, Java uses one object to read streams of data coming in from the keyboard, **System.in**, and another to print output streams to the screen, **System.out**. Java (and also C++) has a temporary memory location to hold input and output which is called the *buffer*. If the program has been giving output, the buffer must be cleared, or flushed, before trying to read input. System.out.flush() is the function needed to be sure the buffer is clear.

Java System input catches one character at a time and assumes it is a character even if we are looking for integers. Therefore, we must specifically change the incoming character to an integer. Remember that the ASCII value of "0" is 48, of "1" is 49, and so forth. Therefore, we can subtract the ASCII value of "0", or 48, from the character to change it into an integer. Example 3.7 will print 5 if 5 is entered. Without the subtraction, it would have printed 53, or the ASCII value of 5.

EXAMPLE 3.7 The following illustrates the use of Java System input and output.

```
System.out.print ("Enter a number");       //give instructions to user
System.out.flush();                        //flush the buffer before reading
num1=System.in.read();                     //read the integer that is typed
num1=num1 - '0';                           // subtract 48 to give the integer
                                           //value, not ASCII
System.out.println ("Your number is"+num1);
```

It should also be noted that System.in.read() will accept only one character. If 999 is entered in the example above, only the first 9 is read. If two items are to be read, and the Enter key is pressed between them, that character must be skipped. The number of characters to skip depends upon the actual implementation. This is demonstrated in Example 3.8. Input and output are easier with Java applets, which is beyond the scope of this book.

EXAMPLE 3.8 The following illustrates more Java System input and output.

```
System.out.print ("Enter a number");
System.out.flush();
num1=System.in.read();                    //user types integer and then presses Enter
num1=num1-'0';
System.out.println ("Your number is"+num1);
System.in.skip(2);                        //skip the Enter key before reading new data
System.out.print ("Enter a number");
System.out.flush();
num1=System.in.read();
num1=num1-'0';
System.out.println ("Your number is"+num1);
```

3.6.3 Visual Basic I/O

Visual Basic I/O is not as complicated as Java and C++. Input and output are not streams of character data, but specific discrete values coming in and going out. There are several ways of managing I/O in a visual environment. VB's object-oriented environment will be discussed further in Chapter 8. In this chapter, only the simplest I/O from a code module will be explained.

The "Visual" part of Visual Basic implies that one can see specific objects on the screen. Input is accomplished through the use of Input boxes, and output through Message boxes. Syntax for these objects is shown in Table 3-7. Another output command, Print, is also described. It will be used in many VB examples in this text. In the VB environment, it prints output to the main program form, or window.

Table 3-7 Visual Basic I/O.

VB Command Syntax	Explanation
variable = InputBox(*prompt*)	*prompt* is message to user, and *variable* is filled with value typed into box by user
MsgBox(*message*)	*message* is displayed in a box on screen
Print *variable or constant list*	Simple print used to print to VB form
Str(value)	Converts numbers into Strings that can be displayed in boxes – usually not necessary with Print
+ or &	Used to connect string parts into a long string to be displayed in boxes or with Print

Input boxes are dialog boxes, with the prompt displayed and a place for the user to respond. The user types a value into the box, and that value is placed into the variable. VB is very flexible. The input comes into the program as a string. However, if the variable destination is an integer or single precision value, the input is converted automatically into the correct data type. Example 3.9 shows examples of two InputBox commands, along with the resulting output.

EXAMPLE 3.9

```
num1=InputBox("Enter a number")

char1=InputBox("Enter a character")
```

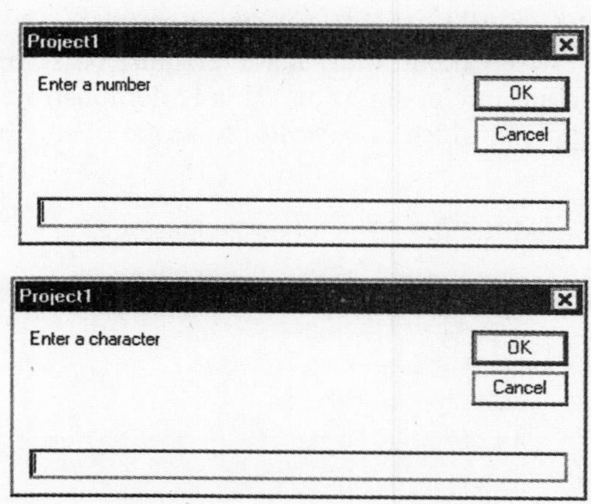

Message boxes display the message in a dialog box and then wait for the user to click OK. There are options for both Input and Message boxes to allow different buttons to be displayed. At the present, however, we will use the default values. The message sent to the Message box must be a string. If integers or floating-point numbers are to be displayed they must be converted into a string with the Str(value) function. All parts of the String message are concatenated with the plus sign or ampersand. Example 3.10 shows several examples of the Message box command with its resulting output. Notice the use of the ASCII character 10 to force the cursor to the next line. This corresponds to the *endl* of C++.

EXAMPLE 3.10

```
MsgBox ("Your number is"+Str(num1))

MsgBox ("Your initial is"+char1)
```

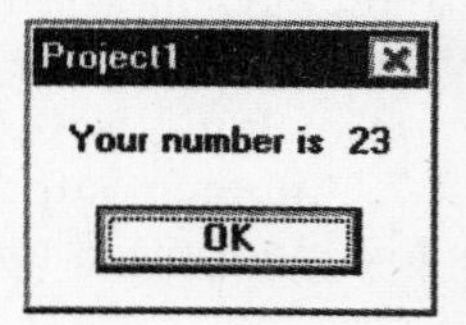

```
MsgBox ("line 1" & Chr(10) & "line 2")
```

```
MsgBox ("The sum of 4 and 5 is" & Str(4+5))
```

3.6.4 C I/O

The most commonly used library functions to do I/O operations in C are printf() and scanf(). The printf() function allows us to write to the standard output device, the video screen, formatted and unformatted data. Likewise, the scanf() function allows us to read values from the standard input device, the keyboard. In Chapter 7, we will use similar instructions to do file I/O. In this chapter, we will illustrate the use of these functions with several examples. The general format of these two functions is as follows:

printf(control string, list of variables)   **scanf**(control string, list of variables)

where control string is a string of characters, enclosed in double quotes, that may contain control specifications. Although the purpose of the control string is very similar for both functions, there are slight differences in their use. The control string in printf () generally indicates how the data are to be formatted for output. That is, it is concerned with the appearance of the data when printed. The control string in scanf() is a conversion control sequence. That is, it specifies the type of data being input by the user. The list of variables in printf() corresponds to those variables or constants that are to be printed. These variables or constants need to be separated by commas. The list of variables in scanf() corresponds to the list of variables whose values will be read in. However, unlike printf(), the scanf() function requires that the addresses of the variables rather than their names be used in the list of variables. Variables in this list also need to be separated by commas. In general, for both printf() and scanf() there is a one-to-one correspondence between the conversion characters and the variables or constants in the list of variables. To use any of these two functions it is necessary to include the header file stdio.h.

All conversion specifications begin with a % character and end with a conversion character. Partial lists of the conversion characters most commonly used in conjunction with printf() and scanf() are shown in Tables 3-8 and 3-9 respectively.

When outputting information to a device like the video screen, in addition to the conversion characters, the control string may contain escape sequences. An escape sequence is a single character that is represented by a combination of two other characters. The first of these two characters is the "\" backslash character; the second character of the escape sequence is a letter. Table 3-10 shows a partial list of escape sequences.

Table 3-8

Conversion Character for printf()	Associated Argument is Printed
c	as character
d	as decimal
f	as floating point
s	as a string

Table 3-9

Conversion Character for scanf()	Associated Argument is Converted to
c	a character
d	a decimal
f	a floating-point number
s	a string
Lf	a double

Table 3-10

Escape Sequence	Effect
\a	make a beep sound
\b	backspace
\f	new page or form
\n	new line
\t	horizontal tab

EXAMPLE 3.11 Write the message "Hello World" to the screen.

To write messages to the screen we can use the printf() function in its simplest form. To print the given message we can use the printf() function as follows:

```
printf("Hello World");
```

This statement will print "Hello World" on the screen beginning at the current position of the cursor. That is, if we assume that the cursor is on column 10 on the screen, this instruction will print the message beginning on column 10. However, if we need to print this message on column 1 on the next line, the instruction needs to be slightly modified as follows:

```
printf("\nHello World");
```

Notice that in this case we have used the escape sequence "\n". As indicated in Table 3-10, the effect of this sequence is to "go to a new line" before printing the message.

EXAMPLE 3.12 Write the message "I am fine" beginning on a new line, five spaces to the right. Call the attention of the user by making a beep sound.

To do all this, the printf() function needs to be written as follows:

```
printf("\n\tI am fine\a");
```

In this statement, the effect of the escape sequences, from left to right, is as follows:

"\n" moves the cursor to a new line.

"\t" moves the cursor to the next "tab". Tabs are separated 5 spaces from each other.

After printing the message, the escape sequence "\a" makes the beep sound.

As indicated before, the printf() function can also be used to control the appearance of the output. This is generally accomplished by means of a combination of control string characters and field width specifiers. A specifier is an integer number, written between the % sign and the control letter, that indicates, among some other things, the number of output columns that are available for writing a variable or a constant. When specifiers are used, numeric values are right-justified and character strings are left-justified. The following example illustrates this.

EXAMPLE 3.13 What is the output of the following printf() statement?

```
printf("The sum of %5d and %5d is %7d", 20, 25, 45);
```

Within the control string there are three control characters; each one of these control characters is associated with one and only one of the constants appearing in the "variable list." The association, from left to right, between the control character, the width specifier, and the constants, is as follows:

%5d is associated with 20	Write the integer 20 using a field 5 columns wide
%5d is associated with 25	Write the integer 25 using a field 5 columns wide
%7d is associated with 45	Write the integer 45 using a field 7 columns wide

Therefore, the output looks like this:

```
The sum of    20 and    25 is      45
```

Notice that all numeric values are right-justified within their fields. What this implies is that the numbers are "written backwards." That is, the last digit of the number gets written in the last column of the field; the remaining digits are "written" moving toward the left. This function writes the number 20 in a field that is 5 columns wide; therefore, there are three blanks at the left of the digit 2. A similar situation occurs with the other constants.

EXAMPLE 3.14 Is there any difference between the output produced by the print statements of column A and the print statements of column B? Assume that the statements, in each column, are executed in the order indicated and independently of the statements in the other column.

Column A	Column B
`printf("\n%d+",1);`	`printf("\n%5d+",1);`
`printf("\n%d",10);`	`printf("\n%5d",10);`
`printf("\n%d",100);`	`printf("\n%5d",100);`
`printf("\n_____");`	`printf("\n_____");`
`printf("\n%d",111);`	`printf("\n%5d",111);`

Notice that the statements under column A do not have a width specifier. In this case, C uses the minimum space to write each of these values. The output produced by the statement of column A is

```
1+
10
100
_____
111
```

Since the statements of column B have width specifiers, each numeric field is right-justified within the space indicated by the specifiers. The output of the statements of column B is

```
    1+
   10
  100
_____
  111
```

EXAMPLE 3.15 What is the output of the following printf() statement?

```
printf("\n%3d %6.2f",1,47.9);
```

The output of this statement looks like this:

1 47.90

The field width specifier 6.2 indicates that its associated number needs to be printed in a field that is 6 columns wide, with two decimal places. Since the number has only one decimal, the output is padded with an extra zero.

If the width specifier is smaller than the number that we want to print, the printf() function ignores the width specifier and uses the minimum number of spaces to print the number. Fractional parts of floating or double numeric values are always printed with the specified number of digits. As Example 3.15 illustrated, whenever the fractional part has fewer digits than specified, the number is padded with extra zeros. If the fractional part has more digits than specified, the number is rounded to the number of decimal places specified in the width specifier.

The scanf() function is the input counterpart of printf(). This function reads characters from the standard input, and interprets them according to the format indicated in the control string. The function stops reading, provided that there are no errors, when it exhausts all its control characters. The variable list of this function indicates the location where the input should be stored. Each of the elements making up this list should be an address.

EXAMPLE 3.16 What is the result of executing the input operation shown below? Assume that the variables num1 and num2 have been declared as integer variables.

```
scanf("%d%d", &num1, &num2);
```

This statement allows a user to input two integer values into the integer variables num1 and num2. The first control character "%d" is matched with the address of the variable num1. Likewise, the second control character "%d" is matched with the address of the variable num2. Notice the use of the operator & to indicate the address of the variables. If we assume that the user types the values 25 and 35 and then hits the Enter key, the value of 25 will be stored into variable num1 and the value 35 will be stored into the variable num2.

The functions scanf() and printf() are generally used together to elicit and capture the user's input. Example 3.17 illustrates this.

EXAMPLE 3.17 Write the necessary instructions to prompt the user to enter two integer values.

To accomplish this task, we need two pairs of instructions. Each pair consists of one printf() to prompt the user and one scanf() to capture the input values. These two instructions may look like this:

```
printf("\nPlease enter the first integer value =>");
scanf("%d",&num1);

printf("\nPlease enter the second integer value =>");
scanf("%d",&num1);
```

Notice that the first printf statement, after skipping to a new line, displays on the video screen something like this:

Please enter the first integer value =>■

where we have indicated with the symbol, ■, the position of the cursor after the first print statement has been executed. Notice that, when the user starts typing the integer number, the typing starts at the position indicated by the cursor. When the user presses the Enter key, whatever value is typed is then stored into the variable num1.

The second pair of instructions behaves exactly the same as the first pair.

EXAMPLE 3.18 Explain the result of executing the following instructions. Assume that the variables have been properly declared and match the control characters indicated in the control string.

```
printf("\n%s\n%s", "Input three values", "An integer, a single character and a float:");
scanf("%d %c %f", &ivar, &cvar, &fvar);
printf("\nYou typed the following: %5d , %c , %7.3f :", ivar, cvar, fvar);
```

Notice the use of the control character "%s" to display the prompts to the user. These two prompts are written in two separate lines. Observe how the escape sequence is being used to obtain this effect. Assuming that the user typed 123 A 3.5, the result of executing these instructions is

Input three values
An integer, a single character and a float: 123 A 3.5
You typed the following: 123, A,   3.500

Notice that, within the control string of the printf, the spaces after each control character are displayed in the output line "as is."

3.7 WRITING A COMPLETE PROGRAM

All that remains is to put everything – input, process, and output – into a whole program that the computer can understand. Again, each programming language does this in a different way. In each example, the program must have a ***main*** section of code to be executed. Chapter 5 deals with other functions and subroutines that can be used along with the main.

3.7.1 C and C++

The ***main*** function in C and C++ is enclosed with curly brackets { } to indicate where it starts and ends. The general order for the statements is, of course:

(1) declare variables
(2) get input
(3) do processing
(4) produce output

EXAMPLE 3.19 The short sample program in Fig. 3-2 uses this general outline as comments. Notice the compiler directive #include must precede the main section.

```
//First Program - gets a number, calculates and prints the square
#include <isostream.h>
void main()
{
    //declare variables
    int num, square;
    //1. Get the number
    cout<<endl<<"Enter the number you want to square=>";
    cin>>num;
    //2. Square it
    square=num*num;
    //3. Print out the square
    cout<<num<<"squared is"<<square<<endl;
}//end main
```

Fig. 3-2 First C++ program – square a number.

In the function heading *void main*( ), the empty parentheses indicate that there is nothing coming into the section, and the *void* shows there is nothing going out. Other functions which have values going in and/or out will be described in Chapter 5.

3.7.2 C

```
// First Program - gets a number, calculates and prints the square
#include <stdio.h>
void main()
{
    int num, square; // declare variables
    // Get the number
    printf("\nEnter the integer number you want to square =>");
    scanf("%d",&num);
    //Square it
    square=num*num;
    //Print the square
    printf("\n%d squared is %d\n",num,square);
  }
```

This program consists of only one function, the main function. As indicated in Chapter 5, this is a required function in any C program since it is the first function to be executed when the program starts running.

3.7.3 Java

Java also uses curly brackets to begin and end its main section. However, Java is fully object-oriented, which means it is class based and even the program itself is a class. Classes will be explained in Chapter 8. For the present, it is important to remember that the class name is also the application name.

EXAMPLE 3.20 Consider the program shown in Fig. 3-3. It is the Java version of the C++ program above.

```
//First Program - gets a number, calculates and prints the square
import java.io.*;
class SquareIt {
   public static void main (String args[]) throws IOException
   {
      //declare variables
      int num,square;
      //1. Get the number
      System.out.print ("Enter a number between 0 and 9 you want to square => ");
      System.out.flush();       //clear buffer before reading
      num=System.in.read();
      num=num – '0';            //change character input to integer
      //2. Square it
      square=num*num;
      //3. Print out the square
      System.out.println (num+" squared is " +square);
   }//end main
}//end class
```

Fig. 3-3 First Java program – square a number.

There are two lines to examine. The first is:

class SquareIt {

This line indicates that the application is called SquareIt. In Java the file must have the same name as the class. Everything in the program is within this class definition. Notice the bracket ending the class is the last line of the file.

The second line to examine is:

public static void main (String args[]) throws IOException

This line obviously begins the main function. It is required to be typed exactly like this. The *void main* (*String args*[]) indicates it is the main function which can receive string messages from the operating system and is not returning a value. The *public* and *static* indicate that the program can be run from outside itself (which obviously is necessary when we start execution) and that it will remain in memory until it is finished. If errors occur in I/O, Java generates an exception to tell us what happened. The final part of the line, *throws IOException*, means that input and output will be performed and we know that an error might occur, but we will ignore these exceptions and let the program crash. Writing code to handle all exceptions is beyond the scope of this book.

3.7.4 Visual Basic

Visual Basic calls its functions Sub's, or subroutines. When writing code modules, instead of using the Visual tools, we are required to have a *Sub main*.

EXAMPLE 3.21 The Visual Basic version of the squaring program is found in Fig. 3-4.

```
'First Program - gets a number, calculates and prints the square

Sub main()
  ' declare variables
  Dim num As Integer, square As Integer

  '1. Get the number
  num=InputBox("Enter the number you want to square =>")

  '2. Square it
  square=num*num

  '3. Print out the square
  MsgBox (Str(num)+" squared is "+Str(square))

End Sub
```

Fig. 3-4 Visual Basic first program – square a number.

Notice the Sub must begin with its name, *main*, and the empty parentheses indicating nothing is coming into the program. When all the code has executed, the Sub must End. Everything else in the Sub is self-explanatory.

Solved Problems

3.1 What would be the ASCII representation of the word "HELLO" in decimal?

By looking at the ASCII chart in Table 3-1, the following values can be found:

H => 72
E => 69
L => 76
L => 76
O => 79

Therefore, the answer would be: 72 69 76 76 79

3.2 What does the following ASCII code represent?

69 97 116 32 118 101 103 103 105 101 115 33

Answer: Eat veggies! Notice the space and the exclamation point are both represented explicitly.

3.3 What does the following ASCII code represent?

51 43 49 61 52

Answer: 3 + 1 = 4

Notice each digit is a character, not a numeric value. Therefore, real arithmetic cannot be performed. 51 plus 49 does not equal 52. This is simply the ASCII representation of the equation.

3.4 The **sizeof(variable)** displays the number of bytes used, and the **&** operator gives the actual address in memory. This address can be different on each computer, or even for each run of the program. What will be the output of the following C++ code section?

```
int int1=1;          short short1=1;     long long1=1;
double d1 = 1.0;     float f1=1.0;       char ch='1';
cout<<"int1\t"<<int1<<' '<<sizeof(int1)<<' '<<&int1<<endl;
cout<<"short1\t"<<short1<<' '<<sizeof(short1)<<' '<<&short1<<endl;
cout<<"long1\t"<<long1<<' '<<sizeof(long1)<<' '<<&long1<<endl;
cout <<"d1\t"<<d1<<' '<<sizeof(d1)<<' '<<&d1<<endl;
cout<<"f1\t"<<f1<<' '<<sizeof(f1)<<' '<<&f1<<endl;
```

int1 1 4 0x0066FDF4
short1 1 2 0x0066FDF0
long1 1 4 0x0066FDEC
d1 1 8 0x0066FDE4
f1 1 4 0x0066FDE0

Answer: Notice the addresses are represented by the computer in hexadecimal notation.

3.5 Write the statements needed to declare the variables and constants for a program to find the circumference and area of a rectangle. Show the declarations in Visual Basic as well as C/C++ and Java.

Visual Basic	C/C++	Java
`Const SIDES=4`	`const SIDES=4;`	`final SIDES=4;`
`Dim length As Integer`	`int length;`	`int length;`
`Dim width As Integer`	`int width;`	`int width;`
`Dim areaOfRect As Integer`	`int areaOfRect;`	`int areaOfRect;`
`Dim circum As Integer`	`int circum;`	`int circum;`

3.6 Write the statements needed to declare the variables and constants for a program to find the circumference and area of a circle. Show the declarations in Visual Basic as well as C/C++ and Java.

Visual Basic	C/C++	Java
`Const PI=3.14`	`const PI=3.14;`	`final PI=3.14;`
`Dim radius As Integer`	`int radius;`	`int radius;`
`Dim areaOfCircle As Single`	`float areaOfCircle;`	`float areaOfCircle;`

3.7 Specify whether these variable names are legal and/or meaningful: (*a*) @amount; (*b*) z; (*c*) side1; (*d*) const; (*e*) my_password.

Variable Name	Explanation
(*a*) @amount	**Illegal** because of @ character
(*b*) z	**Legal**, but should not be used because it is not meaningful
(*c*) side1	**Legal** and meaningful
(*d*) const	**Illegal** because it is a reserved word
(*e*) my_password	**Legal** and meaningful

3.8 Specify whether these constant names are legal and/or meaningful: (*a*) AMT#MONEY; (*b*) X; (*c*) int_rate; (*d*) Boolean; (*e*) MINCOST.

Variable Name	Explanation
(*a*) AMT#MONEY	**Illegal** because of # character
(*b*) X	**Legal**, but should not be used because it is not meaningful
(*c*) int_rate	**Legal** and meaningful, but not correct because constants are usually in all caps
(*d*) Boolean	**Illegal** because it is a reserved word
(*e*) MINCOST	**Legal** and meaningful

3.9 Write a short C++ program implementing a simple Adder program that will add two numbers.

```
#include <iostream.h>

void main()
{

    //declare variables
    int num1, num2, sum;

    //get 2 numbers
    cout<<endl<<"Enter number one=>"; cin>>num1;
    cout<<endl<<"Enter number two=>"; cin>>num2;

    //add them together
    sum=num1+num2;

    //print the result
    cout<<"The sum of"<<num1<<" plus "<<num2<<" is "<<sum<<endl;

}
```

3.10 Write the VB program implementing a simple payroll program. Assume the person makes $10.00 per hour with no extra for overtime.

```
Sub main()
 'declare variables
 Const PERHOUR = 10
 Dim hours As Integer, pay As Integer

 '1. get the number of hours
 hours=InputBox("How many hours?")

 '2. calculate pay
 pay=hours*PERHOUR

 '3. print out pay amount
 MsgBox ("Your pay this week is "+Str(pay))
End Sub
```

3.11 Write a Java program which calculates the area of a small circle with radius between 0 and 9.

```
//Area: calculate the area of a circle with radius between 0 and 9

import java.io.*;

class Area {
 public static void main ( String args[] ) throws IOException
 {
    // declare variables
    final double PI=3.14;
    int radius;
    double area;
```

```
    //1. Get the radius
    System.out.print ("Enter a radius of a circle between 0 and 9=> ");
    System.out.flush();
    radius=System.in.read();
    radius=radius - '0'; //change character to integer

    //2. Calculate area
    area= PI * (radius*radius);

    //3. Print out the square
    System.out.println ("The area of a circle with radius "+radius+" is "+area);
  }// end main
}// end class
```

3.12 In C, display on the video screen the words "It is fun to do I\O".

Since we have to display a message on the screen, we can use the printf() function. Therefore, we may write the following statement

```
printf("\nIt is fun to do I\O");
```

However, if we try to run a program with this statement in it, we will get a warning from the compiler that may read something like this: "warning C4129: 'O' : unrecognized character escape sequence". What this warning means is that the compiler (see Appendix A) could not recognize \O as a valid escape sequence. That is, the compiler "thinks" that we are trying to use an escape sequence instead of writing a backward slash. To remedy this, we need to use a sequence of two consecutive backward slashes. The correct printf statement should look like this:

```
printf("\nIt is fun to do I\\O");
```

3.13 Using only one printf() statement display on the screen, on three separate lines, the message "I came, I saw, and I conquered".

To display this message on the screen we use the printf() function. To write the message on three separate lines, we use the escape sequence "\n". Therefore, the C statement to accomplish this may look like this,

```
printf("\nI came,\nI saw and,\n I conquered");
```

3.14 Write the necessary C statements to print the numbers 1 through 10 and their squares. Align the output.

The code to accomplish this may look like this:

```
for (i=1;i<=10;i++)
  printf("%4d\t%6d\n",i,i*i);
```

Notice the use of the width specifiers to align the results. See page 101 for explanation of for statement.

Supplementary Problems

3.15 What would be the ASCII representation of the phrase "Happy Programming!" in decimal?

3.16 What does the following ASCII code represent?

84 111 109 32 104 97 115 32 36 51 50 46 52 53 46

3.17 What does the following ASCII code represent?

71 111 32 70 105 115 104 108 110 103 33

3.18 Write the statements needed to declare the variables and constants for a program to find the miles per gallon for a specific car. Show the declarations in Visual Basic as well as C++ and Java.

3.19 Write the statements needed to declare the variables and constants for a program to handle an ATM machine. The transactions are specified by "W" for withdrawal or "D" for deposit.

3.20 Which of these identifiers are legal and/or meaningful?

Variables	**Constants**
(*a*) 123	(*e*) pi
(*b*) length	(*f*) MAXSTUDENTS
(*c*) test2	(*g*) RATE!
(*d*) a	(*h*) tempNum

3.21 Write a C++ program to convert a Celsius temperature to Fahrenheit.

3.22 Write a VB program to find the average of three test scores.

3.23 Write a Java program that calculates the quotient and remainder of 97 divided by some integer between 1 and 9.

Answers to Supplementary Problems

3.15 72 97 112 112 121 32 80 114 111 103 114 97 109 109 105 110 103 33

3.16 Tom has $32.45.

3.17 Go Fishing!

3.18 **Visual Basic**

```
Dim milesTraveled As Single
Dim gallonsUsed As Single
Dim mpg As Single
```

C++ and Java

```
float milesTraveled;
float gallonsUsed;
float mpg;
```

3.19 **Visual Basic**

```
Dim transactionType As String
Dim amount As Single
Dim balance As Single
```

C++ and Java

```
char transactionType;
float amount;
float balance;
```

3.20 (*a*) 123 => Illegal, because it is a numeric constant. a123 would be legal but not meaningful.

(*b*) length => Legal and meaningful.

(*c*) test2 => Legal and meaningful.

(*d*) a => Legal, but not meaningful. It would be hard to debug in the program.

(*e*) pi => Legal, but constants are usually printed in all caps.

(*f*) MAXSTUDENTS => Legal and meaningful.

(*g*) RATE! => Illegal because of the !.

(*h*) tempNum => Legal, if that is the desired name. However, if it represents a temporary number that may change values during the program, it would not be a constant.

3.21

```
#include <iostream.h>

void main()
{
    // declare variables
    double fahrenheit, celsius;

    //1. Get the Celsius temperature
    cout<<endl<<"Enter the Celsius temperature=> "; cin>>celsius;

    //2. Calculate the fahrenheit
    fahrenheit= (celsius *(9.0/5))+32;

    //3. Print out the result
    cout<<celsius<<" degrees Celsius is"
        <<fahrenheit<<" degrees fahrenheit"<<endl;
}
```

3.22

```
'Average - finds the average of three test scores
Sub main()
 'declare variables
 Dim test1 As Integer, test2 As Integer, test3 As Integer
 Dim average As Single

 '1. Get the 3 scores
 test1=InputBox("Enter the first score=>")
 test2=InputBox("Enter the second score=>")
 test3=InputBox("Enter the third score=>")

 '2. Calculate the Average
 average=(test1+test2+test3)/3

 '3. Print out the square
 MsgBox ("The average of"+Str(test1)+","+Str(test2)+_
   " and "+Str(test3)+" is "+Str(average))

 'notice the underline character to indicate continuation
End Sub
```

3.23

```
/* Divide - Calculates the quotient and remainder of 97
   divided by any number between 1 and 9 */

import java.io.*;

class Divide {
 public static void main ( String args[] ) throws IOException
 {
  // declare variables
  int num, quotient, remainder;

  //1. Get the divisor
  System.out.print ("Enter a number between 1 and 9=>");
  System.out.flush();
  num=System.in.read();
  num=num - '0'; // change character to integer

  //2. Calculate quotient and remainder
  quotient=97 / num; // integer division
  remainder=97 % num; // modulo arithmetic

  //3. Print out the result
  System.out.println ("When 97 is divided by "+num+" the quotient is "
    +quotient+ "and the remainder is"+remainder);
 }// end main
}// end class
```

Control Structures and Program Writing

4.1 BOOLEAN EXPRESSIONS

George Boole, a mathematician in the nineteenth century, was interested in the relationship between human logic and mathematics. He developed Boolean algebra, which is modeled after human thought patterns. This algebra is widely used today in the design of computer circuits, where all variables have only the values zero or one. A ***Boolean expression*** is a statement that is either true or false, one or the other, but not both at once. A Boolean expression may be a Boolean variable or constant by itself, or it may be constants or variables connected by relational or equality operators. Individual Boolean expressions can be combined into more complex statements by connecting them with the logical operators NOT, AND, and OR.

4.1.1 Boolean Variables and Constants

A Boolean expression may be a Boolean variable or constant. Such variables are often called flags because they can provide signals regarding the status of conditions in the program. It is important to give these variables descriptive names, because descriptive names help in the understanding and debugging of programs. Possible descriptive variable names include dataOK, workDone, or itemFound. Some languages have a built-in Boolean data type. Usually, however, integer variables are used to represent Boolean conditions. For example, in some languages zero (0) signifies false, and other non-zero values signify true. In C, C++, and Java, any value other than zero signifies true, but usually the value one (1) is used. In Visual Basic, negative one (−1) signifies true.

EXAMPLE 4.1 Demonstrate some Boolean variables in C, C++, and Java.

```
const TRUE=1;
const FALSE=0;
int dataOK, workDone, itemFound;
dataOK=FALSE; // set to false, data is NOT OK
workDone=TRUE;// set to true, the work is completed
itemFound=FALSE;// set to false, the item was not found
```

4.1.2 Relational Expressions

Boolean expressions may be constructed by connecting constants or variables by a relational operator. ***Relational operators*** and ***equality operators*** are shown in Table 4-1. Their English equivalents are used in normal speech and are easily understood.

Table 4-1 Relational Operators.

Relational Operators in C, C++ and JAVA	Relational Operators in Visual Basic	English Equivalent
<	<	less than
<=	<=	less than or equal to
>	>	greater than
>=	>=	greater than or equal to
Equality Operators	Equality Operators	
==	=	equal to
!=	<>	not equal to

Arithmetic calculations are always performed before the relational and equality operators are evaluated. For example, in the expression

$$4 + 5 < 20$$

the 4 and 5 would be added together before testing whether the result is in fact less than 20. All calculations and comparisons are performed left to right unless specified otherwise through the use of parentheses. The variables and/or constants connected by relational and equality operators must always be of the same type. For example, consider the values of the following expressions in Table 4-2. In the second column, both x and y have been declared type integer. In the third column both have been declared of type character.

Table 4-2 Examples of Boolean Expressions.

Boolean Expression	Value if x = 3 and y = 4	Value if x = 'b' and y = 'b'	Explanation
x > y	false	false	If x and y are the same, x is not greater than y
x == y	false	true	They are precisely equal to each other
x != y	true	false	They are precisely not equal to each other
x < y	true	false	If x and y are the same, x is not less than y
x <= y	true	true	If they are the same, then x is either less than or equal to y

EXAMPLE 4.2 What is the value of each of these expressions, given the values of x and y?

Boolean Expression	Value if x = 3 and y = 4	Explanation
x − 4 < y	true	(−1) is less than 4
x + 1 == y	true	4 is precisely equal to 4
x != y − 1	false	It is false that 3 is precisely not equal to 3
x + 1 >= y	true	3 is greater than or equal to 3

EXAMPLE 4.3 String variables can also be compared. In this case, the computer looks at the values left to right, character by character, and compares the ASCII value of each letter. Consider the Boolean expressions in Table 4-3.

Table 4-3

Boolean Expression	Value	Explanation
"Ann" < "Annette"	true	The 4th character is considered to be null, which in ASCII is zero, and less than the ASCII value of any other character
"Sam" == "Sam"	true	Each character is precisely the same
"Johnson" <= "Johnsen"	false	The 6th character 'e' is less than 'o', which makes the entire string "Johnsen" less than the entire string "Johnson"

4.1.3 Logical Expressions

Individual Boolean variables or expressions can be combined into more complex statements by connecting them with logical operators. ***Logical operators*** for several languages are shown in the order of precedence in Table 4-4 with English explanations. The basic process for evaluating complex Boolean expressions is:

(1) Evaluate all the individual relational expressions left to right.

(2) Evaluate the logical expressions in parentheses.

(3) Evaluate the logical expressions in the order of precedence.

Table 4-4 Logical Operators.

Logical Operators in C, C++, and Java	English and Visual Basic	Explanation	Associativity
!	NOT	has single operand, and returns its negation (opposite)	Left to right
&&	AND	returns true ONLY if BOTH operands are true, false if EITHER or BOTH operands are false	Left to right
||	OR	returns true if EITHER or BOTH operands are true, false ONLY if BOTH operands are false	Left to right

Table 4-5 demonstrates the order of precedence for all operators, including the arithmetic operators explained in Chapter 3. Each part of a Boolean expression is evaluated in the order indicated.

Table 4-5 Order of Precedence.

Operators	Operation	Order of Precedence	Associativity
( )	Parentheses	1	
^ (VB only)	Exponentiation	2	
! or NOT	Negation	3	Left to right
* /	Multiplication and division	4	Left to right
\(VB only)	Integer division	5	Left to right
% or MOD	Modulus	6	Left to right
+ −	Addition and subtraction	7	Left to right
< <= > >=	Relational operators	8	Left to right
== != or <>	Equality operators	9	Left to right
&& or AND	Logical AND	10	Left to right
‖ or OR	Logical OR	11	Left to right

EXAMPLE 4.4 What is the value of each of these expressions given the values of x and y? Note, each individual Boolean expression is evaluated first, depending upon parentheses. Then the resultant Boolean combinations are evaluated next according to the precedence chart, and finally the whole expression is evaluated.

(*a*) if x = −3 and y = 4

(x == −3) && (y != 3)

```
   T      |    |     Evaluate this expression first, x is −3.
          |    T     Evaluate this expression second, y does not equal 3.
          T          Finally follow the rules for AND, true if both are true.
```

(*b*) if x = 3 and y = 3

(x == −3) && (y != 3)

```
   F      |    |     Evaluate this expression first.
          |    F     Evaluate this expression second.
          F          Finally follow the rules for AND, false if both are false.
```

EXAMPLE 4.5 What is the value of each of these expressions given the values of x and y? Note, each individual Boolean expression is evaluated first, depending upon parentheses. Then the resultant Boolean combinations are evaluated next according to the precedence chart, and finally the whole expression is evaluated.

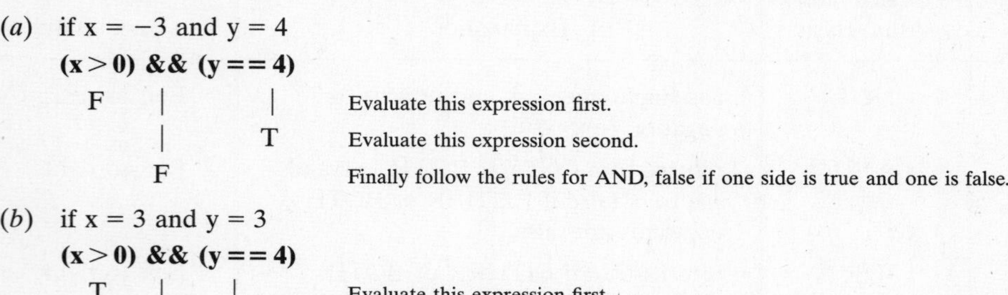

(*a*) if x = −3 and y = 4

(x > 0) && (y == 4)

```
   F   |     |     Evaluate this expression first.
       |     T     Evaluate this expression second.
       F           Finally follow the rules for AND, false if one side is true and one is false.
```

(*b*) if x = 3 and y = 3

(x > 0) && (y == 4)

```
   T   |   |       Evaluate this expression first.
       |   F       Evaluate this expression second.
       F           Finally follow the rules for AND, false if one side is true and one is false.
```

EXAMPLE 4.6 What is the value of each of these expressions given the values of x and y?

(*a*) if x = −3 and y = 4

```
(x > 0) || (y == 4)
   F    |     |         Evaluate this expression first.
        |     T         Evaluate this expression second.
        T               Finally follow the rules for OR, true if one side is true and one is false.
```

(*b*) if x = 3 and y = 3

```
(x > 0) || (y == 4)
   T    |     |         Evaluate this expression first.
        |     F         Evaluate this expression second.
        T               Finally follow the rules for OR, true if one side is true and one is false.
```

EXAMPLE 4.7 What is the value of each of these expressions given the values of x and y?

(*a*) if x = −3 and y = 4

```
(x < 0) || (x == 3) && (y > 0)
   T    |     |     |     |     Evaluate this expression first.
        |     F     |     |     Evaluate this expression second.
        |           |     T     Evaluate this expression third.
        |           F           Evaluate AND before OR, false if either is false.
        T                       Finally follow the rules for OR, true if one side is true and one is false.
```

(*b*) if x = 3 and y = 3

```
(x > 0) || (x == 3) && (y > 0)
   T    |     |     |     |     Evaluate this expression first.
        |     T     |     |     Evaluate this expression second.
        |           |     T     Evaluate this expression third.
        |           T           Evaluate AND before OR, true if both are true.
        T                       Finally follow the rules for OR, true if one side is true and one is false.
```

EXAMPLE 4.8 What is the value of each of these expressions given the values of x and y?

(*a*) if x = 3

```
(x > 0) && (x < 100)
   T    |      |        Evaluate this expression first.
        |      T        Evaluate this expression second.
        T               Finally follow the rules for AND, true if both are true.
```

Note: The algebraic expression **(0 < x < 100)** cannot be used. Each Boolean expression for x must be tested separately.

(*b*) if x = 3

```
!(x > 0) && (x < 100)
    T    |      |       Evaluate this expression first.
 F       |      |       Evaluate this expression second.
         |      T       Evaluate this expression third.
         F              Finally follow the rules for AND, true ONLY if both sides are true.
```

(*c*) if x = 3

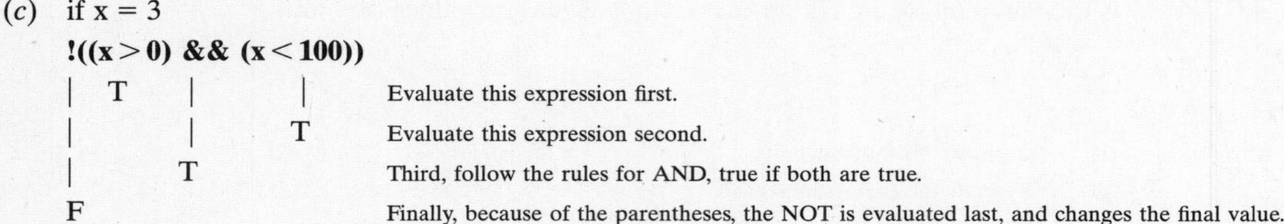

!((x > 0) && (x < 100))
T
T
T
F
Evaluate this expression first.
Evaluate this expression second.
Third, follow the rules for AND, true if both are true.
Finally, because of the parentheses, the NOT is evaluated last, and changes the final value.

4.2 CONTROL STRUCTURES – DEFINITIONS

Computer programs only do what the programmer has told them to do. They execute the instruction statements in three ways: sequence, selection, and repetition. Most of the time, instructions are executed in ***sequence***, one after the other, in the order in which they are written. Figure 4-1 shows the flowchart for sequence.

EXAMPLE 4.9 What will be the value of the variable *c* after this code section?

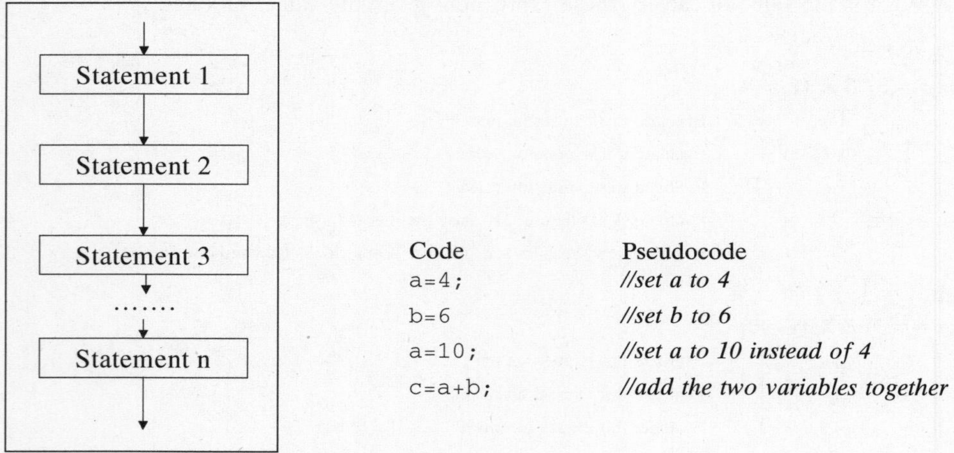

Fig. 4-1 Sequence flowchart.

Each statement is executed in order, so the final value of the variable *c* would equal 16, because the variable *a* was changed before the addition.

Sometimes, the programmer has two or more possible instructions for the computer to execute, with the decision to be made at runtime from the value of a variable or a Boolean expression. In this case, the programmer uses ***selection***. The computer selects only ONE instruction (or set of instructions) to execute from two possible choices depending upon whether the Boolean expression is true or false, or from several possible choices depending upon the value of the specified variable.

Often, the programmer wants to execute one or more instructions over and over, or perform ***repetition***. Once again, a Boolean expression helps to determine how many times the instruction (or set of instructions) will execute.

4.3 SELECTION

Selection allows the computer to choose the instructions to execute. Other instructions may be ignored. A choice may be made between two alternatives, or from many possible alternatives. For readability, the statements within each alternative are usually indented.

4.3.1 Choosing Between Two Alternatives

The computer can choose between two possible alternatives, although the second alternative may just be to ignore the first statement. For example, you might say, "If it is raining, I'll take my umbrella." Implied is the option to ignore the umbrella if it is not raining. Or you might say, "If it is cold outside, I'll drink hot tea. Otherwise, I'll have ice water." The option to drink something is not ignored; there are two clear options from which to choose. Figure 4-2 illustrates the flowcharts for the two kinds of statements.

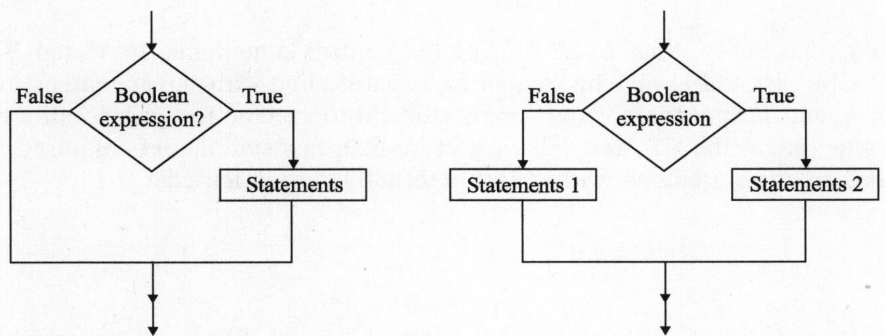

Fig. 4-2 Single "If" and "If...Else" structures.

Most programming languages have single "If" statements, as well as "If...Else" statements. Specific forms are shown in Table 4-6. In C, C++, and Java, the braces may be omitted if there is only one statement.

Table 4-6 If and If...Else Statements.

<table>
<tr><th>C, C++, and Java</th><th>Visual Basic</th></tr>
<tr><td><pre>if (Boolean expression)
{ statement(s)
}
if (Boolean expression)
{   statement(s)
}
else
{   statement(s)
}</pre></td><td><pre>If Boolean expression Then
     statement(s)
End If
If Boolean expression Then
     statement(s)
Else
     statement(s)
End If</pre></td></tr>
</table>

If the Boolean expression is true, the first set of statements will be executed. If the Boolean expression is false, in the single "If" structure, nothing happens, and the control passes to the statements following the "If". In the "If...Else" structure, if the Boolean expression is false, the Else statements will execute.

In Example 4.9 below, notice the difference in the equality testing between C++ and Visual Basic. C, C++, and Java require the double equal sign "==" to test equality. However, if a single equal sign is used no error message is given. The computer assumes it is an assignment statement, puts the value on the right into the variable on the left, and then tests whether the result is zero or non-zero. In debugging a program, one of the first things to look for is the correct use of the double equal sign. In addition, Visual Basic requires that the word "Else" be on a line by itself.

EXAMPLE 4.9 Write an "If" statement that will set a character variable called *message* to "T" if the Boolean variable *raining* is true. Notice the indentation of the statements.

C, C++, and Java:
```
if (raining==true)      // "if (raining = true)" would assign the value true,
    message='T';        // and always execute the if statements
```

Visual Basic:
```
If (raining=true) Then
    message="T"
End If
```

Each language has rules about placement of the control statements. In Visual Basic, as stated previously, the "Else" should always be on its own separate line with the statements to be executed below. In C, C++, and Java, if there is only one statement to execute for each condition, they may be placed on the same line as the "if" and "else." If more than one statement is required, brackets must be used. In that case, the statements within each alternative are indented.

EXAMPLE 4.10 Write an "If...Else" statement that will set a character variable called *drink* to "H" for (Hot Tea) if the Boolean variable *cold* is true, or "W" for (Ice Water) otherwise. Show how the code would be different if the running total of each kind of drink was to be tabulated.

One statement for each alternative:

C, C++, and Java:
```
if (cold==true) drink='H';
else drink='W';
```

Visual Basic:
```
If (cold=true) Then
    drink="H"
Else
    drink="W"
End If
```

More than one statement for each alternative:

C, C++, and Java:
```
if (cold==true)
{
    drink='H';
    hot++;
}
else
{
    drink='W';
    warm++;
}
```

Visual Basic:
```
If (cold=true) Then
    drink="H"
    hot=hot+1
Else
    drink="W"
    warm=warm+1
End If
```

4.3.2 Choosing One From Several Alternatives

Sometimes there are more than two alternatives from which to choose. For example, if it is Monday or Friday, you have class. On Tuesday and Thursday you have lab. Wednesday you work, and Saturday you sleep late. Your activity depends upon which day it is. Most modern languages have two ways to indicate such a choice: a series of "If" statements, or a more efficient case structure. The flowcharts for both structures are illustrated in Fig. 4-3.

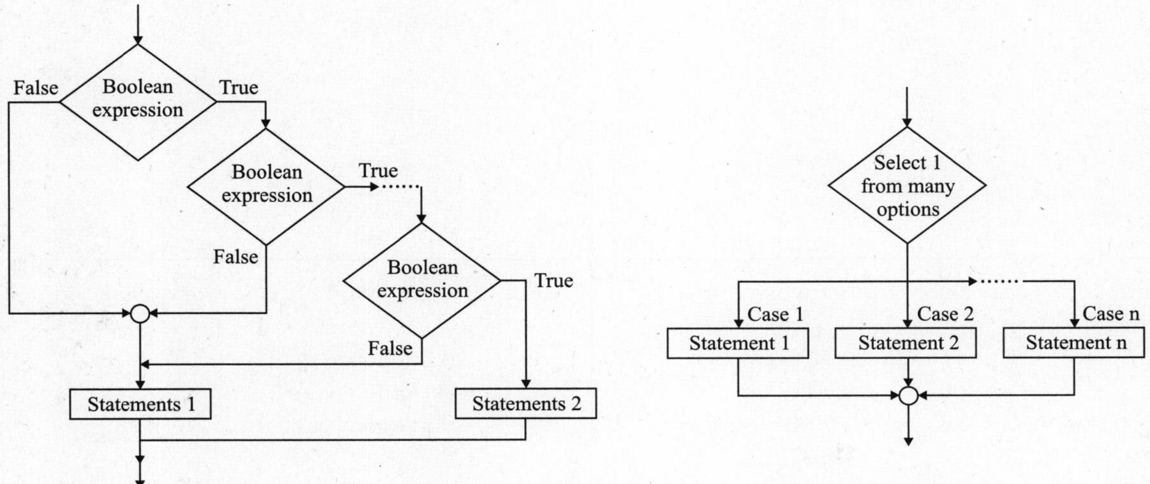

Fig. 4-3 Nested "If" and Case structures.

The case structure examines a variable or expression, and allows the choices to match its possible values. Usually, a default is specified in case none of the possible values is present. The alternate structures for all three languages are shown in Table 4-7.

Table 4-7 Nested Ifs and Case Structures.

<table>
<tr><th>C, C++, and Java</th><th>Visual Basic</th></tr>
<tr><td><pre>
if (Boolean Expression)
...{ statements }
else {
  if (Boolean Expression)
...   { statements }
  else   {
    if (Boolean Expression)
    ...{ statements }
    else
... { statements }
  }
}
</pre></td><td><pre>
If Boolean Expression Then
    Statement(s)
Else
    If Boolean Expression Then
      Statement(s)
    Else
      If Boolean Expression Then
        Statement(s)
...   Else
        Statement(s)
    End If
  End If
End If
</pre></td></tr>
</table>

C, C++, and Java	Visual Basic

if (*Boolean Expression*)
{
   statement(s)
}
else if
{
   statement(s)
}...
else
{
   statement(s)
}
	If *Boolean Expression* Then
	   Statement(s)
	ElseIf *Boolean Expression* Then
	   Statement(s)
	ElseIf *Boolean Expression* Then
	   Statement(s)
	...
	End If

switch (*variable or expression*)
{
  case (*1st value*): statement(s);
                      break;
  case (*2nd^{t} value*): statement(s);
                       break;
...
  default : statement(s);
}
	Select Case *variable or expression*
	   Case (*1st value*)
	      statement(s)
	   Case (*2nd value*)
	      statement(s)
	...
	   Case Else
	      statement(s)
	End Select

It is possible to convert a complex "If...Else" statement to a case structure. Often the logic is more evident using the switch or select case statement, especially if there is a compound condition. Alternate versions are shown in Examples 4.11 and 4.12. Notice the awkward nature of nested ifs in the first version. These three versions demonstrate how much easier the case structure is to write and to understand. The Visual Basic equivalents are shown in Solved Problem 4.4 at the end of the chapter.

EXAMPLE 4.11 Write a section of code that will take in a number 1 through 7, and print out the day of the week.

"If ... Else" version

```
cout<<endl<<"Enter a day of the week - 1 for Sun, etc."; cin>>dayNum;
if (dayNum==1)
        cout<<"Sunday"<<endl;
else {
        if (dayNum==2)
                cout<<"Monday"<<endl;
        else {
                if (dayNum==3)
                        cout<<"Tuesday"<<endl;
                else {
                        if (dayNum==4)
                                cout<<"Wednesday"<<endl;
                        else {
```

```
                                if (dayNum==5)
                                        cout<<"Thursday"<<endl;
                                else {
                                        if (dayNum==6)
                                                cout<<"Friday"<<endl;
                                        else {
                                                if (dayNum==7)
                                                      cout<<"Saturday"<<endl;
                                                else{
                                                      cout<<"Only 1 through 7"<<endl;
                                                }
                                        }
                                }
                        }
                }
        }
}
```

"If ... Elseif" version

```
cout<<endl<<"Enter a day of the week - 1 for Sun, etc."; cin>>dayNum;
if (dayNum==1)
        cout<<"Sunday"<<endl;
else if (dayNum==2)
        cout<<"Monday"<<endl;
else if (dayNum==3)
        cout<<"Tuesday"<<endl;
else if (dayNum==4)
        cout<<"Wednesday"<<endl;
else if (dayNum==5)
        cout<<"Thursday"<<endl;
else if (dayNum==6)
        cout<<"Friday"<<endl;
else if (dayNum==7)
        cout<<"Saturday"<<endl;
else
        cout<<"Only 1 through 7"<<endl;
```

Case Structure version: The variable dayNum is the variable tested for each case.

```
cout<<endl<<"Enter a day of the week - 1 for Sun, etc."; cin>>dayNum;
switch (dayNum)
{
        case 1: cout<<"Sunday"<<endl; break;
        case 2: cout<<"Monday"<<endl; break;
        case 3: cout<<"Tuesday"<<endl; break;
        case 4: cout<<"Wednesday"<<endl; break;
        case 5: cout<<"Thursday"<<endl; break;
        case 6: cout<<"Friday"<<endl; break;
        case 7: cout<<"Saturday"<<endl; break;
        default: cout<<"Only 1 through 7"<<endl;
}
```

EXAMPLE 4.12 Write a section of code that will determine whether a day of the week is a working day or a weekend.

"If...Else" version

```
cout<<endl<<"Enter a day of the week - 1 for Sun, etc."; cin>>dayNum;
if (dayNum==1 || dayNum==7)
        cout<<"Weekend - have fun"<<endl;
else
        if (dayNum>=2 && dayNum<=6)
                cout<<"Weekday - go to work"<<endl;
        else
                cout<<"Only 1 through 7"<<endl;
```

"If ... Elseif" version

```
cout<<endl<<"Enter a day of the week - 1 for Sun, etc."; cin>>dayNum;
if (dayNum==1 || dayNum==7)
        cout<<"Weekend - have fun"<<endl;
else if (dayNum>=&& dayNum<=6)
        cout<<"Weekday - go to work"<<endl;
else
        cout<<"Only 1 through 7"<<endl;
```

Case Structure version: Notice the cases can be combined. Each line will be executed sequentially until it reaches the *break* command.

```
cout<<endl<<"Enter a day of the week - 1 for Sun, etc."; cin>>dayNum;
switch (dayNum)
{
        case 1:
        case 7: cout<<"Weekend - have fun"<<endl; break;
        case 2:
        case 3:
        case 4:
        case 5:
        case 6: cout<<"Weekday - go to work"<<endl; break;
        default: cout<<"Only 1 through 7"<<endl;
}
```

4.4 REPETITION

As indicated before, repetition allows the program to execute one or more instructions over and over. Each repetition statement is controlled by a loop control variable (lcv) which has an initial and a final value. The lcv begins with its initial value and must be incremented, decremented, or changed in some way during the loop body. Each time the loop is executed, the lcv is compared to the final value to test whether to execute the loop once again. The initial and final values must be of the same data type as the lcv. It is possible in compound conditional statements for the loop to have more than one lcv. The loop body is always indented for ease in reading.

4.4.1 Fixed Repetition Statements

Fixed repetition statements are used when you KNOW in advance how many times the loop should be executed. The flowchart for fixed repetition is shown in Fig. 4-4. The lcv is set to the initial

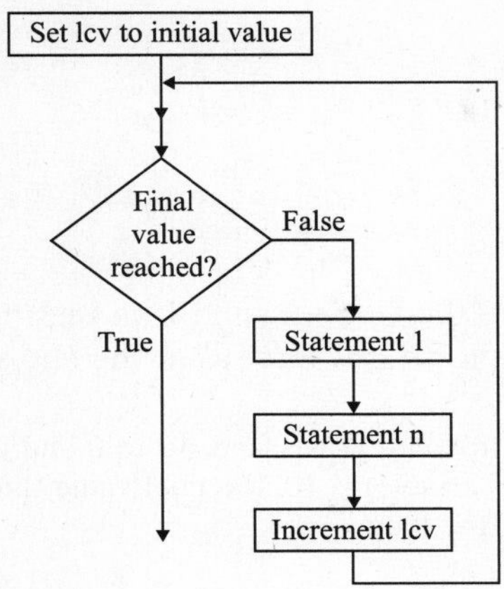

Fig. 4-4 Fixed repetition.

value before the loop is entered. Boolean testing of the lcv against the final value is done BEFORE the loop is entered, so if the initial value already reaches the final value the loop will never be entered. When all the statements in the loop body have been executed, the lcv is automatically incremented by the specified amount.

Table 4-8 shows the structure of a fixed repetition statement in specific languages. Notice in C, C++, and Java the initial and final value, as well as the amount to increment, are all contained in parentheses separated by semicolons. In the Visual Basic version, if the STEP value is omitted the incremental value is set to one by default.

Table 4-8 Fixed Repetition – iv = Initial Value of lcv, fv = Final Value of lcv.

C, C++, and Java	Visual Basic

`for (set lcv to iv; test lcv for fv; change`
`lcv by increment value)`
`{`
`statements`
`}`
	`For lcv=iv TO fv STEP increment value`
	`Statement(s)`
	`Next lcv`

Here is a sample of a C or C++ fixed repetition loop that will print the numbers from one to ten. Before the loop begins, the lcv is set to 1, then tested to see if it is less than or equal to 10. After the lcv is printed, lcv is incremented by 1 and then tested again against the value 10. The last time through the loop, the 10 is printed, lcv is incremented to 11, and, since that is greater than 10, the loop stops. Remember, the value of lcv following this loop will be 11.

```
for (lcv=1; lcv <= 10; lcv++)     //BEFORE the loop begins, lcv is set to 1,
                                   //then tested to see if it is <= 10

    cout<<lcv<<endl;               //AFTER the lcv is printed, lcv is
                                   //incremented by 1 and then tested again
```

The Visual Basic sample of this loop follows the same process. Because the STEP value is left out, lcv is automatically incremented by 1.

```
For lcv=1 To 10        'BEFORE the loop begins, lcv is set to 1, then tested
                       'to see if it is <= 10
   Print lcv
Next lcv               'AFTER the lcv is printed, lcv is incremented by 1
                       'and then tested again
```

The examples below demonstrate the C, C++, and Java versions of fixed repetition loops. Similar examples of Visual Basic loops are shown in exercises at the end of the chapter.

EXAMPLE 4.13 Write a code section to count down from 10 to 0 and then print "Blast off!" In other words, the initial value of the lcv (loop control variable) is 10, the final value that will stop the loop is 0, and the lcv is incremented by (−1) each time through the loop.

```
for (lcv=10; lcv >= 0; lcv--)  //OUTPUT: 10 9 8 7 6 5 4 3 2 1 0 Blast off!
        cout<<lcv<<' ';        //cout the number and then a blank for separation
cout<<"Blast off!"<<endl;
```

EXAMPLE 4.14 Write a section of code to add all the numbers from 0 to 19 and print the sum.

```
sum=0;                          //initialize the sum to 0
for (num=0; num < 20; num++)    //lcv starts at 0, stops at 20, and increments by 1
        sum+=num;               //this is the same as sum=sum+num;
cout<<sum<<endl;                //prints the result, 190
```

NOTE: ++ means add 1 to variable, −− means subtract 1 from variable.

EXAMPLE 4.15 Write a section of code to count by 5's from 0 to 100.

```
for (lcv=0; lcv<101; lcv+=5)   // lcv starts at 0, stops after 100, and increments by 5
        cout<<lcv<<endl;
```

4.4.2 Pretest Repetition Statements

In ***pretest loops*** the Boolean expression is tested FIRST before the body is executed. Use them when you DON'T KNOW how many repetitions are needed.

- The while loop is executed while the Boolean expression is true; the until loop executes until the Boolean expression becomes true.
- The Boolean expression must be changed in the loop, or it results in an infinite loop.
- The Boolean expression can be an EOF marker, a sentinel value, a Boolean flag, or an arithmetic expression.

The unique characteristics of a pretest loop are:

- The Boolean expression must be given an initial value BEFORE the loop starts.
- If the Boolean expression is initially false, the loop is skipped.

The flowchart for a pretest loop is shown in Fig. 4-5. Notice, like fixed repetition, the testing is done before the loop starts. However, unlike fixed repetition, the lcv must be explicitly changed within the loop. It is not done automatically. Two examples are shown. The first is for the C or C++ while and the Visual Basic Do While and the second demonstrates an alternate version available in Visual Basic, the Do Until.

Notice, the "While" version executes AS LONG AS the Boolean expression is true, and the "Until" version executes UNTIL the Boolean version becomes true. Syntax for these loops is shown in Table 4-9.

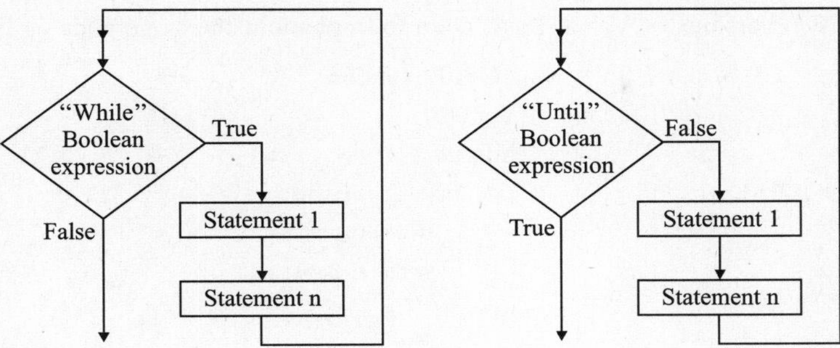

Fig. 4-5 Pretest Loop "While" and "Until".

Table 4-9 Pretest Loops.

C, C++, and Java	Visual Basic	Visual Basic (alternate)

`// set lcv to initial value`
`while (Boolean expression)`
`{`
`    //statement(s)`
`    //change lcv`
`}`
	`'set lcv to initial value`
	`Do While (Boolean expression)`
	`    'statement(s)`
	`    'change lcv`
	`Loop`
		`'set lcv to initial value`
		`Do Until (Boolean expression)`
		`    'statement(s)`
		`    'change lcv`
		`Loop`

EXAMPLE 4.16 Write a C++ section of code to ask the user for a list of numbers and add them until the user wants to stop.

```
sum=0;                                  //initialize sum to 0 to begin
cout<<"Enter an integer, -1 to stop";

cin>>lcv;                               //initial value for lcv
while (lcv !=-1)                        // final value -1 will stop loop
{
    sum+=lcv;
    cout<<"Enter an integer, -1 to stop";

    cin>>lcv;                           //change lcv in loop
}
cout<<sum<<endl;                        //prints the resulting sum
```

Note: if the user enters −1 the first time, the loop will not be entered and the sum will be zero.

EXAMPLE 4.17 Write a C++ section of code to add successive numbers starting with one until the sum is greater than or equal to 1000.

```
num=0;
sum=0;                   //give initial value, in this case sum is the lcv
while (sum<1000)         //sum's final value will be>999
{
    num++;
    sum+=num;            //change sum in the loop
}
cout<<sum;               //sum is 1035 which stops the loop
```

EXAMPLE 4.18 Write two versions of Visual Basic code to implement the same code as Example 4.17.

"While" version:

```
num=0
sum=0
Do While (sum<1000)
      num=num+1
      sum=sum+num
Loop
```

"Until" version

```
num=0
sum=0
Do Until (sum>=1000)
      num=num+1
      sum=sum+num
Loop
```

4.4.3 Posttest Repetition Statements

In ***posttest loops*** the Boolean expression is tested LAST. Use them when you know you want to execute the loop AT LEAST ONCE (e.g. a menu program). Several characteristics are the same as for a pretest loop.

- The while loop is executed while the Boolean expression is true; the until loop executes until the Boolean expression becomes true.
- The Boolean expression must be changed in the loop, or it results in an infinite loop.
- The Boolean expression can be an EOF marker, a sentinel value, a Boolean flag, or an arithmetic expression.

The unique characteristics of a posttest loop are:

- The Boolean expression may get its initial value within the loop.
- Because it is tested after the loop body has executed, the loop is ALWAYS executed at least once, even if the Boolean expression is false.

The flowchart for a posttest loop is shown in Fig. 4-6. Notice the testing is done after the loop finishes executing. However, unlike fixed repetition, the lcv must be explicitly changed within the loop. It is not done automatically. Two examples are shown. The first is for the C/C++ while and the Visual Basic Do While and the second demonstrates an alternate version available in Visual Basic, the Do Until.

Notice, the "While" version executes AS LONG AS the Boolean expression is true, and the "Until" version executes UNTIL the Boolean version becomes true. Syntax for these loops is shown in Table 4-10.

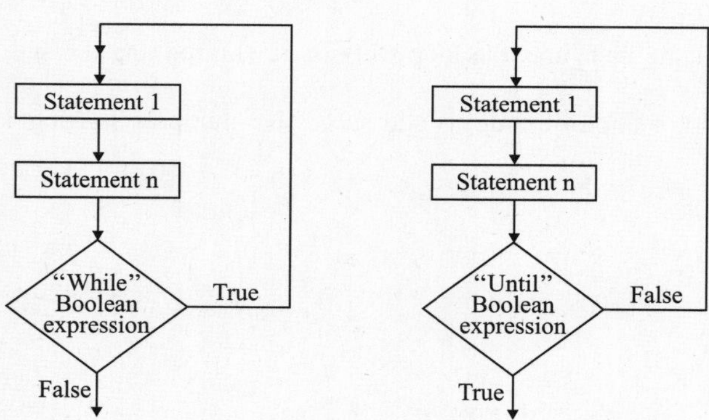

Fig. 4-6 Posttest Loop "While" and "Until".

Table 4-10 Posttest Loops.

C, C++, and Java	Visual Basic	Visual Basic (alternate)

do {
//statement(s)
//change lcv
} while (Boolean expression);
	Do
	'statement(s)
	'change lcv
	Loop While (Boolean expression)
		Do
		'statement(s)
		'change lcv
		Loop Until (Boolean expression)

EXAMPLE 4.19 Write a section of code to ask the user for a list of numbers and add them until the user wants to stop.

```
sum=0;
lcv=0;                     //give lcv initial value, necessary before add
do                         //loop MUST be entered the first time
{
    sum+=lcv;
    cout<<"Enter an integer, -1 to stop";
    cin>>lcv;              //change lcv in loop
} while (lcv!=-1);         //final value of -1 will stop loop
cout<<sum<<endl;           //prints the result
```

EXAMPLE 4.20 Write a section of code to display a menu of arithmetic choices and have the loop continue until the user chooses to quit.

```
do                                  //loop MUST be entered at least once
{
    cout<<"1. Add"<<endl;
    cout<<"2. Subtract"<<endl;
    cout<<"3. Multiply"<<endl;
    cout<<"4. Divide"<<endl;
    cout<<"5. Quit"<<endl;
    cin>>choice;                    // lcv is allowed to change in loop
    //put in switch statement here to handle calculations
} while (choice!=5);                //final value of 5 will stop loop
```

Solved Problems

4.1 What is the value of each of these expressions given the values of a, b, and c and of the Boolean variable done? Remember to follow the order of precedence in Table 4-5.

(*a*) if a = −3 and b = 4 and c = 2

```
(a<c) && (b>c)
  T    |   |          Evaluate this expression first.
       |   T          Evaluate this expression second.

       T              Finally follow the rules for AND, true if both are true.
```

(*b*) if a = −3 and b = 4 and c = 2

```
(a<c) || (c>b)
  T   |   |           Evaluate this expression first.
      |   F           Evaluate this expression second.
      T               Finally follow the rules for OR, true if one or both are true.
```

(*c*) if a = 3 and b = 3 and done = false

```
(a==-3) || (b!=3) && (!done)
  F      |   |     |    |      Evaluate this expression first.
         |   F     |    |      Evaluate this expression second.
         |         |    T      Evaluate this expression third, if done is false, not done is true.
         |         F           AND is evaluated before OR, and follow the rules for AND, true only if both are true.
         F                     Finally follow the rules for OR, false if both are false.
```

4.2 What is the value of each of these expressions given the values of a, b, and c and of the Boolean variable done? Remember to follow the order of precedence in Table 4-5.

(*a*) if a = 8 and b = 9 and done is true

```
(a!=8) && (b!=7) || (!done)
  F     |     |    |    |      Evaluate this expression first.
        |     T    |    |      Evaluate this expression second.
        |          |    F      Evaluate this expression third, if done is true, not done is false.
        F          |           AND is evaluated before OR, and follow the rules for AND, true only if both are true.
                   F           Finally follow the rules for OR, false if both sides are false.
```

(*b*) if a = 8 and b = 9 and c = 5

```
!(a>b) || ((b+c)>=(a-c))
  T    |         |        Evaluate this expression first, if a greater than b is false, then the NOT makes it true.
       |         T        Evaluate this expression second, 17 is greater than 4.
       T                  Finally follow the rules for OR, true if one side is true and one is false, or both sides are true.
```

(*c*) if a = 8 and b = 9 and c = 5

```
!((a<b) && ((b+c)>=(a-c)))
| T      |       |         Evaluate this expression first, a is less than b is true.
|        |       T         Evaluate this expression second, 17 is greater than 4.
|        T                 Follow the rules for AND, true if both sides are true.
F                          Finally, because of the parentheses, the NOT reverses the value of the entire expression.
```

4.3 Write a relational or logical statement in Visual Basic and C/C++ that will express the following:

	Expression
(*a*)	speed is exactly 65 mph
(*b*)	name is less than "JONES"
(*c*)	0<x<100 or, x is between 0 and 100, but not equal to either
(*d*)	x is NOT between 0 and 100
(*e*)	exclusive OR – true if x is true and y is false, or true if x is false and y is true – they are never the same

Solution:

	C/C++	VB
(*a*)	(speed==65)	(speed = 65)
(*b*)	(name<"JONES")	(name<"JONES")
(*c*)	(x>0) && (x<100)	(x>0) AND (x<100)
(*d*)	!((x>0) && (x<100))	NOT((x>0) AND (x<100))
(*e*)	((x && !y) || (!x && y))	((x AND NOT(y)) OR (NOT(x) AND y))

4.4 Write the Visual Basic code for the three kinds of selection structures in Example 4.11.

"If...Else" version

```
'assign dayNum or read in value
If (dayNum=1 OR dayNum=7)
    Print "Weekend - have fun"
Else
    If (dayNum>=2 AND dayNum<=6)
        Print "Weekday - go to work"
    Else
        Print "Only 1 through 7"
    End If
End If
```

"If...Elseif" version

```
'assign dayNum or read in value
If (dayNum==1 OR dayNum==7)
    Print "Weekend - have fun"
ElseIf (dayNum>=2 AND dayNum<=6)
    Print "Weekday - go to work"
Else
    Print "Only 1 through 7"
End If
```

Case Structure version

```
'assign dayNum or read in value
Select Case (dayNum)
   Case 1, 6: Print "Weekend - have fun"
   Case 2 To 7: Print "Weekday - go to work"
                                        'the word "To" means all values 2 through 7
   Case Else: Print "Only 1 through 7"
End Select
```

4.5 What is the output of this section of code?

```
temp=80;
if (temp>80)
   if (temp>90)
      cout<<"Hot";
else
   cout<<"Warm";
cout<<"day"<<endl;
```

OUTPUT: day
Because temp is not greater than 80, the first condition is false, and the second if...else is never executed. The else always goes with the closest if, even if the indentation is not correct. The only time "Warm day" would be the output would be for temp values of 81 through 90.

4.6 Write a Visual Basic code section to count down from 10 to 0 and then print "Blast off!"

```
For lcv=10 To 0 Step -1    'in Visual Basic the For statement goes from the initial
                           'value to the final value, incrementing
   Print lcv               'according to the Step value. If the Step is omitted, the
                           'default is to add 1.
Next lcv
Print "Blast off!"
```

4.7 Write a Visual Basic code section to calculate the value of $1,000 at the end of 5 years, with a simple interest rate of 5% per year.

```
rate=0.05
amt=1000
For year=1 To 5   'year gets values from 1 to 5, with a default increment of +1
   amt=amt+amt*rate
   Print amt
Next year
```

4.8 What is the output of this section of code if the sales amounts are 10, 13, 15, and 20?

```
int row, col, sales;
char response;
cout<<"Do you want to see a graph of your sales?";
cin>>response;
while (response=='y' || response=='Y')
{
```

```
    cout<<"Enter your 4 week sales amounts all on one line "<<endl<<endl;
    for (row=1; row<=4; row++)
    {
        cin>>sales;
        cout<<"Week "<<row<<";
        for (col=0; col<sales; col++)
            cout<<'*';
        cout<<endl;
    }
    cout<<endl<<"Do you want to see another graph of your sales?";
    cin>>response;
}
```

OUTPUT:

```
Do you want to see a graph of your sales?y
Enter your 4 week sales amounts all on one line

10 13 15 20
Week 1 **********
Week 2 *************
Week 3 ***************
Week 4 ********************

Do you want to see another graph of your sales?
```

Loop structures can be nested within other structures. The pretest loop in this example continues as long as the user replies with a Y or y to the question. The two inner loops print the rows and columns of the histogram.

4.9 Write two versions of Visual Basic code to implement the menu in Example 4.20.

"While" version

```
Do
    Print "1. Add"
    Print "2. Subtract"
    Print "3. Multiply"
    Print "4. Divide"
    Print "5. Quit"
    choice=InputBox("Enter your choice")
Loop While (choice<>5)
```

The "not equal to" symbol in Visual Basic is "<>." This menu always prints once, and continues until the user enters 5.

"Until" version

```
Do
    Print "1. Add"
    Print "2. Subtract"
    Print "3. Multiply"
    Print "4. Divide"
    Print "5. Quit"
    choice=InputBox("Enter your choice")
Loop Until (choice=5)
```

4.10 Write a short C++ program which will implement the simple calculator program from Solved Problem 2.3. Use the pseudocode as comments to guide the code-writing process.

Answer:

```
#include <iostream.h>

void main ()
{
    //declare variables
    int num1,num2,result;
    char oper;

    // 1. Get two numbers and the operation desired
    cout<<endl<<"Enter number one=>"; cin>>num1;
    cout<<endl<<"Enter number two=>"; cin>>num2;
    cout<<endl<<"Enter operation=>"; cin>>oper;

    // 2. Check the operation and perform the correct operation
    switch (oper)
    {
        case '+': result=num1+num2; break;
        case '-': result=num1-num2; break;
        case '*': result=num1*num2; break;
        case '/': if (num2==0)
                      {
                          result=0;
                          cerr<<"Number 2 cannot be a zero"<<endl;
                      }
                      else result=num1/num2;
                      break;
        default:
                      cerr<<"Operation must be + - * or /"<<endl;
    }//end switch
    // 3. Print out the result or the error message
    cout<<endl<<"The result of" <<num1<<oper<<num2<<" is "<<result<<endl;
}
```

Supplementary Problems

For all these problems, assume the variables have all been declared properly.

4.11 Write a relational or logical statement in Visual Basic and C/C++ that will express the following:

Expression
(*a*) distance is 200 miles or greater
(*b*) number is evenly divisible by 4
(*c*) x equals y or y equals z but z does not equal x
(*d*) both x and y are positive
(*e*) x is negative or y is positive, but not both

4.12 Write a section of code (in both Visual Basic and C++) to determine whether a year is a leap year. A leap year is any year divisible by 4 unless it is divisible by 100, but not 400.

4.13 Write a section of code (in both Visual Basic and C++) that will print all the perfect squares between 0 and 100.

4.14 Write a section of code in C++ that will print the following designs:

(*a*)

```
*
**
***
****
*****
```

(*b*)

```
*****
****
***
**
*
```

4.15 Repeat the previous exercise using Visual Basic.

4.16 Write a segment of C++ code that will get an integer as input, and then use a posttest loop to print a list of powers of that integer until the power is greater than 10,000.

4.17 Write a segment of Visual Basic code that will get an integer as input, and then use a posttest loop to print the square, then the square of the square, and continue with successive squares until the square is greater than 100,000.

4.18 Indicate what the output will be for the following Visual Basic segments of code:

(*a*)

```
num1=0
num2=10
Do
    num1=num1+1
    num2=num2-1
    Print num1, num2
Loop While num1<num2
```

(*b*)
```
num=1
Do
    Print num, 17 Mod num
    num=num+1
Loop While 17 Mod num<>5
```

(*c*)
```
num1=4
num2=80
Do
    num2=num2/num1-6
    If num2>num1 Then
        num2=num1+20
    End If
Loop While num2>=0
Print num1, num2
```

4.19 Indicate what the output will be for the following C++ segments of code:

(*a*)
```
num=15;
do
{
    cout<<num<<''<<num/3<<endl; //integer division
    num--;
}while (num/3>3);
```

(*b*)
```
num1=2;
do
{
    cout<<num1<<'';
    num1*=2;
} while (num1<=20);
```

(*c*)
```
sum=0;
num1=7;
while (num1<10)
{
    for (num2=num1; num2<=10; num2++)
        sum+=num2;
    num1++;
}
cout<<sum<<endl;
```

4.20 Write the VB program which will implement the hotel checkout program from Solved Problem 2.5. Assume the meal charge is $9.95 per person per night, and the tax rate is 5%.

Answers to Supplementary Problems

4.11 Solution:

	C/C++	VB
(*a*)	(distance>= 200)	(distance>= 200)
(*b*)	(number % 4==0)	(number MOD 4 = 0)
(*c*)	((x==y ‖ y==z) && (y!= z))	((x = y OR y = z) AND (y<>z))
(*d*)	(x>=0 && y>=0)	(x>=0 AND y>=0)
(*e*)	((x<0 && y<0) ‖ (x >=0 && y>=0))	((x<0 AND y<0) OR (x >=0 AND y>=0))

4.12 C++ version:

```
cout<<"Enter the year"; cin >>year;
if (year%4==0)
{
   if (year%100!=0)
      cout<<year<<"is a leap year"<<endl;
   else if (year%400==0)
      cout<<year<<"is a leap year"<<endl;
   else
      cout<<year<<"is NOT a leap year"<<endl;
   }
   else
      cout<<year<<"is NOT a leap year"<<endl;
```

Visual Basic version:

```
year=Val(txtYear)
If (year Mod 4=0) Then
   If (year Mod 100 <> 0) Then
      Print year; "is a leap year"
   ElseIf (year Mod 400=0) Then
      Print year; "is a leap year"
   Else
      Print year; "is NOT a leap year"
   End If
Else
  Print year; "is NOT a leap year"
End If
```

4.13 C++ version:

```
num=0;
numSqr=num*num;
while (numSqr<100)
{
```

```
    cout<<numSqr<<'';
    num++;
    numSqr=num*num;
}
```

Visual Basic version:

```
Do While (numSquare<100)
    Print numSquare
    num=num+1
    numSquare=num*num
Loop
```

4.14 (*a*)

```
for (row=1; row<=5; row++)
{
    for (col=0; col<row; col++)
        cout<<'*';
    cout<<endl;
}
```

(*b*)

```
for (row=1; row<=5; row++)
{
    for (col=6-row; col>0; col--)
        cout<<'*';
    cout<<endl;
}
```

4.15 (*a*)

```
For row=1 To 5
    For col=1 To row
        Print "*";
    Next col
    Print
Next row
```

(*b*)

```
For row=1 To 5
    For col=6-row To 1 Step -1
        Print "*";
    Next col
    Print
Next row
```

4.16

```
power=1;
cout<<"Enter an integer greater than 1=>";
cin>>num;
do
{
   cout<<power<<'';
   power *=num;
}while (power<10000);
```

4.17

```
num=InputBox("Enter an integer greater than 1=>")
num=num*num
Do
    Print num
    num=num*num
Loop While (num<100000)
```

4.18 Output (*a*)

1 9
2 8
3 7
4 6
5 5

Output (*b*)

1 0
2 1
3 2
4 1
5 2

Output (*c*): 4 −6

4.19 Output (*a*):

15 5
14 4
13 4
12 4

Output (*b*): 2 4 8 16

Output (*c*): 80

4.20 VB program:

```
Sub main()
  'Declare variables
  Const MEALCHARGE=9.95
  Const ROOM1PERSON=55
  Const ROOM2PEOPLE=60
  Const ROOM3ORMORE=65
  Const TAXRATE=0.05
  Dim nights As Integer, people As Integer
  Dim meals As Single, total As Single
  '1. Get the number of nights and number of people
  'in the room from the customer
  nights=InputBox("How many nights?")
  people=InputBox("How many people?")
```

```
    '3. Calculate bill
    '3.1. Look up the room charge for that number of people
    '3.2. Multiply by the number of nights
    If (people=1) Then
      total=nights*ROOM1PERSON
    ElseIf (people=2) Then
      total=nights*ROOM2PEOPLE
    ElseIf (people>2) Then
      total=nights*ROOM3ORMORE
    Else 'if number is zero or negative
      total=0
    End If
    '3.3. Add the meal charges
    total=total+(people*MEALCHARGE)
    '3.4. Calculate and add the tax
    total=total=(total*TAXRATE)
    '4. Print the bill
    MsgBox ("Your total cost is" +Str(total))
  End Sub
```

CHAPTER 5

Functions and Subroutines

In any software development process, subroutines and functions play a critical role since they allow the decomposition of the program into logical units or modules. A **subroutine** is a self-contained program structure included within a program. Subroutines are written to solve a particular problem; they have a specific purpose. **Functions**, like subroutines, are also self-contained program structures designed with a single purpose; however, unlike subroutines they all "return" a single value of a particular type. This unique feature allows programmers to use a function in the same context where a variable or expression can be used. The term **subprogram** is commonly used to refer to either a function or a subroutine.

Before concentrating our attention to the specific aspects of functions and subroutines, let us consider how they facilitate program planning. ***Modular programming*** is the application to computer programming of the principle "divide and conquer" used so successfully by other disciplines to solve complex problems. What needs to be "conquered" (or solved) is a particular problem and, to solve it, we divide it into smaller and more manageable subproblems. Each of these subproblems can be, in turn, subdivided even further until they are considered by the programmer to be "elementary" or "sufficiently simple." Since the notion of "elementary" or "simple" is a subjective notion, we will adopt the idea that a task is "elementary" when its function can be described by a sentence that contains a single subject, a single verb, and a single object. For example, see Solved Problems 5.1 and 5.2. As self-contained structures, subroutines and functions can be used as building blocks to construct a program. In this sense, we can use the same routine or function in different programs whenever is appropriate. We can also replace less efficient program components by faster or simpler ones without affecting the execution of the program.

5.1 FUNCTIONS

As indicated before, a function is a program structure that always returns a single value. A function may receive one or more input values. These input values are called **arguments** or **parameters** (see Fig. 5-1).

Functions may be "called" or "invoked" from a main program, function, or subroutine. Functions are called by naming them and passing the appropriate parameters, if any. Whenever a function is called the execution of the main program, subroutine, or function that calls the function is halted. The

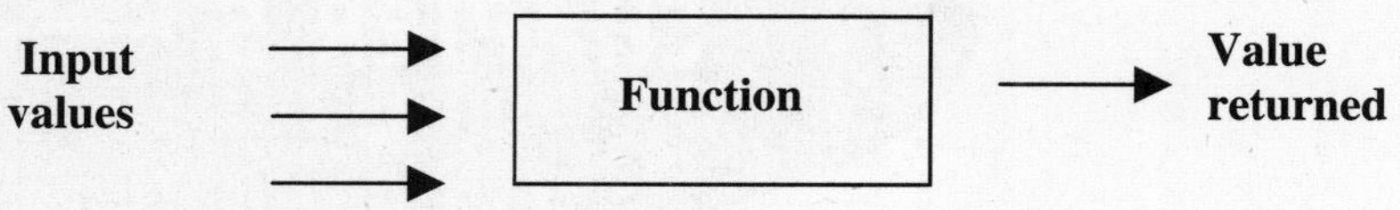

Fig. 5-1 General structure of a function.

control of the program is automatically transferred to the function which, upon completion, returns to the same statement where it was called (its reference point). Functions can be used whenever a variable can be used.

Some of the languages that we use to illustrate the examples in this book require that all functions be "declared" before they get called (see Solved Problem 5.3). This means that we need to specify the function's name, the data type that it returns, the number of arguments or parameters that it receives, if any, the order of these parameters, and their data type. The term argument(s) or parameter(s) refers to the input that the function receives.

Although the syntax rules for declaring functions may vary from language to language, in any function we can always distinguish two basic elements. Using the terminology of the American National Standards Institute (ANSI) we will call these basic elements the **function header** and the **function body** (see Fig. 5-2). The header provides general information about the function's name, the type that it returns, the number of input parameters, if any, the order of these parameters, and their types. Depending on the language, the syntax of the function header may require the use of one or more keywords and some other qualifiers (see Example 5.1). The body is made up of local declarations and some other statements that perform the function's task.

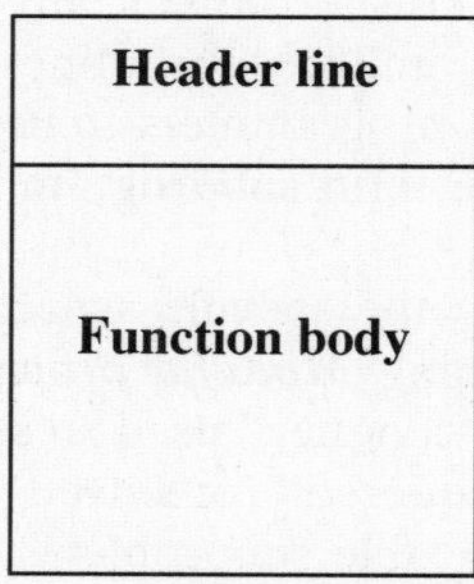

Fig. 5-2 Basic elements of a function.

EXAMPLE 5.1 Distinguish the basic elements of the C/C++ function shown below.

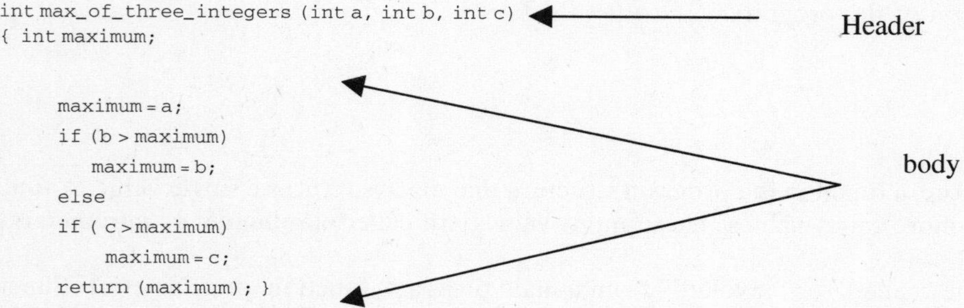

The header of this function is: int max_of_three_integers (int a, int b, int c).

This header indicates:

(1) the name of the function (max_of_three_integers)

(2) the data type that it returns (int)

(3) the number of inputs of the function (int a, int b, int c). This function receives three input integer parameters called a, b, and c, respectively. The variables a, b, c, and their data type are called the **formal parameters** or **arguments** of the function.

The body, enclosed in braces or curly brackets, consists of:

```
{ int maximum;
   maximum=a;
   if  (b>maximum)
       maximum=b;
   else
     if  (c>maximum)
       maximum=c;
return  (maximum);  }
```

(1) a local declaration of the integer variable called maximum.

(2) the instructions that calculate the maximum of the three given integer numbers. In C, the variable or expression indicated in parentheses in the **return** statement is evaluated and "sent back" to its referencing point in the calling procedure. The term "calling procedure" refers to the main program, subroutine, or function that "calls" the function. The following example illustrates this.

EXAMPLE 5.2 Identify the calling program, the calling statement and explain the flow of control in the following program section of a C++ program.

```
int main()
{ int val1,val2,val3, max;
  cin>>val1>>val2>>val3; //input the three integers
  max=max_of_three_integers (val1,val2, val3) //this statement calls the function
  cout<<"The maximum of the three integers is" <<max; //print the maximum
  return (0); }
int max_of_three_integers (int a, int b, int c)
{ int maximum;
  maximum=a;
  if (b>maximum)
    maximum=b;
  else
    if (c>maximum)
      maximum=c;
return (maximum);}
```

The main program (the calling program), after receiving three input values from the user, calls the function max_of_three_integers(val1,val2,val3) to calculate the maximum value of the three integers. The execution of the main program is halted as soon as it reaches the statement that contains the function call. At this moment, the function starts executing. Using computer lingo, we can say that "control is transferred to the function." After the function calculates the maximum value, the function returns to the calling statement (its reference point) and the returned value is assigned to the variable max. The main program then continues executing its remaining statements.

In Example 5.2, notice that when the function gets called the parameter values val1, val2, and val3 are separated by commas and enclosed in parentheses following the name of the function. These values are the input values that the function receives. We say that these values are "passed" to the function and we will call them the **actual parameters**. As Fig. 5-3 shows, the actual parameters are associated with the formal parameters "by position." That is, the value of actual parameter, val1, is assigned to the formal parameter, a, of the function. Likewise, the values of variables val2 and val3 are assigned to the formal parameters b and c respectively.

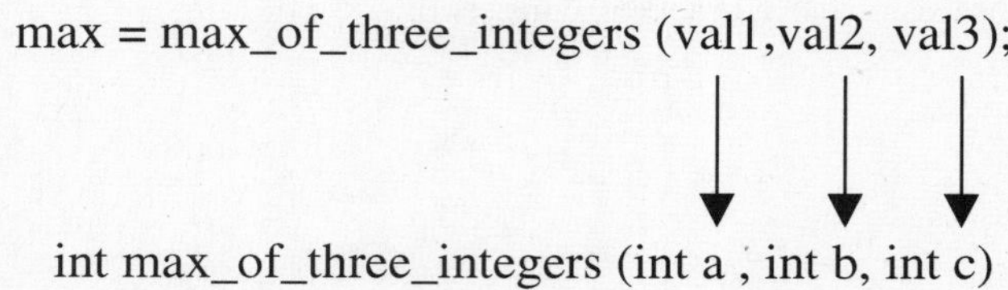
max = max_of_three_integers (val1,val2, val3);
int max_of_three_integers (int a , int b, int c)

Fig. 5-3 Association of actual and formal parameters by position.

Example 5.2 also illustrates the rules that govern the calling of a function. These rules, which apply to any program, subroutine, or function that calls another function, are:

(1) The number of actual parameters in the calling statement must be the same as the number of formal parameters in the header of the function. There are languages like Visual Basic where a parameter can be defined as optional. However, we will not consider this type of parameter in this book.

(2) The type of the actual parameters must be of the same type as its corresponding formal parameters.

(3) Actual parameters are generally associated to formal parameters "by position." Depending on the language, the association may be carried out by pairing the actual and formal parameters from left to right or from right to left or in no particular order.

Visual Basic allows a different mechanism for passing multiple arguments, where the parameters are explicitly named in the call to the function. This new modality eliminates the need for passing arguments according to the order specified in the function header. This feature does not affect the syntax or structure of the function header at all. The following example illustrates this.

EXAMPLE 5.3 Assume that we have the following function declaration which accepts three input parameters and an instance of a call to this function:

Private Function IsAlarmClockSet (iSecs As Integer, iMins As Integer, iHrs As Integer) As Boolean

An instance of a call to this function may be IsAlarmClockSet (30, 45, 13).

Notice that whenever we call this function, we need to remember what these parameters are and what they represent. However, if we use named arguments this is not necessary.

To call the previous function using named arguments, each formal parameter is associated with its formal parameter using the following syntax:

FunctionName(formalPar1 : = actualPar1, formalPar2 : = actualPar2, formalParN : = actualParN)

Using this mechanism, we could call the function as follows:

bVariable = IsAlarmClockSet(iMins : = 45, iHrs : = 13, iSecs : = 30)

or

bVariable = IsAlarmClockSet(iHrs : = 13, iSecs : = 30, iMins : = 45)

Notice that the syntax of the call to the function requires the use of the operator : = to associate a formal parameter with its actual parameter.

In some languages like C and C++ it is required that the function be declared using a **function prototype**. In these languages the prototype gives the name of the function, the value that it returns and the number and type of the formal parameters. The function prototype helps the compiler to do error checking (see Appendix A). A compilation error occurs if the information provided by the prototype does not agree with that of the function header or with the type of the value returned by the function. If a compilation error of this type occurs the program does not get executed. A prototype for the function of Examples 5.1 and 5.2 may look like this:

int max_of_three_integers (int, int, int);

In this function prototype there is no mention of the name of the actual parameters, just their type. However, it is also possible to name the arguments as part of the prototype, as indicated below:

int max_of_three_integers (int x, int y, int z);

In this case the variables x, y, and z are "dummy" arguments. These variables do not need to appear in the function header. We can declare the function used in the two previous examples with this prototype. No changes need to be made either to the calling program or the function itself.

The value that a function returns can be omitted in some languages. In all these cases a predefined value is used as default. In the case of the C language the default value is int. Since this rule may vary from language to language, it is always wise to consult the reference manual of a language to find out whether the default value can be used or not.

The proper place of the function prototype inside the program will be discussed later in this chapter.

In C and C++ the value that the function returns is explicitly indicated by means of a return statement. However, not all languages use this mechanism. The following example shows the implementation of the max_of_three_integers function using Visual Basic.

EXAMPLE 5.4 Identify the basic elements of the following Visual Basic function.

```
Private Function MaxOfThreeIntegers (a As Integer, b As Integer, c As Integer) As Integer
Dim maximum As Integer 'declaration of variable maximum as an integer
  maximum=a
  If b>maximum Then
    maximum=b
  Elseif c>maximum Then
    maximum=c
  End if
MaxOfThreeIntegers=maximum 'Notice that the function name is treated as a variable
End Function
```

The header of this function is

Private Function iMaxOfThreeIntegers (a As Integer, b As Integer, c As Integer) As Integer

The header is comprised of several parts and indicates:

(1) the scope or visibility of the function (see Section 5.3). The word **private** signals that this function is known only within the form or module in which it is defined.

(2) the name of the function. Notice that we have written the name of the function as a combination of upper- and lowercase letters with the letter i as prefix. The letter i is a mnemonic to the programmer or any other reader that the function returns an integer value. This style of writing names is known as the Hungarian notation. The name of the function must be followed by parentheses even if there are no parameters.

(3) the data type that the function returns. The As Integer following the formal parameters states explicitly that this particular function returns an integer.

(4) the number and type of the formal parameters. This function has three input integer parameters a, b, and c. The As Integer allows us to define the data type of the formal parameter.

The body of this function follows the header and ends with the words **End Function**.

The code to calculate the maximum value is almost identical to the code of C and C++ shown before. However, notice that in Visual Basic we must specify the function's return value within the function's body. We do this by treating the function's name as if it were a variable and assigning a value to it.

One interesting exception to a function returning a value is observed in C and C++ with the use of the keyword **void**. This word, when placed before a function's name, indicates that the function will return no value. Although this may seem to be a contradiction of the definition of a function, it is useful in those situations where the programmer is more interested in the effect of the function rather than the value that it returns.

5.2 SUBROUTINES

Subroutines or procedures, as indicated before, are also self-contained program structures. Subroutines, unlike functions, do not have to return a value, and when they do, they use a different mechanism. The declaration of a procedure, for those languages that require it, is similar to that of a function. Likewise, the rules for associating actual and formal parameters are similar to those of a function.

EXAMPLE 5.5 Identify the basic elements in the Visual Basic subroutine shown below.

```
Private Sub EliminateExtraBlanks(txtInputBox As TextBox)
    txtInputBox=RTrim(txtInputBox)
    txtInputBox=LTrim(txtInputBox)
End Sub
```

The header of the subroutine is:

Private Sub EliminateExtraBlanksInTextBox (txtInputBox As TextBox)

The name of the subroutine is EliminateExtraBlanksInTextBox and it receives as an input parameter a TextBox called txtInputBox.

The keyword Private indicates that this subprocedure is known only within the form where it is defined.

The keyword Sub indicates that EliminateExtraBlanks is a subroutine. The body of this subroutine ends with End Sub.

Notice that the body of this subroutine consists of two function calls to the built-in functions Rtrim and Ltrim which eliminate the leading and trailing extra blanks respectively of the input parameter txtInputBox. The actions of these two functions alter the content of the textbox that was passed as an actual parameter (see Section 5.4).

EXAMPLE 5.6 The following C program converts a given Fahrenheit temperature into its Celsius equivalent.

```
#include <stdio.h>
void ConvertToCelsius(void);
double Celsius;
double Fahrenheit;
void main()
{
```

```
  printf ("\nEnter a Fahrenheit temperature :");
  scanf("%lf", &Fahrenheit);
  ConvertToCelsius();
  printf("\n\n %6.2lf Fahrenheit degrees are equivalent to
  %6.2lf Celsius\n\n", Fahrenheit,Celsius);
}

void ConvertToCelsius(void)
{
   Celsius=(Fahrenheit-32.0)*(5.0/9.0);
}
```

Notice that the "subroutine" ConvertToCelsius has been implemented using a function with void as the returning value. ConvertToCelsius operates on the global variables Celsius and Fahrenheit (see Section 5.3).

5.3 SCOPE AND LIFETIME OF IDENTIFIERS

A useful concept in understanding the interaction of the different components of a program is that of the **scope or referencing environment**. This term defines the "visibility" of each variable, constant, function, or subprocedure. That is, the scope determines where a variable or constant can be used and where a function or subroutine can be referenced or invoked. The rules that allow a programmer to determine the referencing environment at any one time are called the **scope rules**. These rules may vary from language to language; however, in all languages we can differentiate between a **global** and **local** scope. When the visibility of a variable, constant, procedure, or function is confined to a section of the program, module, or form we say that the scope is local. Otherwise, we say that the scope is global. For example, if during the execution of a program a variable can be accessed at any time from any function and subroutine, the variable is said to be a global variable. However, if the variable can only be accessed within the function or subprocedure that defines it, the variable is said to be local. The following sections illustrate how these rules apply to C, C++, Java, and Visual Basic.

When a program starts executing, all of its global variables are allocated storage in main memory. Likewise, when a function or subroutine starts executing, all the local variables are allocated storage in main memory. The memory storage allocated to the global variables remains for the entire duration of the program. However, the storage allocated to the local variables of a function or subroutine is released as soon as the function or subroutine finishes executing. The term **lifetime** of a variable or constant refers to the duration of its storage allocation during the execution of the program. In other words, the lifetime determines how long a variable retains its assigned values. Using this definition we can say that the lifetime of global variables is for the entire duration of the program. The lifetime of all local variables, in general, is limited to the execution of the function or subprocedure that defines them.

Before addressing the issues of local versus global variables, let's consider when to use one over the other. The basic rule to remember is that the scope of a variable should be kept as narrow as possible. The main reasons for this are:

(1) Better organization in the program's structure. It has been recognized that the indiscriminate use of global variables may have undesirable side effects. The fact that a variable can be accessed from anywhere in the program also opens the possibility of being able to modify the content of the variable anywhere in the program. If a global variable is changed at several places and its final result is not what we anticipated, it may be difficult to determine where it was changed last. To avoid this problem we need strictly to limit the number of places where a global variable can be changed. Ideally, global variables should be modified in only one place and one place only. This restriction will force us sometimes to look at the program design several times; however, in the experience of the authors it is a worthwhile effort.

(2) Conservation of memory. Since global variables must exist for the entire duration of the program, their storage locations in main memory must be maintained. This obviously increases the amount of memory that the program uses at any one time.

(3) Prevention of access to global variables. Most languages allow users to define variables with the same name at different places of the program. If a local variable is defined inside a procedure or function and its name is shared by a global variable then the global variable is no longer visible inside the function or procedure.

5.3.1 Scope of Identifiers in C/C++ and Java

In C, C++, and Java all variables that are declared outside the body of functions are global; any module can use them. On the other hand, variables declared within the body of a function are always local to that function.

EXAMPLE 5.7 What is the scope of the variables in each of the functions shown below? What is the lifetime of the global and local variables?

```
#include<stdio.h>
void print_double_sum (int, int);
void print_triple_sum (int,int);
int total_value; /* This is a global variable */
int main()
{
 int value1, value2;
 printf("Input two integers:");
 scanf("%d%d", &value1, &value2);
 print_double_sum (value1, value2);
 print_triple_sum (value1,value2);
 return(0);
}
void print_double_sum (int val1, int val2)
{
 total_value=2*(val1+val2);
 printf("The double value of the sum of %d and %d is =%d\n", val1, val2, total_value);
}
void print_triple_sum (int val3, int val4)
{
 total_value=3*(val3+val4);
 printf("The triple value of the sum of %d and %d is =%d\n", val3, val4, total_value);
}
```

The variable total_value is defined before main and any other function in the program. The visibility of this variable is global. That is, it can be referenced from any other function in the program. Observe that this variable can be accessed within the functions print_double_sum and print_triple_sum.

Variables value1 and value2 are defined within the main program and are local to that function. That is, if we try to reference either of these variables outside main we will get an error. For instance, if we try to use these two variables in any of the print statements of the functions print_double_sum or print_triple_sum we will get a compilation error.

Variables val1 and val2 are both defined within the function print_double_sum. They are local variables to this function only. That is, if we try to reference either of these variables outside this function we will get a compilation error.

Likewise, val3 and val4 are both defined within the function print_triple_sum. They are local variables to this function only. That is, if we try to reference either of these variables outside this function we will get a compilation error. Figure 5-4 illustrates this visibility of the variable in this example.

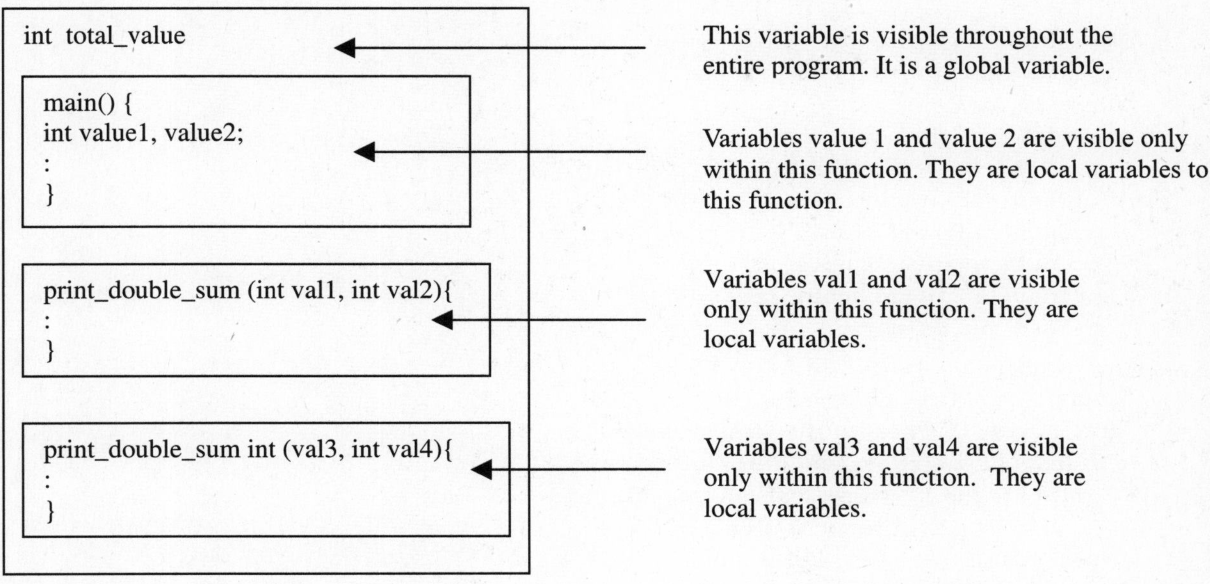

Fig. 5-4 Scope of variables for Example 5.4.

The global variable total_value has storage allocated to it for as long as the program is executing. Local variables val1, val2, val3, val4 are allocated storage as long as the functions in which they are defined are executing. Their storage is released when the functions finish executing. Variables value1 and value2 have storage allocated as long as the program is executing since they are declared in the main function.

Local variables declared with the **static** attribute retain their values even after the function or subroutine in which they are declared has finished executing. Static variables are only visible when the function or subprocedure in which they are defined is executing. These types of variables are generally used to keep track of running totals or in situations where it is necessary to make a decision based upon the number of times that a function has been called. Table 5-1 shows a partial classification of the scope and visibility of variables in the C/C++ languages.

Table 5-1 The Scope and Lifetime of C Variables.

Place of Declaration within the Program	Keyword	Visibility	Lifetime
Before all functions including main		Throughout the program	For the entire duration of the program
Inside a function		Only within the function	While function is executing
Inside a function	Static	Only within the function	For the entire duration of the program

EXAMPLE 5.8 The C function shown below illustrates the use of static variables. This function doubles its previous output every time that it gets called. However, the first time it gets called it prints its initial input parameters and returns a zero.

```
#include<stdio.h>
int double_it(void);
int a=5, b=2;
void main()
{  printf("%d \n", double_it());
   printf("%d\n", double_it());
   printf("%d\n", double_it());
   printf("%d\n", double_it());
   printf("%d\n", double_it());
} /* end of main */
int double_it (void)
{static int previous_value;
 static int number_of_previous_calls=0;
 if (number_of_previous_calls==0) {
   printf("The initial values are %d and %d", a, b);
   number_of_previous_calls++;
   return(0); }
else if (number_of_previous_calls==1) {
   previous_value=2*a*b;
   number_of_previous_calls++;
   return (previous_value); }
 else {
   number_of_previous_calls++;
   previous_value=2*previous_value;
   return(previous_value); }
} /* end of function double_it*/
```

Notice that in the function double_it the variable number_of_previous_calls is declared and initialized to zero. The first time the function double_it is invoked, number_of_previous_calls has the value of zero since it was initialized to this value. After the first call to the function the static variable is no longer initialized and retains whatever value it was assigned during the last call to the function.

5.3.2 Scope of Identifiers in Visual Basic

5.3.2.1 Global Scope

The widest scope that you can give to any variable or constant in VB is through the use of the keyword **Public**. The general format declaration for variables or constants is:

Public **Const** ConstantName [As data type] = Value

or

Public VariableName [As dat type]

The square brackets indicate that the specification of the data type is optional. However, it always better specify the data type of all constants and variables. This book will follow this convention.

After a public constant or variable has been declared, it can be referenced anywhere in the project. However, there are restrictions as to where in your program you can declare Public variables or constants. Depending upon where the variable or constant is declared, there may be some restrictions on how they are referenced.

Public variables can only be declared in the General Declaration section of a Class, Standard, or Form module.

Public constants can only be declared in the General Declaration section of a Standard module.

EXAMPLE 5.9 Assume that you declare a VB Public integer variable iTotalCount. What is the scope of this variable?

The answer to this question depends on where you declare the variable. If the variable was declared in a Standard module then all modules within the application can access the variable just by using its name. For example,

iTotalCount = 15

If the variable was declared in a Class or Form module, then the variable is considered as properties of the Class or Form. For example, if the variable is declared within a form called frmInitialForm, then the variable can be referenced as follows:

frmInitialForm.iTotalCount = 15

Notice that this feature will allow you to declare variables with identical names in all forms of the project. To reference any of these variables outside the form we would need to precede them with their corresponding form's name.

5.3.2.1.1 Private Variables

Variables declared **Private** within the General Declaration of a Form, Class, or Standard Module cannot be referenced outside the Form, Class, or Standard module where they were defined.

5.3.2.2 Local Scope

All variables declared inside an event procedure, general procedure, or function are considered local to that procedure or function. All variables declared using the keyword Dim are local variables. Another way of declaring local variables is through the use of the keyword Static.

EXAMPLE 5.10 The following subroutine changes to uppercase the text that the user types in a textbox called txtCategory.

```
Private Sub txtCategory_KeyPress (KeyAscii As Integer)
Dim stCharacter As String
   stCharacter=Chr(KeyAscii)
   stCharacter=Ucase(stCharacter)
   keyAscii=Asc(stCharacter)
End Sub
```

The KeyPress event occurs whenever the user presses a key that has an ASCII code. This procedure receives as its input an integer parameter that represents the ASCII code of the character pressed by the user. The name of this input parameter is KeyAscii.

The initial action of this procedure is to convert to a character the integer input parameter KeyAscii. This is carried out using the built-in function Chr which returns the ASCII character whose code is given by KeyAscii. The local variable stCharacter holds this character. The content of the variable stCharacter is then changed to an uppercase character using the built-in function Ucase. Finally, the integer ASCII code representing the uppercase character is assigned to the variable KeyAscii.

The code used in this procedure can be used whenever it is necessary to convert input text to all uppercase as the user types into a textbox. The string variable stCharacter is local to this subprocedure regardless of how many times the same code is used in similar procedures associated with other textboxes. The variable stCharacter cannot be referenced outside this procedure.

5.3.3 Scope of Procedures

In Visual Basic, procedures follow scope rules similar to the rules already defined for variables. There are two levels of scope rules for procedures within an application. Functions or procedures defined as Private can only be called from some other procedures or functions within the same Form, Class, or Standard module. Public procedures or functions can be called from anywhere within a project.

EXAMPLE 5.11 The Visual Basic procedure shown below accepts a name from a user and displays it all in uppercase as soon as the user presses the Enter key. This VB program uses public and private procedures. The pseudo algorithm for the program is shown below:

```
If KeyPress=ReturnKey Then
  Display Name In UpperCase
  Clear Name
Else
  Save Input Character
End If
```

The implementation of this algorithm in Visual Basic uses the following form and objects.

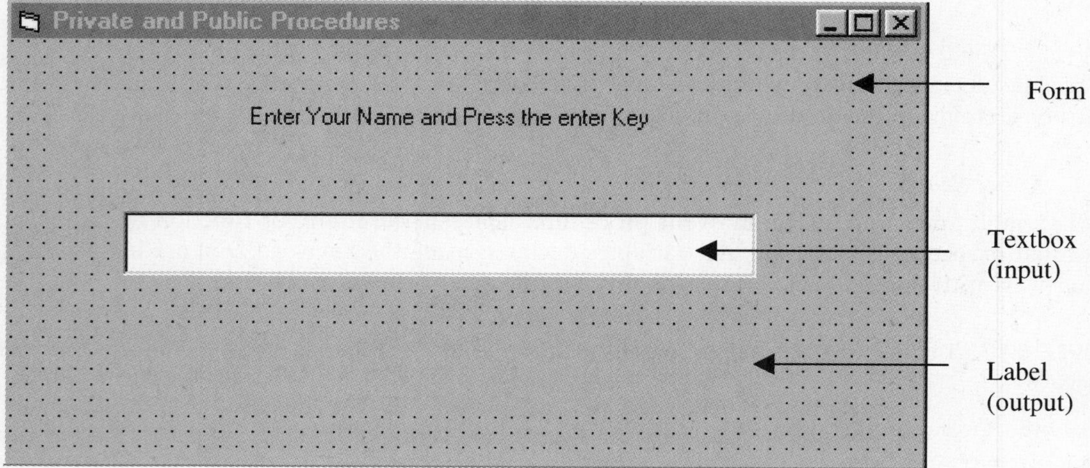

- The textbox is named txtName.
- The label, where the name in uppercase is displayed, is named lblUpperName.
- The form is called frmName.

The general module section of the program should look like this:

```
Option Explicit
Public stName As String
Public Sub SaveInputCharacter (KeyAscii As Integer)
  If KeyAscii <> vbKeyBack Then
    stName=stName & UCase(Chr(KeyAscii))
  End If
End Sub
```

'This procedure clears name typed by the user in the textbox

```
Public Sub ClearName()
  stName=""
  frmName!txtName.Text=""
End Sub
```

In the form module the code section should look like this:

When the user presses the Enter Key (Return Key) the procedure displays the name of the user in caps on the label underneath the textbox. All other characters are converted into uppercase and saved until the user presses the return key.

```
Private Sub txtBox1_KeyPress(KeyAscii As Integer)
  If KeyAscii=vbKeyReturn Then
    DisplayNameInUpperCase
    ClearName
  Else
    SaveInputCharacter (KeyAscii)
  End If
End Sub
```

'This procedure, as its name indicates, displays the name typed by the user.

```
Private Sub DisplayNameInUpperCase()
    lblUpperName.Caption=stName
End Sub
```

Every time the user presses a key in the textbox the program checks to see if the pressed key is the Enter Key. Notice that we compare the code of the input key given (by keyAscii) with the global VB constant vbKeyReturn (ASCII code 13). If the Enter key is detected the program displays the message and clears the content of the textbox.

The Public procedure SaveInputCharacter changes every input character to its uppercase equivalent. The procedure uses the global variable stName to save the user's keystrokes. It does this by concatenating, that is, by putting together, each new input character with the previous input characters. In this case we have also ignored the backspace key. This way, if the user happens to use the backspace key, we avoid displaying a character that looks like this **I** as part of the user's name.

The Public procedure DisplayNameInUpper writes the content of the global variable stName into the caption of the label used to display the name.

The Public procedure ClearName sets the global variable stName and the content of the textbox to the Null string, therefore clearing their contents. Notice that to set the property of the textbox to the Null string, the textbox name has to be preceded by the form's name.

5.4 PARAMETER-PASSING MECHANISMS

The term **parameter-passing** mechanism refers to the different ways in which parameters are passed to or from a function or procedure. As we indicated in Section 5.1, a procedure or function can call any other procedure that is visible to it. The procedure that makes the call is called the "calling procedure" and the procedure that is invoked is the "called procedure." There are two basic models of how data transfers take place between functions or procedures. In one model, actual values are physically moved from the calling function or procedure to the called function or procedure. In the second model, an access path is transmitted to the called function or procedure. What get transmitted are the addresses in memory where the actual parameters are.

5.4.1 The Pass-by-Value Mechanism

When an actual parameter is **passed by value**, the value of the actual parameter is used to initialize the corresponding actual parameter. In other words, the formal parameter receives a copy of the value of the actual parameter. Any changes made to the value of this formal parameter do not affect the value of the actual parameter.

Pass-by-value is the parameter-passing mechanism by default in C, C++, and Java.

The following diagram illustrates this parameter-passing mechanism:

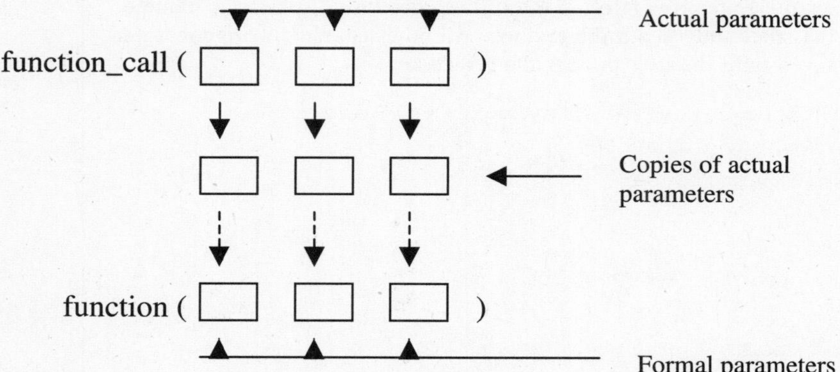

The called function only receives a copy of the actual parameters. Therefore, any changes made to the formal parameters do not affect the original values of the actual parameters.

EXAMPLE 5.12 The following C program reads in the numerical value for n and doubles it.

```
#include <stdio.h>
void DoubleNumber(int);
void main()
{
  int iValue;
  printf("\nEnter an integer value: ");
  scanf("%d", &iValue);
  printf("\n\nThe actual parameter is %d", iValue);
  DoubleNumber(iValue);
  printf("\n\nThe value of the actual parameter after the function call is %d\n\n", iValue);
} /* End of main function*/
void DoubleNumber(int n)
{
  printf("\n\nThe value assigned to the formal parameter is %d\n\n", n);
  n=2*n;
  printf("\n\nThe double of the input parameter is %d\n\n", n);
} /*End of the function DoubleNumber */
```

The main function calls the procedure DoubleNumber to calculate the double of the input number iValue. The value of iValue is printed before and after the function is called. As the user can verify, the value of iValue is unchanged. Notice that the formal parameter n is changed in the called function.

EXAMPLE 5.13 Write Visual Basic code that calculates the absolute value of a given number n. The main form is shown below.

Absolute Value

Enter a number and Press Enter

The absolute value is

- The form is called frmAbsolute.
- The textboxes are called txtInput and txtOutput respectively.

The code for implementing this program is:

```
Private Sub txtInput_KeyPress(KeyAscii As Integer)
 Dim stInput As String
 If KeyAscii=vbKeyReturn Then
   If IsNumeric(txtInput.Text) Then
     txtInput.BackColor=vbWhite
       CalculateAbsoluteValue (Val(txtInput.Text))
   Else
       MsgBox "Input is not numeric", vbInformation, "Invalid data"
       txtInput.Text=""
       txtInput.BackColor=vbYellow
   End If
 End If
End Sub
Private Sub CalculateAbsoluteValue(ByVal InputValue As Single)
 If InputValue>=0 Then
   txtOutput.Text= Str(InputValue)
 Else
   InputValue=-InputValue
   txtOutput.Text=Str(InputValue)
 End If
End Sub
```

The subprocedure txtInputKeyPress determines whether the input value is numeric. If the input value is numeric the subprocedure CalculateAbsoluteValue determines the absolute value of the given input. If the input value is not numeric the program displays an error message and set the background of the textbox to yellow. When the user enters a correct value the background color is set to white. The built-function IsNumeric, as its name indicates, is used to verify that the user's input is numeric. The user is notified of any invalid input by means of a message box.

Notice that the formal parameter InputValue is declared with the keyword ByVal. This way the subprocedure CalculateAbsoluteValue only gets a copy of the input value. The actual parameter is not changed, even though the formal parameter is assigned a value with an opposite sign inside the procedure. The formal parameter InputValue has been declared as a Single data type. This data type is generally used for storing values that may contain a fractional part.

5.4.2 The Pass-By-Reference Mechanism

When an actual parameter is passed to a function or subprocedure using the **pass-by-reference** mechanism, the address of the actual parameter is passed to the formal parameter. This way, the actual and formal parameters refer to the same memory location. As a consequence, any changes made to the formal parameter affect the value of the actual parameter. This is the default mechanism for passing arguments in VB. In C and C++ this mechanism is implemented using "pointers." Java does not use these pointers. A pointer is nothing more than a variable that can hold the address of an object, which can be either a variable, subprocedure, or function.

As we indicated in Section 1.2.1, every location has a unique address associated with it. The address of a variable remains constant throughout the execution of a program, whereas the content of the variable may change many times while the program is executing.

EXAMPLE 5.14 The following C program illustrates the difference between the address and content of a variable.

```
#include<stdio.h>
void main ()
{ int value1;
  printf("\nThe address of the integer variable value1 is:");
  printf("%x",&value1);
  value1=15;
  printf("\nThe new value of variable value1 is:");
  printf("%d",value1);
  value1=15;
  printf("\nThe new value of variable value1 is:");
  printf("%d",value1);
  printf("\nThe address of the integer variable value1 is: ");
  printf("%x\n\n",&value1); }
```

The output of this program is:

The address of the integer variable value1 is: 65fdf4
The new value of variable is: 15
The address of the integer variable value1 is: 65fdf4

Notice that the address of the variable is printed using the address operator &. This operator, when used in conjunction of a variable as illustrated in this program, is a reference to the address of the memory location occupied by the variable. The conversion specification %x used in the control string of the first and third call to printf indicates that the value should be printed in hexadecimal. The content of the variable changes twice during the execution of the program but its address remains the same. The & operator is commonly used in the scanf function.

5.4.3 Pointers

In C and C++ each data type has a corresponding pointer data type. For example, the statement shown below declares a pointer to a variable of type integer. This variable is capable of holding the address of any integer variable used throughout the program.

int * iPtr; /* declaring an integer to an integer variable */

The * placed to the immediate left of the variable iPtr is an unary operator called the **indirection** or **dereferencing** operator. If we assume that an integer variable called iValue has been defined in the program, the statement shown below assigns the address of this variable to the pointer variable. Notice the use of the address operator to reference the address of the variable iValue.

iPtr = &iValue; /* assigning the address of variable iValue to iPtr */

In this case we say that the variable iPtr "points to" the memory location iValue. The following diagram illustrates this.

The pointer variable points to the address of the first byte of the memory location of the integer variable iValue (shown in the diagram as occupying four consecutive bytes).

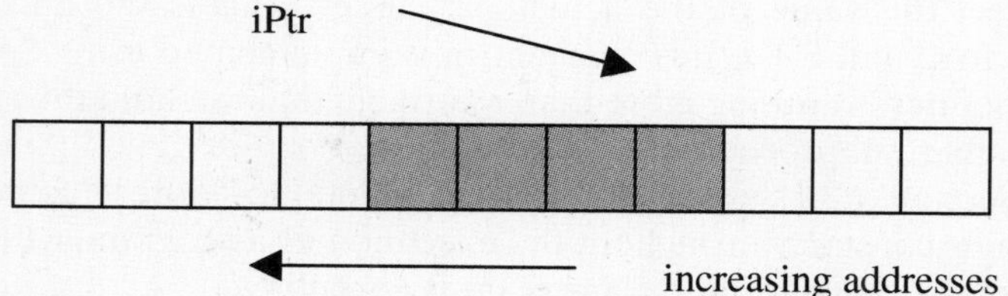

When the dereferencing operator is used with a pointer variable, it accesses the content of the variable that it points to. The following section of code illustrates the use of both operators.

```
int x, y;           /* declaration of variables x and y */
int * iPtr;         /* pointer to an integer variable */
x = 10;             /* new content of variable x */
iPtr = &x           /* variable iPtr points to variable x */
y = *iPtr;          /* variable y is assigned the content of variable x */
```

In this last statement *iPtr refers to the content of variable x. The value of this variable, 10, is assigned to variable y.

5.4.4 Function and Procedure Arguments Using Pointers

In languages like C++ and C the pass-by-reference mechanism is implemented using pointers. In this method the address of the actual parameter is passed to a subprogram. The address itself is not modified, but the called function or procedure may modify the content of that address. Whenever an address is passed as an actual parameter, the corresponding formal parameter in the subprogram must be declared as a pointer.

EXAMPLE 5.15 The following C program swaps the value of two given integer variables using pointers.

```
#include <stdio.h>
void swap_values(int *, int *); /* function prototype */
int a=5, b=2;
void main()
{
  printf("\nThe initial values of the variables a and b are %d and %d respectively", a,b);
swap_values (&a,&b); /* swap content of variables */
printf("\n\nThe final values of the variables a and b are %d and %d respectively\n", a,b);
} /* end of main */
void swap_values (int * iPtr1, int * iPtr2)
{
  int temp;
  temp=*iPtr1;
  *iPtr1=*iPtr2;
  *iPtr2=temp;}
```

Notice that the addresses of the actual parameters were passed to the subprocedure using the dereferencing operator and that the corresponding formal parameters were defined as pointers.

In the function prototype **void swap_values (int *, int *);** the data type of both parameters is defined as "pointers to integers." There is no mention of the name of the parameters. This prototype could have been defined as shown below without affecting the execution of the program.

```
void swap_values(int * x, int * y);
```

As we indicated before, the role of the variables x and y in the prototype is that of placeholders. No formal or actual parameter has to be named after any of these variables.

EXAMPLE 5.16 The following program illustrates the swap function from Example 5.15 above in C++. It shows an alternate way to pass arguments by reference. It uses the &, or address operator, instead of the * pointer.

```
void swap_values (int& iPtr1, int& iPtr2)
{
  int temp;

  temp=iPtr1;
  iPtr1=iPtr2;
  iPtr2=temp;}
```

Notice that C++ formal parameters use the & to indicate that the memory location is being passed from the calling program. The variables sent as actual parameters will be changed. The line needed to call this function does not send the pointers, but the variables themselves.

swap_values (a,b); /* swap content of variables */

In Visual Basic the default parameter mechanism is pass-by-reference. The following example illustrates this.

EXAMPLE 5.17 The following procedure changes ASCII lowercase characters to uppercase.

Assume that there is a textbox called txtUserInput. The subprocedure associated with the event KeyPress is shown below. As its name indicates, this event occurs only when a user presses a key that has a corresponding ASCII code.

```
Private Sub txtUserInput_KeyPress (KeyAscii As Integer)
Dim Character as String

  Character=Chr(KeyAscii) 'convert input value to character
  Character=Ucase(Character) 'convert character to uppercase
  KeyAscii=Asc(Character) 'convert character to ASCII code

End Sub
```

The input value to this procedure is the integer variable KeyAscii. This variable represents the ASCII code of the key pressed by the user.

The subprocedure initially converts the input integer value to a character using the built-in function Chr(). This character is then transformed to an uppercase character using the built-in function Ucase(). Finally, the uppercase character is converted to its equivalent ASCII code using the built-in function Asc(). Although we have used three separate statements to perform these transformations, it is possible to combine all three functions in a single statement as follows

KeyAscii = Asc(Ucase(Chr(KeyAscii)))

Notice that the changes to the input parameter are reflected immediately, since the actual and formal parameters are referring to the same address.

5.4.5 Parameter Passing in Java

Java is not a procedural language like C or C++. In Java, every function, or method, is part of a larger class. See Chapter 8 for a full explanation of the Java language class structure. Java functions look and behave in a similar way as C++ functions, except that all class objects are passed by reference, and all simple types are passed by value. Neither the ampersand (&) nor the asterisk (*) is ever used. Only simple Java functions will be illustrated here, not the class calling code.

EXAMPLE 5.18 Write a Java function to return a double value representing the area of a circle, given the integer radius as a parameter.

Using 3.14 as the value of π and the area of a circle as π*radius^2. The function may look like this.

```
public double FindAreaCircle(int radius)
{
  final double PI=3.14;
  return (PI*radius*radius);
}
```

Solved Problems

5.1 The narrative shown below describes the tasks of a subprogram. Is this an appropriate description for a function? If it is not, can it be an appropriate description for a subprocedure?

"The subprogram reads a sequence of integers typed by the user and returns the average, maximum, and minimum values of the sequence."

This is not an appropriate description for a function. A function can return only a single value and this narrative calls for a subprogram that returns three possible different values.

This is not an appropriate description for a subprocedure either. Subprocedures and functions should perform single tasks. The narrative describes four individual tasks to be carried out by a single subprogram. Each of these actions should be carried out by an individual subprogram. The sequence of values should be read by a subprocedure. The average, the maximum, and the minimum should be calculated by three individual functions.

5.2 The following narrative describes the tasks of a subprogram. What type of subprogram should perform these actions?

"The subprogram reads a sequence of characters into a series of consecutive memory locations and eliminates leading (blanks at the front) and trailing blanks (blanks at the back). It also eliminates a sequence of one or more intervening blanks (blanks in the middle) by a single blank."

Functions and subprocedures should perform actions that can be described by a sentence containing a single subject, a single verb, and a single object. Following this convention, it is better to subdivide the task called for by this narrative into several subtasks. Each subtask, in turn, should be performed by a single subprogram. Therefore, there should be a single subprocedure to perform each of the following activities: read the characters into the consecutive memory locations, eliminate leading blanks, eliminate intervening blanks, and eliminate trailing blanks. From a design point of view, each of these procedures should be considered as a building block. Once these subprocedures have been written, they can be used in subsequent programs to perform similar tasks.

5.3 Write the function prototype for the C functions described below.

(*a*) Function name: random number generator
Return data type: integer
Input data types: none

(*b*) Function name: greatest common divisor
Return data type: integer
Input data types: two integer values

(*c*) Function name: delete leading blanks
Return data type: none
Input data types: none

(*d*) Function name: string concatenation
Return data type: void
Input data type: pointer to a character, a pointer to a character constant

Names of identifiers in the C language are written with no intervening blanks. We will use a combination of upper- and lowercase to write the function names.

(*a*) int RandomNumberGenerator (void);
Since the function returns an integer we can use the keyword int to specify the return data type. The keyword void indicates that no input parameters are expected.

(*b*) int GreatestCommonDivisor (int, int);
This function returns an integer value, therefore, we can use the keyword int to specify the return data type. There are two integer inputs, therefore, we need to write the keyword int twice separated by a comma. There is no need to write the name of any identifier in the function prototype; however, this prototype could have been written as

int GreatestCommonDivisor (j int, k int);

None of the identifiers in the function header needs to be called either j or k.

(*c*) void DeleteLeadingBlanks (void);
This function does not return any value nor receive any input. Therefore, we need to use the keyword void to indicate that no returning value should be expected from this function. Likewise, we indicate that no input parameter should be expected using the keyword void.

(*d*) void StringConcatenation (char * , const char *);
The keyword void indicates that the function does not return any value. The first parameter to this function is a pointer to a character variable or string. The second parameter is a pointer to a character constant.

5.4 Write a Visual Basic program that prompts the user for an input string and translates each of the characters of the input sequence into Morse code using the equivalence table given below. Use a function that returns the Morse equivalent of each letter.

Morse Code

A	•_	**J**	•___	**S**	•••
B	_•••	**K**	_•_	**T**	_
C	_•_•	**L**	•_••	**U**	••_
D	_••	**M**	__	**V**	•••_
E	•	**N**	_•	**W**	•__
F	••_•	**O**	___	**X**	_••_
G	__•	**P**	•__•	**Y**	_•__
H	••••	**Q**	__•_	**Z**	__••
I	••	**R**	•_•		

Assume that there is only one form called frmMorse with two textboxes called txtPlainText and txtMorseCode. To limit the length of the output Morse code to less than 80 characters, limit your input line to 30 characters maximum.

Morse Code

Input an English sentence or phrase (30 characters max.)

Equivalent Morse Code

The code for this program is:

```
Option Explicit
Private Sub txtPlainText_KeyPress(KeyAscii As Integer)
 Dim Character As String
  Character=txtMorseCode.Text & "  " & EnglishToMorse (Chr(KeyAscii))
  txtMorseCode.Text=Character
End Sub
Private Function EnglishToMorse(stInputCharacter As String) As String
Select Case stInputCharacter
 Case Is="A", "a"
   EnglishToMorse="· _"
 Case Is="B", "b"
   EnglishToMorse="_ · · ·"
 Case Is="C", "c"
   EnglishToMorse="_ · _ ·"
 Case Is="D", "d"
   EnglishToMorse="_ · ·"
 Case Is="E", "e"
   EnglishToMorse="·"
 Case Is="F", "f"
   EnglishToMorse="· · _ ·"
 Case Is="G", "g"
   EnglishToMorse="_ _ ·"
 Case Is="H", "h"
   EnglishToMorse="· · · ·"
 Case Is="I", "i"
   EnglishToMorse="· ·"
```

```
    Case Is="J", "j"
      EnglishToMorse="· _ _ _"
    Case Is="K", "k"
      EnglishToMorse="_ · _"
    Case Is="L", "l"
      EnglishToMorse="· _ · ·"
    Case Is="M", "m"
      EnglishToMorse="_ _"
    Case Is="N", "n"
      EnglishToMorse="_ ·"
    Case Is="O", "o"
      EnglishToMorse="_ _ _"
    Case Is="P", "p"
      EnglishToMorse="· _ _ ·"
    Case Is="Q", "q"
      EnglishToMorse="_ _ · _"
    Case Is="R", "r"
      EnglishToMorse="· _ ·"
    Case Is="S", "s"
      EnglishToMorse="· · ·"
    Case Is="T", "t"
      EnglishToMorse="_"
    Case Is="U", "u"
      EnglishToMorse="· · _"
    Case Is="V", "v"
      EnglishToMorse="· · · _"
    Case Is="W", "w"
      EnglishToMorse="· _ _"
    Case Is="X", "x"
      EnglishToMorse="_ · · _"
    Case Is="Y", "y"
      EnglishToMorse="_ · _ _"
    Case Is="Z", "z"
      EnglishToMorse="_ _ · ·"
    Case Else
      EnglishToMorse=""
    End Select

  End Function
```

The function EnglishToMorse translates, character by character, the input typed by the user. The function EnglishToMorse receives as its input the ASCII character code of keys pressed by the user. In all other cases the function generates a null character. The Select Case statement allows the function to choose the appropriate Morse code for any letter of the English alphabet. Notice that the output characters are separated by a blank.

5.5 Implement the swap algorithm in Visual Basic.

The initial input screen of this program may look like this:

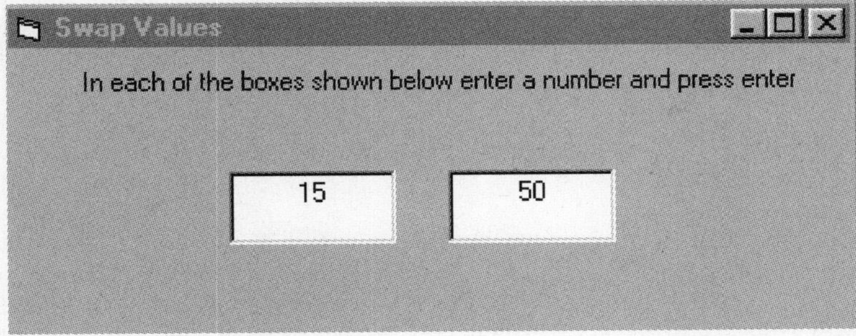

The code to implement this program is shown below:

```
Option Explicit
    Private Sub TxtVal1_KeyPress(KeyAscii As Integer)
    Dim Character As String

    If KeyAscii=vbKeyReturn Then
      If IsNumeric(txtVal1.Text) Then
        txtVal2.SetFocus
      Else
        MsgBox "Enter a numeric value", vbInformation, "Invalid Input"
        txtVal1.SetFocus
      End If
    End If
End Sub
    Private Sub TxtVal2_KeyPress(KeyAscii As Integer)
    Dim Character As String

    If KeyAscii=vbKeyReturn Then
      If IsNumeric(txtVal2.Text) Then
        SwapValues txtVal1, txtVal2
      Else
        MsgBox "Enter a numeric value", vbInformation, "Invalid Input"
        txtVal1.SetFocus
      End If
    End If

    Private Sub SwapValues(iBox1 As TextBox, iBox2 As TextBox)
    Dim temp As String

        temp=iBox1.Text
        iBox1.Text=iBox2.Text
        iBox2.Text=temp
End Sub
```

Observe that the code associated with each of the textboxes verifies that the user has typed a numeric value by means of the built-in function Val. If the value typed by the user is not numeric, the program warns the user of this fact by means of a message box, and the focus remains in the textbox. This program assumes that the user proceeds in an orderly fashion and it never attempts to start typing in the second textbox.

5.6 What is wrong with the following header declaration in C?

```
int function_header(int x, y, float z)
```

This is an erroneous declaration since each parameter needs to be declared separately. If the user wants to declare two integer formal parameters, each parameter has to be preceded by the qualifier int. Therefore, the correct format is

```
int function_header(int x, int y, float z)
```

5.7 If val1, val2 and val3 are integer variables, is it incorrect to invoke the function of Example 5.1 as max_of_three val1,val2, val3?

Calling the function max_of_three_integers as indicated above will produce an error since the parameters to the function need to be passed enclosed in parentheses.

5.8 What is wrong with the following C function?

```
//function to calculate the maximum of two given integer values
int maximum_of_two (int x, int y)
{
 int temp ;

   if ( x>y )
      temp=x;

   if (y>x)
      temp=y;
}
```

There are two types of error in this function. The first is syntactical, since the function does not return a value. This can be corrected by writing

return temp

before the closing curly bracket. In this particular function there is no need to use a temporary variable. We could have used **return x** or **return y** to simplify the code.

The second type of error is a little bit more difficult to discover. Notice that the function does not consider the case that the two input variables may have the same value. In other words, assuming that the function is syntactically correct, the function will return the maximum of the two input variables only when these variables are different. To correct this error one of the two if conditions needs to be changed so it tests for values that are "greater or equal." Therefore, the function can be written as follows:

```
int maximum_of_two (int x, int y)
{
 if ( x>=y)
  return x;

 if ( y>x)
    return y;
}
```

5.9 Are there any errors in the following function declarations and function calls? If there are, correct them. After correcting the program, try to run it using a C compiler. Are there any warnings? If there are, correct them.

```
//Function prototypes
float square (int x);
float triple_it (int y);

//Function calls
dval1=square ( value1); // assume that value1 is an integer variable and dval1 a double
                        //variable
dval2=triple_it (value1); // dval2 is a double variable

//Function declarations
void square ( int w)
{
  return w *w;
}

float triple_it (int x)
{
  return square(x) * x;
}
```

The header of the square function has been declared with the void qualifier whereas its prototype has been declared as returning a float. Correct this error by changing the function header to float.

If we run this program after correcting it, we will see that the C compiler produces a warning about a possible loss of data during conversion. This refers to the fact that the input parameters are integers but the function returns a float. To correct this, short of changing the type of the input parameters, we can use a **cast operator** to convert the results of the operations before returning any value to the calling program. To do this, change the return statements as indicated below.

return w *w; ⟹ return (float) w *w;

return square(x) * x; ⟹ return (float) square(x) * x;

Notice that in the function triple_it we have used the square function as if it were any other variable.

5.10 Assume that the following declarations appear in a C++ program. Are these declarations illegal? Can these two declarations appear in the same program?

```
int triple_it (int x);          ← different functions with identical names
                                  in the same program.
double triple_it(double x);
```

No. These declarations are not illegal. C++ allows the declarations of two or more functions with the same name and in the same program provided that these functions have different sets of parameters. This means that if the parameters are all of the same type then the number of parameters in both functions must be different. If both functions have the same number of parameters then, in one of the functions, at least one of the parameters must be of different type. This is known as **function overloading**. This feature of C++ and some other languages allows the programmer to operate on different data types using functions with identical names. The combination of function name and number of parameters is known as the **signature of the function**. Using this terminology, we can say that C++ allows function overloading provided that the signatures of the functions are different.

5.11 Write function prototypes in C to match the following descriptions.

(*a*) a function named ValidateNumber has three arguments. The first argument is an integer, the second argument is a float number and the third argument is a double. The function returns a float.

(*b*) a function named ValidRange operates on three global variables and returns a float value in the range of −1 to 1 if the number is in the valid range.

(*c*) a function PowerOfTwo accepts a floating-point argument and returns the result of raising the argument to the second power.

(*a*) Since the ValidateNumber function returns a float value and has three arguments, its skeleton looks like this:

```
float ValidateNumber( x,y,z);
```

Replacing the placeholders x, y, and z with their corresponding data types, the function prototype is

```
float ValidateNumber (int, float, double);
```

We can also write this prototype as float ValidateNumber(int x, float y, double z);.

(*b*) Since the function ValidRange operates on three global variables, it does not need any arguments. Knowing that the function returns a float value we can write its prototype as

```
float ValidRange (void)
```

The fact that the function returns a value between −1 and 1 cannot be expressed as part of the prototype. It is the responsibility of the programmer to ensure that the function meets this requirement.

(*c*) Since the function PowerOfTwo returns a float value and accepts a single argument, its skeleton is float(x). Replacing the placeholder x with the data type of the input parameter, the prototype for this function is

```
float PowerOfTwo (float);
```

This function prototype can also be written as

```
float PowerOfTwo ( x float);
```

5.12 Write function headers in Visual Basic to match the descriptions shown below. Assume that all functions are private.

(*a*) A function named factorial accepts an integer parameter and returns an integer.

(*b*) A function named ValidRange accepts as input a double value and returns True or False depending on whether or not the value is within a given range.

(*c*) A function named ConvertToNumeric accepts as input a text string representing an integer value and returns its numerical equivalent.

(*a*) As indicated before, the data type for functions and variables in Visual Basic is indicated using the As Data type clause. According to this, the header of the factorial function may look like this

```
Private Function Factorial (iValue as Integer) As Integer
```

(*b*) Since the function ValidRange returns true or false, its data type must be Boolean. Therefore, the function header may look like this:

```
Private Function ValidRange (dValue As Double) As Boolean
```

(*c*) The function ConvertToNumeric accepts as input the text string representation of an integer and returns its numerical representation. Therefore, the function header may look like this:

```
Private Function ConvertToNumeric (stInputValue as String) As Integer
```

5.13 Write a Visual Basic program that accepts two integer values from the user and determines whether the first input value is multiple of the second. Use a function named IsMultiple that returns true or false as appropriate.

We could use a simple form with two textboxes to accept the user inputs. The result (True or False) can be displayed on the form by assigning it to the caption of a label on the form. In addition, we may have a command button to do the calculations and another one to end the program. The form may look like this:

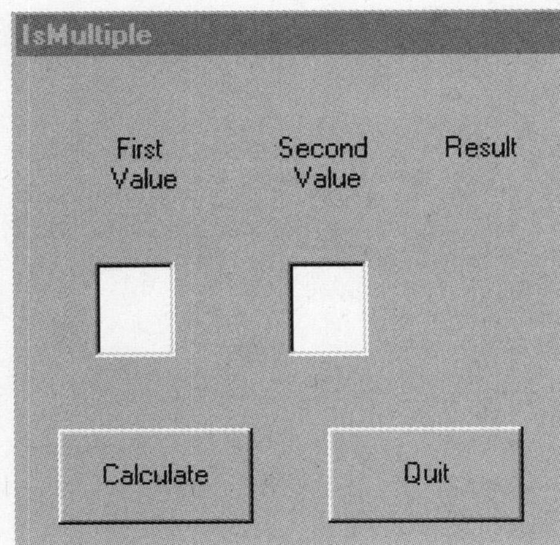

The code associated with the command button Calculate is shown below.

```
Private Sub Calculate_Click()
 Dim i As Integer
 Dim j As Integer

 i=Val(txtVal1)
 j=Val(txtVal2)

 If IsMultiple(i, j) Then
  lblMultiple.Caption=True
 Else
  lblMultiple.Caption=False
 End If

End Sub
```

The values of the textboxes are initially converted to their numerical equivalents using the built-in function Val. Although the IsMultiple function could have been called as follows: IsMultiple(Val(txtVal1),Val(txtVal2)), it is better to transform the contents of the textboxes outside the function call to make the code a little bit more readable.

The code associated with the Quit function is very simple since it consists of a single statement, the End statement, which, as its name indicates, ends the execution of the program:

```
Private Sub Quit_Click()
 End
End Sub
```

The function IsMultiple uses the Mod operator to determine whether the first argument is a multiple of the second argument. This operator returns the remainder of the division of the first argument by the second argument. Notice that we compare the result of the Mod operation to zero since it is a mathematical fact that a number is a multiple of another if the remainder of dividing the first number by the second is equal to zero.

```
Private Function IsMultiple(iVal1 As Integer, ival2 As Integer) As Boolean
  If (iVal1 Mod ival2)=0 Then
    IsMultiple=True
  Else
    IsMultiple=False
  End If
End Function
```

5.14 Write the function of the previous exercise in C++.

In the C family, including C++, there is no Boolean data type as defined in Visual Basic. However, we will consider that the function returns a true value if it returns a 1 and false if it returns a zero. With this in mind, we can write the program as follows:

```
#include <iostream.h>
int IsMultiple(int, int); //function prototype
void main()
{ int i,j;
    cout<<"\nEnter the first integer value:";
    cin>>i;
    cout<<"\nEnter the second integer value:";
    cin>>j;
    if (IsMultiple(i,j)==0)
        cout<< "\nThe first value is multiple of the second\n\n";
    else
        cout<< "\nThe first value is not multiple of the second\n\n";}
int IsMultiple(int x, int y)
{
    if (x % y==0)
      return 1;
    else
      return 0;}
```

Notice that the C++ operator % is equivalent to the Mod operator of Visual Basic.

5.15 Write a function in Visual Basic that accepts as input a value between zero and 100 and returns a letter grade according to the grading scale shown below.

Numerical Grade	Letter Grade
90 through 100	A
80 through 89	B
70 through 79	C
60 through 69	D
less than 60	F

We will assume that the function is private and part of a much larger program not shown here.

```
Private Function LetterGrade(Grade As Double) As String
  Select Case Grade
  Case 90 To 100
    LetterGrade="A"
    Case 80 To 89
    LetterGrade="B"
  Case 70 To 79
    LetterGrade="C"
  Case 60 To 69
    LetterGrade="D"
  Case 0 To 59
    LetterGrade="F"
  End Select
End Function
```

In this case we use the Select statement because it allows us to test for ranges of values in a more compact and more understandable way than a set of nested if statements.

5.16 Using the program skeleton shown below, determine the scope of all declared variables in C.

```
int price_per_unit;
float interest_rate;
double earnings;

void main()
{ int stock_type;
  float commission;
  int rating;
  :
  :
}

double depreciation (int val1, int val2)
{ double index_deval;
  float earnings;
    :
    :
  return(index_deval);
}

int internal_revs(float val1, float val2)
( int rating;
  float commission;
    :
    :
  return(interest_rate*(rating-(val1/val2)));
)
```

Variables price_per_unit and interest_rate are both global variables that can be referenced by any of the functions of this program.

The global variable earnings can be referenced by all functions except by the depreciation function. Notice that this function has a local variable by the same name.

Variables stock_type, commission, and rating are all local to main. No other function can reference these variables.

Variables index_deval, earnings, val1, and val2 are local variables to the depreciation function. No other function can reference these variables.

Variables rating, commission, val1, and val2 are local variables to the internal_revs function. No other function can reference these variables.

Notice that the formal parameters val1 and val2 are known only within this procedure and do not have anything in common with the formal parameters of the same name in the depreciation function. Similar comment can be made with respect to the variables rating and commission in this function and the variables by the same names in the main function.

5.17 What is the scope of the following variables in the program skeleton shown below? What global variables can be referenced in both main and function1?

```
int a,b;
char c,d;
void main()
{ float a, d;
:
}
int function1 (int a)
{char d;
 int b;
:
}
```

Only variable c can be referenced simultaneously by main and function1. Notice that in main there are two local variables named a and d. When these variables are referenced in main they always refer to the local variables, not the global variables. The global variable b can be referenced inside main since there is no local variable with this name.

Similarly, function1 has three local variables named a, b, and d. Within this function, any reference to any variable with any of these names will always refer to the local variables and not the global variables. Since none of the local variables of function1 is called c, we can always refer to this global variable.

5.18 In the programming languages of the C family, if value1 is an integer variable, what is the meaning of &value1?

value1 is a named memory location. We refer to the content of this memory location whenever we reference value1. &value1 is the address of the memory location value1. As Example 5.14 illustrates, there is a difference between the content of a variable and the address of such a variable

5.19 Write the appropriate C statements that correspond to the following situations.

(*a*) iptr is a pointer to an integer variable.

(*b*) the variable pointed to by iptr is an integer.

(*c*) the variable pointed to by cptr is a character variable.

(*d*) the integer variable whose address is in value_ptr.

(*a*) and (*b*) refer to the same situation although they are phrased a little bit differently. int *iptr declares iptr as a pointer variable to an integer.

(*c*) char *cptr declares that cptr is a pointer to a character variable. In other words, the variable pointed to by cptr is a character variable.

(*d*) If value_ptr is a pointer to an integer variable and it contains already the address of a particular variable, we can always refer to the variable as *value_ptr. This can be better illustrated as follows:

```
int j, *value_ptr;
:
value_ptr=&j;
:
*value_ptr=*value_ptr+1; // the content of variable j is incremented by 1.
```

5.20 Consider the following set of memory locations and C-like instructions. What is the content of the variables and pointers after executing the instructions shown below in sequence? Assume that all variables are of the same type and that the Ptr variables are pointers to that type of variables.

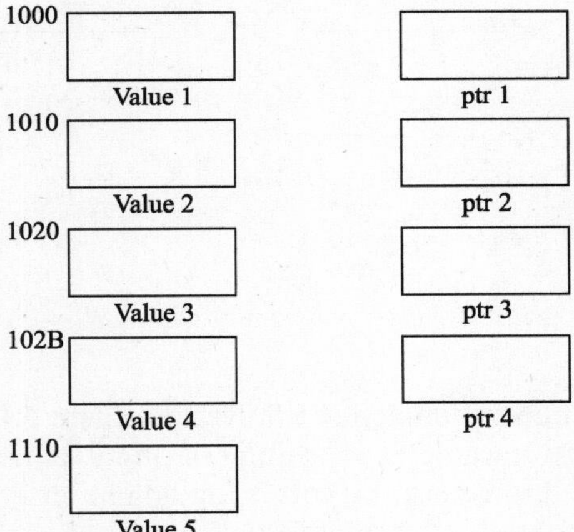

(*a*) value3 = 15
(*b*) value4 = 12
(*c*) Ptr3 = &value4
(*d*) Ptr1 = &value1
(*e*) value1 = *Ptr3 + 2
(*f*) Ptr2 = &value3
(*g*) value2 = *Ptr2 + *Ptr3
(*h*) Ptr4 = &value2
(*i*) value5 = *Ptr1 +*Ptr2+*Ptr3*Ptr4

Instructions (a) and (b) set the content of variables value3 and value4 to 15 and 12 respectively.

Instructions (c) and (d) copy the addresses of variables value4 and value1 into the pointer variables Ptr3 and Ptr1 respectively. According to the diagram, the content of Ptr1 is now 1000 and the content of Ptr3 is 102B.

Instruction (e) sets the content of variable value1 to the contents of variable value4 plus 2. Notice that *Ptr3 is the content of the variable whose address is currently stored in Ptr3. Observe that the current content of Ptr3 is 102B. This is the address of variable value4. *Ptr3 is the content of the variable value4, which, according to the diagram, is 12. Therefore, the content of variable value1 is $12 + 2$.

Instruction (f) copies the address of variable value3 into Ptr2. The new value of Ptr2 is 1020.

Instruction (g) adds the contents of the variables whose addresses are in Ptr2 and Ptr3. Since the content of variable value3 (address 1020) is 15 and the content of variable value4 (address 102B) is 12, the content of variable value2 is 27.

Instruction (h) copies the address of variable value2 into Ptr4.

Instruction (i) adds the content of variables value1, value2, value3, and value4 and stores the result into variable value5. The new content of variable value5 is 68.

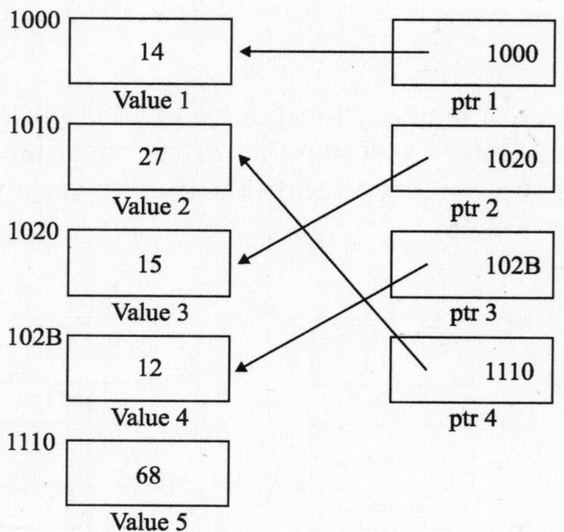

5.21 Write a C++ subprocedure to implement Solved Problem 5.15. Write the subprocedure with two parameters; the first parameter is a numeric input parameter between 0 and 100. The second parameter is used to return the corresponding letter grade. Pass the first parameter by value and the second parameter by reference.

A subprocedure to accomplish this task is shown below. Notice that the first input parameter is a float variable (passed by value) and the second parameter is a pointer to a character variable (passed by reference). Therefore, when the subprocedure is called the address of the character variable grade needs to be passed as an actual parameter. In this procedure a set of nested if ... else if statements is used instead of the case statement of problem 5.15 because the switch statement in C++ does not allow us to test for a range of values.

```
#include<iostream.h>
void GetLetterGrade(float, char*);

float score;
char grade;

void main()
{ cout<<"\nPlease enter a score between 0 and 100: ";
 cin>> score;
 GetLetterGrade(score,&grade);
 cout<<"\nThe letter grade is "<<grade<<endl<<endl;}
```

```
/*This procedure receives as input a value between 0 and 100 and "returns"
a letter grade corresponding to the grade. The first parameter is passed by
value; the second parameter is passed by reference. Ptr is a pointer to a
character variable.*

void GetLetterGrade(float i, char* ptr)
{
 if (i>=90 && i<=100)
     *ptr='A';
 else if (i>=80 && i<=89)
     *ptr='B';
 else if (i>=70 && i<=79)
     *ptr='C';
 else if (i>=60 && i<= 69)
     *ptr='D';
 else if (i>=0 && i<=59)
     *ptr='F';
}
```

5.22 Write a C++ subprocedure that accepts as input a number of nickels, dimes, and quarters and returns the corresponding dollar amount. Pass the variable corresponding to the dollar amount by reference.

```
#include<iostream.h>

void HowManyDollars(int,int,int,float&);

void main()
{ float dollar_amount;
 int nickels, dimes, quarters;

 cout<<"\nPlease enter number of nickels:";
 cin>>nickels;
 cout<<"\nPlease enter number of dimes:";
 cin>>dimes;
 cout<<"\nPlease enter number of quarters:";
 cin>>quarters;
 HowManyDollars(nickels,dimes,quarters,dollar_amount);
 cout<<"\nThe total amount in dollars is "<<dollar_amount<<endl<<endl;
}

void HowManyDollars(int n, int d, int q, float& t)
{
 t=(float)(n*0.05+d*0.10+q*0.25);
}
```

Notice that we have used the cast operator to convert the entire result to a float value. C++ converts the integer values to double before doing the individual multiplication operations. The resulting addition is of type double. If we do not use the cast operator the compiler will produce a warning.

5.23 Write a Java function to return the double value of miles per gallon, given the integer distance and the integer gallons used as a parameter.

```
public double FindMPG (int distance, int gallonsUsed)
 {
   return (double)distance/gallonsUsed;
 }
```

5.24 Write a Java method that implements the problem in Solved Problem 5.22. The function should accept a number of nickels, dimes, and quarters and return the corresponding dollar amount. Remember that Java can only return a value directly using the return function.

```
public float HowManyDollars (int nick, int dime, int quart)
{
   return (float)(nick*0.05+dime*0.10+quart*.25);
}
```

Supplementary Problems

5.25 The following narrative describes the task of a subprogram. Can this task be accomplished by a single function? What tasks seem to be more appropriate for a subroutine than for a function?

"The subprogram reads a sequence of characters and verifies that there are no duplicate words next to each other unless they are separated by a period. If there are duplicate words the program deletes the second word. In addition, the program should verify that the first word following a period begins with a capital letter."

5.26 The following narrative describes the task of a subprogram. Can this task be accomplished by a single function?

"The subprogram receives as its input a pointer to a character string and returns the number of words in the string. A word is any sequence of alphanumeric characters separated by at least one blank. Some of the words are written in uppercase letters."

5.27 Example 5.15 swaps the values of two integer variables with the parameters being passed by reference. Can this subprocedure swap the two input parameters if the parameters are passed by value instead?

5.28 Write the prototype for the following C functions:

(*a*) Function name: Cubic Root
Return data type: double
Input data types: two input values of type double

(*b*) Function name: Copy String
Return data type: pointer to a character
Input data type: pointer to character string, pointer to character string, integer value

(*c*) Function name: Polynomial
Return data type: none
Input data type: pointer to character string, pointer to character string, pointer to character string, pointer to character string

5.29 What is the difference between formal and actual parameters?

5.30 Write function headers for the following Visual Basic functions:

(*a*) Function name: ConvertToCharacter
Return data type: character
Input data type: an integer value between 0 and 9

(*b*) Function name: TimeDifference
Return data type: string of characters
Input data type: a couple of strings of the form hh:min:secs

5.31 If variables ptr1 and ptr2 are both integer pointer variables, what is the difference, if any, between the statements ptr1 = ptr2 and *ptr1 = *ptr2?

5.32 Is it true that for any variable x, the expression *&x can be considered synonymous?

5.33 Write a Java method that implements the problem in Solved Problem 5.13, a function that receives two integer values as parameters and determines whether the first value is a multiple of the second. Java supports the simple data type "boolean."

5.34 Write a Java function to implement the grade problem in Solved Problem 5.15.

5.35 What does the Mystery function do?

```
#include<stdio.h>
void Mystery (int, int *);
void main()
{
    int a,b;

    a=12;
    b=15;

    Mystery (a,&b);
    printf("\n%d %d\n",a,b);
}
void Mystery(int x, int* y)
{
    int z;
    z=x;
    *y=*y+z;
    x=*y;
}
```

5.36 Mark the order of execution of the statement in the following program:

```
#include <stdio.h>
void f1 (int *, int *);
void main()
{
    int val1,val2;
```

```
    printf("\n Write the order of execution"); // No.______
    f1(&val1,&val2); // No.______
    printf("\nThe value read in are %4d and %4d", val1,val2); // No.______
 }
 void f1 (int * i, int * j)
{
    printf("\nEnter the first integer number:"); // No.______
    scanf("%d",i); // No.______

    printf("\nEnter the second integer number:"); // No.______
    scanf("%d",j); // No.______

    *i=*i+2; // No.______
    *j=*j+5; // No.______
}
```

5.37 Write a C++ function that takes as parameters three integers, and returns the minimum of the three.

5.38 Write a C function to calculate the power i^n where i and n are both integers.

Answers to Supplementary Problems

5.25 No! A function should perform single tasks. This narrative requires that multiple tasks be performed by a single function. There should be at least two subroutines: one for reading the sequence of characters and one for deleting consecutive double words. A function can be used to determine if two consecutive words are identical. However, a subprocedure is more appropriate for this task since the subprocedure may "return" a Yes/No indication that the words are duplicate and, if they are, a pointer to the word that needs to be eliminated.

5.26 Yes! This subprogram performs a single task. The function should return the number of words in the given string.

5.27 No! When the parameters are passed by value the subprocedure operates on copies of the input parameters. Therefore, any changes to the formal parameters will not be reflected on the actual parameters.

5.28 (*a*) double CubicRoot (double, double);

(*b*) char *CopyString (char *, char *, int);

(*c*) void Polynomial (char *, char *, char *, char *);

5.29 Formal parameters are used in the declaration of the function or subprocedure. They are local to the subprogram in which they are defined. Actual parameters are the values passed to the subprogram.

5.30 (*a*) Private Function ConvertToCharacter (iValue As Integer) As String

(*b*) Private Function TimeDifference (stTime1 As String, stTime2 As String) As String

5.31 These two sets of statements are totally different. Assume that the content of variable ptr1 is 10FF. The statement ptr1 = ptr2 makes both variables point to the same location. That is, the content of both variables is 10FF. The statement *ptr1 = *ptr2 copies the value of the memory location pointed to by ptr2 into the location pointed to by ptr1. That is, assume that the content of the variable pointed to by ptr2 is 555. After this instruction is executed the variable pointed to by ptr1 is also 555.

5.32 True. The expression *&x always refers to the content of variable x.

5.33
```
public boolean IsMultiple(int x, int y)
{
    if (x%y==0) return true;
    else return false;
}
```

5.34
```
public char GetLetterGrade(int grade) //receives integer as parameter, returns char
  {
    char lettergrade='';
    if (grade>=90 && grade<=100)
        lettergrade='A';
    else if (grade<90 && grade>=80)
        lettergrade='B';
    else if (grade<80 && grade>=70)
        lettergrade='C';
    else if (grade>=60 && grade<70)
        lettergrade='D';
    else if (grade<60 && grade>=0)
        lettergrade='F';
    return lettergrade;
  }
```

5.35 The function Mystery adds the contents of variables a and b and assigns the sum to variable b.

5.36
```
    void main()
{
    int val1,val2;

    printf("\n Write the order of execution"); // No. 1
    f1(&val1,&val2); // No. 2
    printf("\nThe value read in are %4d and %4d", val1,val2); // No. 9
}
void f1 (int * i, int * j)
{
    printf("\nEnter the first integer number:"); // No. 3
    scanf("%d",i); // No.4
```

```
    printf("\nEnter the second integer number:"); // No. 5
    scanf("%d",j); // No. 6

    *i=*i+2; // No. 7
    *j=*j+5; // No. 8
}
```

5.37

```
int min_of_three_integers (int a, int b, int c)
{ int minimum;

    minimum=a;
    if (b<minimum)
        minimum=b;
    else
      if ( c<minimum)
        minimum=c;
    return (minimum); }
```

5.38

```
int Power (int num, int exp)
{
    int i;
    int product=1;
    for (i=1; i<=exp; i++)
        product=product*num;
    return product;
}
```

Arrays and Strings

6.1 INTRODUCTION TO ARRAYS

An ***array*** is a group of memory locations all of the same type that have the same name. Previously, in a program to calculate employee pay, the user would type in the employee number, the pay rate, and the number of hours worked. There would be one variable to hold each piece of information as shown in Fig. 6-1, and then the gross pay would be calculated.

employeeNum	hourlyRate	hoursWorked	grossPay
101	6.25	40	

Fig. 6-1 Individual variables for payroll.

If there were more than one employee, the program could have a loop for the user to type in the information into the same variables for the second employee and calculate that person's gross pay, then the third, and so forth. However, a problem would arise if the employer wanted to have a report containing a list of the weekly pay for all the employees, the average pay for the week, and then a list of all the employees who received above the average pay. The average could not be calculated until all the employees' information was submitted. In order to compare each person's pay to the average, all the information would need to be entered a second time.

One solution to this problem would be to have a different variable for each employee, as shown in Fig. 6-2. Each person's pay could be compared to the average. This would be possible if there were only two or three employees, but completely impractical to declare separate variables for twenty or a hundred or a thousand employees.

The solution to this problem is to use an array. Arrays allow the storing and manipulating of large amounts of data. Three arrays are declared, one to hold all the employee numbers, another for all the hourly rates and a third for all the hours worked, as shown in Fig. 6-3. The information is entered in such a way that the employee whose number is in box 2 receives the rate in box 2 and worked the number of hours in box 2. Each person's gross pay is calculated and the average is found. Each person's data is still in memory and can quickly be examined to produce the list of people with pay above the average.

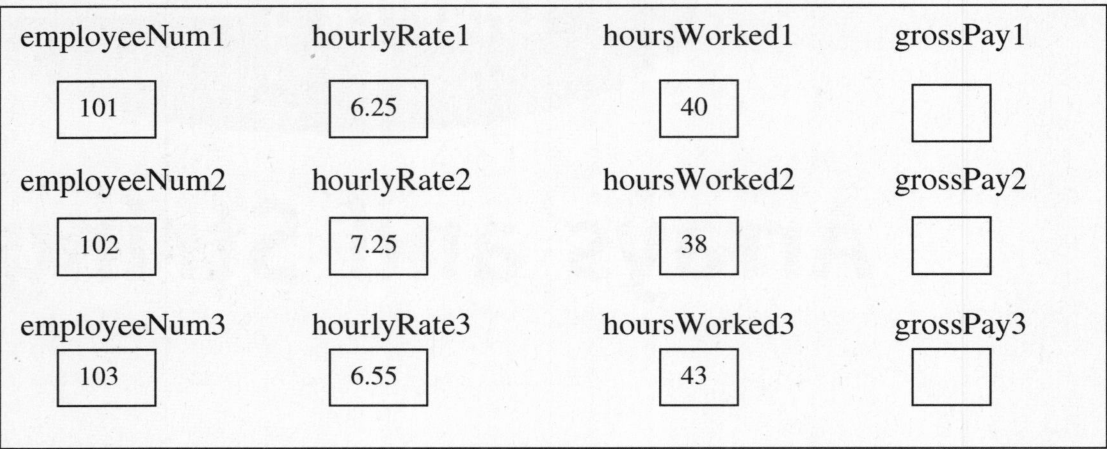

Fig. 6-2 Individual variables for three employees.

employeeNums		hourlyRates		hoursWorked		grossPay	
[0]	101	[0]	6.25	[0]	40	[0]	
[1]	102	[1]	6.55	[1]	38	[1]	
[2]	103	[2]	7.25	[2]	42	[2]	
[3]	104	[3]	7.15	[3]	40	[3]	
[4]	105	[4]	6.25	[4]	37	[4]	
..	...	..	...	..	...	..	
[n-1]	...	[n-1]	...	[n-1]	...	[n-1]	

Fig. 6-3 Array variables for any number (n) of employees.

6.1.1 Manipulating Arrays

The entire array is declared once and known by one name. When it is declared, the exact number of memory locations to be set aside is specified. All the locations must contain data of the same type. Each ***element***, or individual memory location in the array, is accessible through the use of its ***subscript*** or index number. For example, in Fig. 6-3 employeeNums[3] refers to the element in box number 3 of the employeeNums array which contains "104," or hourlyRates[4] would access the element in box 4 of the hourlyRates array which contains "6.25." The subscripts usually begin with 0.

Input and output for an array is accomplished through the use of loops. Each time through the loop a different box in the array is filled or printed.

EXAMPLE 6.1 Pseudocode for a loop to fill or print an array of *n* items would look like this:

```
loop from lcv = 0 to lcv = n – 1 where n is the total number of items in the array
    input or output array[lcv]
end loop
```

EXAMPLE 6.2 Most other processing of arrays also entails loops. One common example is to calculate the sum of all the items in an integer array. Pseudocode for summing an array would look like this:

```
set the sum to 0 before the loop starts
loop from lcv = 0 to lcv = n − 1 where n is the total number of items in the array
    add the array[lcv] to the running sum
end loop
```

Specific processing of arrays in Visual Basic, C, C++, and Java is demonstrated later in this chapter. Each language handles them in a slightly different way. However, in all languages the programmer must be careful not to try to process past the end of the array. For example, if there are 10 items in the array called grossPay, located in boxes [0] through [9], a statement including grossPay[20] would cause serious problems because there is no memory location with that designation.

6.1.2 Multi-Dimension Arrays

Regular single-dimension arrays are good for processing lists of items. Sometimes, however, two-dimensional arrays are necessary.

mySales

	[0]	[1]	[2]
[0]	250	300	325
[1]	350	325	400
[2]	220	315	210
[3]	210	310	295

Fig. 6-4 Two-dimensional array for sales.

EXAMPLE 6.3 A sales representative might have a report of the sales for each month of each quarter, as shown in Fig. 6-4. The rows [0] through [3] represent the four quarters of the year. The columns [0] through [2] represent the three months in each quarter. Each element of the array is accessed through two subscripts, one for the row and one for the column, in that order. For example, in Fig. 6-4 the contents of entry mySales[1][2] is "400."

Two-dimensional arrays follow the rules of single-dimension arrays. The array is declared specifying the number of memory locations desired by stating the number of rows and the number of columns. Each item in the array must contain the same type of data. The entire array has one name and each element is accessible through the use of its row and column numbers.

Most processing of these arrays is accomplished through the use of nested loops, one for the row and one for the column.

EXAMPLE 6.4 The pseudocode for printing a two-dimensional array looks like this:

```
loop from row = 0 to row = n − 1 where n is the number of rows in the array
    loop from col = 0 to col = m − 1 where m is the number of columns in the array
        print out array[row][col]
    end col loop
end row loop
```

Arrays of more than two dimensions are possible, but rarely used. See Solved Problems 6.4 and 6.5 at the end of the chapter for an example.

6.1.3 Strings – A Special Kind of Array

The array examples we have seen so far have been numeric. It is also possible to manipulate arrays of characters. These arrays, usually called ***strings***, are a special type of array because they are used so frequently. An array of strings is implemented as a two-dimensional array of characters.

EXAMPLE 6.5 Draw single-dimension arrays to contain the following strings: "JOAN," "CHICAGO," and "MAY." In addition, draw a two-dimensional array to contain the strings: "corn," "wheat," and "rye."

The result is shown in Fig. 6-5.

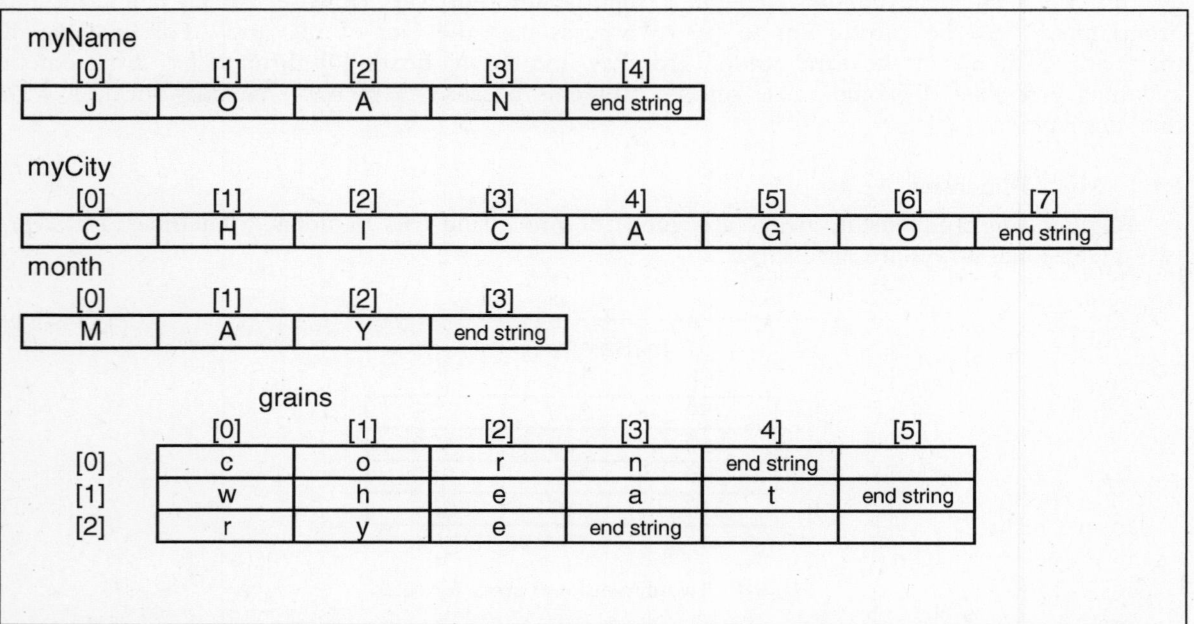

Fig. 6-5 Strings in one and two dimensions.

Each language implements and manipulates strings differently. Usually special kinds of processing commands are available. Many require some indication of where the string ends, as shown in the previous example.

The following sections explain the use of arrays in specific languages. In each of these languages we have considered the following topics: declaring arrays, manipulating arrays, two-dimensional arrays, string processing, and arrays as parameters to functions.

6.2 ARRAYS IN VISUAL BASIC

6.2.1 Declaring Arrays

In Visual Basic, arrays are declared like other variables, using the Dim statement. The number of memory locations to be used is placed in parentheses immediately following the array name.

EXAMPLE 6.6 An integer and a floating point array would be declared in this way:

```
Dim testScores (10) As Integer 'an array to keep 10 integer test scores from 0 to 9
Dim cashAvailable (12) As Currency 'an array to keep 12 months record of cash from 0 to 11
```

Unlike most other languages, Visual Basic allows the lowest subscript of the array to be set to a value other than 0. The subscripts may even be negative, but it is best to have all subscripts be integer values. For these non-zero-based arrays, both the lowest and the highest subscripts are specified in the Dim statement.

EXAMPLE 6.7 Declare an array from 1 to 12 to hold monthly income. Declare an array of integer values with subscripts from −20 to 20.

```
Dim monthlyIncome (1 to 12) As Currency    '12 items in the array
Dim values (−20 to 20) As Integer          '41 items in the array
```

If the program attempts to access an invalid element of the array, Visual Basic stops and gives an error message, *Subscript out of range*. If the program uses non-standard subscript ranges, it is very important to verify that the element accessed really exists.

6.2.2 Manipulating Arrays

Most Visual Basic processing with arrays is accomplished using the For...Next loops.

EXAMPLE 6.8 Write a Visual Basic program to read in a set of ten test scores, find the average, and print out the average and the scores that are above average.

Figure 6-6 shows a section of code that would accomplish this task. In each section, the For...Next loop goes through the entire array to fill or process each element.

```
Dim lcv As Integer    'loop control variable
Dim sum As Integer
Dim scores(1 To 10) As Integer
Dim avg As Single
'read in scores
For lcv=1 To 10        'read in the entire array
   scores(lcv)=InputBox("Enter the number")
Next lcv
'find the average
sum=0
For lcv=1 To 10
   sum=sum+scores(lcv)              'add each to sum
Next lcv
avg=sum/10
'print those above average
Print "The average is"; avg
For lcv=1 To 10
  If scores(lcv)>avg Then         'only print the ones above average
    Print scores(lcv)
  End If
Next lcv
```

Fig. 6-6 Visual Basic test scores.

6.2.3 Two-dimensional Arrays

Two-dimensional arrays are declared with the row boundaries and the column boundaries in the same parentheses, separated by a comma. In each case, if no lower boundary is specified, a lower bound of zero is assumed.

EXAMPLE 6.9 Declare an array to keep track of daily temperatures for 31 days in 12 months. Declare an array to monitor 5 test scores for each person in the class numbered from 101 to 110. Declare a two-dimensional array of strings with 4 rows and 26 columns.

```
Dim dailyTemperatures (1 to 12, 1 to 31) As Integer    '12 monthly rows, 31 daily columns
Dim classScores (101 to 110, 1 to 5) As Integer        'student numbers 101 to 110, 5 scores
Dim nameTable (3, 25) As String                        'rows 0 to 3, 0 to 25
```

Processing of two-dimensional arrays is accomplished using nested For..Next loops, as shown in Fig. 6-7.

EXAMPLE 6.10 Write a Visual Basic program where four weeks of temperatures are entered and printed in a well-documented chart. Remember that the Dim statement always indicates rows first and then columns.

The code to implement this program is shown in Fig. 6-7.

```
Dim row As Integer, col As Integer
Dim temps(1 To 4, 1 To 7) As Single
Dim message As String
'read in temps
For row=1 To 4
  For col=1 To 7
    message="Enter the temperature for week "+Str(row)+" and day "+Str(col)
    temps(row, col)=InputBox(message) 'see chapter 3 to review explanation of message
  Next col
Next row
'print chart - heading first
Print "DAY:", "Sun", "Mon", "Tue", "Wed", "Thu", "Fri", "Sat"
For row=1 To 4                'do everything for each row in this loop
  Print "Week"; row,          'label for each row followed by comma for next column
  For col=1 To 7              'do everything for each column in this loop
    Print temps(row, col),    'each temp followed by comma for next column
  Next col
  Print                       'take cursor to next line for next row
Next row
```

Fig. 6-7 Temperatures in Visual Basic.

The output for the code in Fig. 6-7 with sample data entered looks like this:

Temperatures

DAY:	Sun	Mon	Tue	Wed	Thu	Fri	Sat
Week 1	55	56	57	59	60	52	49
Week 2	45	42	45	42	35	30	26
Week 3	21	25	26	32	36	39	40
Week 4	45	48	52	53	57	51	49

6.2.4 String Processing

Visual Basic provides a special data type called **String** to handle arrays of characters. The String type makes it easier for the programmer to process because the String variable can expand or contract to be the length needed for any given String value. The programmer does not have to keep track of the end of the string. Visual Basic also provides the necessary functions to manipulate strings.

EXAMPLE 6.11 Look at this section of code.

```
Dim myName As String
myName="Joe"
Print myName; " is "; Len(myName); " characters long"
myName="Alexander the Great"
Print myName; " is "; Len(myName); " characters long"
```

The output would be:

```
Joe is 3 characters long
Alexander the Great is 19 characters long
```

The built-in Len() function returns the exact length of the string, not including the end of string mark. Visual Basic takes care of marking the end of string, making programming less complex.

Arrays of strings can be declared to make the two-dimensional array of characters more understandable. Remember, in VB only the number of strings in the list need to be declared, not the length of each string.

Other string processing functions available in VB include:

- Len(*string*) returns the length of the *string*.
- Right(*string*, *n*) returns the rightmost *n* characters.
- Left(*string*, *n*) returns the leftmost *n* characters.
- Mid(*string*, *p*, *n*) returns the middle *n* characters beginning at position *p*.

EXAMPLE 6.12 Write a Visual Basic program that examines an array of strings and determines the following: (a) the length of each string, (b) the leftmost character, (c) the rightmost three characters, and (d) the middle two letters.

Figure 6-8 shows the code using the Visual Basic functions.

```
Dim myNames(1 To 4) As String
Dim lcv As Integer, middle As Integer
myNames(1)="Joe"
myNames(2)="Alexander the Great"
myNames(3)="Susan B. Anthony"
myNames(4)="Louis XIV"
For lcv=1 To 4
 Print myNames(lcv); " is "; Len(myNames(lcv)); " characters long"
 Print "The first letter is "; Left(myNames(lcv), 1)
 Print "The last three letters are "; Right(myNames(lcv), 3)
 middle=(Len(myNames(lcv)) / 2)
 Print "The middle two letters are ' "; Mid(myNames(lcv), middle, 2); "'"
 Print
Next lcv
```

Fig. 6-8 String processing in Visual Basic.

The output for this code is shown below. Notice that a space is considered a character. It is listed as one of the middle two characters for both "Susan B. Anthony" and "Alexander the Great."

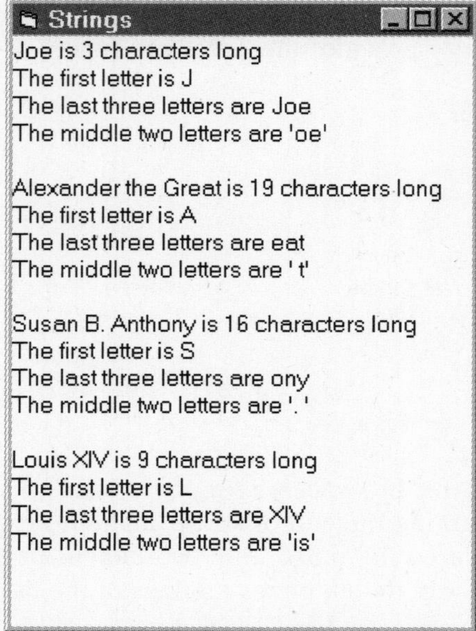

Strings
Joe is 3 characters long
The first letter is J
The last three letters are Joe
The middle two letters are 'oe'
Alexander the Great is 19 characters long
The first letter is A
The last three letters are eat
The middle two letters are ' t'
Susan B. Anthony is 16 characters long
The first letter is S
The last three letters are ony
The middle two letters are '. '
Louis XIV is 9 characters long
The first letter is L
The last three letters are XIV
The middle two letters are 'is'

6.2.5 Arrays as Parameters to Functions

An entire array can be sent to a function as a parameter in Visual Basic. This is often done if the same function needs to be applied to several different arrays to keep from repeating code.

EXAMPLE 6.13 Write a generic Visual Basic function to find the average of the numbers in an integer array. That function can receive an array of temperatures, an array of scores, or any other integer array, as long as the number of elements in the array is also sent.

Figure 6-9 shows this function and also some sample code calling that function with different arrays as parameters.

6.3 ARRAYS IN C/C++ AND JAVA

Recall from Chapter 5 that ***pointers*** are variables that contain memory addresses as their values. A variable name *directly* references a value and a pointer *indirectly* references the value.

6.3.1 Declaring Arrays in C/C++

A pointer to an array is shown in Fig. 6-10. When implementing arrays in C, C++, and Java, the array name is the same as a pointer that points to the FIRST object in the array.

Figure 6-10 demonstrates how an array can be declared in C and C++. The first statement:

```
int ar[6];
```

tells the compiler to set aside 6 memory locations (0 through 5) for integer data types. All subscripts in C and C++ begin with 0. Each location is specified through the use of square brackets (e.g., array[2]) instead of the parentheses used in VB.

The function is:

```
Private Function FindAvg(arr() As Integer, length As Integer) As Single
 Dim sum As Integer, lcv As Integer
  For lcv=1 To length
    sum=sum+arr(lcv)
  Next lcv
  FindAvg=sum/length 'returns value of function as single
End Function
```

One part of the calling code:

```
Dim lcv As Integer 'loop control variable
Dim scores(1 To 10) As Integer
Dim numScores As Integer, numIn As Integer
Dim avg As Single
'handle scores
lcv=1
numIn=InputBox("Enter the score (-1 to stop)")
Do While (lcv<10 And numIn>0) 'stop at 10 or -1
    numScores=numScores+1
    scores(lcv)=numIn
    numIn=InputBox("Enter the score (-1 to stop)")
    lcv=lcv+1
Loop
avg=FindAvg(scores, numScores) 'send exact number of scores
Print "The average score is "; avg
```

Another part of the calling code:

```
'handle temps
 Dim temps(1 To 7) As Integer
 For lcv=1 To 7
    numIn=InputBox("Day"+ Str(lcv)+" Enter the temperature")
    temps(lcv)=numIn
Next lcv
avg=FindAvg(temps, 7) 'send 7 days
Print "The average temperature this week is "; avg
```

Fig. 6-9 Functions with array parameters in Visual Basic.

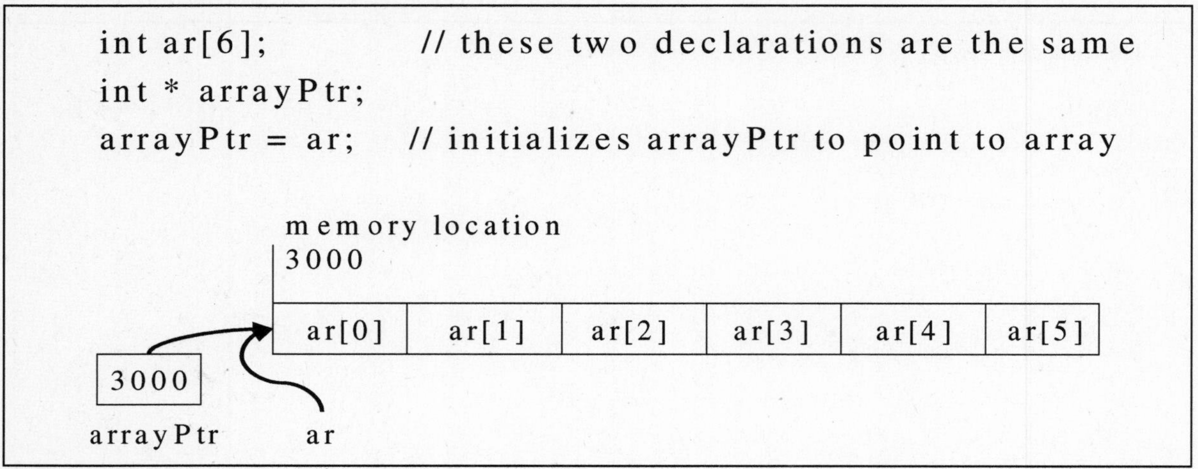

Fig. 6-10 Pointers and array names in C and C++.

EXAMPLE 6.14 Write a statement that would set up the array of 6 spaces and actually put values into each space:

```
int ar[6]={5,10,15,20,25,30};
```

It is possible to declare and initialize C and C++ arrays at the same time. The compiler usually gives an error if more than the specified number of values are listed. If fewer than that number are listed, many compilers will fill in the rest with zero.

It is also possible to initialize all elements of the array to zero at the same time, like this:

```
int ar[6]={0};
```

6.3.2 Declaring Arrays in Java

Declaring an array in C/C++ allocates the appropriate number of memory locations. Declaring arrays in Java is more explicit. First, the program declares the array and then it allocates memory. This task can be accomplished either in one step or in two.

EXAMPLE 6.15 Write the declaration from Fig. 6-10 in Java.

```
   int ar[];                 // declaring array
   ar=new int[6];            // allocating memory
or int ar[]=new int[6];      // declaring and allocating in one statement
```

It is possible to declare, allocate, and initialize Java arrays at the same time. This statement would set up the array of 6 spaces and actually put values into each space:

```
int ar[]={2, 3, 4, 1, 2, 6};
int ar[]={0};
```

The compiler only allocates the number of items that are listed. The first array above has 6 items, 0 through 5. The second has only 1, array space zero. Java never automatically allocates or fills any memory locations. That is the responsibility of the program.

6.3.3 Manipulating Arrays in C, C++, and Java

As in Visual Basic, arrays are usually processed in C, C++, and Java using loops. One of the dangerous aspects of C++ is that if the loop attempts to access locations not in the array, most compilers will not give an error message. The program simply uses whatever happens to be in that location, which is often undefined. In computer lingo, we refer to the content of these locations as "garbage." Programmers must be very careful, especially when using loops to access the array items, to be sure that the loop does not go beyond the end of the array.

EXAMPLE 6.16 Write a short section of code in C++ that declares an array of six integers with the value of each element double its index and then try to print ten elements of the array.

Figure 6-11 illustrates this code.

```
int ar[6], i;
for (i=0; i<6; i++)
    ar[i]=2*i;
for (i=0; i<10; i++)
    cout<<ar[i]<<"";
cout<<endl<<endl;
```

Fig. 6-11 Manipulating C++ arrays.

Notice that the array was declared with 6 elements and subscripts 0 through 5. However, the second loop tries to print out up to the subscript 9. Beyond the sixth location, the contents are garbage. Some C and C++ compilers will simply print out in integer form whatever happens to be in those locations. The output might look like this:

0 2 4 6 8 10 6684216 4208633 1 7867264

Once the array was accessed past where it had been initialized, whatever happened to be in those particular locations was printed out. If the array is used in calculations of any kind the results would be completely unpredictable. Java offers more help to the programmer. Trying to access any locations beyond the bounds of an array always results in an error message. The message below specifies that the program tried to go beyond the array, and it was the index 5 that caused the problem.

java.lang.ArrayIndexOutOfBoundsException: 5

In order to prevent this kind of error in C and C++, many programmers use constants to signify the number of locations, and then use the constant as a boundary in every loop. Using this convention in Java also results in code that is much clearer.

EXAMPLE 6.17 Write a short section of code to declare an array of 6 integers using the constant MAX and use this constant to control execution of a loop that initializes the contents of each element to the same value as its index.

The C/C++ and Java code would look like this:

C/C++

```
const int MAX=6;
int ar[MAX], i;
for (i=0; i<MAX; i++)
  ar[i]=i;
```

Java

```
final int MAX=6;
int ar[], i;
ar=new int[MAX];
for (i=0; i<MAX; i++)
  ar[i]=i;
```

EXAMPLE 6.18 Write a C++ program that reads in integers and keeps track of how many are entered.

Another way to keep track of the items in the array is to allocate a separate variable containing the number of items in the array. Figure 6-12 demonstrates this using the variable *size* to keep track of how many are entered into the array. The constant *MAX* assures that the program never processes past the end of the array. The same concept could be implemented in Java.

```
const int MAX=6;
int ar[MAX], i;
int num, size=0;
cout<<"Enter a number, -1 to stop"<<endl;
cin>>num;
while (num !=-1 && size<MAX) //stop the loop with -1 or if it gets too big
{
    ar[size]=num;
    size++;
    cout<<"Enter a number, -1 to stop"<<endl;
    cin>>num;
}
for (i=0; i<size; i++)
    cout<<ar[i]<<" ";
cout<<endl<<endl;
```

Fig. 6-12 Keeping track of the size of an array in C++.

6.3.4 Two-dimensional Arrays

Two-dimensional arrays in C, C++, and Java require the row and column size in separate brackets.

EXAMPLE 6.19 Write declarations in C/C++ and Java for an array with 3 rows and columns, and an array with 4 rows and 6 columns.

C/C++	Java
`int mySquare[3][3];`	`int mySquare[ ][ ];` `mySquare=new int [3][3];`
`int myTable[4][6];`	`int myTable[ ][ ];` `myTable=new int [4][6];`

EXAMPLE 6.20 Write the statements in C/C++ and Java that declare two two-dimensional arrays and initialize them as they are declared. Use the following data: (a) the contents of each element in each row of the first array is the row number plus 1, (b) the contents of each element of the second array is the (row number times 10) plus (the column number plus 1).

Two-dimensional arrays can also be initialized as they are declared in C, C++, and Java. Figure 6-13 shows an initialization in C/C++ and one in Java, as well as the resulting arrays.

C/C++	`int mySquare[3][3]={ {1,1,1},{2,2,2}, {3,3,3} };`	[0] [1] [2] [0] 1 1 1 [1] 2 2 2 [2] 3 3 3
Java	`int myTable[][]={ {1,2,3,4,5,6}, {11,12,13,14,15,16}, {21,22,23,24,25,26}, {31,32,33,34,35,36} };`	[0] [1] [2] [3] [4] [5] [0] 1 2 3 4 5 6 [1] 11 12 13 14 15 16 [2] 21 22 23 24 25 26 [3] 31 32 33 34 35 36

Fig. 6-13 Initializing two-dimensional arrays.

EXAMPLE 6.21 Given the following arrays, write the nested loops that will initialize them as indicated below.

	[0]	[1]	[2]
[0]	1	2	3
[1]	2	4	6
[2]	3	6	9

	[0]	[1]	[2]	[3]	[4]	[5]
[0]	0	1	2	3	4	5
[1]	1	2	3	4	5	6
[2]	2	3	4	5	6	7
[3]	3	4	5	6	7	8

As in Visual Basic, processing is done using nested loops, one for the row and one for the column. The loops shown in Fig. 6-14, which would be the same in C, C++, and Java, show these two initializations using nested loops.

```
for (row=0; row<3; row++)
  for (col=0; col<3; col++)
    mySquare[row][col]=(row +1)*(col+1);
for (row=0; row<4; row++)
    for (col=0; col<6; col++)
        myTable[row][col]=row+col;
```

Fig. 6-14 Processing two-dimensional arrays.

6.3.5 String Processing in C and C++

The processing of strings is the one area completely different in C/C++ and Java, so they will be addressed in separate sections. In C and C++, string processing is very cumbersome. There is no separate data type called string. The ***string*** is an array of characters, ending in the null character '\0'. An array of strings is a two-dimensional array of characters, with each row ending in the null character '\0'. Recall that some C/C++ compilers allow array elements to be processed that are beyond the bounds of the declared array. When dealing with strings, this can be very frustrating. C/C++ provides a string-handling library that sometimes helps in handling strings, but the programmer still needs to be very careful that the null character actually is present to indicate the end of each string.

EXAMPLE 6.22 The short C++ program in Fig. 6-15 demonstrates some of the C/C++ string-handling capabilities. Each program section is explained below.

```
#include<iostream.h>
#include <string.h>
void main ()
{
    //Section 1
    char word[3];
    strcpy (word,"my");     //alternate declaration:    char * word="my";
    cout<<word<<endl;
    cout<<strlen(word)<<endl;    //prints out 2
    //Section 2
    char word2[]={'S','t','o','r','y','\0'};
    cout<<word2<<endl;
    cout<<strlen(word2)<<endl; //prints out 5
    //Section 3
    char word3[]="is good";
    cout<<word3<<endl;
    cout<<strlen(word3)<<endl;    //prints out 7
    if (strcmp(word2, word3)) cout<<"They are not the same"<<endl;
    else cout<<"The strings are identical"<<endl;
    //Section 4
    char *greetings[3]={"I love you", "Be mine", "Valentine"};
    for (int i=0; i<3; i++)
        cout<<greetings[i]<<" is "<< strlen(greetings[i])<< " characters long"<<endl;
    //the strings are 10, 7, and 9 characters long respectively
    cout<<endl;
}
```

Fig. 6-15 String example in C++.

The first section shows that the most common way of declaring a string is as a simple array of characters. Be sure that the array size is one more than the number of characters in the word to allow for the null character at the end. In this example, *word* is declared as 3 characters long which does include the null character. Once the array is declared, it cannot be filled by using a simple assignment statement. A loop could be used, but the string.h library provides for the string copy *strcpy(destination, source)* function. The *strcpy()* function automatically appends the null character at the end of the string.

The example also shows an alternate type of declaration. An array of characters can also be declared without specifying its length through the use of the asterisk to indicate a pointer to a group of characters. Many programmers find it easier not to be required to specify the length of the string. However, it is usually easier and safer in C/C++ to declare the length explicitly.

An array of characters is the one kind of array that can be printed out without accessing each item in the array individually. The *cout* statement knows to print the characters until it comes to the null character. The *strlen(string)* function returns the number of characters in the string, NOT COUNTING the null character. If the programmer wants to process each character in the string by using a loop, the strlen could be used as the upper bound as in this code:

```
for (i=0; i<strlen(word); i++) cout<<word[i];
```

The second section demonstrates how to declare a string and initialize it at the same time. If each character is listed with single quotes, then the null character MUST be listed explicitly at the end. Note that C/C++ is consistent in enclosing a character in single quotation marks and a string in double quotation marks.

The third section shows an alternate way of declaring a string and initializing it at the same time. If the string is listed as a single group of characters surrounded by double quotation marks, the null character is automatically added at the end. Note that a space is a character and is counted in the length of the string.

The *strcmp(str1, str2)* is a string-handling function that compares two strings to see if they are the same or different. The function returns a zero if they are the same, a 1 if the first string is greater than the second one, and a −1 if the second string is greater than the first one. The ASCII value of each character (see Chapter 3) is compared. Therefore, all capital letters are less than all the lowercase letters. Therefore, the programmer must be sure that the case is the same for each string being compared.

The last section demonstrates an array of strings. In reality, this statement is declaring an array of 3 pointers, each pointing to a character at the beginning of a string. The actual two-dimensional array is shown in Fig. 6-16. The brackets indicate the array, and the asterisk indicates that the array is of pointers to characters. Each element in the array of strings can be printed individually using *cout*.

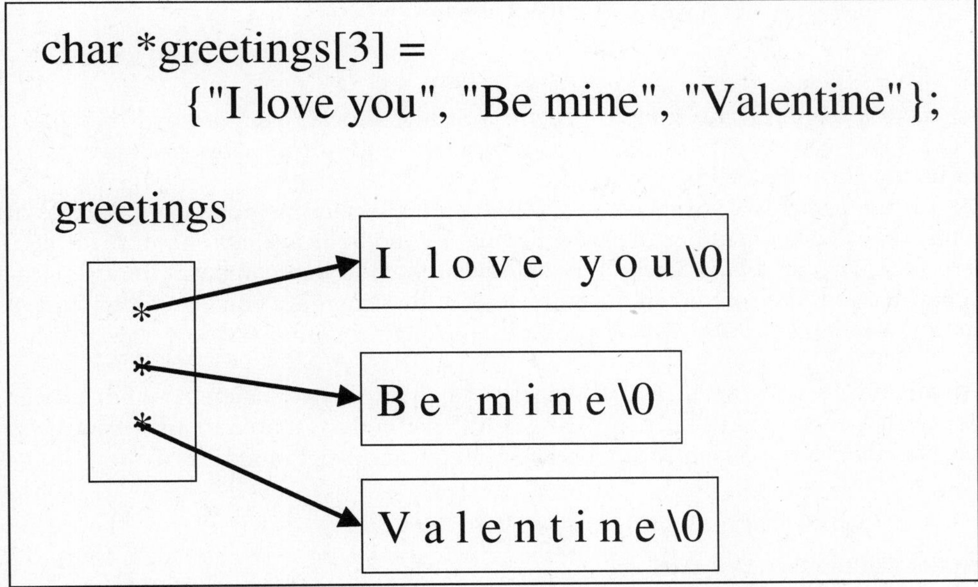

Fig. 6-16 Array of strings in C/C++.

6.3.6 String Processing in Java

String processing in Java is much different from C/C++. There is a built-in String class (see Chapter 8 for a complete explanation of classes) which behaves much like the String data type in Visual Basic. However, unlike C/C++, the programmer does not need to deal with the null character indicating the end of the string. Because this class is quite complex, only the most basic string processing will be explained in this section.

EXAMPLE 6.23 Figure 6-17 shows some Java code implementing strings. Each program section will be explained below.

```
//Section 1
String myStr="me";              //declare and allocate memory
System.out.println (myStr);
System.out.println (myStr.length());
//Section 2
String newStr;                  //declare
newStr=new String("you");       //allocate memory
System.out.println (newStr);
System.out.println (newStr.length());
if (myStr.equals(newStr)) System.out.println("The strings are identical");
else System.out.println("They are not the same");
//Section 3
String listOfNames[]=new String[3];    //declare array of Strings
listOfNames[0]=("Robert Redford");     //allocate memory
listOfNames[1]=("Willie Nelson");
listOfNames[2]=("Sophia Loren");
for (int i=0; i<3; i++)
  System.out.println(listOfNames[i]+" is "+ listOfNames[i].length()+" characters long");
```

Fig. 6-17 String example in Java.

The first section demonstrates how to declare a String, allocate memory and initialize it in one statement. The String can report its own length through the use of the *StringName.length()* method (Java's term for functions belonging to a class).

The next section declares a String in one line and then allocates memory and initializes the String in the next line. There are a number of String comparing methods available to each string. The one demonstrated here, *String1.equals(String2)*, is a Boolean method that compares the two strings using the ASCII chart to see if they are equal. It returns *true* if the strings are equal and *false* if they are not. Another method available, *String1.equalsIgnoreCase(String2)*, is often of more value than the pure equals().

The last section declares an array of Strings, and then allocates memory and initializes each element. Notice that each item in the array can use the methods available to any String. Many other methods are available to the String class. See Fig. 6-30 for another example.

6.3.7 Arrays as Parameters to Functions

An entire array can be sent to a function as a parameter in C, C++, and Java, just as in Visual Basic. Remember that the name of the array is just a pointer, or reference, to the first item in the array. Therefore, arrays are always sent by reference. Any changes made to the array in the function will be retained in the calling code.

EXAMPLE 6.24 Write a generic function to find the average of the numbers in an integer array. That function can receive an array of temperatures, an array of scores, or any other integer array, as long as the number of elements in the array is also sent.

Figure 6-18 illustrates this function.

```
//C, C++ and Java Functions are identical
float FindAvg(int arr[], int length)
{
    int sum=0, lcv;
    for(lcv=0; lcv<length; lcv++)
        sum=sum+arr[lcv];
    return (float)sum/length;      //returns value of function as float
}
//portion of C++ calling program
    const int MAX=6;
    int ar[MAX], i;
    for (i=0; i<MAX; i++)
        ar[i]=i+10;
    float avg=FindAvg(ar, MAX);
//portion of Java calling program
    final int MAX=6;               //difference in declaration of constant
    int ar[]=new int[MAX];         //difference in declaration of array
    int i;
    for (i=0; i<MAX; i++)
        ar[i]=i+10;
    float avg=FindAvg(ar,MAX);
```

Fig. 6-18 Arrays as parameters to functions.

The Java, C, and C++ function is the same, and the Java version of the calling program listed shows only minor differences from the C++ version. Notice that only the array name is included in the calling statement. The function heading contains the brackets to indicate that an array is an incoming parameter. Other parts of the code are self-explanatory.

6.4 SEARCHING

One of the main goals in programming is to save time and energy through the reuse of code. Several generic functions like searching and sorting arrays can be written in such a way that they are useful in many different applications. A number of different algorithms for sorting and searching arrays have been designed and can be implemented in any language. Two searching algorithms and three sorting algorithms will be illustrated here.

6.4.1 Sequential Search

The simplest algorithm for searching an array is the ***sequential search***. In the sequential search the array is examined, one element at a time, until the target value is found or the end of the array is reached without finding the target value. The sequential search is often the best choice in either of these two instances:

- The array size is small (less than 100 elements).
- The elements in the array are in no particular order.

EXAMPLE 6.25 Write a sequential search function in Visual Basic that takes in as parameters the array to be searched, its length, and the target value to search for. It returns the index number of the element holding the target value or -1 if the target is not in the array.

Figure 6-19 illustrates a possible implementation of this function.

```
'Sequential Search Function
 Private Function SequentialSearch(ar() As Integer, length As Integer, _
                                     target As Integer) As Integer
'This function searches 1 through length of the incoming array for the target value.
'It returns the index of the element holding that value.
'If the target is not in the array, the function returns -1
  Dim lcv As Integer, targetIndex As Integer
  Dim found As Boolean
  found=False                   'set initial flag to false
  targetIndex=-1                'default value in case target is not found
  For lcv=1 To length
    If ar(lcv)=target Then
       found=True               'set flag to true when found
       targetIndex=lcv
    End If
 Next lcv
 SequentialSearch=targetIndex 'send back the target Index or -1
End Function
'portion of calling program
 const MAX=10
 Dim lcv As Integer            'loop control variable
 Dim response As Integer, target As Integer
 Dim scores(1 To MAX) As Integer
'read in scores
For lcv=1 To MAX
  scores(lcv)=InputBox("Enter the number")
Next lcv
'get the target value
target=InputBox("What number will you search for?")
response=SequentialSearch(scores, MAX, target)
If (response>=0) Then
   Print target; "is in the array at location"; response
Else
   Print target; "is not in the array"
End If
```

Fig. 6-19 Sequential search in Visual Basic.

There are several reasons that this algorithm is not very efficient. First, if the array had more than 100 elements, the search process would take a lot of time. Second, the loop in the search function goes through the entire array every time, even if the item is found at the first index. Third, if the target is in the array more than once, the function will return only its last index.

EXAMPLE 6.26 A small modification of the loop in the function, shown in Fig. 6-20, enables it to stop as soon as the target value is found. Instead of a For ... Next loop which executes until the lcv reaches the length, a Do While loop is used which stops as soon as the item is found. In this example, if the target is in the array more than once, the function will return only the FIRST index. An alternate search function which returns the number of times the item is in the loop is shown in Solved Problem 6.10 at the end of this chapter.

```
'alternate form of loop for the sequential search function
Private Function SequentialSearch(ar() As Integer, length As Integer, _
                     target As Integer) As Integer
'This function searches 1 through length of the incoming array for the target value.
'It returns the index of the element holding that value.
'If the target is not in the array, the function returns -1
  Dim lcv As Integer, targetIndex As Integer
  Dim found As Boolean
  found=False                   'set initial flag to false
  targetIndex=-1
  lcv=1
  Do While (lcv<=length And (Not found))    'use do while to stop when item is found
    If ar(lcv)=target Then
      found=True
      targetIndex=lcv
    End If
    lcv=lcv+1
  Loop
  SequentialSearch=targetIndex 'send back the target Index or -1
End Function
```

Fig. 6-20 More efficient sequential search.

EXAMPLE 6.27 One more modification can be made to the sequential search of the previous example to increase efficiency if the target is not in the array.

If the incoming array is IN ASCENDING ORDER, as soon as an element is seen that is greater than the target, the array could stop. This requires that only one line be changed, the Do While statement:

```
Do While (lcv<=length And (Not found) AND ar(lcv) <target)
```

Figure 6-21 demonstrates the number of times the loop would execute for each of the sequential search algorithms for a target that is in the array and one that is not.

Version 1: For lcv = 1 To length

target = 4 -goes through loop 6 times
target = 5 -goes through loop 6 times

ar[0]	ar[1]	ar[2]	ar[3]	ar[4]	ar[5]
9	7	2	4	8	6

Version 2: Do While (lcv <= length And (Not found))

target = 4 -goes through loop 4 times
target = 5 -goes through loop 6 times

ar[0]	ar[1]	ar[2]	ar[3]	ar[4]	ar[5]
9	7	2	4	8	6

Version 3: Do While (lcv <= length And (Not found) AND ar(lcv) < target) with ORDERED array

target = 4 -goes through loop 2 times
target = 5 -goes through loop 3 times

ar[0]	ar[1]	ar[2]	ar[3]	ar[4]	ar[5]
2	4	6	7	8	9

Fig. 6-21 Comparison of sequential search test conditions.

6.4.2 Binary Search

The last modification is obviously the best possible improvement on a sequential search for an ordered array. However, even that algorithm would take a long time to search a large array, such as one with 10,000 elements. A better solution for finding a target value in an ordered array with no duplicates is to use the binary search algorithm.

In the ***binary search*** the middle element is examined first.

- If that element is the target being sought, then the middle index is returned.
- If the middle element is less than the target, then because the array is in order the entire first half of the list can be ignored.
- If the middle element is greater than the target, then the entire last half of the list is ignored.

The array sections are successively cut in half, eliminating large numbers of elements until the target is found or there is only one element in the section being examined. The binary search is usually the best choice if the array size is large. The elements in the array must be in order, so extra time would be needed if the array must be sorted first. Sorts will be examined in the next section.

EXAMPLE 6.28 Write the code necessary to implement the binary search function in C/C++. The function takes the same parameters as the sequential search: the array, the length of the array, and the target value.

Figure 6-22 illustrates this function. The Java version of this function would be identical except for the marked line.

Figure 6-23 shows a walk-through of the code for two different target values. If the array is small, not too much time is saved. If, however, the array had 1000 items, the first examination would eliminate half of the items, which would save a considerable amount of time. The binary search is a very fast search, but the array must be in order. If the array is not in order, it must be sorted before the binary search can be applied. If it cannot be sorted, then the sequential search is the only choice.

6.5 SORTING

Both the binary search and the most efficient of the sequential search algorithms require that the array be sorted in ascending order. Many applications also depend upon keeping various lists in numeric or alphabetical order. Many algorithms for sorting arrays have been designed, some of which are very complex. Three sorting algorithms will be explained in this section: bubble sort, selection sort, and insertion sort. These are often not the most efficient sorting algorithms, but are usually the easiest to understand and code.

6.5.1 Selection Sort

The concept of the selection sort algorithm is fairly simple. Successive passes are made through the array to find the largest element, and then put it in its proper place. The algorithm is:

(1) Pass 1: Examine the entire array and find the largest element.

(2) Place it in its proper spot at the end of the array.

(3) Pass 2: Examine the entire array except for the last element (already placed) and find the next largest element.

(4) Place the next largest in the spot second from the end.

(5) Continue the passes until there is only one element left. The last pass is not necessary because the last item left must be the smallest and already at the beginning of the array.

In each pass through the array all the elements are examined from the beginning until reaching the point where an element has already been placed in its proper spot.

```
//C/C++ version of Binary Search (with Java change)
int BinarySearch(int ar[], int length, int target)
//This function searches 0 through length-1 of the incoming array for the target value.
//It returns the index of the target value if is in the array
//If the target is not in the array, the function returns -1
{
    int mid, targetIndex=-1;
    int lowerBound=0;
    int upperBound=length-1;
    int found=false;  //the Java version would be boolean found=false;
    while (lowerBound<=upperBound && !found)
    {
        mid=(upperBound+lowerBound)/2;
        if (target<ar[mid])         //eliminate the upper half of this section
            upperBound=mid-1;
        else if (target>ar[mid])    //eliminate the lower half of this section
            lowerBound=mid+1;
        else                        //(target==ar[mid]) means it is found
        {
            targetIndex=mid;
            found=true;
        }
    }//end while
    return targetIndex;
}
//portion of C++ calling program:
    const int MAX=10;
    int ar[MAX], target, i, item;
    //get values
    cout<<"Enter "<<MAX<<" values separated by a space"<<endl;
    for (i=0; i<MAX; i++) cin>>ar[i];
    //get the target
    cout<<"What number should you search for in the array?";
    cin>>target;
    //perform the search
    item=BinarySearch(ar, MAX, target);
    if (item >=0) cout<<"The item is in location "<<item<<endl;
    else cout<<"The item is not in the array"<<endl;
```

Fig. 6-22 Binary search in C/C++.

EXAMPLE 6.29 Trace the algorithm and show how it would sort an array of characters {S, A, N, Z, B} and then write a Visual Basic subprogram that performs the selection sort on an array of strings.

Figure 6-24 illustrates the tracing of the selection sort algorithm. Figure 6-25 shows the Visual Basic code.

while (lowerBound <= upperBound && !found)

Trace through the code:

ar[0]	ar[1]	ar[2]	ar[3]	ar[4]	ar[5]
2	4	6	7	9	10

target = 4	**upper**	**lower**	**mid = (upper+lower)/2**
set values	5	0	2
examine ar[2] ---- 4 < 6			
eliminate upper half	1	0	0
examine ar[0] ---- 4 > 2			
eliminate lower half	1	1	1
examine ar[1] ---- 4==4		FOUND	

target = 8	**upper**	**lower**	**mid = (upper+lower)/2**
set values	5	0	2
examine ar[2] ---- 8 > 6			
eliminate lower half	5	3	4
examine ar[4] ---- 8 < 9			
eliminate upper half	3	3	3
examine ar[1] ---- 8 > 7	lower == upper so NOT FOUND		

Fig. 6-23 Tracing the binary search algorithm.

In the Visual Basic code, each pass through the array is performed by the outer loop which executes length−1 times. The inner loop examines each element in the array from the beginning to the limit of this particular pass to find the largest. After the inner loop stops, the largest element (maxIndex) is swapped with the item in the last spot of this pass (limit). In this particular algorithm, if maxIndex and limit are the same spot, it swaps them anyhow. This could be avoided by using an If statement to test whether the largest element is already in its proper spot:

```
If (maxIndex<>limit) Then
    temp=ar(limit)
    ar(limit)=ar(maxIndex)
    ar(maxIndex)=temp
End If
```

6.5.2 Bubble Sort

The algorithm for the bubble sort also makes use of successive passes through the array. However, instead of searching for one largest element, the bubble sort compares each successive pair of elements

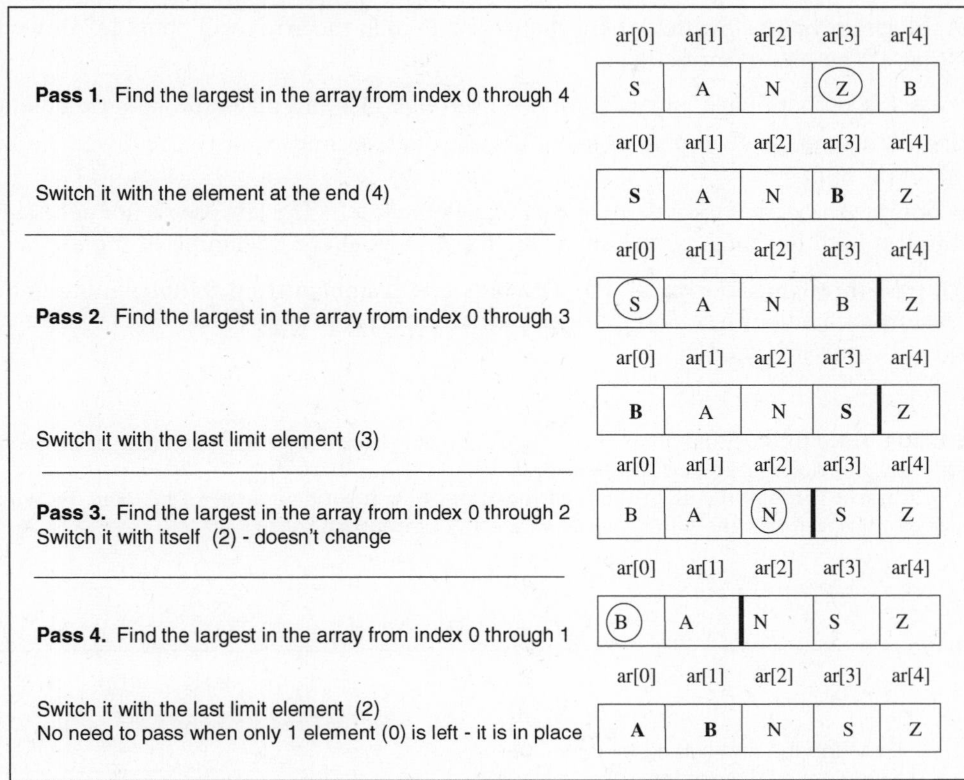

Fig. 6-24 Tracing the selection sort algorithm.

```
Sub SelectionSort(ByRef ar() As String, ByVal length As Integer)
'............................................................
'Takes in an array of integers and the length of the list
'Returns list sorted into ascending order
'............................................................
  Dim maxIndex As Integer          'Index of largest num in each pass
  Dim limit As Integer             '"limit" for each pass - last item not placed
  Dim i As Integer
  Dim temp As String
  For limit=length-1 To 1 Step-1 'begin each pass
    maxIndex=0
    For i=1 To limit               'in this pass, examine each element
      If ar(i)>ar(maxIndex) Then
        maxIndex=i                 'find the maximum
      End If
    Next i
    temp=ar(limit)                 'swap the largest with the current limit
    ar(limit)=ar(maxIndex)
    ar(maxIndex)=temp
  Next limit
 End Sub
```

Fig. 6-25 Visual Basic selection sort.

and places the larger one below the other. The largest item in the array will "bubble" down to the end on the first pass. The algorithm is:

(1) Pass 1: Compare each pair of items first through last and place the larger element second.
(2) Pass 2: Compare each pair of items first through second from last and put the larger item second.
(3) Continue the passes until there is only one element left. The last pass is not necessary because the last item left must be the smallest and already at the beginning of the array.

In each pass through the array all the elements are examined from the beginning until reaching the point where an element has already been placed in its proper spot.

EXAMPLE 6.30 Trace through the bubble sort algorithm and show how it sorts an array of integers {4, 8, 2, 0, 6}. Then write a C++ function to perform this sort.

Figure 6-26 traces through the algorithm and illustrates how it sorts an array of integers. Figure 6-27 shows a C++ function that performs the bubble sort on an array of integers.

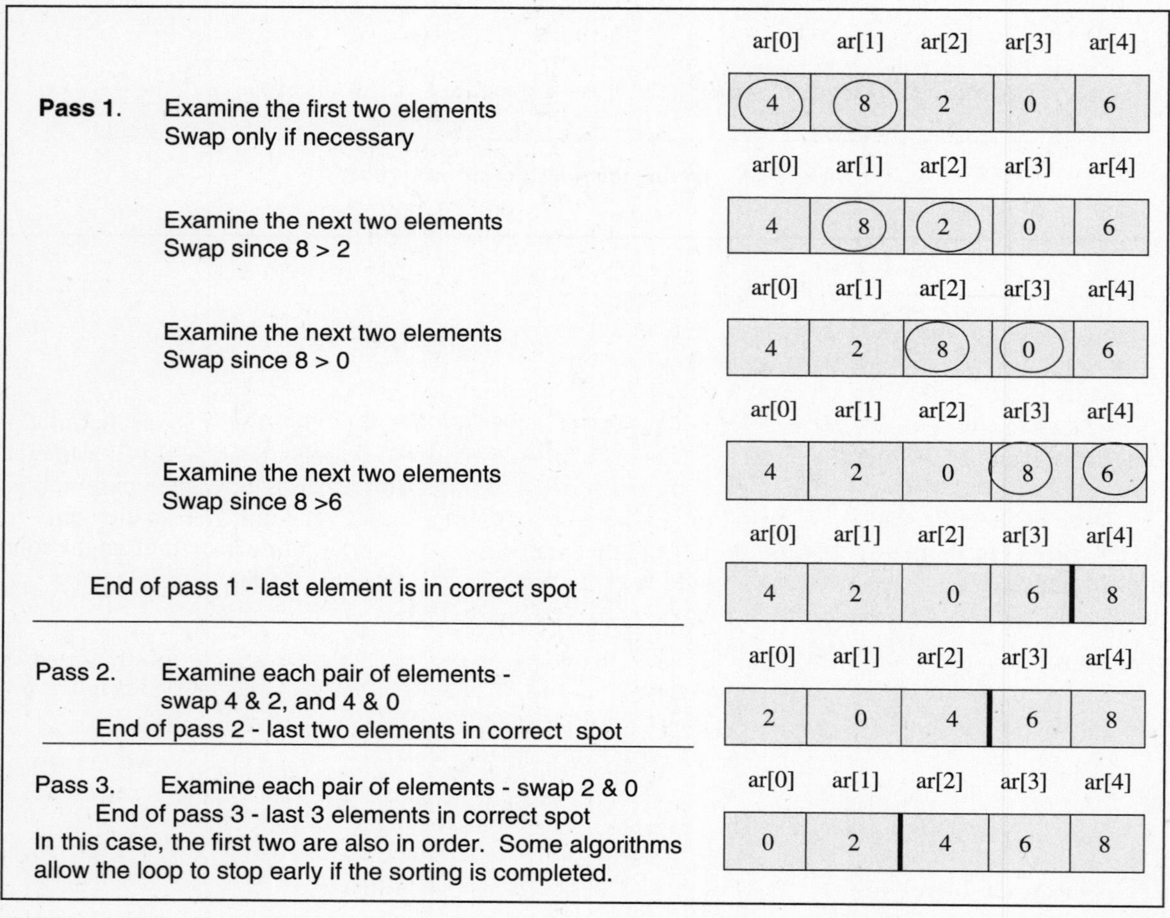

Fig. 6-26 Tracing the bubble sort algorithm.

```
// swap function can be used by several sorts
void Swap(int& num1,int& num2 )
  //.........................................
  //Takes in 2 numbers and swaps their contents
  //.........................................
{
  int temp=num1;
  num1=num2;
  num2=temp;
}
void BubbleSort( int ar[], int length )
  //.....................................................
  //Takes in an array of integers and the length of the list
  //Returns list sorted into ascending order
  //.....................................................
{
  int limit;                     //"limit" for each pass
  int i;
  limit=length-1;
  while (limit>0) {              //each pass through the array
    for (i=0; i<limit; i++)      // successive comparisons in this pass
      if (ar[i]>ar[i+1])
          Swap(ar[i], ar[i+1]);  // calls swap function above
      limit--;
  }
}
```

Fig. 6-27 C/C++ bubble sort.

Notice that the code above uses a more modular approach to sorting by using a separate function to perform the swap. This function can be called from any sort function. Since the incoming parameters are being switched, it is important that they come into the function as call by reference parameters.

In the C++ code, each pass examines all the pairs of elements up to the limit where elements are already placed in their correct spot, even if the items are already in order. For arrays that might come into the function already sorted, this would take an unnecessary amount of time.

EXAMPLE 6.31 It is possible to speed up the sorting, especially for lists that are already mostly sorted, by reducing the number of passes. If the array is sorted, then no swaps are necessary. The Java function in Fig. 6-28 demonstrates the more efficient version of the bubble sort.

In the Java code of Fig. 6-28, if the array is already in order, only one pass is made with no swaps and the loop ends. There is no way to make the selection sort this efficient, so if the array comes in mostly sorted, the bubble sort is more efficient.

6.5.3 Insertion Sort

The bubble sort can be coded to recognize an already sorted list and stop before executing all the length−1 passes. However, if even only a few elements are out of order, it could take several passes

```
void BubbleSort( int list[], int length )
  //..........................................................
  // Takes in an array of integers and the length of the list
  // Returns list sorted into ascending order
  //..........................................................
{
  int limit;              //"limit" for each pass
  int i;
  boolean swaps=true;     //boolean variable to see if there were swaps
  limit=length-1;
  while (limit>0 && swaps)
  {
    swaps=false;          //set initially to false
    for (i=0; i<limit; i++)
      if (list[i]>list[i+1])
      {
          int temp=list[i];
          list[i]=list[i+1];
          list[i+1]=temp;
          swaps=true;     //a swap occurred in this pass
      }
    limit--;              //if no swaps occurred, swaps is still false to stop loop
  }
}
```

Fig. 6-28 Java version of more efficient bubble sort.

and a large number of comparisons to perform the sort. The insertion sort algorithm takes greater advantage of the partial ordering of an array. The algorithm for the insertion sort is:

(1) Pass 1: Examine the first two elements and place them in the proper order with respect to each other.

(2) Pass 2: Starting at the third element, find its correct spot relative to the first two. If necessary, move the elements above down accordingly.

(3) Continue the passes starting with the next element, the limit element, until the last element is placed in its proper spot.

The bubble and selection sort place the largest items in their spots first. The insertion sort does not look for the largest elements. Instead, it moves the others down looking for the place to insert the next item until the correct spot is found. After EACH pass, all the elements that have been considered so far are in their proper order.

EXAMPLE 6.32 Trace through the insertion sort algorithm as it sorts an array of strings {"Tom", "Joe", "Sue", "Low", "Ann"}. Then write a Java function to implement the insertion sort.
Figure 6-29 traces through the algorithm and illustrates how it sorts the array of strings. Figure 6-30 shows a Java function that performs the insertion sort on an array of strings.

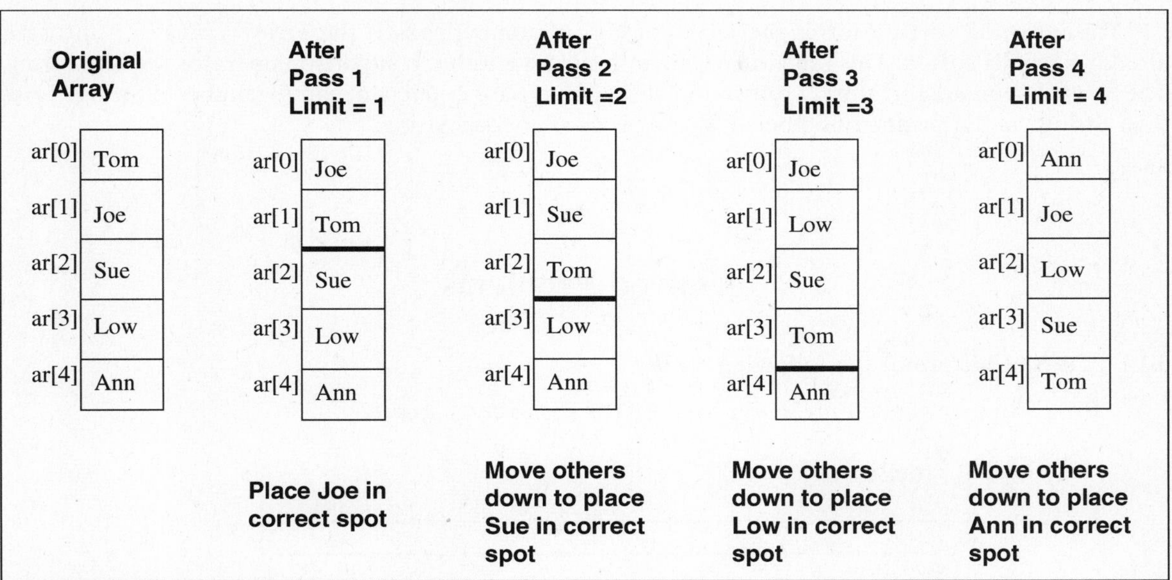

Fig. 6-29 Tracing the insertion sort algorithm.

```
void InsertionSort( String list[], int length )
  //.......................................................
  //Takes in an array of Strings and the length of the list
  //Returns list sorted into ascending order
  //.......................................................
{
  String itemToInsert;        //item to insert in each pass
  boolean stillLooking;       //Boolean variable to control loop
  int limit, j;
  for (limit=1; limit<length; limit++)
  {
        //walk backwards through the list looking for slot to insert list[i]
        itemToInsert=list[limit];
        j=limit-1;
        stillLooking=true;
        while (j>=0 && stillLooking)
        {
            if (itemToInsert.compareTo(list[j])<0) //<0 if 1st is greater than 2nd
            {
                list[j+1]=list[j];
                j--;
            }
            else stillLooking=false;
        }//end while
        list[j+1]=itemToInsert;
    }//end for
}
```

Fig. 6-30 Java insertion sort.

The insertion sort performs the least amount of comparisons if the array comes into the array already partially sorted. This function also demonstrates another comparison operator for Java Strings. The *String1.compareTo(String2)* returns a 0 if the strings are equal, a negative number if String1 is less than String2 and a positive number if String1 is greater than String2.

Solved Problems

6.1 Draw a picture of the following arrays:

(*a*) An array called *myScores* to keep track of 5 tests scores.

myScores

[0]	[1]	[2]	[3]	[4]

Arrays can be pictured either vertically or horizontally. In the computer the elements are consecutive memory locations.

(*b*) An array called *myClass* to keep track of 5 test scores for a class of 10 people.

myClass

	[0]	[1]	[2]	[3]	[4]
[0]					
[1]					
[2]					
[3]					
[4]					
[5]					
[6]					
[7]					
[8]					
[9]					

6.2 Given an array called *myArray* declared with 10 items, or boxes from [0] to [9], which of the following designations would be legal calls? Assume X = 5.

(*a*) `myArray[X]`

(*b*) `myArray[2*X]`

(*c*) `myArray[0]`

(*d*) `myArray[X-6]`

(*e*) `myArray[4*X]`

(*a*) Legal because there is a box 5.

(*b*) Illegal because there is no box 10.

(*c*) Legal because there is a box 0.

(*d*) Illegal because there is no box −1.

(*e*) Illegal because there is no box 20.

6.3 Draw a picture of an array called *deskItems* that contains a list of items usually found on a desk. The items are: paper clips, rubber bands, pens, and pencils.

deskItems

	[0]	[1]	[2]	[3]	4]	[5]	[6]	[7]	[8]	[9]	[10]	[11]	[12]
[0]	p	a	p	e	r		c	l	l	p	s	end string	
[1]	r	u	b	b	e	r		b	a	n	d	s	end string
[2]	p	e	n	s	end string								
[3]	p	e	n	c	l	l	s	end string					

Notice in this example that a space, as in row 0 column 5, is a character. Also, if some strings are short like "pens," and some are long like "rubber bands," the array must be large enough for the largest string even if memory locations are wasted following the shortest element.

6.4 Draw a picture of a three-dimensional array called *book* that contains 4 pages with 10 *lines* of 15 integers on each page.

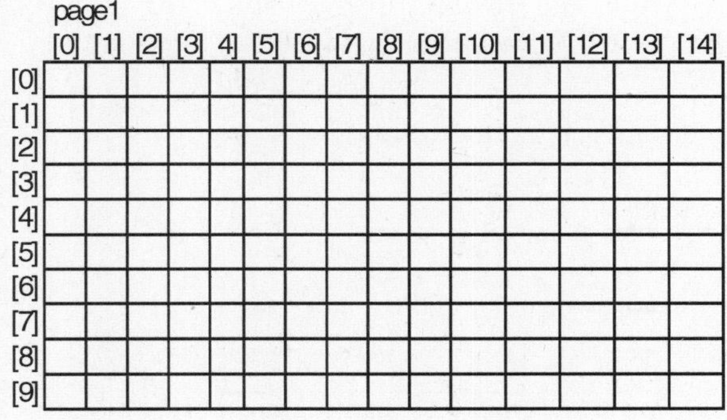

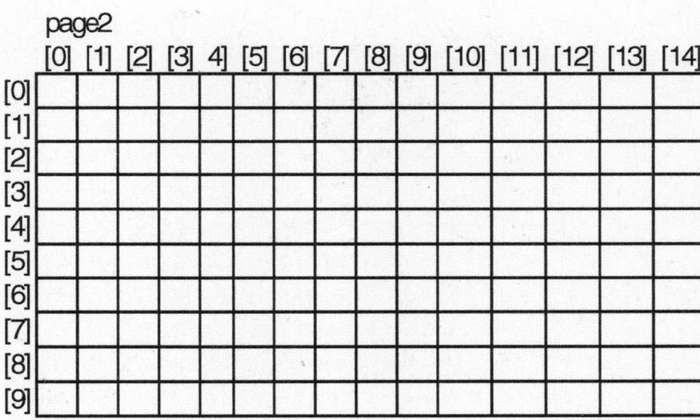

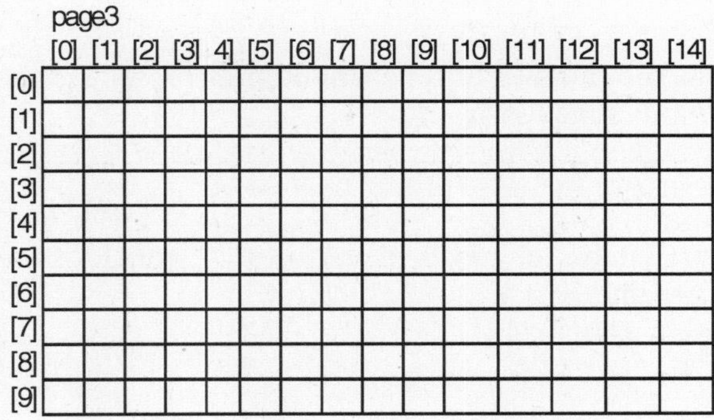

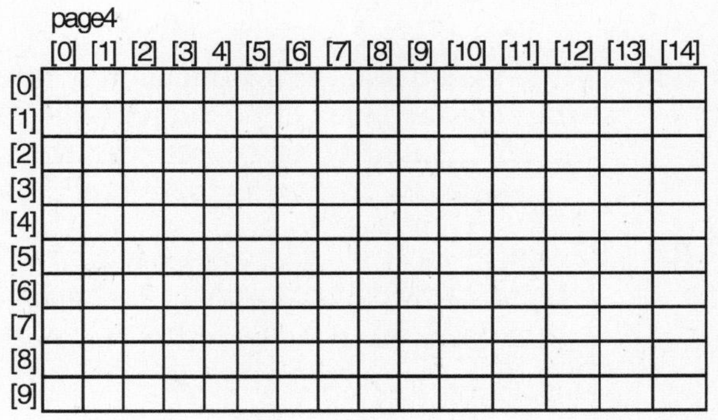

6.5 Write the Visual Basic, C/C++, and Java code to declare the three-dimensional array in the previous problem.

(*a*) VB: `Dim book (4, 10, 15) As Integer`

(*b*) C/C++: `int book[4][10][15];`

(*c*) Java:

```
int book [][][];
book=new int[4][10][15];
```

6.6 Write the Visual Basic declaration statements for both arrays in Solved Problem 6.1 above.

(*a*) `Dim myScores (5) As Integer` or `Dim myScores (0 to 4) As Integer`

(*b*) `Dim myClass (10, 5) As Integer` or `Dim myClass (0 to 9, 0 to 4) As Integer`

In Visual Basic, if the lower subscript is not given, it is assumed to be 0. The two Dim statements in each part produce identical results.

6.7 Write the C/C++ declaration statements for both arrays in Solved Problem 6.1 above.

(*a*)
```
int myScores [5];      //C/C++ uses the brackets instead of parentheses
```

(*b*)
```
int myClass [10][5];   //C/C++ defines the rows and columns in separate
                         brackets
```

6.8 Write the Java declaration statements for both arrays in Solved Problem 6.1 above.

(*a*)
```
int myScores [ ];             //declare the array
myScores=new int [5];         //allocate the memory space
```

(*b*)
```
int myClass [ ][ ];           //declare the array
myClass=new int [10][5];      //allocate the memory space
```

6.9 Write the Visual Basic, C/C++, and Java declaration statements for the string array in Solved Problem 6.3. For C++ and Java, assign the values when memory is allocated.

(*a*) VB: `Dim deskItems(1 To 4) As String`

(*b*) C/C++:
```
char *deskItems[4]={"paper clips", "rubber bands",
        "pens", "pencils"};
```

(*c*) Java:
```
String deskItems[]=new String[4];
    deskItems[0]="paper clips";
    deskItems[1]="rubber bands";
    deskItems[2]="pens";
    deskItems[3]="pencils";
```

Remember, in C and C++ there is no built-in String type in most compilers. The structure must be an array of pointers to strings.

6.10 Write a sequential search function that returns the number of times the item is present in the array, not the index of the target value. Write this function in C/C++.

```
int SequentialSearch(int ar[], int length, int target)
{
//This function searches 0 through length-1 of the incoming array for the target value.
//It returns the number of times the target value is in the array
//If the target is not in the array, the function returns 0
    int lcv, count=0;
    for (lcv=0; lcv<length; lcv++)
        if (ar[lcv]==target) count++;
    return count;
}
```

Notes:

- There is no reason to try to end the loop early, since the entire array must be searched to find the number of target elements present.
- Remember the comparison statement in C and C++ needs two equal signs, not one.
- The Java code is identical.

6.11 Write a Visual Basic function that receives a String array and its length as parameters, finds the largest element in the array and returns its index.

```
Function FindLast(list() As String, length As Integer) As Integer
  Dim i As Integer
  Dim maxIndex As Integer
  maxIndex=0
  For i=1 To length
    If list(i)>list(maxIndex) Then
      maxIndex=i
    End If
  Next i
  FindLast=maxIndex
End Function
```

Note: The largest element in the array of strings is usually the one falling the farthest to the end of the alphabet. Remember, however, that strings are compared using their ASCII values and all the lowercase letters come after the uppercase letters. All the strings should be in the same case for this code to work correctly.

6.12 Given an array in the order shown below, trace the selection sort algorithm and show what the array would look like after each successive pass.

Selection Sort

	ar[0]	ar[1]	ar[2]	ar[3]	ar[4]	ar[5]	ar[6]
Original Array	5	14	8	9	22	4	7
After Pass 1. Last 1 in its spot	5	14	8	9	7	4	22
After Pass 2. Last 2 in correct spots	5	4	8	9	7	14	22
After Pass 3. Last 3 in correct spots	5	4	8	7	9	14	22
After Pass 4. Last 4 in correct spots	5	4	7	8	9	14	22
After Pass 5. Last 5 in correct spots	5	4	7	8	9	14	22
After Pass 6. All correct	4	5	7	8	9	14	22

6.13 Given an array in the order shown below, trace the bubble sort algorithm and show what the array would look like after each successive pass.

Bubble Sort

	ar[0]	ar[1]	ar[2]	ar[3]	ar[4]	ar[5]	ar[6]
Original Array	5	14	8	9	22	4	7
After Pass 1. Last 1 in its spot	5	8	9	14	4	7	22
After Pass 2. Last 2 in correct spots	5	8	9	4	7	14	22
After Pass 3. Last 3 in correct spots	5	8	4	7	9	14	22
After Pass 4. Last 4 in correct spots	5	4	7	8	9	14	22
After Pass 5. Last 5 in correct spots	4	5	7	8	9	14	22
After Pass 6. All correct	4	5	7	8	9	14	22

6.14 Given an array in the order shown below, trace the insertion sort algorithm and show what the array would look like after each pass.

Insertion Sort

	ar[0]	ar[1]	ar[2]	ar[3]	ar[4]	ar[5]	ar[6]
Original Array	5	14	8	9	22	4	7
After Pass 1. First 2 in order	5	14	8	9	22	4	7
After Pass 2. First 3 in order	5	8	14	9	22	4	7
After Pass 3. First 4 in order	5	8	9	14	22	4	7
After Pass 4. First 5 in order	5	8	9	14	22	4	7
After Pass 5. First 6 in order	4	5	8	9	14	22	7
After Pass 6. All in order	4	5	7	8	9	14	22

Supplementary Problems

6.15 Draw a picture of an array called *cashOnHand* that will keep track of the amount of cash at the end of each month in the year.

6.16 Draw a picture of an array called *listOfNames* that will contain a list of people's names. The names are: W. C. Fields, Cary Grant, and Jane Fonda.

6.17 Write the Visual Basic declaration statements:

(*a*) For an array with subscripts from 1990 to 1999 that will contain the name of the Employee Of The Year for each year

(*b*) For an array to keep the sales data at the end of each quarter for 10 parts with part numbers starting at 1101. The parts are numbered consecutively.

6.18 Write the C/C++ and Java declaration statements for the array described in Supplementary Problem 6.15 above.

6.19 Write the C/C++ and Java declaration statements for the array described in Supplementary Problem 6.16 above.

6.20 Write the more efficient sequential search algorithm from Fig. 6-19 in Java.

6.21 Write a binary search function for a string array in Visual Basic.

6.22 Write a C/C++ function that receives an integer array and its length as parameters, finds the smallest element in the array and returns its index.

6.23 Given an array in this initial order, trace the selection sort algorithm and show what the array would look like after each successive pass.

ar[0]	ar[1]	ar[2]	ar[3]	ar[4]	ar[5]	ar[6]
cat	rat	dog	pig	cow	pup	bat

6.24 Using the array from Supplementary Problem 6.23 (in the same initial order), trace the bubble sort algorithm and show what the array would look like after each successive pass.

6.25 Using the array from Supplementary Problem 6.23 (in the same initial order), trace the insertion sort algorithm and show what the array would look like after each successive pass.

Answers to Supplementary Problems

6.15 Array:

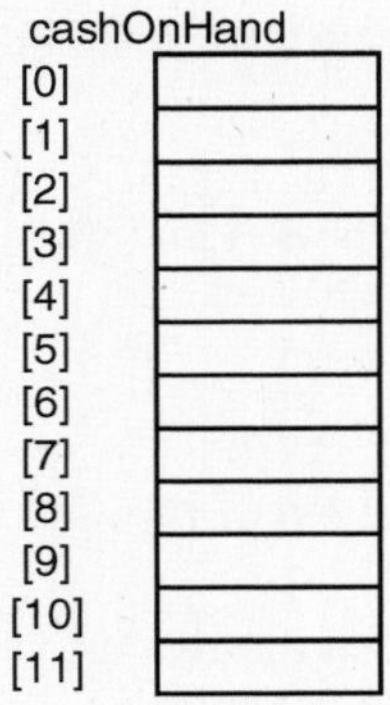

cashOnHand	
[0]	
[1]	
[2]	
[3]	
[4]	
[5]	
[6]	
[7]	
[8]	
[9]	
[10]	
[11]	

6.16 Array:

listOfNames

	[0]	[1]	[2]	[3]	4]	[5]	[6]	[7]	[8]	[9]	[10]	[11]	[12]
[0]	W	.		C	.		F	I	e	l	d	s	end string
[1]	C	a	r	y		G	r	a	n	t	end string		
[2]	J	a	n	e		F	o	n	d	a	end string		

6.17 (*a*) `Dim empOfYear (1990 to 1999) As String`

(*b*) `Dim partSales (1 to 4, 1101 to 1110) As Currency`

6.18 (*a*) C/C++: `int cashOnHand[12];`

(*b*) Java: `int cashOnHand[ ]=new int [12];`

6.19 (*a*) C/C++: `char *listOfNames[3] ={"W. C. Fields", "Cary Grant", "Jane Fonda"};`

(*b*) Java: `String listOfNames[]=new String[3];`

```
listOfNames[0]="W. C. Fields";
listOfNames[1]="Cary Grant";
listOfNames[2]="Jane Fonda";
```

6.20 The Java code for sequential search:

```
int SequentialSearch (int ar[], int length, int target)
{
//This function searches 0 through length-1 of the incoming array for the target value.
//It returns the index of the target value if it is in the array
//If the target is not in the array, the function returns -1
    int lcv, targetIndex=-1;
    boolean found=false; // boolean type is available in Java
    lcv=0;
    while (lcv<length && !found )
    {
        if (ar[lcv]==target)
        {
            found=true;
            targetIndex=lcv;
        }
        lcv++;
    }
    return targetIndex;
}
```

6.21 The Visual Basic code for binary search:

```
Function BinarySearch(ar() As String, length As Integer, _
                    target As String) As Integer
'This function searches 1 through length of the incoming array for the target value.
'It returns the index of the element holding that value.
'If the target is not in the array, the function returns -1
  Dim mid As Integer, lowerBound As Integer, upperBound As Integer
  Dim targetIndex As Integer
  Dim found As Boolean
  'set initial values
  targetIndex=-1
  found=False
  lowerBound=0
  upperBound=length-1
  Do While (lowerBound<=upperBound And Not found)
    mid=(upperBound+lowerBound) / 2
    If (target<ar(mid)) Then
      upperBound=mid-1 'eliminate the upper half of this section
    ElseIf (target>ar(mid)) Then
      lowerBound=mid+1 'eliminate the lower half of this section
    Else
      targetIndex=mid 'target is found
      found=True
    End If
  Loop
  BinarySearch=targetIndex
End Function
```

6.22 The C/C++ code for finding the minimum value in an integer array:

```
int FindMin(int ar[], int length)
{
//This function searches 0 through length-1 of the incoming array for the
//lowest value.
//It returns the index of the lowest value
    int lcv, lowest=0;
    for (lcv=1; lcv<length; lcv++)
        if (ar[lcv]<ar[lowest]) lowest=lcv;
    return lowest;
}
```

6.23 The selection sort trace:

Selection Sort

	ar[0]	ar[1]	ar[2]	ar[3]	ar[4]	ar[5]	ar[6]
Original Array	cat	rat	dog	pig	cow	pup	bat
After Pass 1. Last 1 in its spot	cat	bat	dog	pig	cow	pup	rat
After Pass 2. Last 2 in correct spots	cat	bat	dog	pig	cow	pup	rat
After Pass 3. Last 3 in correct spots	cat	bat	dog	cow	pig	pup	rat
After Pass 4. Last 4 in correct spots	cat	bat	cow	dog	pig	pup	rat
After Pass 5. Last 5 in correct spots	cat	bat	cow	dog	pig	pup	rat
After Pass 6. All correct	bat	cat	cow	dog	pig	pup	rat

6.24 The bubble sort trace:

Bubble Sort

	ar[0]	ar[1]	ar[2]	ar[3]	ar[4]	ar[5]	ar[6]
Original Array	cat	rat	dog	pig	cow	pup	bat
After Pass 1. Last 1 in its spot	cat	dog	pig	cow	pup	bat	rat
After Pass 2. Last 2 in correct spots	cat	dog	cow	pig	bat	pup	rat
After Pass 3. Last 3 in correct spots	cat	cow	dog	bat	pig	pup	rat
After Pass 4. Last 4 in correct spots	cat	cow	bat	dog	pig	pup	rat
After Pass 5. Last 5 in correct spots	cat	bat	cow	dog	pig	pup	rat
After Pass 6. All correct	bat	cat	cow	dog	pig	pup	rat

6.25 The insertion sort trace:

Insertion Sort

	ar[0]	ar[1]	ar[2]	ar[3]	ar[4]	ar[5]	ar[6]
Original Array	cat	rat	dog	pig	cow	pup	bat
After Pass 1. First 2 in order	cat	rat	dog	pig	cow	pup	bat
After Pass 2. First 3 in order	cat	dog	rat	pig	cow	pup	bat
After Pass 3. First 4 in order	cat	dog	pig	rat	cow	pup	bat
After Pass 4. First 5 in order	cat	cow	dog	pig	rat	pup	bat
After Pass 5. First 6 in order	cat	cow	dog	pig	pup	rat	bat
After Pass 6. All in order	bat	cat	cow	dog	pig	pup	rat

CHAPTER 7

Data Files

7.1 INTRODUCTION

The file system is an essential component of any computer. Most of the applications and their data reside in files stored in a hard disk, diskette, or some other appropriate storage medium. In computer terminology, anything that can be stored in a diskette or hard disk is a file. Files are given unique names and may contain data of any type. In general, files are named using the following convention:

[pathname]filename[.extension]

where the square brackets indicate that the filename may include an optional pathname, and an optional extension. For most personal computers, the **pathname** starts with a single drive letter and a directory. The drive letter, followed by a colon, indicates the disk drive where the file resides. Following the drive letter, pathnames may include a directory and some subdirectories that explicitly state the location of the file in the computer system. Directories start at the root directory and, depending on the system, each subdirectory may be separated from the previous one by either a backslash or frontslash. The **filename** is a sequence of characters consisting of letters, numbers, and some punctuation symbols such as a blank, hyphen, or an underscore. In some computer systems, the name given to a file cannot exceed more than eight characters. In some other systems, only letters and numbers can be part of a file name. File names should be chosen to indicate both the type of data contained in the file and the application for which it is being used. Following the filename there may be a **file extension**. This extension, separated from the file name by a period, is generally an optional three-character sequence used to describe the content of the file. This file name convention is sometimes referred to as the first name, middle name, and last name of the file. In this case, the first name is the file name, the middle initial is the period and the last name is the extension. Files names are unique within a particular folder or subdirectory. In other words, no system will allow two files with identical first name, middle initial, and last name in the same folder or subdirectory.

EXAMPLE 7.1 Identify the elements of the following filenames:

(*a*) C:\Acme Company\Data\Employee Reccord.dat

(*b*) D:\My Documents\tax records.dat

The components of file name described in (*a*) are:

C:\Acme Company\Data\ EmployeeRecord.dat

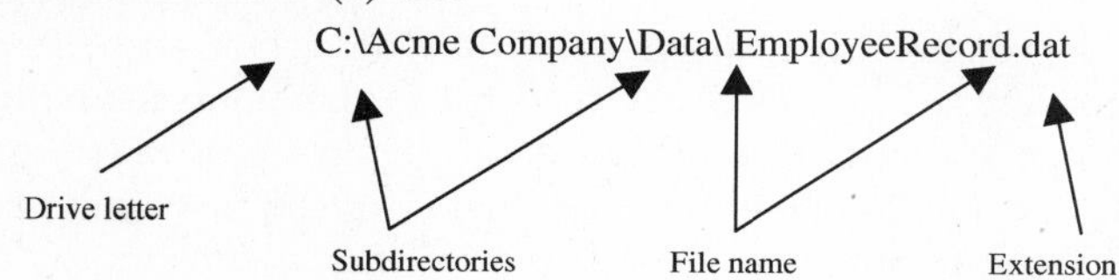

The elements of the file name described in (*b*) are:

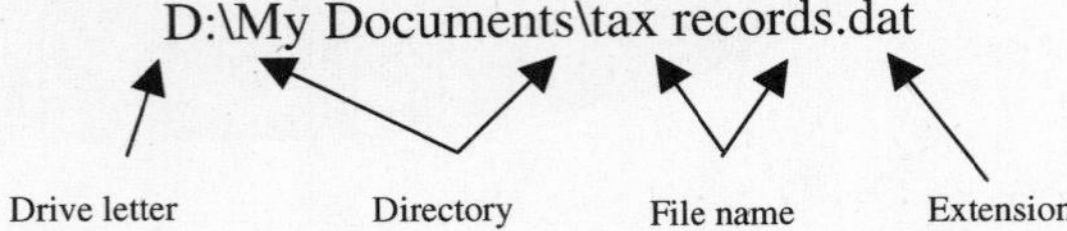

EXAMPLE 7.2 Determine whether or not the following sequences are valid file names:

(*a*) TaxDocuments.doc (*b*) AveryLongNameForADataFile.exe (*c*) ?>.doc

Names (*a*) and (*b*) are valid for most computer systems or applications. However, there may be applications where these names are illegal because they are longer than eight characters. Name (c) is illegal because it contains invalid characters such as the ? or the >.

Depending upon the convention being used, the extension of a file may determine its type. Example 7.3 clarifies this.

EXAMPLE 7.3 Classify the files shown below according to their extension.

(*a*) BirthDate.doc (*b*) List.txt (*c*) Employee.mdb (*d*) tax.dat

The extension .doc is generally used to identify **doc**uments created with word processors such as MS Word.

The extension .txt is generally used to identify files created with **text** editors such as MS NotePad. Files with a .txt extension are generally referred to as "plain text" or ASCII files.

The extension .mdb is generally used to identify **d**ata**b**ase files created using a database management system such as MS Access.

The extension .dat of problem (*d*) is generally used to store "**dat**a" of some sort.

Files do not need to have an extension; however, some applications require that a particular extension be used if we want to launch the application in some systems by double clicking on a file. For example, if we want to launch the MS C++ compiler automatically by double clicking on a source file, the file must have a .c or .cpp extension.

7.2 DATA TERMINOLOGY

Files are made up of **records**. Generally, there is one type of record per file. Records are made up of **fields**. For example, consider the file made up of employee records as shown in Table 7-1. There is one record per employee. Each row of this table constitutes a record.

Table 7-1

Id	Last Name	First Name	Department	Salary	Email
0155	Johnson	Michael	Accounting	45,000	johnmic@ccnet.com
0352	Heffner	Lois	Marketing	38,000	heffloi@ccnet.com
9461	Tsu	Tan	M.I.S.	35,000	tsutan@ccnet.com
9830	Hudson	Michael	Accounting	45,000	hudsmic@ccnet.com

The fields of these records are Id, Last Name, First Name, Department, Salary, and Email. All records share the same structure. That is, every record has the same fields and every field appears, within the record, in the same order. Records in data files are generally organized according to a particular field called the key. The **key field** serves a dual purpose. First, it is used uniquely to identify each record. Secondly, the key field is used to sort the records, according to their values in this field, in ascending or descending order. For instance, Id is the key field in Table 7-1. Notice that the records, in this case, are sorted on the Id field in ascending numerical order. A key field may be numerical or it may be a string of characters.

Files have special markers to indicate where they begin and where they end. These two markers are generally called **BOF** (**B**eginning **O**f **F**ile) and **EOF** (**E**nd **O**f **F**ile) respectively. When a file is empty, that is, when it does not have any records in it, both markers coincide.

The reader needs to be aware that not every programming language uses or even has the notion of a record. For instance, C++ does not impose any structure on files. Therefore, the notion of a "record" does not exist in C++. In C++, a file is nothing more than a sequence of bytes that ends in a special character called the **end-of-file** marker or after a specific number of bytes recorded in an administrative data structure.

7.3 FILE ORGANIZATION

This term refers to the way data are organized, stored, and retrieved. There are basically two types of file organization: **sequential** and **random**. A sequential organization indicates that the records are stored one after another in some sequence. When these records are retrieved or **read** they must be retrieved in the same order in which they were stored. This implies that in order to read the fifth record of a sequential file we must first retrieve the previous four records. In a random file we can read the records in any order. Although this offers more flexibility than a sequential organization, it requires that all records be of the same length. In a sequential file the individual records may be of different lengths.

7.4 TEXT AND BINARY FILES

In addition to their organization, files can be classified according to the way their constituent bytes are interpreted by the computer system. There are two basic modes: text and binary. In **text files**, each byte is interpreted as an ASCII character. In **binary files**, the bytes are not interpreted in any manner. In this case it is necessary to know beforehand the content of the file. That is, we must know what was stored in the file in the first place. Binary files cannot be read by word processors or text editors. Text files, on the contrary, can be read and created with any text editor. A text file can also be created with a word processor provided that the file is saved as "text" or ASCII.

7.5 OPENING AND CLOSING FILES

There is no standard way to operate on files across the different programming languages. In general, each language has its own peculiar way to handle files. Moreover, programming languages are not even required to provide any I/O mechanisms. For example, C does not have built-in capabilities for performing I/O. It is up to the manufacturers of the C compilers to provide all the necessary I/O capabilities. Recall from Chapter 3 that Java programs can be either applets for use on Web pages or stand-alone applications. For security reasons, Java applets cannot read from or write to local drives. Java applications, however, make extensive use of class objects for file input and output. Classes will be explained in Chapter 8, but the complexity of Java file input and output classes is beyond the scope of this book.

Regardless of the language, there are some "common file operations" that need to be performed when working with files. Before using a file, and depending on the language, it is necessary to associate with the file a unique numerical identifier or a pointer by which the file will be referred to later during the execution of the program. This unique identifier is sometimes called a "file handler." The association between a file and its handler usually occurs when the file is **opened**. This association ceases to exist when, at the end of the program, the file is **closed**.

7.5.1 Opening Files in Visual Basic

The format of the instruction that allows us to open a file in Visual Basic is as follows:

Open "filename" For {Input | Output | Append | Random} As "#filenumber" [Len = RecLength]

where filename must be enclosed in double quotes and may include the entire path to the file. The curly braces in the instruction indicate that we have to choose one and only one of the options enclosed by the braces; the vertical bars separate the different options from which we can choose. That is, we need to open the file *in one and only one* of the four **modes** as indicated in the instruction. Table 7-2 explains the purpose of the different modes. The filenumber can be any integer from 1 to 511. The Len = RecLength option applies to random files only. A record can be up to 32,767 characters long.

Table 7-2

Mode	Type of File	Action Required to
Input	Sequential	read records from a file.
Output	Sequential	write records to a file starting at the BOF. Previous data are overwritten.
Append	Sequential	write records to the end of the file (append).
Random	Random	read/write records in any order.

The filenumber is uniquely associated with a file as long as the file is opened. Once the file is closed, this number can be assigned to another file that needs to be opened.

EXAMPLE 7.4 Write the necessary Visual Basic instructions to open the file InFile.dat for input and the file OutFile.dat for output. Assume that both files are located in a subdirectory called C:\vb\project.

```
Open "C:\vb\project\InFile.dat" for Input as #1
Open "C:\vb\project\OutFile.dat" for Output as #2
```

The input and output file have been assigned the numbers #1 and #2 respectively; however, if both files need to be opened simultaneously in the same program, any two different integer numbers between 1 and 511 could have been assigned to these files.

7.5.1.1 The FreeFile Function

As previously indicated, to open a file a user can assign to the file any integer number between 1 and 511. This is an easy task when there are few files to manipulate; however, when there are a large number of files, it is better to use the FreeFile function to assign the next available number to a file. This way the user avoids the inconveniences of assigning the same number to more than one file at the same time. The use of the FreeFile function is illustrated in the next example.

EXAMPLE 7.5 Rewrite the instructions of the previous example using the FreeFile function.

```
Dim iInFile As Integer 'This variable is used to open the input file
Dim iOutFile As Integer 'This variable is used to open the output file
iInFile=FreeFile
Open "C:\vb\project\InFile.dat" for Input as #iInFile
iOutFile=FreeFile
Open "C:\vb\project\OutFile.dat" for Output as #iOutFile
```

The FreeFile function is called *before* each open instruction to obtain the next available number. In each case, the value returned by the FreeFile function is assigned to an integer variable that is then used in the open statement.

7.5.1.2 The Close Statement

When a program has finished processing a file, the file needs to be closed. There are two instructions that can be used to do this.

Close #filenumber closes the file to which it was assigned the integer filenumber. All other files, if any, remain opened.

Close closes all opened files. Notice that in this case we do not have to specify any file number.

7.5.1.3 Reading Data From Sequential Files

As indicated before, the data in any sequential file are read in the same order in which they were written. As Example 7.6 shows, when a sequential file is open, the user starts reading from the beginning of the file. The instruction that allows us to read records from a sequential file has the following format:

Input #Filenumber, field1, field2,.......,fieldn

where **Input** is a keyword that indicates that we are reading (inputting) data from a file which was opened in Input mode. Filenumber is the integer number assigned to the previously opened file from which we are reading.

When preparing a sequential file for input, character strings are enclosed in double quotes and separated by commas. Sequential files are usually created with an editor or with a word processor. However, when created with a word processor, sequential files need to be saved as text.

EXAMPLE 7.6 Assume that a sequential file (models.dat) contains the different car models that Silverado Motors has currently on stock. Write a Visual Basic procedure that reads this sequential file and displays its content in a listBox called lstModelsOnStock. Use the test file shown below.

Input Text file:

"Xavier LTD", "Cougar 100", "El Dorado Special", "Silver Bullet 2000",
"Bronco all terrain", "Ford Globe Trotter", "Audi 2000", "Chevrolet El Camino"

The code of the procedure may look like this:

```
Private Sub ReadModels()
 Dim stModels As String 'This variable is used to read the models in
 Dim iLoopIndex As Integer 'This variable is used as index of the for loop
 Open "C:\temp\Vbjunk\models.dat" For Input As #1
  For iLoopIndex=0 To 7
    Input #1, stModels
  DisplayForm.lstModelsOnStock.AddItem stModels, iLoopIndex
Next iLoopIndex
```

In this example, we have assumed that the listBox appears on a form called DisplayForm. Notice that the .AddItem method has been used to fill in the listBox. The variable iLoopIndex serves a dual purpose. First, it is used to control the execution of the loop. Secondly, since the loop index starts at zero it serves also as an index to the list. A list index in Visual Basic begins at zero. Since there are eight models in the input file, the iLoopIndex variable varies from 0 to 7. The general format of the instruction to fill the listBox is as follows:

```
Object.AddItem value [,index]
```

The square brackets indicate that we have the option of using an index.

The code of Example 7.6 assumes that there are exactly eight different models in the input file. Solved Problem 7.2 shows a more general method to read data from a file without requiring to know beforehand the number of records in the file.

7.5.1.4 Writing Data To a Sequential File

To write data to a sequential file use the **Write** instruction. The general format of this instruction is:

Write #Filenumber, field1, field2, field3, ...fieldn

where #Filenumber is a file already opened in Output or Append mode and field1, field2,. . .fieldn are the different fields that we want to write to that file. We refer collectively to all these fields as the "list of fields." When Visual Basic writes these fields to disk, it separates them with commas. String data are enclosed in double quotes and numerical data are written "as is." After writing the last element of the list, Visual Basic automatically inserts a carriage return and a line feed into the file.

Table 7-2 shows the two different modes that can be used to write records to a file: Output and Append. When **output** mode is used, the data are written to the file starting at the beginning of the file. This mode overwrites any data already on the file. When **append** mode is used, the data are added at the end of the file following the last piece of information previously written to the file.

7.5.1.5 The End Of File Function

In Example 7.6, to execute the program correctly we needed to know the exact number of elements that needed to be entered into the list. A more general approach to fill in the list is to read the different car models until we run out elements in the input file. In other words, we read the different car models until we reach the end of the file. The EOF function allows us to detect when we have reached the end of the file. The general format of the EOF function is as follows:

EOF (Filenumber)

where Filenumber is the integer associated with a previously opened file in input mode.

The function EOF() returns a True value when the end of file marker has been detected. This occurs after the last data in the file has been read in or as soon as we try to read from a file that is originally empty. Solved Problem 7.2 illustrates the use of the EOF function.

7.5.2 Files in C++

C++ views files as a stream of bytes. Although this view is shared by all the compiler manufacturers, as of the writing of this book there is not a definite standard on the specification of the I/O system. In this section, we will discuss the most commonly used I/O system. This system, called the C++ I/O stream, is based on three different classes: the **i**stream for input, the **o**stream for output and the **io**stream for input/output. These classes allow the user to define and manipulate files. The topic of classes will be addressed more formally in Chapter 8.

Whenever we start a C++ program, there are four different class variables that are created automatically. These classes are indicated in Table 7-3.

Table 7-3

Variable	Use
cin	Console **In**put/generally assigned to the keyboard
cout	Console **Out**put/generally assigned to the screen
cerr	Console **Error**/ generally assigned to the screen
clog	Console **Log**/ generally assigned to the screen

All these class variables are defined in the header file <iostream.h>. It is important to keep in mind that we need to select the appropriate version or mode of the stream class when doing disk I/O. The I/O stream classes, indicated in Table 7-4, are included in the header file <iostream.h>.

Table 7-4

Classes	Use
ifstream	**I**nput **F**ile **Stream**/represents a stream of characters coming from an input file
ofstream	**O**utput **F**ile **Stream**/represents a stream of characters going out to an output file
fstream	**F**ile **Stream**/ represent I/O streams from and to a file (random file)

7.5.2.1 Declaring File Streams

In C++, it is necessary to declare the stream variables before using them. The following example illustrates this. Always include the header *fstream.h* whenever you are doing disk I/O.

EXAMPLE 7.7 Write the C++ declarations for the files InputFile and OutputFile which, as their names indicate, will be used for inputting and outputting data respectively.

```
#include <fstream.h>   //this header needs to be included to do disk I/O
:
ifstream InFile;       //declaration of the input stream variable
ofstream OutFile;      // declaration of the output stream variable
```

This section of code declares two stream variables. One of them, InFile, will be associated with an input file. That is, a file from which we will be reading data. Likewise, the variable OutFile will be associated with an output file. That is, a file to which we will write or append some data.

7.5.2.2 Opening and Closing Files in C++

Opening a file in C++ serves a dual purpose. First, it associates a physical file with a stream variable defined in the program. Secondly, depending upon the mode of the file (input or output file), the reading marker is set to the beginning or to the end of the file.

EXAMPLE 7.8 Write the necessary instructions to open the files defined in the previous example.

Using the previous declaration, repeated here for the convenience of the reader, we have that there are two stream variables:

ifstream InFile;
ofstream OutFile;

To open these two files we can use the open function as shown below:

InFile.**open**("externalInputFile.dat");
OutFile.**open**("externalOutputFile.dat");

The file name that we pass as a parameter to the open function needs to be enclosed in double quotes. Notice that, even though we use the same open function, the first instruction is associated with the *ifstream* while the second is associated with the *ofstream*. Observe the use of the dot notation when calling the open function.

Both instructions set the corresponding file markers. For the input file, the reading marker is set to the beginning of the file provided that the file already exists. If the input file does not exist, an error will occur. If the output file already exists, the writing marker is set to the end of the file. If the file does not exist, the open function creates a new file and the writing marker is set to the beginning of the file. The string enclosed in quotation marks in the open instructions indicates the location and name of the file on disk. If that string does not include anything but the file name itself, the file is created in the current directory.

After processing the files, we need to close them. To do this we use the instructions

```
InFile.close();
OutFile.close();
```

The execution of these two instructions will free resources that can be used by some other programs.

7.5.2.3 Using Files in Input and Output Instructions

When working with files we can still use the same constructors that we used when working with cin and cout, as shown in the next example.

EXAMPLE 7.9 Use the file of the two previous examples to input the number of times a loop needs to be executed and output the different values of the index of the loop.

```
#include<iostream.h>
#include<fstream>
void main()
{ int i;
  int loopIndex;      /
  ifstream inFile ;   //declaration of the input file
  ofstream outFile;   //declaration of the output file
  inFile.open("c:/temp/data.dat");    //location of the input file
  outFile.open("c:/temp/data.out");   //location of the output file
  inFile>>i; //read the upper limit of the loop index
  for (loopIndex=1; loopIndex<=i; loopIndex++)
           outFile <<loopIndex<<endl;
  inFile.close();
  outFile.close();}
```

Observe that in the specification of the path for both the input and output files we have used the character "/" instead of the usual "\". If we do not this the compiler will generate a warning because, in the family of C-like languages, the character "\" is interpreted as the escape character.

7.5.3 Files in C

To reference a file in C, the user needs to declare a variable of type File. The general format for declaring variables of this type is

FILE * variable_name;

where FILE is a special type of data structure contained in the standard header file *stdio.h* that contains information about the current status of the file. Variable_name refers to the name of the pointer variable selected by the user.

EXAMPLE 7.10 Declare two file variables named InFile and OutFile.

According to format indicated above, these two variables can be declared as follows:

FILE * InFile;
FILE * OutFile;

This example assumes that *stdio.h* has been included at the beginning of the program.

7.5.3.1 Opening Files in C

In C, the open file instruction serves a dual purpose. First, it establishes a physical connection between the program and the data file. Secondly, it equates the external name of the file with the pointer variable declared in the program.

To open a file in C we use the function fopen(). This function takes, as indicated below, two arguments and returns a pointer to the file if the operation succeeded. If the file cannot be opened, fopen() returns a NULL. A filename may or may not include the entire path to the file.

fopen("filename","access mode");

The access mode indicates the type of operations that the user intends to perform on a file. Table 7-5 shows the complete set of options for accessing a file. In this book we will only consider the **r**, **w**, and **a** options.

EXAMPLE 7.11 Using the declarations of the previous example, open the file InFile for reading and open the file OutFile for writing. Assume that the locations and names of the input and output files are "C:/temp/inData.dat" and "C:/temp/OutData.dat" respectively.

We can open these two files as follows:

```
InFile=fopen("C:/temp/inData.dat","r");
OutFile=fopen("C:/temp/OutData.dat","w");
```

Table 7-5

Mode	Use
r	Opens the file for read operations only.
w	Opens the file for writing. If the file already exists, its contents are erased. Otherwise the file is created.
a	Opens the file for appending. If the file does not exist it is created.
r+	If the file already exists it opens it for both reading and writing. Otherwise, it returns an error.
w+	Creates a file and opens it for both reading and writing. If the file already exists, its contents are erased.
a+	Opens the file for reading and appending if the file already exists. Otherwise, it creates a new file.

7.5.3.2 Using Files in Input and Output Instructions

Once the files have been opened we can use the functions fscanf(), fgets(), or fgetc() to read from the file. Likewise, we can use the functions fprintf(), fputs(), or fputc() to write to the file. In the remainder of this chapter we will use the functions fscanf and fprintf to do I/O operations since they are more flexible than fgets, fgetc, fputs, or fputc. The general format of fscanf and fprintf is as follows:

fscanf(pointer_to_file,format_string, &arguments)

fprintf(pointer_to_file,format_string, arguments)

EXAMPLE 7.12 Assume that you have an input file that contains the data shown below. Write the necessary C instructions to read four records from the input file and write these records to another output file according to the given formats.

Input file (indata.dat)	Output File (outdata.dat)
Smith Joe	Joe Smith
Randall George	George Randall
Weaver Earl	Earl Weaver
Ford James	James Ford

In this program, we have assumed that both the first and last names are limited to a maximum of 20 characters each. We have also used the function fscanf() to read the strings from the input file and the function fprintf() to write the strings to the output file. Notice also that to specify the path of both the input and output files we have used the frontward slash "/" instead of the backward slash "\". In, addition, we have made provision to exit the program if there is an error when opening the file.

```
#include<stdio.h>
#include<stdlib.h>
#include<string.h>
void main()
{ int loopIndex;
char Fname[20], Lname[20]; //arrays to hold first and last names
FILE *inFile;
FILE *outFile;
outFile=fopen("c:/temp/outdata.out","w");//open file for output
/*open file for input. If there is an error, exit program*/
if ((inFile=fopen("c:/temp/indata.dat","r"))==NULL)
{ printf("\nFailed to open input file");
  exit (1); }
/*Read strings from the input file and write them to the output file*/
for(loopIndex=1; loopIndex<=4; loopIndex++)
{ fscanf(inFile,"%s %s",Fname,Lname);
  fprintf(outFile,"%s %s\n",Lname,Fname); }
} //end of program
```

Solved Problems

7.1 Write a Visual Basic procedure that saves in a file whatever the user types in a text box. The text is saved to the file when user presses the Enter key. Assume that all inputs are saved to a file located in the temp folder of the C drive. All messages are written using characters of the English alphabet. Assume also that the file is opened at the form load event. Show the code to open the output file.

We can use the KeyPress event of the text box to detect when the user has pressed the Enter key. The integer input parameter KeyAscii of the KeyPress event contains the ASCII value of the character representing the pressed key. The KeyPress event only takes effect (triggers) if the key pressed by the user represents an ASCII character. To know exactly when the user has pressed the Enter key we compare the value of the input parameter KeyAscii with the Visual Basic predefined constant vbKeyReturn. This constant represents the ASCII code for the Enter key. Assuming that the text box is called txtInputBox, the code for this procedure may look as shown below. The skeleton for this procedure is automatically created by Visual Basic simply by double clicking on the textbox.

```
Private Sub TxtInputBox_KeyPress(KeyAscii As Integer)
  If KeyAscii=vbKeyReturn Then
    Write #1, txtInputBox.Text
  End If
End Sub
```

It is fairly common for files to be opened at the form load event. The code to open the file is shown below. Notice that we have used the FileFree function to obtain the next available file number. Since the output file is opened in append mode the file retains its previous content.

```
Private Sub Form_Load()
  Dim iFileNumber As Integer
    iFileNumber=FreeFile
    Open "C:\temp\OutFile.txt" For Append As #1
End Sub
```

7.2 Generalize the code of the Visual Basic procedure shown in Example 7.6 to allow the procedure to read from the input file until all its content has been exhausted.

```
Private Sub ReadModels()
  Dim stModels As String 'This variable is used to read the models in
  Dim iFileNumber As Integer
  iFileNumber=FreeFile
  Open "C:\temp\Vb\Projects\models.dat" For Input As #iFileNumber
    Do Until EOF(iFileNumber)
      Input #1, stModels
     DisplayForm.lstModelsOnStock.AddItem stModels, iLoopIndex
  Loop
End Sub
```

To allow the procedure to read from the models.dat file until all its values have been exhausted, we will use the EOF function. This function returns a value of True when the end of file has been detected. This occurs right after the last record has been read. Since the condition of the Do Until is evaluated at the top of the loop, the instruction comprising the body of the loop is not executed after the last record is read. The code of Example 7.6 was also modified to illustrate the use of the variable iFileNumber when testing for the EOF condition.

7.3 Write a Visual Basic Procedure that reads string values from an input file called C:\notes.txt. Include in the procedure the necessary instructions to detect errors like "drive is not available" or "file does not exist."

In Visual Basic, to detect if an error has occurred when opening a file we can use the **On Error instruction**. Visual Basic provides an Err object that contains information about the current error. The number that identifies the error is saved in the Err.number property. To determine the type of run-time error that has occurred and to take the appropriate actions, we need to intercept or trap the error. To do this we need to:

(1) Enable the error-handling feature using the On Error instruction. This instruction specifies the line that will be executed if an error occurs. That is, the line that the program will "go to" if there is an error. The format of this instruction is

On Error Goto labeled_line

(2) Create a labeled line that marks the beginning of the error handler. A labeled line is a name followed by a colon. Nothing else should appear in this line.

(3) Write the error handler. That is, the code that will be executed if an error occurs.

(4) Determine if the program is to continue executing after the error. If so, determine how and where execution should start.

```
Private Sub Form_Load()
  Dim iFileNumber As Integer
  Dim stLine As String
  Dim ErrorMessage As String
  iFileNumber=FreeFile
  On Error GoTo HandleError 'This instruction corresponds to step 1 above
  Open "C:\temp\Notes.txt" For Input As #1
  Do Until (iFileNumber)
    Input #iFileNumber, stLine
  Loop
HandleError:                    'labeled line that corresponds to step 2 above
  Select Case Err.Number        'Here begins the error handler of step 3
  Case 53
    ErrorMessage="File does not exist"
  Case 68
    ErrorMessage="Drive is not available"
  Case 71
    ErrorMessage="Disk is not ready"
  End Select
  MsgBox ErrorMessage, vbInformation, "Missing File"
  Exit 'Instruction that indicates next action to follow after error has been detected.
    'It corresponds to step 4
End Sub
```

The Select statement shows the value of some of the predefined Visual Basic constants that we can use to introduce minimal error-handling capabilities into the program. The user should consult the appropriate manuals if other cases need to be considered.

7.4 Write the necessary Visual Basic instructions to read the fifth record from the random file C:\Data\employee.dat and increase the salary of the fifth employee by $100.00. Assume that each employee record has the following structure.

Last Name 15 characters

First Name 15 characters

Department 5 characters

Salary Number

Since all the records in a random file have the same length, it is necessary to set up the structure of the record using the **Type** and **Type End** statements. After the record structure has been set up, we can declare a record variable of that type.

The structure of the employee record indicated above can be defined as follows:

```
Private Type EmployeeRecord
  stLastName As String*15
  stFirstName As String*15
  stDepartment As String*5
  cSalary As Currency
End Type
Dim mEmployee As EmployeeRecord
```

The variable mEmployee has been declared to be of an EmployeeRecord type. The prefix letter m indicates that the variable is a **m**ember of the EmployeeRecord structure.

To specify that the string fields have a fixed length we have followed each string declaration with an asterisk and an integer number. This integer number indicates the maximum number of characters that the string can hold. Whenever the content of a field does not fill the entire string, Visual Basic adds extra blanks (pads the field) to make the content of the field fit the length of the string. If the number of characters assigned to a string variable is longer than the maximum number of characters that the variable can hold, Visual Basic will truncate (chop off) the extra characters.

To open the file we can use the same instruction that we used for opening sequential files except that now we also have to include the length of the records. The latter action is required for all random files. The instruction to open the file is

Open "C:\Data\employee.dat" For Random As #1 Len = Len(mEmployee)

where the right-hand side of the expression Len = Len(mEmployee) is a call to the Length function. This function returns the length (in bytes) of the record mEmployee.

To read the records from the random file we can use the **Get** instruction. The format of this instruction is

Get #Filenumber, [RecordNumber], RecordName

where the square brackets indicate that we have the option of specifying the number of the record that needs to be read. Records numbers start at record 1.

To write a record to the random file we use the **Put** instruction. The format of this instruction is

Put #Filenumber, [RecordNumber], RecordName

where the square brackets indicate that we have the option of specifying the number of the record that needs to be written. Records start at record 1.

We now have all the elements to read the record of the fifth employee and increase the salary by $100.00. The instructions to do this may look like this:

```
Get #iFileNumber, 5, mEmployee //read the fifth record
mEmployee.cSalary=mEmployee.cSalary+100.00 //increase salary
Put #iFileNumber,5,mEmployee //write fifth record back to file
```

Notice that to access the cSalary field we have to qualify the field by preceding it with the record name and a period. In this set of instructions, we have made the assumption that the file is not empty and that it has been opened successfully.

7.5 How can we determine the end of a random file in Visual Basic?

In a random file, we determine the end of the file indirectly through the use of the function **LOF** (**L**ength **Of** **F**ile). This function returns the length of the file in bytes. If we divide the value returned by LOF by the length of a single record, we can calculate the highest record number in the file. We can use this value and compare it with the number of the current record being processed to determine if we have already reached the last record of the file. The formula to calculate the highest record in a random file is

Number of records in file = LOF(Filenumber)/Len(variable)

7.6 Assume that a sequential file contains information about the different employees of a company. The order in which the information appears in the file (C:\Dta\emp.dat) and some sample data are shown below. Write a Visual Basic procedure that reads from this sequential file and separates the employees according to the department in which they work. Each department should have its own output file.

SSN	Name	Department	Salary
512-23-0987	Alice McPearson	Accounting	45000
345-90-1234	Andrew Antonelli	Marketing	32000
123-56-7898	Darlene Bartlow	Sales	30000
890-78-2345	Benjamin Nichols	Accounting	38000
340-34-1234	Mark Felton	Sales	35000

The input file can be prepared with any text editor. Each record in the input file (C:\Data\emp.dat) should have the following format:

"512-23-0987", "Alice McPearson", "Accounting", 45000.

A procedure to separate the employees into the different departments is shown below. This procedure uses four private variables, one for each of the fields that we want to read from the input sequential file. In addition, the procedure, in each of the write statements, makes use of a global variable that contains the integer number associated with a department output file. As the employees are read in, they are separated into their different departments through the use of a Select statement. The procedure to open the input and output files is also shown below.

```
Private Sub SeparateEmployeesIntoDepartments()
  Dim stSSN As String
  Dim stName As String
  Dim stDepartment As String
  Dim cSalary As Currency
  Do Until EOF(1)
    Input #1, stSSN, stName, stDepartment, cSalary
    Select Case stDepartment
     Case "Accounting"
      Write #iAccountingFile, stSSN, stName, cSalary
     Case "Marketing"
      Write #iMarketingFile, stSSN, stName, cSalary
     Case "Sales"
      Write #iSalesFile, stSSN, stName, cSalary
    End Select
  Loop
End Sub
  Private Sub OpenDataFiles()
    Open "C:\temp\emp.dat" For Input As #1
    iMarketingFile=FreeFile 'Get file number for the marketing file
    Open "C:\temp\mrktng.dat" For Output As #iMarketingFile
    iSalesFile=FreeFile 'Get file number for the sales file
  Open "C:\temp\sales.dat" For Output As #iSalesFile
  iAccountingFile=FreeFile 'Get number for the accounting department
  Open "C:\temp\acctng.dat" For Output As #iAccountingFile
End Sub
```

7.7 What does the Visual Basic procedure shown below do? Assume the existence of the following user-defined data type.

```
Type EmployeeRecord
  LastName as String * 20
  FirstName as String * 20
  Salary As Currency
End Type
  Private Sub GuessWhatIdo()
  Dim iFileNumber As Integer
  Dim Employee As EmployeeRecord
  iFileNumber=FreeFile
  Open "C:\temp\emp.dat" For Random As #iFileNumber Len=Len(Employee)
  Employee.LastName="Scott"
  Employee.FirstName="George"
  Employee.Salary=23000
  Put #iFileNumber, 10, Employee
End Sub
```

The code of this procedure writes to the random file C:\temp\emp.dat an employee record in the 10th position of the file. This new employee record is for George Scott who has a salary of 23,000.

7.8 Assume that there is a sequential file that contains character strings (one per line) that are preceded or followed by an unknown number of blanks. Write a Visual Basic program that eliminates these extra blanks surrounding each string and copies the resulting string to a new file.

The execution of this program is controlled by the procedure Main. Since there is no form associated with this program a Main procedure is mandatory. Automatically Visual Basic starts the execution of the program with this procedure.

Each of the procedures that comprise the program performs a single function.

The procedure ProcessFiles reads the input file, calls the procedure to eliminate the blanks and writes to the output file. In this procedure, we have used the function EOF to read the input file until all its content has been exhausted.

The procedure EliminateSurroundingBlanks makes use of the TRIM(string) function to get rid of the leading and trailing blanks of any string. The TRIM() function preserves any blanks embedded in the strings. Observe the use of the input parameter in the assignment statement where the TRIM() function is used. Since the parameter is passed by reference, any changes to this parameter are immediately reflected in the actual parameter.

The procedure CloseFiles does exactly what its name indicates: it closes the files. In this procedure, we have closed the files individually. However, we could have closed both files by means of the Close instruction.

```
Option Explicit
 Dim inFile As Integer
 Dim outFile As Integer
Private Sub EliminateSurroundingBlanks (stInString As String)
 stInString=Trim(stInString)
End Sub
```

```
Private Sub OpenFiles()
 inFile=FreeFile
  Open "C:\temp\blanks.dat" For Input As #inFile
 outFile=FreeFile
  Open "C:\temp\noblanks.dat" For Output As #outFile
End Sub

Public Sub Main()
 OpenFiles
 ProcessFiles
 CloseFiles
End Sub

Private Sub ProcessFiles()
 Dim stLine As String
 Do Until EOF(inFile)
  Input #inFile, stLine
  EliminateSurroundingBlanks (stLine)
  Write #outFile, stLine
 Loop
End Sub

Private Sub CloseFiles()
 Close #inFile
 Close #outFile
End Sub
```

7.9 Assume that a file contains a series of character strings. Each string can be up to 80 characters long. Each string is a sequence of digits and letters from the English alphabet. Each string occupies one line. Write a C++ program that reads the strings from the file "C:/temp/sequence.dat" and counts the number of letters and digits present in each string. Write the output of this program to the file "C:/temp/count.dat".

This program consists of four functions: main, openfiles, countcharacters and closefiles. The role of the main function is to call the other three functions in sequence. The function openfiles does exactly that. It opens the files for reading and writing. Likewise, the function closefiles closes all files that were opened in the program. The countcharacters function reads one line at a time from the input file and examines each character to see if it is a letter or a digit. The funcion isalpha() is used to determine if the current character is a letter or not. Likewise, the function isdigit() is used to determine if the current character is a digit. If the current character is a letter or a digit, the corresponding counters are incremented. After examining the characters of the input line, the program writes each line to the output file.

```
#include<iostream.h>
#include<fstream.h>
#include<stdlib.h>
#include<ctype.h>

void openfiles (void);      //function prototypes
void countcharacters(void);
void closefiles(void);

const int Line_Size=80;     //variables that define the input line
char InLine [Line_Size];
```

```
ifstream InFile;            //file variable declaration
ofstream OutFile;
void main()
{ openfiles();
  countcharacters();
  closefiles();
}
void openfiles(void)
{
  InFile.open ("c:\temp\sequence.dat");
  if (InFile.bad())
  { cerr<<"Error: Could not open input file\n";
    exit (8); }
  OutFile.open("c:\\temp\\count.dat");
 if (OutFile.bad())
  { cerr<<"Error: Could not open output file\n";
    exit (1); }
}
void countcharacters(void)
{ int i, digits, letters;
  while(!InFile.eof())
  { digits=0;
    letters=0;
    InFile.getline(InLine,sizeof(InLine),'\n');//read input line
    for(i=0; i<Line_Size; i++)
      { if (isalpha(InLine[i])) // Is character a letter?
              letters++;
        else
              if (isdigit(InLine[i])) //Is character a digit?
              digits++;
        }
      i=0;
      OutFile<<"Input Line:"; //write line to output file
      while(InLine[i]!='')
        { OutFile<<InLine[i];
          i++;
        }
      OutFile<<endl<<"Letters="<<letters;
      OutFile<<endl<<"Digits="<<digits<<endl;
      OutFile<<endl;
     }
      OutFile<<endl;
}
void closefiles(void)
{
 InFile.close();
 OutFile.close();
}
```

7.10 Write a C++ procedure that reads a student name and his class grades from the file C:\exams.dat. Write the student's name and his average to an output file C:\grades.dat. Use the input sample data and output guidelines indicated below.

Sample Input Data	Sample Output Data
Anita Jones 89 92 75 92	Anita Jones 87
Joseph Martin 82 89 93 91	Joseph Martin 88.75
Albert Smith 83 82 90 91	Albert Smith 86.5

The C++ program may look like the one shown below. There are three functions in addition to the main function. The openfiles and closefiles functions perform the tasks indicated by their names. The calculategrades() function reads the grades of each student and determines the corresponding average.

```
#include<fstream.h>
#include<stdlib.h>
void openfiles (void);
void calculate_grades(void);
const int totalexams=4;
float exams [totalexams];
char firstname[10];
char lastname[10];
ifstream InFile;
ofstream OutFile;
void main()
{
  openfiles();
  calculate_grades();
  closefiles(0;
}//end of main
void openfiles(void)
{
InFile.open ("c:\\temp\\exams.dat");
if (InFile.bad())
 {
 cerr<<"Error: Could not open input file\n";
 exit (8);
 }
 OutFile.open("c:\\temp\\grades.dat");
if (OutFile.bad())
  {
   cerr<<"Error: Could not open output file\n";
   exit (1);
  }
  }//end of openfiles
```

```
void calculate_grades(void)
{ int i;
  float average,sumofgrades;
  while(!InFile.eof())
  {
    InFile>>firstname>>lastname; //read student's first and last names
    sum=0;
    for(i=0; i<totalexams; i++)
    {
      InFile>>exams[i]; //read grades
      sumofgrades=sumofgrades+exams[i]; //keep running total
    }
      average=sumofgrades/totalexams; //calculate average
      OutFile<<firstname<<" "<<lastname << " "<<average<<endl;
  }
}//end of calculate_grades
void closefiles(void)
{
  InFile.close();
  OutFile.close();
}
```

7.11 Write a C++ program that reads a string of data from an input file and replaces every vowel in the string with some other characters according to the substitution rules indicated below.
Substitute:

a,A for ? e,E for * i,I for # o,O for % u, U for ^

The program to accomplish this task may look like the one shown below. The program, in addition to the main function, has three functions that perform specific tasks. The openfiles function does exactly what its name indicates. It opens the input and output files and notifies the user of any error that may occur while opening these files. Likewise, the closefiles function closes the input and output files. The Convertdata function reads a line and replaces each vowel in the line according to the given specifications. Notice the use of the switch–case construct to change each of the vowels. The clearline function is necessary to erase any leftover characters of any previously read line that happens to be longer than the current line.

```
#include<fstream.h>
#include<stdlib.h>
void openfiles (void); //function prototypes
void convertdata(void);
void clearline(void);
void closefiles(void);
const int maxlength=80; //This variable will hold the input lines read from the file
char line [maxlength];
ifstream InFile;        //file variable declaration
ofstream OutFile;
void main()
{
  openfiles();
  convertdata();
  closefiles();
} // end of main
```

```
void openfiles(void)
{
 InFile.open ("c:\\temp\\convdata.dat");
 if (InFile.bad())
 {
     cerr<<"Error: Could not open input file\n";
     exit (8);
 }
 OutFile.open("c:\\temp\\convout.dat");
 if (OutFile.bad())
 {
     cerr<<"Error: Could not open output file\n";
     exit (1);
 }
}//end of openfiles
void convertdata(void)
{ int i;
 while(!InFile.eof())
{
 InFile.getline(line,sizeof(line),'\n');
 OutFile<<"In: "<<line<<endl;
 OutFile<<"Out:";
 for(i=0; i<maxlength; i++) //Is character a vowel?, if so, change it
 {
     switch (line[i])
                 {
     case 'a':
     case 'A':
     line[i]='?';
     break;
     case 'e':
     case 'E':
     line[i]='*';
     break;
     case 'i':
     case 'I':
     line[i]='#';
     break;
     case 'o':
     case 'O':
     line[i]='%';
     break;
     case 'u':
     case 'U':
     line[i]='^';
     break;
             }// end switch
```

```
  OutFile<<line[i];
}//end for
OutFile<<endl;
      clearline();
    }//end of while
  }//end of convertdata
void clearline(void)
{ int i;
  for (i=0 ; i<maxlength; i++)//replace any existing character with a blank
    line[i]=' ';
}//end of clearline
void closefiles(void)
{
  InFile.close();
  outFile.close();
}//end of closefiles
```

7.12 Write a C++ program that reads a line from an input file and writes the line backward to an output file. Make sure that the input and its corresponding "backward" line are shown in the output file.

```
#include<fstream.h>
#include<stdlib.h>
void openfiles (void);
void printbackward(void);
void clearline(void);
void closefiles(void);
const int maxlength=80;
char line [maxlength];
ifstream InFile;
ofstream OutFile;
void main()
{ openfiles();
   clearline();
 printbackward();
}//end of main
void openfiles(void)
{
  InFile.open ("c:\\temp\\inline.dat");
  if (InFile.bad())
  {
      cerr<<"Error: Could not open input file\n";
      exit (8);
  }
```

```
  OutFile.open("c:\\temp\\outline.dat");
  if (OutFile.bad())
  {
     cerr<<"Error: Could not open output file\n";
     exit (1);
  }
}//end of openfiles
//This procedure starts copying from the last character in the input line and moves
//toward the front of the array.
void printbackward(void)
  { int i;
    while(!InFile.eof())
    {
      InFile.getline(line,sizeof(line),'\n');
      OutFile<<"In: "<<line<<endl;
      OutFile<<"Out:";
      for(i=maxlength-1; i >=0 ; i--)
      { OutFile<<line[i];
       }//end for
      OutFile<<endl;
      clearline();
    }// end of while
  }//end of printbackward
  void clearline(void) // replace existing characters with blanks
  { int i;
  for (i=0 ; i<maxlength; i++)
    line[i]=' ';
  }
  void closefiles()
  {
    InFile.close();
    OutFile.close();
}//end of closefiles
```

7.13 Write a C++ program that reads a string line from a file and determines if the input line is a palindrome. Assume that every string is a sequence of characters with no intervening blanks. Use the following sample data and make sure that the input characters are all of the same case. That is, all uppercase or all lowercase.

Sample Data

RADAR
AREPERA
11111111
11113333

The procedure palindrome locates the first nonblank character starting from the last character of the input line. The location of this nonblank character is then used as the starting-point for the comparison of the string characters. Notice that it is necessary to compare the characters in pairs. That is, we need to compare the first character of the string with the last; then the second character with the next to last and so on. This procedure is repeated until all the characters have been examined and all the pairs match or until there is a pair that does not match. The other procedures of this program are similar to the ones used in the previous solved problems.

```
#include<fstream.h>
#include<stdlib.h>
#include<ctype.h>
void openfiles (void);
void palindrome(void);
void clearline(void);
void closefiles(void);
const int maxlength=80;
char line [maxlength];
ifstream InFile;
ofstream OutFile;
void main()
{
  openfiles();
  clearline();
  palindrome();
}//end of main
void openfiles(void)
{
    InFile.open ("c:\\temp\\inline.dat");
  if (InFile.bad())
   {
        cerr<<"Error: Could not open input file\n";
        exit (8);
   }
  OutFile.open("c:\\temp\\outline.dat");
  if (OutFile.bad())
  {
        cerr<<"Error: Could not open output file\n";
        exit (1);
  }
}//end of openfiles
void palindrome(void)
{ int i,j,k;
  while(!InFile.eof())
  {
    InFile.getline(line,sizeof(line),'\n');
    OutFile<<"In: "<< line<<endl;
    /* find first nonblank character starting from the
      last character and moving to the first */
```

```
    for(i=maxlength-1; i<=0; i--)
          if (line[i] !=' ')
          {
          j=i;
          break;
       }
    k=0;//this variable is used to flag if the string is not a palindrome
    j--;//adjusting variable to position of last character of the string
//compare first and last character, then compare second and next to last until all
//characters match or there is a pair of characters that do not.
  for( i=0; i<j; i++)
  {
    if (line[i] !=line[j-i])//set the flag k if the pair does not match
      { k=1;
        break;
      }
    }//end for
  if (k==1)
    OutFile<<"The input line is not palindrome"<<endl;
  else
    OutFile<<"The input line is a palindrome"<<endl;
    clearline() ;
  }//end of while
}//end of printbackward
void clearline(void)
{ int i;
  for (i=0 ; i<maxlength; i++)
      line[i]=' ';
}
void closefiles()
{
  InFile.close();
  OutFile.close();
}
```

7.14 Is it necessary to verify that a file has been opened correctly before using it? Is there an easier way to verify that the file has been opened correctly?

It is always convenient to verify that a file has been opened successfully because, in general, the compilers of the C-like family may not report all errors in an accurate manner or may not report the error at all. If there is an error file, the program may not work at all and it may not be clear why the program failed. Another way to determine if a file has been opened successfully in C++ is through the use of the function assert(file variable). This function, which requires the inclusion of the header file <assert.h>, aborts the program in case of an error. Although this is not the most elegant way to terminate a program, it provides an easier mechanism to verify that a file has been opened correctly. If a file opens successfully, the file variable, such as InFile or OutFile, evaluates to a nonzero value, otherwise the function returns a zero. This can be illustrated using the open statement of Solved Problem 7.13. The code to open the InFile needs to be modified as follows:

```
<assert.h> //This header needs to be included at the top of the program
ifstream InFile("c:\\temp\\inline.dat");//
assert (InFile); // verify that the open file has not been opened correctly
⋮
ofstream OutFile ("c:\\temp\\outline.dat");
assert (OutFile);
```

If there is an error opening the input file InFile, the compiler will generate an error such as

Assertion failed: InFile, file D:\backward\backwards.cpp, line 04

Some compilers give us the option of aborting the process, ignoring the error or retrying the statement to open the program.

7.15 **Write a C++ procedure that reads an input file (C:\taxdata.dat) and displays its content "one screen at a time." Assume that there are 24 lines per screen.**

```
void WriteToScreen(void)
{
 int const screensize=24;
 char inputline[80];
 int linecounter=0;
 ifstream InFile ("C:\\temp\\taxdata.dat");
 assert(InFile);
while (! InFile.eof())
{
 InFile.getline(inputline,sizeof(inputline),'\n');
 cout<<inputline<<endl;
 if ((++linecounter % screensize)==0)
  {
    cout<<"--MORE--";
    cin.get();
  }
 }
InFile.close();
}//end of procedure WriteToScreen
```

7.16 **Write a C program that reads a file containing a list of items and their prices. There is one item per line and each item is followed by its price.**

To read from the input file, first, we need to declare a variable of type FILE as shown below. Once the file variable has been declared it is necessary to open the file. To do this we need to pass two parameters to the fopen function. The first parameter is the path and name of the file. The second parameter to the fopen function is the mode. Since we want to read a file we use the "r" mode. Following the fopen function the program tests that the file has been opened correctly. If the input file does not exist, the fopen function returns the NULL value. If an error occurs, the program displays an error message on the screen and the execution terminates. The program reads from the file until all its content has been exhausted. Notice how the program tests for the end of file (EOF) condition. To read each of the input lines the program uses the fscanf function. Notice that this function has three parameters: the filename, the descriptors (one per variable), and the variables that need to be read in. The %s descriptor reads strings separated by blanks, tabs, or new line characters. After the last line is read in, the program detects the EOF marker. The while condition fails after the EOF has been detected and no other line is read in from the input file. As the items and their prices are read in, the program displays them on the screen. To ensure that the items and the prices are nicely separated, the output has been formatted so that the items are left-justified in an output field 17 characters long. Prices are displayed with two decimals. After the file has been read, the program finishes by closing all files.

```
#include<stdio.h>
#include<stdlib.h>
void main()
{
  char item[15];
  float price;
  FILE *InFile; //variable file
  InFile=fopen("C:/temp/items.dat","r");
  if(InFile==NULL) //was the file opened successfully?
  {
      printf("\nCould not open input file\n");
      exit (1);
  }
  //read the file until its content is exhausted
  while(fscanf(InFile,"%s %f", item, &price)!=EOF)
    printf("%-17s %5.2f\n",item,price);
fclose(InFile);
}
```

7.17 Write a C program that prompts the user for a file name and then proceeds to open the file for writing. Exit the program if an error occurs while opening the file.

The code to implement this file may look like this:

```
  #include<stdio.h>
  #include<stdlib.h>
  void main()
  {
  char fileToOpen[1b5];
  FILE *OutFile; //file variable
  printf("Print the name of the file to open:"); //prompt user for file name
  scanf("%s", fileToOpen); //read name typed by user
  OutFile=fopen(fileToOpen,"w"); //file opened for writing
  if(OutFile==NULL) //was the file opened successfully?
  {
      printf("\nCould not open input file\n");
      exit (1);
  }
  fprintf(OutFile,"\nThe file was opened successfully");
  fclose(OutFile); //close file
}
```

7.18 **Write a C program that accepts input lines typed by the user and saves them to an output file. The program finishes when the user types N to the question "Do you want to continue?"**

The heart of the program is a continuous loop whose condition always evaluates to true. Within this loop, the user is prompted twice: the first time to enter an input line, the second time to check if he wants to continue inputting data. If the answer is no, the program finishes executing and notifies the user that it finished at his request. Notice that the responses of the user are converted to uppercase to account for the lower- or uppercase "n." This single-letter response is captured using the getchar() function. However, since this function only reads one character at a time, it is also necessary to capture the new line or "return" character generated when the user presses the Enter key after typing Y or N. This is the reason for calling the getchar() function again at the bottom of the while loop.

```
#include<stdio.h>
#include<stdlib.h>
void main()
{
  char Line[80]; //this variable holds the user input
   char answer; //this variable holds the answer typed by the user
   FILE *OutFile; // file variable

  OutFile=fopen("C:\\temp\\dataout","w"); // open file for output
   if( OutFile==NULL)
    {
      printf("\nCould not open output file\n");
      exit(1);
    }
  while ( 1==1 ) // Continuous loop. This condition always evaluates to true
    {
     printf("Enter input lines\n"); // prompt user
     gets(Line);
     fprintf(OutFile,"%s\n",Line);

     printf("Do you want to continue(y/n)? :"); //Continue executing the loop?
     answer=getchar(); // get single letter response
     if(toupper(answer) == 'N') // exit if user does not want to continue
     {
         printf("Program ended at user request\n");
         fclose(OutFile);
         exit(0);
     }
         answer=getchar(); // capture the new line (return) character
    }//end of while (1==1)
}//end of main
```

7.19 **Is there anything wrong with this program?**

```
#include<stdio.h>
void main()
{
  int * OutFile;
  int loopindex;
```

```
  OutFile=fopen("c:\dta.dat");
  if( OutFile=NULL)
  {
     printf("\nCould not open output file\n");
     exit(1);
  }
  fputs (outFile, "What is wrong with me?");
}
```

Yes! There is. The program is missing #include<stdio.h>. If we do not include this the program will generate an error like d:\Project\lines.cpp(17) : error C2065: 'exit' : undeclared identifier. In addition to this, the file variable OutFile has been declared as int instead of type FILE and the open function is missing the mode. The condition of the if statement is incorrect. Since we are making a comparison, we should have used == instead of =. In the puts statement the name of the file has been misspelled. Remember that C is case-sensitive and that outFile is not the same as OutFile. A more subtle error is that of not closing the file.

7.20 Write a utility that copies one file to another and returns the number of characters copied.

The code for this function may look like the one shown below. The function reads the source file, one character at a time, using the getc() function. The source file is copied to the destination file, one character at a time, using the putc() function. If the function finishes its work satisfactorily, it returns the number of characters copied from the source to the destination file. Otherwise, it returns a negative value.

```
long fileCopy (void)
{
   FILE *source;        /*source file pointer*/
   FILE *destination;   /*destination file pointer*/
   char nextchar;       /*next input character*/
   long charcount=-1L;  /*variable to count number of characters copied*/
   if ((source=fopen("c:\\project\\indata.dat","r"))==NULL)
    printf("Can't open source file for reading\n");
   else
   {
    if ((destination=fopen("c:\\project\\outdata.dat","w"))==NULL)
       printf("Can't open output file for writing\n");
    else
       {
        charcount=0L; //initialize counter
        while ((nextchar=getc(source)) !=EOF)
        {
          charcount++;
          putc(nextchar,destination); //copy characters to destination file
        }
        fclose(destination);
       }
        fclose(source);
     }
  return charcount;
}//end of function
```

7.21 Write a C program that prompts the user for two files, compares these two files and determines if their contents are identical.

```
#include<stdio.h>
#include<stdlib.h>
#include <string.h>
void CompareFiles(FILE*,FILE*);
const int MaxLength=80; // length of the input lines
void main()
{
  char firstfileToOpen[80];
  char secondfileToOpen[80];
  FILE *FirstFile; //file variables
  FILE *SecondFile;
  printf("Enter first file to compare:"); //prompt user for file name
  scanf("%s", firstfileToOpen); //read name typed by user
  printf("Enter second file to compare:"); //prompt user for file name
  scanf("%s", secondfileToOpen); //read name typed by user
  FirstFile=fopen(firstfileToOpen,"r"); //file opened for writing
  if(FirstFile==NULL) //was the file opened successfully?
  {
      printf("\nCould not open first file\n");
      exit (1);
  }
  SecondFile=fopen(secondfileToOpen,"r"); //file opened for writing
  if(SecondFile==NULL) //was the file opened successfully?
  {
      printf("\nCould not open first file\n");
      exit (1);
  }
  CompareFiles(FirstFile,SecondFile);
      fclose(FirstFile); //close files
      fclose(SecondFile);
  }
  void CompareFiles(FILE* file1, FILE* file2)
  {
      char line1 [MaxLength];
      char line2[MaxLength];
      char* ptrline1;
      char* ptrline2;
      ptrline1=fgets(line1,MaxLength,file1);
      ptrline2=fgets(line2,MaxLength,file2);
      if(feof(file1) !=0 || feof(file2) !=0)
      {
      printf("\nOne of the files is empty and cannot be compared\n");
      exit(0);
      }
```

```
else
{
    while (ptrline1 !=NULL && ptrline2 !=NULL)
    {
        if (strcmp(line1,line2) !=0)
        {
            printf("\nFound two different lines\n");
          exit(1);
        }
        if(feof(file1)==0)
          ptrline1=fgets(line1,MaxLength,file1);
        else break;
        if(feof(file2)==0)
          ptrline2=fgets(line2,MaxLength,file2);
        else break;
    }
    printf("\nFiles are identical\n");
    exit(0);
  }
}//end of function CompareFiles
```

Supplementary Problems

7.22 Assume that we have saved a Visual Basic program in the temp directory of the C drive. Is it appropriate to refer to this program as a file?

7.23 What would happen in Visual Basic if you try to write to a file that was opened for input? Can this error be trapped and handled by the user?

7.24 What would happen if a file that is meant to be opened as an input file is opened as an output file? Is it possible to recover from this error?

7.25 Modify the procedure of Solved Problem 7.6 to keep track of the annual salary paid to the employees of the different departments. In addition, write to a new file all the information present in the input file of any employee not working for the marketing, accounting, or sales department.

7.26 What type of file is it necessary to use to read or write ASCII text files in Visual Basic?

7.27 What does the following section of code do?

```
iFileNumber = FreeFile
Open "C:\Data.dat" for Input as #iFileNumber
txtInputBox.Text = Input (LOF(iFileNumber), iFileNumber)
```

7.28 What does the following section of code do? What happens if the file is currently empty?

```
iFileNumber = FreeFile
Open "C:\Data\Text.txt" for Append as #iFileNumber
Write #iFileNumber, txtInputBox.Text
```

7.29 Assume that we have a Random file and that we want to read the entire content of file. Can we use a For Next loop to read the entire file one record at a time?

7.30 Modify the program of Solved Problem 7.8 to eliminate the leading blanks of each input string. Leading blanks are the blanks that appear before the strings.

7.31 Modify the program of Solved Problem 7.10 so that, in addition to the average grade, the student also receives a letter grade. Use the following scale for assigning grades.

Grade	Letter Grade
90–100	A
80–89	B
70–79	C
60–69	D
0–59	F

7.32 Modify Solved Problem 7.9 so that it skips and does not print any input blank to the output file.

7.33 Modify the printbackward procedure of Solved Problem 7.12 so that there are no leading blanks in any of the lines of the output file. That is, do not print any trailing blanks of the input lines.

7.34 Modify the procedure palindrome of Solved Problem 7.13 to eliminate the restriction that all input characters need to be of the same case.

7.35 In C, to test if a file has been successfully opened, we have used instructions like the ones shown below. Can these instructions be combined within a single if statement?

```
inFile=fopen("C:\temp\fileToOpen.dat","r");
if (inFile==NULL)
{
  printf("\nProgram failed to open the input file");
  exit(1);
}
```

7.36 In Solved Problem 7.18, the user was prompted to check if he wanted to continue inputting lines to the output file. The answer typed by the user was converted to an uppercase to account for the possibility of the user typing "n" instead of "N". Can this possibility be accounted for without having to convert the user response to an uppercase? Can you modify the if statement to take care of the new line character?

Answers to Supplementary Problems

7.22 Yes, we can say that a saved program located in the hard disk is a file. A computer science purist may argue that a program is not the same as a file since the program is contained in the file. However, for all practical purposes, we can say: "That file is a C program." This is particularly true when looking at files with any file management tool.

7.23 Visual Basic will report a "bad file mode" run-time error. Yes! This error can be trapped and handled by the user. Its number is error 54.

7.24 The contents of the file are erased. No, it is not possible to recover from this error unless there is a copy of the file saved somewhere else.

7.25 Declare four additional global variables to keep track of the department salaries. Initialize these variables to zero and modify each of the different cases of the select statements to include an instruction like cAccoutingSalaries = cSalary + cAccoutingSalaries. In addition, add an Else condition to the Select statement to account for all employees who are not part of the accounting, sales, or marketing departments. Whenever this Else condition is satisfied, write to the new file.

7.26 Sequential files are used to read or write ASCII text files.

7.27 This instruction reads the entire content of the file into the textbox txtInputBox. The Input function takes two parameters: The first parameter, LOC(iFileNumber), indicates the number of bytes that need to be read from the file. The second parameter indicates the file number from which the values will be read. Since the function returns (in bytes) the total length of the file, all characters in the file will be read in.

7.28 This code appends the text property of a textbox called txtInputBox to the file C:\Data\Text.txt. If this file is currently empty, the text will be written at the start of the file. If the file is not empty, the text will be added to the end of the file.

7.29 Yes! We can use a For Next loop to read the entire file. Calculate the highest record number in the file (see Solved Problem 7.5) and use this value as the upper limit of the For Next loop. The starting value of the loop index should be 1.

7.30 Replace the Trim() function with the Ltrim() function. This function deletes any sequence of blanks to the left of the string.

For instance, C++ does not impose any structure on files. Therefore, the notion of a "record" does not exist in C++. In C++, a file is nothing more than a sequence of bytes that ends in a special character called the **end-of-file** marker or after a specific number of bytes recorded in an administrative data structure.

7.31 The modified procedure may look like this. We have added one character variable to hold the grade assigned to the student.

```
void calculate_grades(void)
{ int i;
  char lettergrade;
  float average,sum;
```

```
    while(!InFile.eof())
    {
     InFile>>firstname>>lastname;
     sum=0;
        for(i=0; i<totalexams; i++)
        {
         InFile>>exams[i];
         sum=sum+exams[i];
        }
        average=sum/totalexams;
        if (average>=90 && average<=100)
            lettergrade='A';
        if (average>=80 && average<=89)
            lettergrade='B';
        if (average>=70 && average<=79)
            lettergrade='C';
        if (average>=60 && average<=69)
            lettergrade='D';
        if (average>=0 && average<=59)
            lettergrade='F';
        OutFile<<firstname<<" "<<lastname <<" "<<average;
        OutFile<<" "<<lettergrade<<endl;
    }
}//end of calculategrades
```

7.32 Add a function that tests for blank lines. If there is a blank line do not do anything and continue reading the input file. The code for this new procedure may look like the one shown below. The code for the blankline function is not shown here.

```
void convertdata(void)
{ int i;
  while(!InFile.eof())
  {
    InFile.getline(line,sizeof(line)-1,'\n');
    if (blankline () == 0) //testing if there is a blank line
      {
        OutFile<<"In: "<<line<<endl;
        OutFile<<"Out:";
          for(i=0; i<maxlength; i++)
            {
              switch (line[i])
              {
                case 'a': //upper or lowercase a
                case 'A':
                line[i]='?';
                break;
                case 'e': //upper or lowercase e
                case 'E':
                line[i]='*';
```

```
                break;
                case 'i': //upper or lowercase i
                case 'I':
                line[i]='#';
                break;
                case 'o': //upper or lowercase o
                case 'O':
                line[i]='%';
                break;
                case 'u': //upper or lowercase u
                case 'U':
                line[i]='^';
                break;
            }// end switch
    OutFile<<line[i];
                }//end for
    OutFile<<endl;
      clearline();
      }//end of if
   }// end of while
} //end of convertdata
```

7.33 To avoid printing any trailing blank of the input line, examine the characters of the input line beginning at the last character of the line. If the character is a blank character, ignore it until a nonblank character is encountered. Keep track of the position of this nonblank character and use it as the initial value of the loop that writes the characters to the output file. A modified printbackward procedure may look like this:

```
void printbackward(void)
{ int i,j;
  while(!InFile.eof())
  { InFile.getline(line,sizeof(line),'\n');
    OutFile<<"In: "<<line<<endl;
    OutFile<<"Out:";
        for(i=maxlength-1; i>=0 ; i--)   //find first nonblank character
          {                              //starting from the last position
            if( line[i] != ' ' )
              { j=i;
                break;
              }
          }//end for
        for(i=j-1; i>=0 ; i --) // write characters to output file
          { OutFile<<line[i];
          }//end for
          OutFile<<endl;
          clearline();
      }//end of while
} //end of printbackward
```

7.34 Only one line of the procedure needs to be modified to eliminate the restriction that all input characters have to be of the same case. The trick here is to transform the input characters, within the program, to the same case before they get to be compared. That is, we can change the case of each pair of characters to all upper or lower *before* we get to compare them. In the following section of code we change all input characters to uppercase using the toupper(character) function. We could have also used the tolower(character) function. In both cases, make sure that the header <ctype.h> is included at the top of the program.

```
if (toupper(line[i]) != toupper(line[j - i])) //set the flag k if the pair does not match
{ k=1;
  break;
}
```

7.35 Both statements can be combined in a single if statement as follows:

```
if (( inFile=fopen("C:\temp\fileToOpen.dat","r"))==NULL)
  {
    printf("\nProgram failed to open the input file");
    exit(1);
  }
```

7.36 Yes! it is possible to account for upper- or lowercase "n" simply by changing the condition within the if statement. The code to accomplish this may look like that shown below. At the same time it is possible to account for the new line character using the getchar() function again and moving it to be the "body" of the else part of the if statement. Notice the use of the getchar() function to "consume" the new line character.

```
if(answer == 'N' || answer == 'n') // exit if user does not want to continue
  {
    printf("Program ended at user request\n");
    fclose(OutFile);
    exit(0);
  }
else
  getchar();
```

CHAPTER 8

Object-Oriented Programming

8.1 INTRODUCTION TO OBJECT-ORIENTED PROGRAMMING

The programming concepts throughout this book have all been based on traditional ***procedural programming***. That is, through the use of procedures and functions the program obtains its input, processes that input in a specific way, and then produces the required output. The order in which instructions are executed is predetermined by the programmer, so that you can easily identify which procedures or parts of procedures are performing each task.

There are at least three potential problems with procedural programming.

- It is up to the programmer to handle all possible input and output. In every program, the programmer must try to predict what mistakes a user might make and then write code to handle this input. Each type of output must be formatted carefully.
- Debugging can often be difficult. Making one change in any line can produce a series of errors elsewhere that must be hunted down and fixed.
- It may be difficult to reuse procedures in other code, since they were usually created and formatted for a specific program.

Over the last several years, computer scientists have been focusing their attention on ***object-oriented programming (OOP)***, or creating objects with attributes and behaviors instead of writing procedures. OOP is one way of addressing some of the problems of procedural programming. There are three main definitions needed to understand this kind of programming: objects, classes, and inheritance.

8.1.1 Object

An ***object*** is an abstract definition of something, identified by two subparts inextricably tied together. First, an object has attributes, sometimes called ***states*** or ***properties***, which describe the object. Second, an object has behaviors, sometimes called ***functions***, or ***methods***, which describe what the object can do. For example, a cat, a dog, a car, a couch, and a watermelon are all objects. Some possible attributes and behaviors for each object are listed in Table 8-1. The attributes all describe the object itself, and the behaviors describe what it can do.

Table 8-1 Attributes and Behaviors of Objects.

Object	Possible Attributes	Possible Behaviors
A cat	name, size, color, breed	eat, meow, sleep, catch mice, purr
A dog	name, size, color, breed	eat, bark, sleep, chase cars
A car	make, model, year, color, speed	accelerate, brake, honk
A couch	fabric, color, size, style	recline, open into a bed
A watermelon	color, size, number of seeds	grow, dry up, spoil

Objects defined in this abstract way are called ***abstract data types*** (ADTs). There are two things to notice about ADTs. First, the list of attributes and behaviors is not exhaustive. Only selected categories are included. Second, the attributes are general categories without values. For instance, the first row is not referring to a specific cat, but to any cat in general. Any cat might have a name and color and be able to eat and sleep. To describe a specific cat, one would have to fill in the values for each attribute and behavior. A specific cat might be a large white cat named Snowball, who meows softly and purrs loudly.

An ADT can be generally illustrated as in Fig. 8-1. There are two distinct kinds of behaviors:

- Actions of the object
- Setting or returning attributes

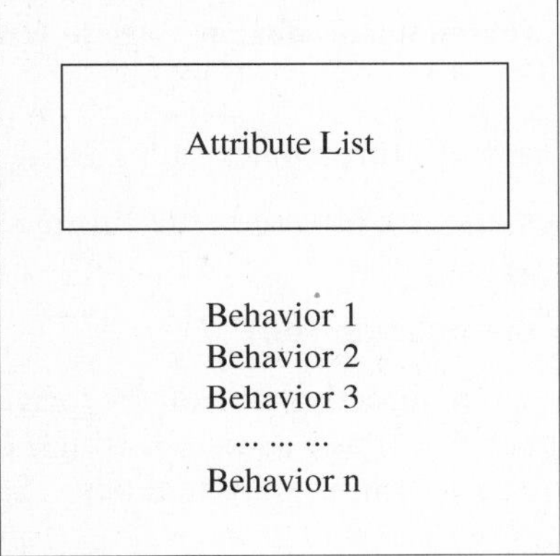

Fig. 8-1 Illustration of an object.

To protect the attributes, or variables, from corruption, such as receiving incorrect values, they are usually only accessible through the member functions. In addition to their regular actions, most classes have specific behaviors for setting and printing out the values of the member attributes. The complete collection of member functions is called the ***interface***.

Usually a program contains several objects. The heart of object-oriented programming is the fact that, in contrast to procedural programming, objects usually do not do anything without being asked. ***Messages***, or function calls, are sent from one object to another, invoking the member functions of the interface.

EXAMPLE 8.1 Draw a picture of a Thermostat object and a Furnace object. The Thermostat controls the Furnace.

Examine the objects in Fig. 8-2. A message comes to the Thermostat to check the current temperature. If the current setting is for heat, and the current temperature falls below the desired temperature, the Thermostat object sends a message to the Furnace object to turn on the heat.

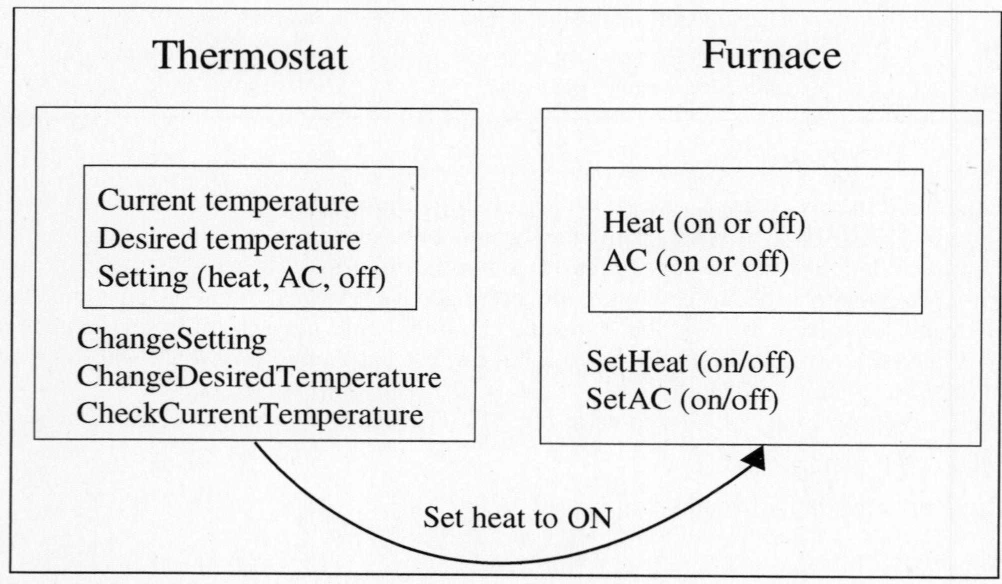

Fig. 8-2 Thermostat sending message to furnace.

As illustrated in this example, there are three parts to a message.

(1) The object to which the message is addressed (the Furnace)

(2) The function to execute (SetHeat)

(3) The parameters needed by the function (on)

Notice that the Thermostat does not directly control the private attributes of the Furnace. It merely sends a message for the Furnace to change its own settings. It is up to the Furnace to be sure that the heat and air conditioning are not operating simultaneously. See Solved Problem 8.11 for a Java implementation of these two classes.

8.1.2 Class

A ***class*** is a prototype definition of an object in a specific programming language. The class definition does not include all possible attributes and behaviors, only the ones that would be needed for the specific program. For example, a program may be comparing the speed of different makes of car objects. If the color is irrelevant, that attribute does not need to be included in the definition.

Once the class is defined, the programmer must ***instantiate*** it, or declare one specific instance of that class. This process corresponds to declaration of built-in variable types. For example, the ADT of integer is available to the programmer. An integer in general has unique attributes (e.g., whole value, no fractional part) and behaviors (e.g., integer division). However, an integer cannot be used until a memory location is set aside for it through a variable declaration. Only then can the location be given a value. In the same way the ADT of the class prototype is available, but cannot be used until it is instantiated and given values. Each object-oriented language handles this process differently, as shown later in this chapter.

8.2 INHERITANCE AND DATA ABSTRACTION

Classes that can be defined in terms of other classes are called ***subclasses***. The ***superclass*** is the defining class.

EXAMPLE 8.2 Define a *car* and a *truck* as subclasses of the parent or superclass *motor vehicle*.

In Fig. 8-3 inheritance occurs when the specific subclass of a more general superclass has access to variables and functions from the parent superclass. All motor vehicles have wheels and headlights. The car and the truck, and even a motorcycle, do not need to repeat these attributes in their individual definitions. They can inherit the attributes from the parent class.

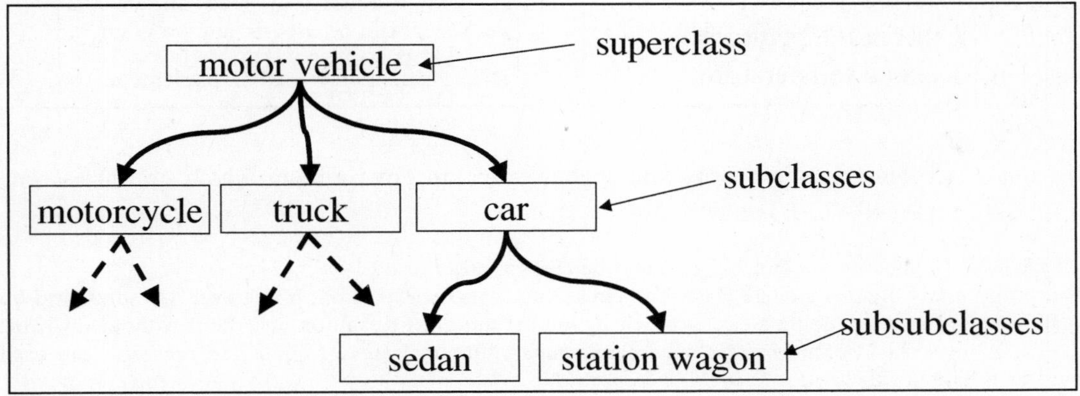

Fig. 8-3 Superclass and subclass.

In many languages a subclass can also be a superclass of another class. As shown above, *car* would be the superclass for the subclasses *sedan* and *station wagon*. All cars have four wheels, but only station wagons have a rear tailgate. Some languages also allow for a subclass to inherit attributes and methods from two different parents. Multiple inheritance is both complex and language specific, and thus will not be addressed in this book.

Superclasses are general, subclasses are more specific. The subclass inherits everything from its superclass, and does not need to redefine the same attributes. The subclass definition only contains what is unique to it.

Some programming languages allow for a superclass to be an abstract class with possibly undefined methods. Each subclass can define the method as needed. This is called ***polymorphism*** and is beyond the scope of this book.

One of the most important goals of object-oriented programming is ***data abstraction***, or keeping WHAT an object can do separate from HOW it does it. The interface of the class (the group of member functions) gives the other objects and programs information about what it can do, not how. The thermostat doesn't need to know how the furnace actually works, just how to turn it on. A list object might have a sorting function, but the program calling that function does not need to know whether it is a bubble sort or a selection sort.

8.3 ADVANTAGES OF OBJECT-ORIENTED PROGRAMMING

The advantages of object-oriented programming are easy to identify by going back to the problems of procedural programming explained at the beginning of this chapter. OOP provides a direct response to each problem. Table 8-2 describes the advantages of object-oriented programming over procedural programming.

Table 8-2 Advantages of OOP.

Procedural Programming	Object-Oriented Programming
The programmer must handle all possible input and output, writing code to handle all input and formatting all output.	The object is responsible for its own input and output, protecting the variables from invalid values and appropriately formatting all output.
Debugging can often be difficult, especially finding errors because of changes to code.	Debugging is much easier. Since the object is programmed to behave in a specific fashion, it is easy to pinpoint errors.
It is difficult to reuse procedures in other code, since they are usually program specific.	It is easy to reuse code. Once an object is defined, it can be used in any program.
Data abstraction is hard to implement.	Data abstraction is easy to implement.

In summary, object-oriented programming provides an environment which optimizes reuse of code, and allows for future changes.

EXAMPLE 8.3 Explain how a circle class could be created and reused.

The programmer creates a circle class. The circle knows its own location, how to set its radius, and how to draw itself. Any program needing a circle can easily import this class definition and use it without rewriting any other code. Also, a class definition of a superclass *shape* with subclasses of *circle* and *rectangle* can easily be extended by adding a subclass for *triangle* or *trapezoid*.

The next three sections will describe some of the object-oriented features and the use of classes in Visual Basic, C++, and Java. C is an older language that has no object-oriented features, so it will not be addressed.

8.4 OBJECT-ORIENTED ENVIRONMENT IN VISUAL BASIC

Even though Visual Basic is not a true object-oriented programming language, the programmer is working in an object-oriented environment. Microsoft calls Visual Basic an ***event-driven*** programming language. In event-driven programming, the user determines the sequence of instructions to be executed, not the programmer. The program screen is built using various buttons and boxes and the user creates *events* by pressing keys or moving the mouse. The program is not a precise sequence of instructions to be executed, but a collection of procedures that contain the code needed to respond to events.

EXAMPLE 8.4 A program screen in Visual Basic might look like the one shown in Fig. 8-4. Explain some of its event-driven features.

The user enters numbers into the boxes and clicks on the command button called *Add*. The program then executes the code that was written to handle the adding process. Code is generally written for all the buttons to handle any possible choice the user might make, but no code is actually executed until the user triggers the event by clicking the button.

In Visual Basic, the program window, or ***form***, and all the items placed inside it, are objects. As in OOP, each object has behaviors and attributes. The behaviors, called ***Subs*** in Visual Basic, are the code segments written to handle a variety of events. The attributes, called ***properties***, can be set by the programmer during the design phase of programming, or may be set by code.

In Fig. 8-4, the form contains ten objects: four command buttons, three text boxes, and three labels. Text boxes are used for user input/output, and labels for explanation purposes. Command buttons can contain code to respond to events such as a mouse click, a double click, or a mouseover. All these

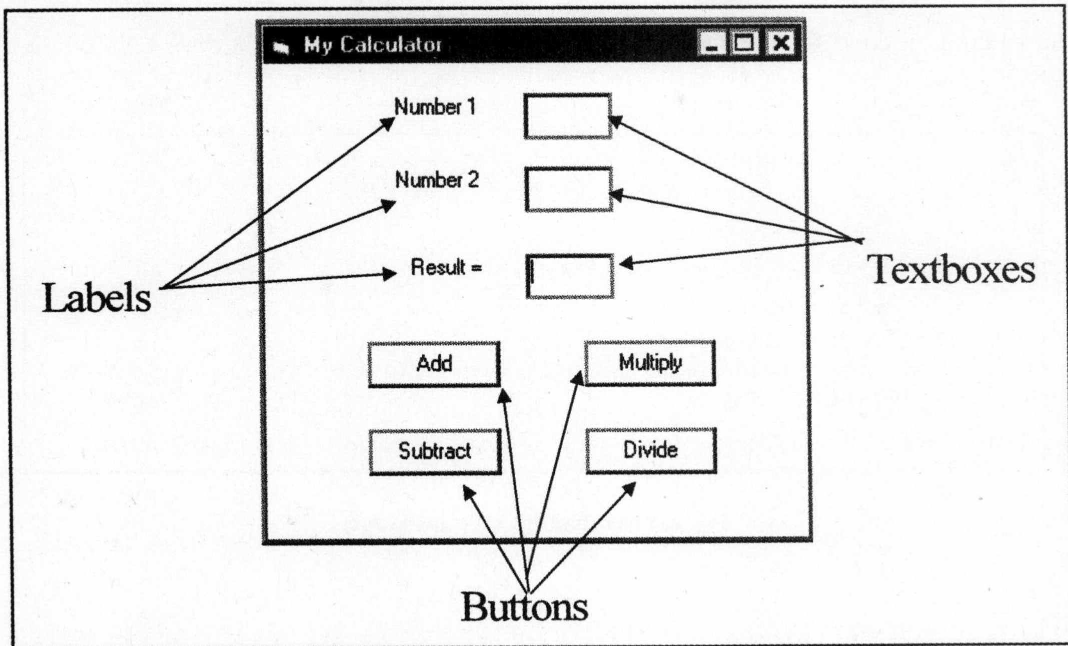

Fig. 8-4 Visual Basic calculator example.

objects have properties such as name, color, and size. Forms, labels, and buttons have captions, and textboxes of course have text. Many other control objects are also available.

In the Visual Basic environment, the programmer manipulates built-in screen objects, setting their properties and programming their behaviors. In C++ and in Java, the programmer has the ability to create classes and subclasses, to specify which attributes and behaviors will be used, and to define inheritance precisely.

8.5 CLASSES AND INHERITANCE IN C++

Classes do not exist in C. The addition of objects was one of the reasons for developing the C++ language. The C++ terminology for object-oriented programming concepts is shown in Table 8-3.

Table 8-3 Terminology for OOP in C++.

OOP	C++
Object	Class instance or class object
Instance variable or attribute	Private data member
Method	Public member function
Message passing	Function calls to public member functions

C++ is a mixture of procedural and object-oriented programming. Classes are defined and implemented. However, there must also be a *main()* procedure to start the program and initiate the function calls.

In C++, the definition of the class includes the definitions for both the member variables (attributes) and the member functions (behaviors). To provide for as much data abstraction as possible, the declaration of the class is in a different section, or even a different file, from the implementation, or code, for the member functions. The general format of a class definition is shown in Fig. 8-5.

```
//class definition (located in classname.h file)
class classname
{
   member variables list
   member function list (usually prototypes, or headings only)
}; //notice semicolon after closing brace
-----------------------------------------------------------------
//class implementation (located in classname.cpp file)
complete code for each function
```

Fig. 8-5 Format for class definition.

8.5.1 Class Header File (.h)

The code where the class object is defined is usually contained within a file with the extension **.h**, which stands for header.

EXAMPLE 8.5 Write C++ definition of a class *Light*. The light may be on or off. A program must be able to print out the current status of the light and to flip the light switch.

For a specific example of this C++ class, look at Fig. 8-6.

```
//class definition (Light.h file)
class Light
{
   private:
      int status;             //Light is on(1) or off(0)
   public:
      Light();                //default constructor
      Light(int statusIn);    //constructor to specific status
      int flipSwitch();       //change the status
      void printStatus();     //print the current status
};
```

Fig. 8-6 Light.h.

The header file, or file ending in **.h**, provides the interface for how this class will interact with the outside world. The access specifiers ***public*** and ***private*** determine specific access rights. Variables or functions defined as public can be accessed from anywhere, and those defined private are accessible only within the class itself. For security purposes, usually the variables are private, protected from change by any other section of code except by member functions. The functions are usually public so the class can be used by other code segments.

In this example, the name of the class is *Light*. The usual convention is to begin class names with a capital letter. The body of the definition, within the braces, lists the member variables and functions. The only variable is the status of the light, on or off. Functions are defined to flip the switch (turn it off or on) and to print out the current status of the light.

Note the functions that have the same name as the class and no return type. These are ***constructors***, functions called automatically when an instance of the ADT is declared. In this case, there are two, one without any parameters and one with an incoming integer parameter. Before examining these functions, first consider an integer. You may declare an integer with or without a value.

```
int num1;            //no initial value given
int num2=9;          //initial value of 9 given
```

Since **integer** is a built-in data type, the compiler knows in both of these instances to set aside a memory location for type integer, and in the second case to put in a value of 9. We are defining classes that will later be used by a program. Therefore, we must specify what to do when an object of our class is declared. In this case, we are allowing an object to be declared with or without an initial value specified. Specifying two or more functions with the same name is an example of ***overloading*** functions. When functions are overloaded, they **must** differ in the number and/or type of parameters. Usually there are at least two constructors, one of which is the default constructor without parameters. If an array of the class objects will be declared, there must be a default constructor.

Because we have specified both types of constructors, we will allow both kinds of ADT object declaration:

```
Light myLight;         //call default constructor to set aside a memory location
Light yourLight(1);    //set aside a memory location and set initial value to on
Light anotherLight(0); //set aside a memory location and set initial value to off
```

8.5.2 Class Implementation File (.cpp)

The header file provides the interface, or WHAT the class can do. The implementation file, ending in **.cpp**, shows HOW each function is implemented. The member functions have access to all the member variables. However, because the implementation is in a separate file, a connection must be made between the definition and the implementation. The header file is included with the compiler directive (#) at the top. If the file were not in the same directory, the entire pathway would be enclosed in the quotation marks. The code for Light.cpp is shown in Fig. 8-7.

Member functions follow all the rules of other C++ functions, with two exceptions. First, as stated before, the constructors do not have a return type. Second, all the function names are preceded by the class name and the **scope resolution operator (::)** which identifies the function as a member of a specific class. Every member function implemented in the **.cpp** file must have its prototype, or heading, listed in the **.h** file.

8.5.3 Using the C++ Class

The header and implementation files together completely define the new ADT. The class is now ready to be used by a calling program.

```
#include <iostream.h>          //library necessary to use cout
#include "Light.h"             //necessary to connect to header file

//class implementation (Light.cpp file)
Light::Light()                 //default constructor
{
   status=0;                   //0 means off, begin with it off
}

Light::Light(int statusIn)  //constructor to specific status
{
   status=statusIn;
}
int Light::flipSwitch()        //change the status
{
   status=!status;
   //if it is off, turn it on. if it is on, turn it off
   return status;
}

void Light::printStatus()   //print the current status
{
   if (status==0) cout<<"The Light is off";
   else cout<<"The Light is on";
   cout<<endl;
}
```

Fig. 8-7 Light.cpp.

EXAMPLE 8.6 Write a simple C++ program to declare instances of the class Light and print the values, then change the values and print their values again.

The implementation of this simple program is shown in Fig. 8-8.

```
#include<iostream.h>           //necessary to use cout
#include "Light.h"             //necessary to connect to header file
void main ()
{
   Light myLight;              //invokes default constructor
   Light yourLight(1);         //invokes constructor with a parameter

   myLight.printStatus();   //prints current values, off and on
   yourLight.printStatus();

   myLight.flipSwitch();    //changes values
   yourLight.flipSwitch();

   myLight.printStatus();   //prints current values, on and off
   yourLight.printStatus();
}
```

Fig. 8-8 Using class Light.

The output from this main() function would be:

The Light is off
The Light is on
The Light is on
The Light is off

In order to declare instances of the class *Light*, the header file must be included. Then two specific instances are created. The first, *myLight*, is initially set to off by the default constructor. The second, *yourLight*, is specifically set to on when it is created. (Remember, 1 is on, 0 is off.)

The member functions are invoked through the use of the **dot operator (.)**. The general form is ***object.function()*** or ***object.variable***. In this program, it is impossible to access the status directly (as in `myLight.status=1;`) because the member variable was declared private. By allowing the member variables only to be changed by member functions, the class protects itself from accidental changes or invalid data.

If the calling program wanted to declare an array of ten Lights, each item in the array is accessible through the subscript. The declaration would look like this:

```
Light myLights[10];
```

After setting some values, each individual light could be accessed and printed out using a loop:

```
for (j=0; j<10; j++) myLights[j].printStatus();
```

8.5.4 Inheritance in C++

C++ allows for inheritance, where subclasses can be derived from a superclass, as shown in Fig. 8-9. The derived classes inherit the member variables and functions from the parent class.

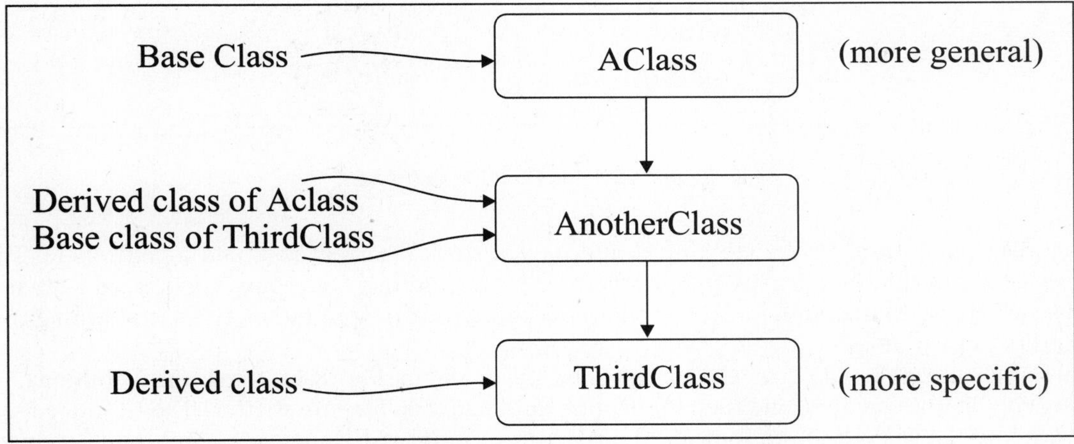

Fig. 8-9 Base and derived classes.

However, if any of the members have been declared as *private*, then even the derived class cannot access them. For example, a car could have a member variable of color inherited from the superclass motor vehicle, but it would not be able to access that value with its member functions. If the members of the parent class were declared as public, then the derived class could access them, but so could any other code segments, and the element of protection and data hiding would be lost. Therefore, C++ allows another level of access specifier in addition to *public* and *private*, that of ***protected***. When a member is declared as *protected*, it can be inherited and accessed by any subclasses, but is still inaccessible from other code segments.

EXAMPLE 8.7 Construct an ADT *Jeans* that is a more specific type of *Clothing*.

To illustrate the concept of inheritance in C++, consider Fig. 8-10. *Clothing* would be the superclass and *Jeans* would be the derived class. Possible member variables and functions are shown.

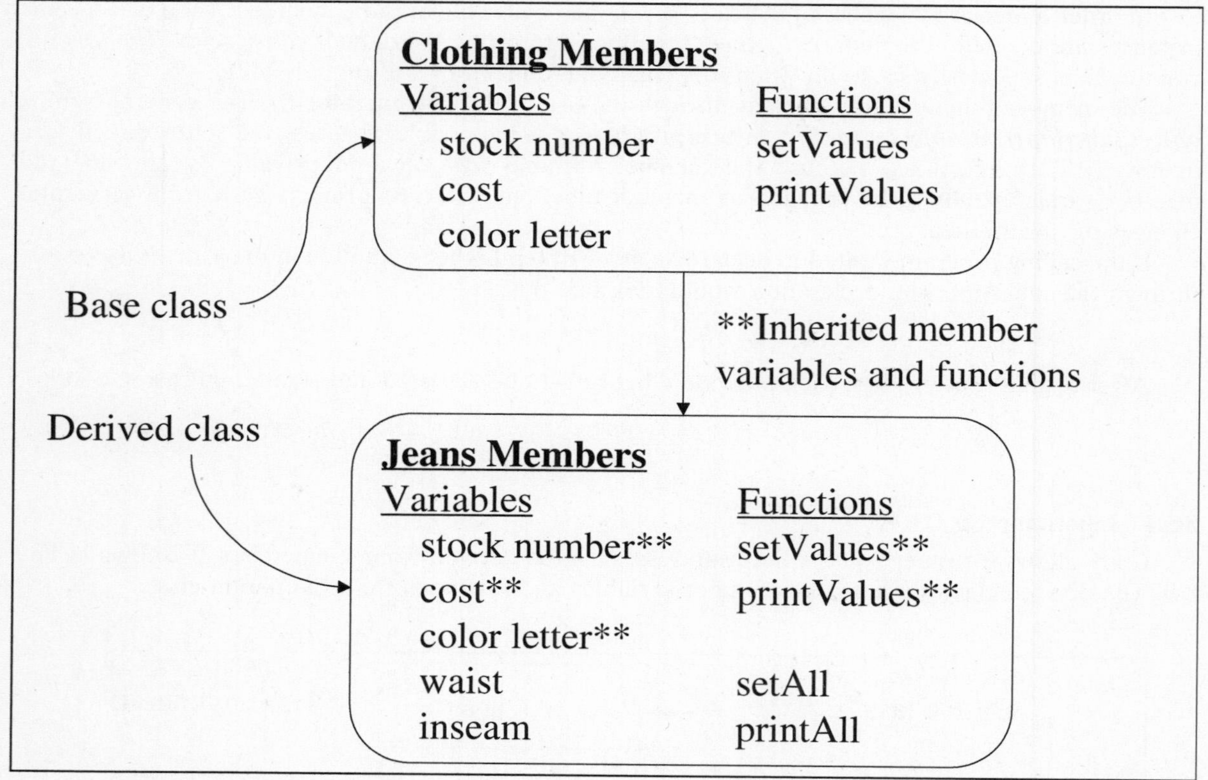

Fig. 8-10 ADT for Clothing and Jeans.

In a particular store, all the clothing would have a stock number, cost, and a color code. These variables would be inherited by any subclass derived from Clothing. Only jeans might need a waist size and inseam length. Shirts would need a collar size and sleeve length. Other types of clothing might need additional variables.

To implement this ADT in C++, consider the code in Fig. 8-11. First the Clothing.h and Clothing.cpp files are created, and then the Jeans.h and Jeans.cpp files are written. The Clothing.h must be included in the Jeans.h file to indicate the source of the inherited members, and then specified in the first line of the class definition in this form:

```
class subclassName : classAccess parentClassName
```

Because the instance variables in the Clothing class are protected, they are accessible in the Jeans class. The Jeans::setAll(...) function could have included the code:

```
stockNum=n; cost=c; colorID=col;
```

That code is not there because it is much easier for the derived class to make use of the parent's setValues(...) function. Notice, however, that no inherited data members are set in the *Jeans* constructor. The *Clothing* constructor is automatically called first when a *Jeans* object is instantiated.

```
//Clothing.h-header for superclass for clothing

class Clothing
{
  protected:
        int stockNum;
        double cost;
        char colorID;
  public:
        Clothing();                 //constructor
        void setValues (int numIn, double costIn, char colorIn);
        void printValues();
};      double reportCost();
```

```
//Clothing.cpp-implementation of superclass

#include<iostream.h>
#include"Clothing.h"

Clothing::Clothing()                //constructor-zero values
{       stockNum=0; cost=0.0; colorID='';}

void Clothing::setValues (int numIn, double costIn, char colorIn)
//allow the setting of all Clothing values
{       stockNum=numIn; cost=costIn; colorID=colorIn: }

double Clothing::reportCost()       //report the cost
{ return cost;   }

void Clothing::printValues()        //print out the Clothing Info
{       cout<<"Item "<<stockNum<<" costs "<<cost
        <<" with color code "<<colorID;
}
```

```
//Jeans.h-definition for the Jeans class

#include "Clothing.h"

class Jeans:public Clothing         //indicates superclass
{
  protected:
        int waist;
        int inseam;
  public:
        Jeans();                    //constructor
        void setAll(int n, double c, char col, int w, int i);
        //set all values for Jeans
        void printAll();            //print all info
};
```

```
//Jeans.cpp-implementation of Jeans class

#include <isostream.h>
#include "Jeans/h"

Jeans::Jeans()                      //constructor
{       waist=0; inseam=0; }

void Jeans::setAll(int n, double c, char col, int w, int i)
//set all values for Jeans
{
  setValues(n, c, col);             //calls superclass function
  waist=w; inseam=i;                //sets subclass unique values
}

void Jeans::printALL()              //print unique info
{       printValues();              //calls superclass function
        cout<<" waist="<<waist<<" and inseam="<<inseam;
}
```

Fig. 8-11 Clothing class and Jeans class.

A short testing main() function could be written as shown in Fig. 8-12. The Clothing.h is not included in the main because it is only needed in the Jeans.h file. When the object *myPants* is instantiated, first the *Clothing* constructor is called and then the *Jeans* constructor. The output from this main() would be:

Item 55 costs 24.99 with color code b waist = 34 and inseam = 30

```
// main() to test jeans

#include <iostream.h>
#include "Jeans.h"

void main ()
{
    Jeans myPants;
    myPants.setAll(55, 24.99, 'b', 34, 30);      //sets all values
    myPants.printAll();                           //prints all
    cout<<endl;
}
```

Fig. 8-12 Testing the Jeans class.

C++ allows for base and inherited classes. However, it is not a pure object-oriented language because it still needs the main() function to issue the calls to the classes. Java is one step further toward a true object-oriented language.

8.6 CLASSES AND INHERITANCE IN JAVA

In C++, programmers can create classes, but the basic unit of each program is the function. In Java, however, everything is a class. Java programmers concentrate on creating classes, which are all based upon the Java superclass **Object**. These classes perform tasks and send messages to other classes. Java is able to accomplish this because of its unique compiling/interpreting nature.

Before looking at the syntax of Java classes, it is important to point out the two environments under which Java programs run. The source code (both definition and implementation) for each class is saved in a file with the extension **.java**. The **.java** file is compiled into files of bytecode with the extension **.class**. The **.class** files can then be interpreted on the local machine in two ways. First, Java classes can be run as stand-alone applications. Second, Java classes can be created as applets to run on a Web page (under an HTML document). These two program types are unique classes that inherit methods (behaviors) from different Java objects. The manner of compiling varies depending upon the type of compiler. Interpreting, however, can be accomplished by any Java interpreter on any machine. This is one of the reasons for the portability of Java programs.

8.6.1 Java Applications

First, we will examine a simple Java application class.

EXAMPLE 8.8 Write a Java class which prints out " This is a Java application. It is a class called to perform printing tasks."

Figure 8-13 shows a short introductory Java code section. The Java I/O libraries are included, so the output can be written directly to the console, and the "throws IO Exception" is a standard way of dealing with I/O errors, which is beyond the scope of this book. Just consider this as something that should be typed in the heading of a Java application.

```
//First.java - first Java Class to examine

import java.io.*;

class First {
  public static void main ( String args[] ) throws IOException
  {

    System.out.print ("This is a Java application.\n");
    System.out.print ("It is a class called to perform printing tasks.\n");

  }//end main
}//end class
```

Fig. 8-13 First Java application (First.java).

The class contains a main() method, inherited from the Java **Object** base class, which executes when the program is run. The heading of the main() allows for the possibility of receiving an array of strings as command-line input from the operating system. The "\n" messages correspond to *endl* in C++ and send the cursor to the next line. The output of this program would look like this:

This is a java application.
It is a class called to perform printing tasks.

8.6.2 Java Applets

The second way to program in Java is to create classes which inherit from the Java **Applet** class, which, in turn, inherits functionality from the Java **Object** base class. These classes are run on Web pages under HTML documents.

EXAMPLE 8.9 Write a Java applet to print the same message as Example 8.8 above.

Figure 8-14 shows the *FirstApp.java* file written as an applet. Notice that two classes are included: the **Applet** class and the **Graphics** class. The *paint()* function, inherited from the **Applet** class, uses an object of the **Graphics** class to print strings to the screen. The numbers following the strings give the x and y locations on the screen.

```
//FirstApp.java - first Java Applet to examine

import java.applet.Applet;  //import Applet class
import java.awt.Graphics;   //import Graphics class for writing

public class FirstApp extends Applet {
  public void paint( Graphics g)
  {

     g.drawString("This is a Java applet.", 25, 25);
     g.drawString
           ("It is a class called to print on a Web page.", 25, 40);

  }//end paint
}//end class
```

Fig. 8-14 First Java applet (FirstApp.java).

Once the Java applet has been compiled into a class, it can be viewed on any Web browser by a call within an HTML file, as shown in Fig. 8-15. The width and height of the applet space must be enough to contain everything the applet will print to the screen.

```
<html>
<applet code="FirstApp.class" width=275 height=70>
</applet>
</html>
```

Fig. 8-15 HTML file to call applet (First.html).

The output of this short HTML file would look like this:

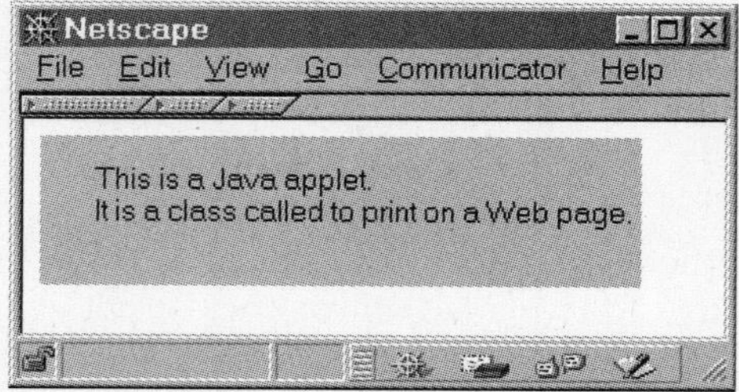

8.6.3 Using Classes in Java

Besides the application and applet classes, other classes can be created as in C++ and then used by the applications and applets.

EXAMPLE 8.10 Write the Light class from Example 8.5 in Java.

The *Light.java* file is shown in Fig. 8-16. Java allows the use of boolean variables. Most classes used by Java applets should have a way of returning the instance variables as strings, as in **toString()**, because the Graphics object prints only strings to the screen. Also, notice that, as in C++, the variables are private and the methods are public.

```
//class definition (Light.java file)
public class Light
{

    //instance variables
    private boolean status;             //Light is on(true) or off(false)

    //methods
    public Light()                      //default constructor
    { status=false; }                   //false means off, begin with it off

    public Light(boolean statusIn)      //constructor to specific status
    { status=statusIn; }

    public boolean flipSwitch()         //change the status
    {   status=!status;                 //if it is off, turn it on. if it is on, turn it off
        return status;
    }

    public String toString()            //returns the current status
    {
        if (status) return "on";
        else return "off";
    }
}
```

Fig. 8-16 Light.java.

An applet that could use the *Light.java* class is shown in Fig. 8-17. First, objects of class Light are declared. In the *init()* method inherited from the Applet class, the objects are instantiated through the use of **new**. Then the objects can be used in the *paint()* method.

```
//LightApp.java - applet to use Light class

import java.applet.Applet;
import java.awt.Graphics;

public class LightApp extends Applet {

    //declare variables
    private Light myLight;
    private Light yourLight;

    public void init()
    {
        myLight=new Light();
        yourLight=new Light(true);
    }//end init

    public void paint( Graphics g )
    {
        g.drawString ("My Light is" +myLight.toString(), 25, 25);
        g.drawString ("Your Light is" +yourLight.toString(), 25, 40);

        myLight.flipSwitch();
        yourLight.flipSwitch();

        g.drawString ("My Light is" +myLight.toString(), 25, 55);
        g.drawString ("Your Light is" +yourLight.toString(), 25, 70);

    }//end paint
  }
```

Fig. 8-17 LightApp.java.

Remember, the applet must run within an HTML document. The Light.html is shown in Fig. 8-18, along with the output that would be shown in the Web browser.

```
<html>
<applet code="LightApp.class" width=275 height=100>
</applet>
</html>

My Light is off
Your Light is on
My Light is on
Your Light is off
```

Fig. 8-18 Light.html and output.

This chapter has presented an introduction to object-oriented programming and its advantages. Visual Basic operates in an object-oriented environment, C++ allows a hybrid between OOP and procedural programming, and Java extensively uses classes. There are some languages like Smalltalk, developed by Xerox at Palo Alto Research Center (PARC), which are pure object-oriented languages. Since each language implements OOP concepts differently, more extensive explanations should be incorporated into the study of a particular language.

Solved Problems

8.1 List possible attributes and behaviors for the following objects: a light switch, a bicycle, an orange, a building, a student.

Some answers, many others are possible:

Object	Possible Attributes	Possible Behaviors
A light switch	status (on, off)	turn on, turn off, check status
A bicycle	model, gear status, color	brake, change gear
An orange	sweetness, color, type	peel, rot, squeeze
A building	temperature, number of floors	turn on heat, open door
A student	name, address, gpa, ss#	change gpa, change address, graduate

8.2 Show the superclass *food* and some of its subclasses.

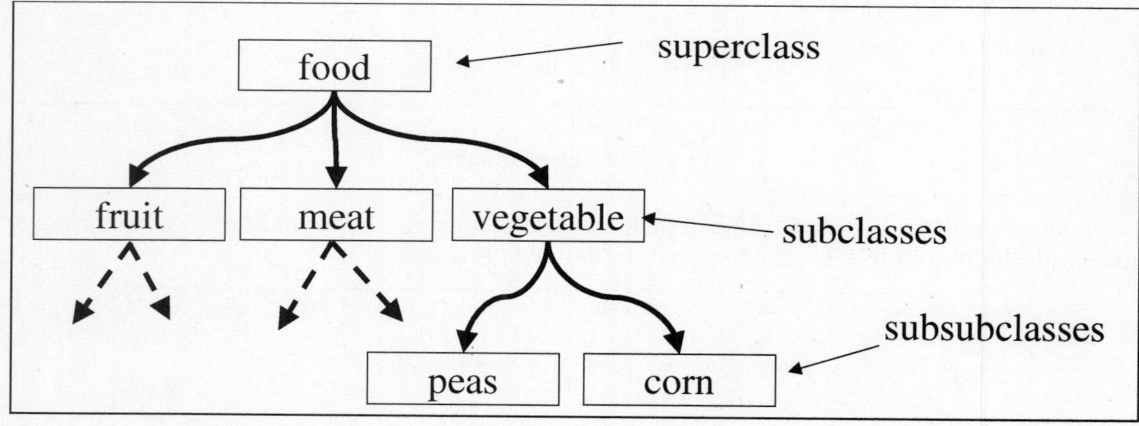

8.3 State whether the following applications would normally be examples of procedural or object-oriented programming:

(*a*) A program asks for the hours worked, calculates the correct amount of pay and prints a check.

(*b*) A program manipulates a house, allowing the user to set the number of doors and windows, and click a button to draw the model.

(*c*) A program simulates a college campus, tracking students as the user moves them from building to building.

(*d*) A program sequentially presents a number of questions and calculates the user's score, displaying the number correct at the end.

(*a*) Procedural – the program works sequentially, in the same order every time it is run.

(*b*) Object-oriented – the attributes of the house object are modified, and then the object displays itself.

(*c*) Object-oriented – the user instigates the movement and the program responds.

(*d*) Procedural – the code automatically executes in the same sequence each time it is run.

8.4 Identify the objects on this Visual Basic form.

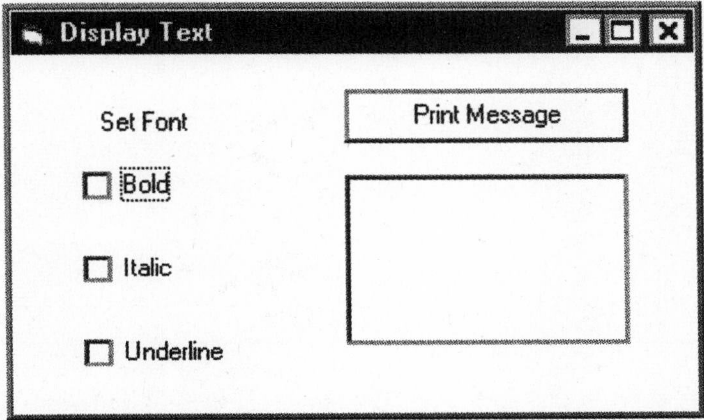

Answer:

Three checkboxes – Bold, Italic and Underline, used for input choices

One label – "Set Font," used to give information

One button – "Print Message," used to accept user action

One picture box – Empty box often used to print output

8.5 Create the C++ .h file definition for an ADT called *Calculator* which has two integer member variables called *num1* and *num2*, and one character operator called *oper*. There should be a default constructor, functions to set the numbers and the operator, a function to perform the calculation, and one to print out the entire problem nicely.

Answer:

```
//Calculator.h
//Calculator class header file

class Calculator
{

    private:
        int num1, num2; //numbers to manipulate
        char oper;      //operation to perform
```

```
    public:
        Calculator();                    //default constructor
        void setNums(int a, int b);      //set the numbers
        void setOper(char operIn);       //set the operation
        int calculate();                 //perform operation and return result
        void printCalculation();         //show the current calculation
};  //remember the semicolon
```

8.6 Write the .cpp file for the ADT *Calculator*. The default constructor should set both numbers to 1 and the operator to '+'. The *calculate()* function should check for a valid operator and should not try to divide by zero. If there is an error, it can return some flag such as −999. Then the *printCalculation()* function can call the *calculate()* function.

Answer:

```
//Calculator.cpp
// Calculator class implementation file
#include<iostream.h>
#include "Calculator.h"

Calculator::Calculator()                     //default constructor
{       num1=1;
        num2=1;
        oper='+';
}

void Calculator::setNums(int a, int b)       //set the numbers to manipulate
{       num1=a; num2=b;}

void Calculator::setOper(char operIn)        //set the operation
{ oper=operIn; }

int Calculator::calculate()                  //perform operation and return result
{
    int temp;
    switch (oper)
    {
        case '+': temp=num1+num2; break;
        case '-': temp=num1-num2; break;
        case '*': temp=num1*num2; break;
        case '/': if (num2 !=0) temp=num1 / num2; //integer division
                  else
                  {   temp = −999;
                      cerr<<"Cannot divide by zero"<<endl;
                  }
                  break;
        default: temp = −999;
                 cerr<<"Error in operator"<<endl;
    }// end switch
    return temp;
}

void Calculator::printCalculation() //calculate and show print the entire calculation
{
    char blank=' ';                       //used to help format output
    int temp=calculate();                 //calls the member function calculate()
    if (temp>-999)
    cout<<num1<<blank<<oper<<blank<< num2<<blank<<"="<<temp<<endl;
}
```

8.7 Write a short main() program to test the Calculator class. Be sure to try to divide by zero and test an illegal operator.

Sample main(): **Output from each line**

```
#include<iostream.h>
#include "Calculator.h"

void main()
{
    Calculator calc;
    calc.printCalculation();     1 + 1 =2
    calc.setNums(5,3);
    calc.setOper('-');
    calc.printCalculation();     5 - 3 =2
    calc.setOper('*');
    calc.printCalculation();     5 * 3 =15
    calc.setOper('p');
    calc.printCalculation();     Error in operator
    calc.setNums(5,0);
    calc.setOper('/');
    calc.printCalculation();     Cannot divide by zero
    calc.setNums(12,4);
    calc.setOper('/');
    calc.printCalculation();     12 / 4 =3
}
```

8.8 Create the **.h** file for C++ base class Vehicle, and a derived class Truck from the following specifications. The truck may have a bedsize of 6 or 8 feet, and a cabType of supercab (s) or regular (r).

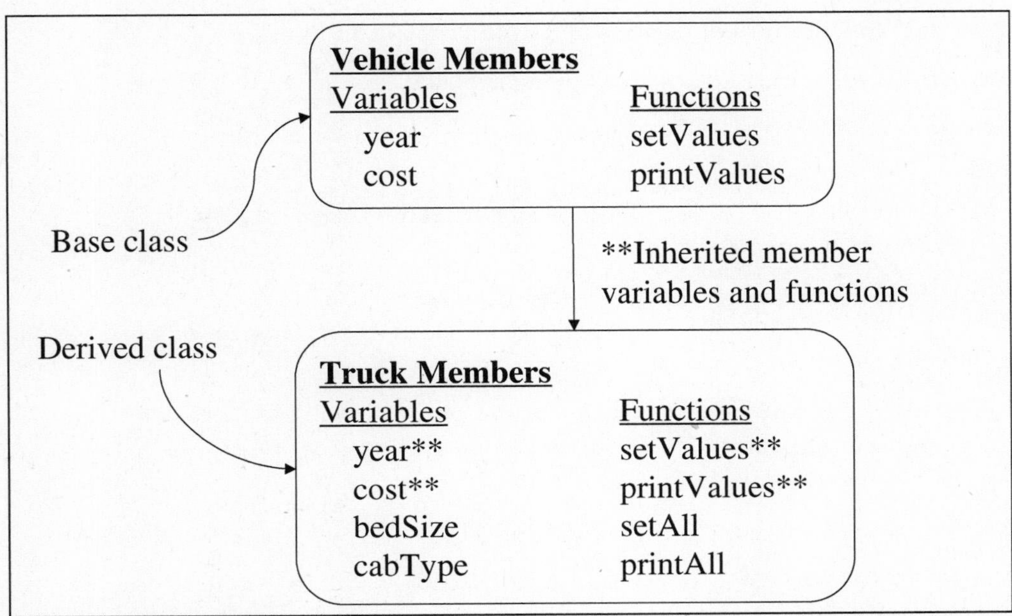

Code:

```
//Vehicle.h - header for superclass for Vehicle

class Vehicle
{
   protected:
      int year;
      double cost;
   public:
      Vehicle();                  //constructor
      void setValues (int yearIn, double costIn);
      void printValues();
};
//Truck.h - definition for the Truck class inheriting from Vehicle

#include "Vehicle.h"

class Truck : public Vehicle
{
   protected:
      int bedSize;
      char cabType;

   public:
      Truck();                    //constructor
      void setAll(int n, double cstIn, int b, char cab);
                                  //set all values for Truck
      void printAll();            //print all info
};
```

8.9 Create the **.cpp** files for both classes in Solved Problem 8.8.

```
//Vehicle.cpp - implementation of superclass

#include<iostream.h>

#include "Vehicle.h"
Vehicle::Vehicle()                //constructor - zero values
{     year=0; cost=0.0; }

void Vehicle::setValues (int yearIn, double costIn)
                                  //allow the setting of all Vehicle values
{     year=yearIn; cost=costIn; }

void Vehicle::printValues()       //print out the Vehicle Info
{     cout<<"Vehicle of year "<<year<<" costs "<<cost;
}

// Truck.cpp - implementation of Truck class

#include<iostream.h>
#include "Truck.h"
```

```
Truck::Truck()                    //constructor
{     bedSize=0; cabType=' '; }

void Truck::setAll(int n, double cstIn, int b, char cab)
// set all values for Truck
{
    setValues(n, cstIn);          //calls superclass function
    bedSize=b; cabType=cab;       //sets subclass unique values
}

void Truck::printAll()            //print unique info
{
    printValues();                //calls public function from superclass
    cout<<"Bed size="<<bedSize<<" and cab type is "<<cabType;
}
```

NOTE: The function setAll() should contain the code to check for proper data values.

8.10 Write a short Java application class to read in a person's favorite digit and print out a message.

```
//Message.java Simple Java application class

import java.io.*;

class Message {
  public static void main ( String args[] ) throws IOException
  {
    //declare variables
    int digit;
    //1. Get the number
    System.out.print ("Enter your favorite digit=>");
    System.out.flush();
    digit=System.in.read();
    digit-='0';

    //3. Print out the message
    System.out.println ("I'm glad you like the number "+digit);
  }//end main
}// end class
```

8.11 Create a Java class to implement the **Furnace** in Fig. 8-2, and a Java applet to implement the **Thermostat** that sends messages to the Furnace.

(*a*) The Furnace object has variables to show whether the heat and air conditioning are on or off. The constructor starts the object with either turned on. There are methods to set the heat on or off, to set the air conditioning on or off, and to report the string values of the head and air conditioning.

```
// class definition (Furnace.java file)
public class Furnace
{

    //instance variables
    private boolean heat;         //Furnace is on(true) or off(false)
```

```
    private boolean ac;           //Air Conditioning is on or off
    // methods
    public Furnace()              //default constructor
    {
        heat=false;               //false means off,
        ac=false;                 //begin with both off
    }
    public void setHeat(boolean status) //change the status
    {   heat=status;                   //set heat
        ac=false;                      //if heat is turned on or off, turn off ac
    }
    public void setAC(boolean status)   //change the status
    {   ac=status;                      //set AC
        heat=false;                     //if AC is turned on or off, turn off ac
    }
    public String toString()      //returns the current status
    {
       String message;
       if (heat) message="heat on";
       else message="heat off";
       if (ac) message+=" and AC on";
       else message+=" and AC off";
       return message;
  }
}
```

(*b*) The Thermostat applet object sets all the necessary constants including the desired setting and declares variables representing the current temperature and the Furnace setting. The *init()* sets the initial values and instantiates the myFurnace object. The *paint()* allows for 15 time periods and calls the *CheckAndChangeTemperature()* function, which checks the current temperature and adjusts the heat and air conditioning by sending messages to the Furnace object.

```
//ThermoApp.java - applet to use Furnace class

import java.applet.Applet;
import java.awt.Graphics;

public class ThermoApp extends Applet {

    //declare constants
    final int NOTHINGON=0;
    final int HEATON=1;
    final int ACON=-1;
    final int DESIREDTEMP=72;
    final boolean ON=true;
    final boolean OFF=false;

    //declare variables
    private Furnace myFurnace;
    int currentTemp;
    int setting;
```

```
  public void init()
  {
     myFurnace=new Furnace();
     currentTemp=64;
     setting=NOTHINGON;
  }// end init

  public void CheckAndChangeTemperature() //check and set Furnace
  {// temperature changes according to what is currently turned on
     if (setting==ACON) currentTemp--;
     if (setting==HEATON) currentTemp++;

     if (currentTemp<DESIREDTEMP)
     {
       myFurnace.setHeat(ON);
       setting=HEATON;
     }
     if (currentTemp>DESIREDTEMP)
     {
       myFurnace.setAC(ON);
       setting=ACON;
     }
  }

  public void paint( Graphics g )
  {
     for (int i=1; i<16; i++)
     {
       g.drawString ("At time "+i+" the temperature is "
            +currentTemp+" with " +myFurnace.toString(), 25, i*15);
       CheckAndChangeTemperature();
     }
  }//end paint
}//end class
```

(*c*) The output of this applet embedded in an HTML document would be:

```
At time 1 the temperature is 64 with heat off and AC off
At time 2 the temperature is 64 with heat on and AC off
At time 3 the temperature is 65 with heat on and AC off
At time 4 the temperature is 66 with heat on and AC off
At time 5 the temperature is 67 with heat on and AC off
At time 6 the temperature is 68 with heat on and AC off
At time 7 the temperature is 69 with heat on and AC off
At time 8 the temperature is 70 with heat on and AC off
At time 9 the temperature is 71 with heat on and AC off
At time 10 the temperature is 72 with heat on and AC off
At time 11 the temperature is 73 with heat off and AC on
At time 12 the temperature is 72 with heat off and AC on
At time 13 the temperature is 71 with heat on and AC off
At time 14 the temperature is 72 with heat on and AC off
At time 15 the temperature is 73 with heat off and AC on
```

Supplementary Problems

8.12 List possible attributes and behaviors for each object in the chart below.

Object	Possible Attributes	Possible Behaviors
A circle A rectangle A book A truck An employee		

8.13 Show a superclass *reading material* and some of its subclasses.

8.14 State whether the following would normally be examples of procedural or object-oriented programming:

Application	Programming Type
(*a*) A program monitors the number of cars passing an intersection, adding one every time a car runs over an input cord. (*b*) A program maintains inventory weekly by getting input from a transaction file, and adding or subtracting items from a master inventory list. (*c*) A program allows users to play solitaire, responding to clicks on the cards on the screen. (*d*) A program mimics a vending machine, counting the money entered, and dispensing the drink requested.	

8.15 Identify the objects on this Visual Basic form.

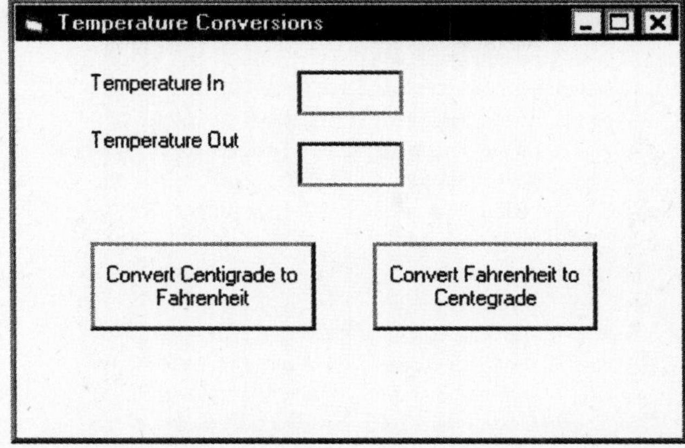

8.16 Create the .h file definition for an ADT called *Student*. Member variables should include an integer ID, an integer array of 10 test scores, and an integer which records how many tests are entered into the array. Member functions should include a default constructor, functions to set the ID, to add scores to the list, to calculate and return a floating point number for the average score, and to print out all the student information.

8.17 Create the .cpp file for all the functions in the ADT *Student*. The default constructor should set the ID, the number of scores, and all the scores in the array to zero. The function to calculate the average should return zero if there are no scores in the array.

8.18 Create a main() function to test the *Student* class which creates an array of five students, sets their IDs to the integers 0 through 4, adds some dummy scores and prints the information for the students in the array.

8.19 Write the .h files to implement the base class Square and the derived class Rectangle as defined below. The Square has the x and y locations of the upper left corner, and the length of each side. The Rectangle inherits those values and adds a width.

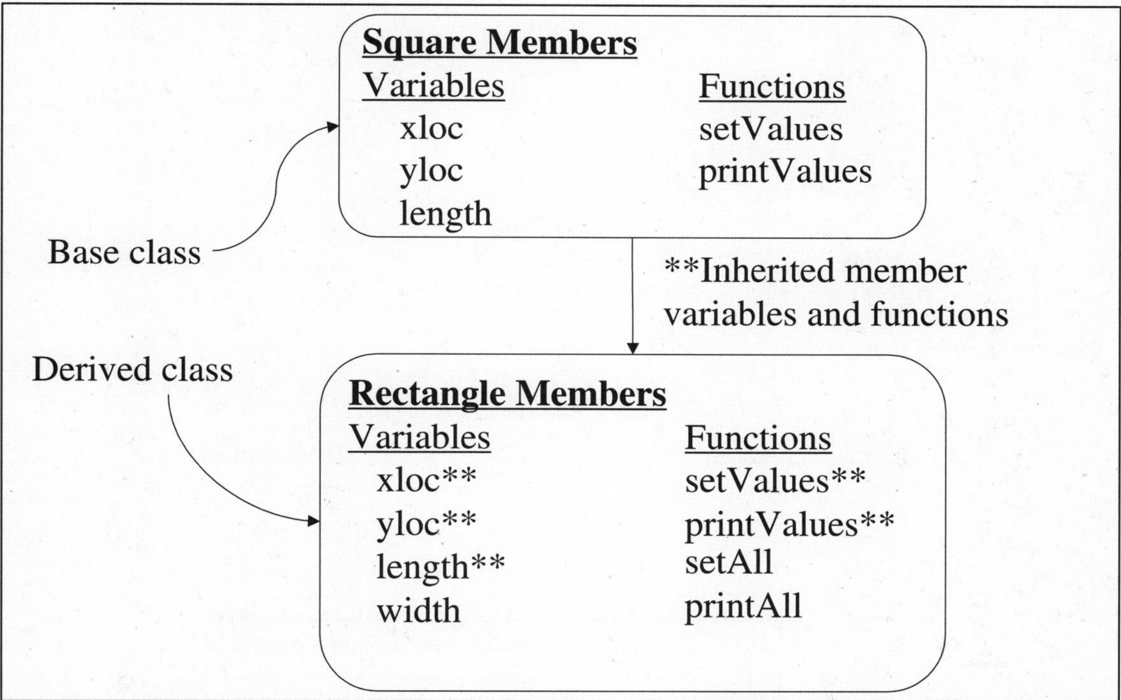

8.20 Write the .cpp files for the Square and Rectangle classes.

8.21 Write a simple Java application class that will read in one digit and print its powers from 0 to 10. Show the output of your program with the digit 2 entered.

8.22 Create a Java class **Car**, which has variables of *model*, *year*, and *mpg*. Write a Java applet **Trip** that will print out the distance two cars could go if the tank had 2, 4, 6, or 8 gallons in it. Show the output for cars with 25 and 35 miles per gallon.

Answers to Supplementary Problems

8.12 Some answers, many others would be possible

Object	Possible Attributes	Possible Behaviors
A circle	radius, color, location	calculate area, draw circle, change color, change location
A rectangle	length, width, color, location	calculate area, draw rectangle, change color, change location
A book	number pages, font type and size, words per page	print out, change font and size, change number of pages
A truck	model, color, weight, gear	accelerate, brake, change gears
An employee	name, address, ss#, pay rate, hours worked	change address, change pay rate calculate net pay

8.13 One possible answer

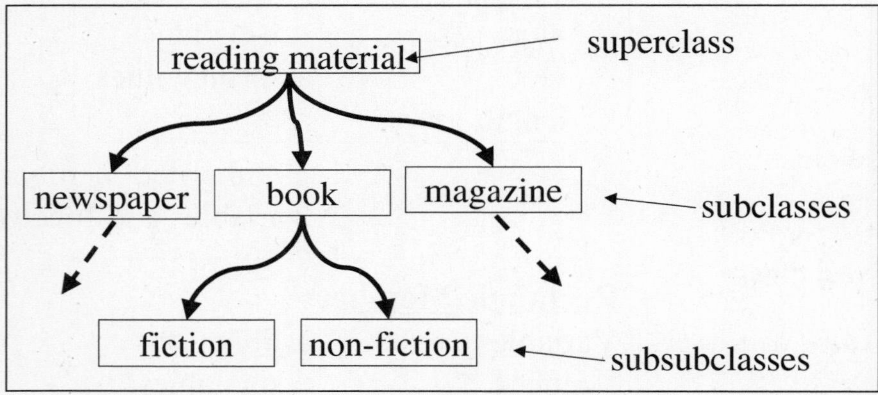

8.14

Application	Programming Type
(*a*) cars	Object-oriented
(*b*) inventory	Procedural
(*c*) solitaire	Object-oriented
(*d*) vending machine	Object-oriented

8.15 Two buttons – "Convert...."
Two textboxes – empty
Two labels – "Temperature..."

8.16 Student.h:

```
//Student.h - header file for Student class

class Student
{
   private:
       int ID;
       int scores[10];
       int numberScores;
   public:
       Student();                     //default constructor
       void setID(int IDin);          //set the ID
       void addScore(int scoreIn);//add score to list
       float calcAvg();               //calculate and return average score
       void printStuInfo();           //print all current information
};
```

8.17 Student.cpp:

```
//Student.cpp - implementation for class Student

#include<iostream.h>
#include "Student.h"

Student::Student()                          //default constructor
{
   ID=0;
   numberScores=0;
   for (int i=0; i<10; i++) scores[i]=0;
}

void Student::setID(int IDin)               //set the ID
{   ID=IDin;    }

void Student::addScore(int scoreIn)   //add score to list
{
   scores[numberScores]=scoreIn;
   numberScores++;                          //add 1 to number of scores
}

float Student::calcAvg()                    //calculate and return average score
{
   float avg=0, sum=0;
   if (numberScores>0)
   {
       for (int i=0; i<numberScores; i++) sum +=scores[i];
       avg=sum / numberScores;
   }
   return avg;
}
```

```
void Student::printStuInfo()          //print all current information
{
    cout<<"Student number "<<ID<<" had "<<numberScores<<
        " grades and an average of "<<calcAvg()<<endl;
}
```

8.18 Main() to test Student class:

```
//main() to test Student class

#include<iostream.h>
#include "Student.h"

void main()
{
    int i, j;
    Student myClass[5];               //declare an array of students
    for (i=0; i<5; i++)
    {
        myClass[i].setID(i);          //set ID equal to i
        for (j=0; j<i+1; j++)
            myClass[i].addScore(j+3); //add some dummy scores
        myClass[i].printStuInfo();    //print the info
    }
}
```

Output from the main() above:

Student number 0 had 1 grades and an average of 3
Student number 1 had 2 grades and an average of 3.5
Student number 2 had 3 grades and an average of 4
Student number 3 had 4 grades and an average of 4.5
Student number 4 had 5 grades and an average of 5

8.19 Header files for Square and Rectangle:

```
//Square.h - header for superclass for Square

class Square
{
    protected:
        int xloc;
        int yloc;
        double length;

    public:
        Square();                     //constructor
        void setValues (int xIn, int yIn, double lengthIn);
        void printValues();
};
```

```
//Rectangle.h - definition for the Rectangle class inheriting from Square
#include "Square.h"

class Rectangle : public Square
{
   protected:
      double width;

   public:

      Rectangle();                        //constructor
      void setAll(int x,int y, double l, double w);
                                          //set all values for Rectangle
      void printAll();                    //print all info
};
```

8.20 Implementation files for Square and Rectangle:

```
//Square.cpp - implementation of superclass

#include<iostream.h>
#include "Square.h"

Square::Square()                          //constructor - zero values
{   xloc=0; yloc=0; length=0.0; }

void Square::setValues (int xIn, int yIn, double lengthIn)
// allow the setting of all Square values
{   xloc=xIn; yloc=yIn; length=lengthIn; }

void Square::printValues() // print out the Square Info
{   cout<<"Four sided shape at location x= "<<xloc<<" y= "<<yloc
    <<" with side lengths of "<<length;
}
//Rectangle.cpp - implementation of Rectangle subclass

#include<iostream.h>
#include "Rectangle.h"

Rectangle::Rectangle()                    //constructor
{   width=0.0; }

void Rectangle::setAll(int x,int y, double l, double w)
//set all values for Rectangle
{
   setValues(x, y, l);                    //calls superclass function
   width=w;                               //sets subclass unique values
}

void Rectangle::printAll()                //print unique info
{
   printValues();                         //calls public function from superclass
   cout<<" and width of "<<width;
}
```

8.21 PowerIt class:

```
//PowerIt.java – class gets a digit, calculates and prints its powers from 0 to 10

import java.io.*;

class PowerIt {
  public static void main ( String args[] ) throws IOException
  {
    //declare variables
    int num;
    int product;

    //1. Get the number
    System.out.print ("Enter a number between 0 and 9=>");
    System.out.flush();
    num=System.in.read();
    num=num-'0'; // change character to integer
    product=num;

    //2. Print out the 0th power
  System.out.println (num+" to the 0 power is "+1);

    //3. Print out the powers
    for (int i=1; i<=10; i++)
    {
        System.out.println (num+" to the "+i+" power is "+product);
        product *= num;
    }// end for loop
  }// end main
}// end class
```

The output with 2 entered would be:

2 to the 0 power is 1
2 to the 1 power is 2
2 to the 2 power is 4
2 to the 3 power is 8
2 to the 4 power is 16
2 to the 5 power is 32
2 to the 6 power is 64
2 to the 7 power is 128
2 to the 8 power is 256
2 to the 9 power is 512
2 to the 10 power is 1024

8.22 Implementation for Car and Trip:

```
//class definition (Car.java file)
public class Car
{
```

```
    //instance variables
    private String model;
    private int year;
    private int mpg;

    //methods
    public Car(String m, int y, int mpgIn)   //constructor with values
    {
        model=m;
        year=y;
        mpg=mpgIn;
    }

    public int getMPG()                      //sends back private variable mpg
    { return mpg; }

    public String toString()                 //returns the current status
    {
        String message;
        message="The car is a "+year+" "+model +
            " which gets "+mpg+" miles per gallon";
        return message;
    }

}
//TripApp.java - applet to use Car class

import java.applet.Applet;
import java.awt.Graphics;

public class TripApp extends Applet {

    //declare variables
    private Car myCar, yourCar;

 public void init()
 {
    myCar=new Car("Ford", 1997, 25);
    yourCar=new Car ("Volvo", 1996, 35);
 }// end init
 public void paint( Graphics g )
 { int i, yloc=15;
    g.drawString (myCar.toString(), 25, yloc);
    for (i=2; i<=8; i +=2)
    {
      yloc += 15;
      g.drawString ("With "+i+" gallons it will travel "
           +myCar.getMPG() * i+" miles", 25, yloc);
    }

    yloc += 30;
    g.drawString (yourCar.toString(), 25, yloc);
```

```
    for (i=2; i<=8; i += 2)
    {
        yloc += 15;
        g.drawString ("With "+i+" gallons it will travel "
                +yourCar.getMPG() * i+" miles", 25, yloc);
    }
  }// end paint
}// end class
```

Output:

```
The car is a 1997  Ford which gets 25 miles per gallon
With 2 gallons it will travel 50 miles
With 4 gallons it will travel 100 miles
With 6 gallons it will travel 150 miles
With 8 gallons it will travel 200 miles

The car is a 1996  Volvo which gets 35 miles per gallon
With 2 gallons it will travel 70 miles
With 4 gallons it will travel 140 miles
With 6 gallons it will travel 210 miles
With 8 gallons it will travel 280 miles
```

CHAPTER 9

Data Structures

9.1 INTRODUCTION TO DATA STRUCTURES

Computer programs are made up of algorithms and data structures. Algorithms have been used extensively in this book to provide the step-by-step instructions of what a program will do. The data or variables are the raw materials with which the algorithms work. A single variable represents one memory location that can hold a variable of a simple type such as integer or character. A ***data structure*** is a group of memory locations used to represent the information used by the algorithm.

Some data structures have already been examined. For example, an array is a fixed-length data structure that sets aside a group of locations called by one common name, each containing the same type of data. Almost all languages provide for the use of arrays. A class is a data structure called by one name that can contain variables of different types, as well as the group of behaviors possible for that class. Classes are built in to some languages and recognized by the compiler. Sometimes, however, programs require other kinds of data structures that do not exist in a particular language. The programmer can build representations of such structures, and then use them in any program that requires that particular type of data.

This chapter examines three common data structures used by computer scientists: linked lists, stacks, and queues. These structures are not built in to most languages, although they may be included in some supplementary libraries. Usually they must be created. Classes are ideal building blocks for the creation of other structures because the programmer can package all the required variables and behaviors together for use by any program. Therefore, in each case, the structures will be created using classes in C++ or Java.

There are two ways to implement these structures: (1) using static data types (arrays), and (2) using dynamic data types (pointers). Static data types use a fixed amount of memory even if not all locations are filled. Dynamic data types use pointer variables, and grow and shrink during the run of the program through the allocation and deallocation of memory. Linked lists will be described using both static and dynamic structures. However, since dynamic structures are usually employed, stacks and queues will be implemented only dynamically.

9.2 LINKED LISTS

A ***linked list*** abstract data type (ADT) is a list or chain of items where each item points to the next one in the list. Each item in a linked list is called a ***node***. Each node contains the needed data and also the location of the next item. The data can be in any form, such as an integer, an array, or even another class object, and is usually maintained in some kind of order depending upon the specific application. The content of the link varies depending upon the implementation.

EXAMPLE 9.1 Draw an abstract representation of a single node and a linked list.

Consider the representation shown in Fig. 9-1.

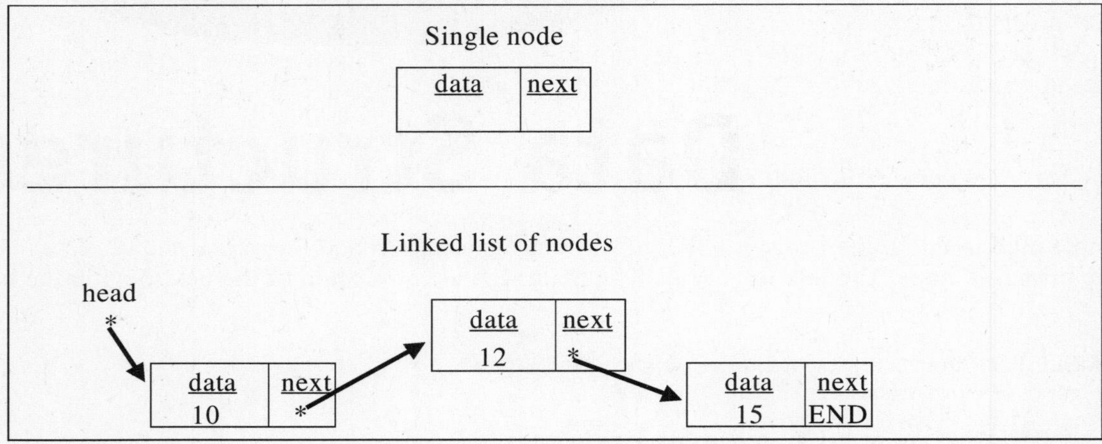

Fig. 9-1 A node and a linked list.

The linked list ADT usually contains member variables for the location of the beginning of the list and the size of the list. The minimum linked list functions needed are to construct the list, insert an item into the list, delete an item from the list, and print the contents of the list. Other functions may be added if needed, such as to report the size of the list, print the kth item, search the list, and so forth. The actual code for insert and delete varies according to whether the list is maintained in order. If the list is in order, an item is inserted in its proper spot. All that is needed is to create the node and then adjust the pointers, as shown in Fig. 9-2.

Linked lists have a distinct advantage over simple arrays. When inserting or deleting an item in an ordered linked list, only the pointers are adjusted. In an array, all items below the insertion point

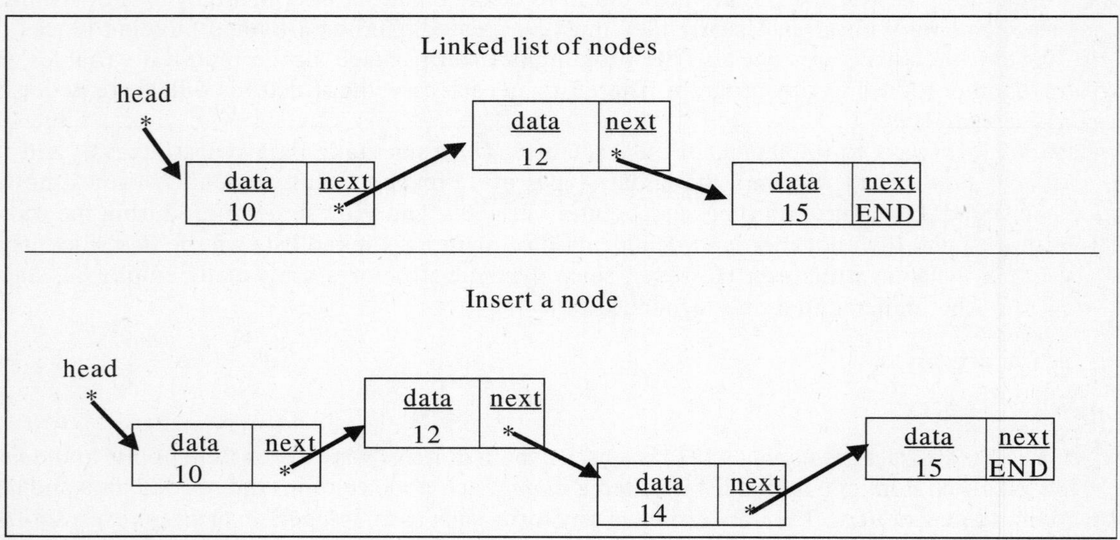

Fig. 9-2 Inserting a node into a linked list.

must be moved up or down to keep the proper order. However, in an array, one can find any specific item directly (e.g., arrayName[31]). In order to find kth item in a linked list, the list must be traversed by following the pointer of each node to the location of the next node. It is impossible to find a single item without traversing the entire list. Therefore, arrays are faster for finding a specific item and linked lists are more efficient for insertions and deletions. The specific implementation of most data structures results in some kind of trade-off between space and time.

9.2.1 Static Implementation of Linked List

The technique for implementing a static linked list involves using an array for the list space. The example used in this section is an unordered list, with items inserted at the end of the list. Each item in the array is a node. The link of each node contains the array location of the next item in the list.

EXAMPLE 9.2 Draw a representation of a static linked list.
Figure 9-3 shows this example.

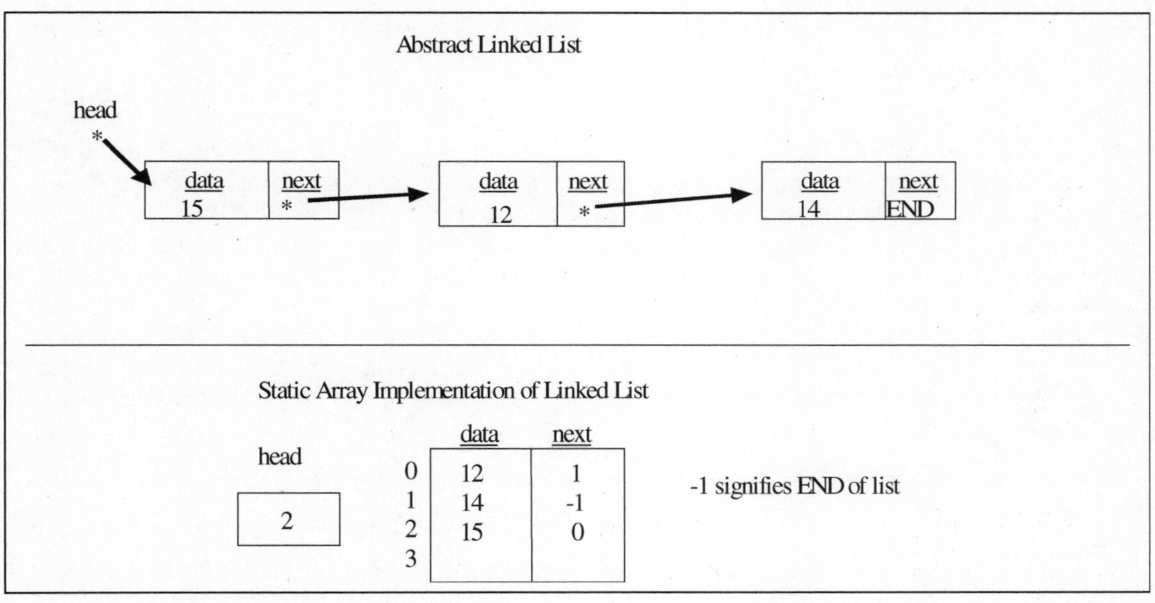

Fig. 9-3 Static linked list.

Notice two things about this implementation. First, the array space is a pool of available nodes which also is a linked list. When inserting an item, the first available node is chosen. In Fig. 9-3, if another item is inserted into the list it would be placed in spot 3. The list needs to keep track of the next available node. Second, the array contains a finite number of locations and must be big enough for all possible lists. For example, an array may be used for course lists. The largest course has 100 students and the smallest has 20. Students add to and drop from the list. The given array space might have 200 locations. Therefore, there are three numbers that must be tracked: the maximum available in the array, the maximum to be used in any given list, and the index of the current number in the list.

EXAMPLE 9.3 Implement in C++ a static linked list of integers.

This is implemented in C++ through the use of the LinkedList class. The LinkedList.h file is shown in Fig. 9-4a. All the member variables and functions needed for the list are included. The functions are implemented in Fig. 9-4b and explained below.

```
/*
 *class LinkedList
 */
typedef int Item;
const int MAX = 8;              //maximum possible in the array
const int END=-1;               //constant signifies the end of any list

class Node
{
  public:
    Item value;
    int link;
};

class LinkedList
{
  private:
    Node space[MAX];
    int head;     //address of the first node in list
    int avail;    //address of first node available to be used
    int maxSize;  //maximum number of items in the current list
    int size;     //number of items in current list
public:
    LinkedList(int n);          //Initializes the LinkedList as empty with maximum size n.
    int Size() {return size;}; //returns size of list - use of inline function
    void Insert(Item x);        //Inserts an item x in first available spot
    void Delete(Item x);        //Removes the item x - Prints error if x was not in the list
    void PrintList(char mode); //prints the list in two ways for testing - either
                                //mode=(o) list in order or (a) print array contents
};
```

Fig. 9-4a LinkedList.h.

```
//LinkedList.cpp - implementation of LinkedList class

#include<iostream.h>
#include "LinkedList.h"
LinkedList::LinkedList(int n)
//Initializes the LinkedList as empty with maximum size n.
{
    head=END;
    size=0;
    avail=0;
    maxSize=n;
    for (int i=0; i<MAX; i++)       //set up all the spaces
    {     space[i].value=END;
          space[i].link=i+1;
    }

    space[MAX-1].link=END;          //end the total list
    space[n-1].link=END;            //end the list of available nodes for the current list
}
void LinkedList::Insert(Item x)
//insert x in first available spot and hook at end of list
{
    int p, current;
    //get the first spot
  if (avail==END) cout<<"\n LinkedList::Insert -- list is full \n";
  else
  {
    p=avail;
    avail=space[avail].link;        //next available spot
    space[p].value=x;               //fill values
    space[p].link=END;
    //find the end to hook it up
    if (head==END) //hook it at the beginning
        head=p;
    else
    {
        current=head;
        while (space[current].link !=END)
            current=space[current].link;
        //now current points to last item
        //hook it up
        space[current].link=p;
    }//end else hook at end
    size++;
  }//end else list is full
}
    void LinkedList::Delete(Item x)
    {
        //find the item
      int prev, current;
      if (head==END) cout<< "\n LinkedList::Delete - List is empty \n";
      else
      {
```

Fig. 9-4b LinkedList.cpp.

```
      prev=head;
      current=head;
      while (space[current].link !=END && space[current].value !=x)
      {
          prev=current;
          current=space[current].link;
      }
      if (space[current].value==x) //item is found
      {
          //unhook it
          //check to see if it is first in list
          if (current==head) head=space[current].link;
          else space[prev].link=space[current].link;

          //return space to avail
           space[current].link=avail;
           avail=current;
           size--;
      }
      else cout<< "\n LinkedList::Delete "<<x<<" not found \n";
}//end else list is not empty
  }

  void LinkedList::PrintList(char mode)
  //prints the list either mode=(o) list in order or (a) print array contents
  {
      int i=0;
      switch (mode)
      {
      case 'o':
          cout<<"\nTHE LIST:\n";
          i=head;
          if (i==END) cout<<"Empty\n";
          else
              while (i !=END)
              {
                  cout<<space[i].value<<endl;
                  i=space[i].link;
              }
          break;
      case 'a':
          cout<<"\nTHE LIST: starts in spot "<<head<<endl;
          cout<<"The first available spot is "<<avail<<endl;
          for (i=0; i<MAX; i++)
              cout<<'['<<i<<']'<<'\t'<<space[i].value<<'\t'<<space[i].link<<endl;
          break;
      default:
          cout<<"LinkedList: PrintList - error in mode\n";
      }
      cout<<endl;
  }
```

Fig. 9-4b (*continued*)

LinkedList(int n): The constructor sets up the needed items for an empty list that may ultimately grow only to size n. The head of the list is set to -1 to signify an empty list. The first available spot is location 0, and the list of available nodes all point to the empty location following. For each node, the value is arbitrarily initialized to END. (The initialization could be set to 0, or 999, or any other number chosen to represent an undefined value.) Finally, the last item in the array and the last item in the available list are both set to END.

Insert(Item x): The Insert function checks to see if the list is full (needed for static structures of finite size), gets the next available spot, adjusts the available list, and then adds the item x at the end of the list. A different algorithm could be written to insert the item at the beginning. Also, if the list were ordered, an algorithm would be written to insert the item into its proper location. These functions are shown in the exercises at the end of this chapter. Since this implementation keeps track of the size of the current list, the *size* variable is incremented.

Delete(Item x): The Delete function first checks to see if the list is empty. If the list is not empty, the function searches for the item to be deleted. Two external pointers are needed: one to point to the current node and one to point to the previous node. The previous pointer follows the current pointer through the list so that when the item is found it can be deleted through the adjustment of two pointers. See Fig. 9-5 for an example. Once the item is found, the item must be removed from the list and the location returned to the list of available nodes so it can be used again.

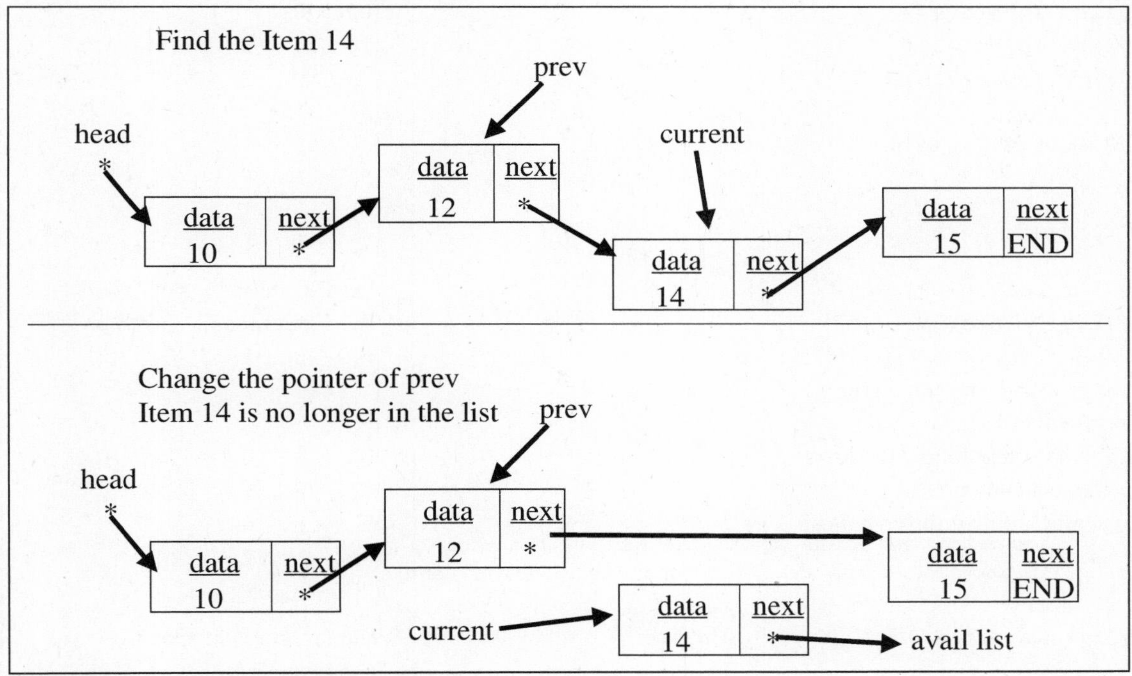

Fig. 9-5 Deleting an item from the list – abstract view.

PrintList(char mode): Usually the Print function would print the contents of the list in order. However, this Print function prints the list in two ways for the purposes of explanation and program testing. When the mode comes in as ‘o’ the values of the list are printed in the order in which they occur in the list. With the mode as ‘a’, the entire array is printed. This print function could be tailored to print in whatever way needed by a particular application.

EXAMPLE 9.4 Write a section of C++ code to use the LinkedList structure.

Shown below are some consecutive code sections in a *main()* function and a picture of the list and the array after each section.

Code	mylist.PrintList('o');	mylist.PrintList('a');

`LinkedList mylist(5);`
 	
//sets up empty list with:
//MAX of array = 8 (see .h file)
//max size of this list = 5
	The list:
	Empty
		The list: starts in spot −1
		The first available spot is 0
		[0] −1 1
		[1] −1 2
		[2] −1 3
		[3] −1 4
		[4] −1 −1
		[5] −1 6
		[6] −1 7
		[7] −1 −1

`mylist.Insert(10);`
`mylist.Insert(14);`
`mylist.Insert(9);`
`mylist.Insert(3);`
`mylist.Insert(15);`
 	
//list is now full, so avail = −1
	The list:
	10
	14
	9
	3
	15
		The list: starts in spot 0
		The first available spot is −1
		[0] 10 1
		[1] 14 2
		[2] 9 3
		[3] 3 4
		[4] 15 −1
		[5] −1 6
		[6] −1 7
		[7] −1 −1

`mylist.Delete(10);`
`mylist.Delete(3);`
 	
/* Start with 1 and follow the links for the list.
Start with 3 and follow the links for the available nodes.
Remember, only 0 through 4 can be used*/
	The list:
	14
	9
	15
		The list: starts in spot 1
		The first available spot is 3
		[0] 10 −1
		[1] 14 2
		[2] 9 4
		[3] 3 0
		[4] 15 −1
		[5] −1 6
		[6] −1 7
		[7] −1 −1

`mylist.Insert(25);` /* Again, start with 1 and follow the links for the list. Start with 3 and follow the links for the available nodes.*/	The list: 14 9 15 25	The list: starts in spot 1 The first available spot is 0 [0] 10 −1 [1] 14 2 [2] 9 4 [3] 25 −1 [4] 15 3 [5] −1 6 [6] −1 7 [7] −1 −1

9.2.2 Dynamic Implementation of Linked List

The static implementation of the linked list above had two problems. First, the array had to be created large enough for any possible application, even if not all the spaces were used in a given list. Also, the list of available nodes had to be maintained by the class itself. In the dynamic implementation, the available space is all of memory, which is called ***heap space***, and the available locations are tracked by the computer. Nodes are created as needed and returned to the heap space for later use. The list class only needs a pointer to the head of the list and an integer to keep track of the size.

EXAMPLE 9.5 Write the Java code to implement an ordered linked list.

In an ordered list, each node is less than or equal to the node that follows it. In this case, the Node is a separate class that handles its own operations. These functions allow the LinkedList class to access the Node class variables. There are two constructors: one to create a Node with a null link, and one to create a Node pointing to another node. Figure 9-6a contains the Node class and Fig. 9-6b shows the LinkedList class.

```
//class definition (Node.java file)

public class Node
{
    int value;
    Node link;                    //pointer to itself is implicit in Java

    Node (int x) this(x, null);} //constructor to create a node with data of x

    Node(int x, Node next) //constructor creates node with data of x and points to next in list
    {
      value=x;
      link=next;
    }

    int getValue() {return value;}               //return the value of the node

    Node getLink() {return link;}                //returns the next node in the list

    void setLink(Node newLink) {link=newLink;}  //resets the value of link
}
```

Fig. 9-6a Java Node class.

```
//class definition (LinkedList.java file)

public class LinkedList
{
  //instance variables
  private Node head;          //only head of list needed - all memory is available
  private int size;           //current size of list
  //methods
  public LinkedList(){ head=null; }        //default constructor

  int getSize (){ return size; }           //returns size of list

  public void Insert(int x)                //inserts x and hooks to begining of list
     {   Node p, prev, current;
         if (head==null)                   //list is empty
        head=new Node(x);
        else                               //insert in order
        {
           //find spot to insert
           current=head;
           prev=head;
           while (current.getLink() !=null && current.getValue() <x)
           {
```

Fig. 9-6b Java LinkedList class.

```
            prev=current;
            current=current.getLink();
        }
        if (current==head && current.getValue()>x)              //hook at front
            head=new Node(x,head);
        else if (current.getLink()==null && current.getValue() <x)//hook at end;
        {
            p=new Node(x);
            current.setLink(p);
        }
        else //hook in middle
        {
            p=new Node(x, current);     //set p before current node
            prev.setLink(p);            //hook prev to p
        }
    }
    size++;
  }

  public void Delete(int x)            //removes x from list, does nothing if not
in list
  {
    Node current, prev;
    if (head !=null)                   //list is empty
    {
        //find item
        current=head;
        prev=head;
        while (current.getLink() !=null && current.getValue() !=x)
        {
            prev=current;
            current=current.getLink();
        }
        //if found unhook from list
        if (current==head)
        {
            head=current.getLink();     //unhook from front
            size--;
        }
        else if (current.getValue()==x)
        {
            prev.setLink(current.getLink());//unhook from middle
            size--;
        }
    }                                  //if not found, nothing is done
    }//end delete

    public String toString()           //returns the current list as a string
    {
      Node p;
      String message=" ";
      p=head;
      while (p !=null)
      {
        message=message+p.getValue() +" ";
        p=p.getLink();
      }
      return message;
    }
}
```

Fig. 9-6b (*continued*)

The LinkedList class has the same methods as the C++ implementation shown in the previous section with a few minor differences.

Insert(int x): The Insert function maintains the list in order. Methods that insert nodes only at the front or back are shown in the exercises at the end of this chapter.

toString(): The *toString()* function does not directly print the list, but creates a String for the *paint()* method of the applet to print. If this were a regular Java application instead of an applet, this method could be coded to do the actual printing.

EXAMPLE 9.6 Write a section of Java code to use the LinkedList class.

Shown below are some consecutive code sections in a *paint()* function and the output after each *g.drawstring()* is executed.

Consecutive sections of Code	Output of paint()
`myList=new LinkedList();`	
`int yloc=0;`	
`myList.Insert(25);`	
`myList.Insert(10);`	
`myList.Insert(50);`	
`g.drawString ("The list is ",25, yloc+=15);`	The list is
`g.drawString (myList.toString(), 25,yloc+=15);`	10 25 50
`myList.Delete (25);`	
`myList.Delete (50);`	
`g.drawString ("The list is ",25, yloc+=15);`	The list is
`g.drawString (myList.toString(), 25, yloc+=15);`	10
`myList.Insert (20);`	
`myList.Insert (1);`	
`myList.Insert (14);`	
`g.drawString ("The list is ",25, yloc+=15);`	The list is
`g.drawString (myList.toString(), 25, yloc+=15);`	1 10 14 20

This section has explained the ADT called linked list. Each node in the list contains a field pointing to the location of the next node in the list. The structure can be an ordered or unordered list. Nodes can be inserted in order, at the beginning, or at the end of the list, depending upon the specific application. Other ADTs that can be built using the same linked structure are stacks and queues.

9.3 STACKS

A ***stack*** is a particular type of linked list where the items are always added to the top and removed from the top. The stack is usually called a *last-in, first-out* (LIFO) structure. One can have a stack of cards, a stack of plates, or a stack of clothing. In each case, the only available item is the one on the top. Many applications, such as the parsing of input data, rely on stacks. The computer also uses stacks during the processing of subroutine calls to keep track of the calling sequence.

EXAMPLE 9.7 Write a C++ implementation of a stack.

A C++ Stack class is shown below. The Stack.h interface file is in Fig. 9-7a and the Stack.cpp implementation is in Fig. 9-7b. This stack implements dynamic memory and a stack of characters rather than the integers shown in the linked lists of the previous section. In C++, a pointer variable is declared using an asterisk (e.g., Node *p;) and then the fields of the node are accessed through the "->" operator (e.g., p->value = 'a';) instead of through the dot operator shown above in Java.

```
//Stack.h - dynamic version of stack

#include <iostream.h>
typedef char Item;

class Node

{
public:
    Item value;
    Node *link;
};

class Stack
{
private:
    Node *stackTop; //a pointer to the top Node of the stack (or NULL if empty)

public:
    Stack();                //initializes a new stack as empty
    void Push(Item x);      //pushes the item x onto the stack

    Item Pop();             //pops and returns the top item from the stack

    Item Top();             //returns the top item from the stack without popping it

    int Size();             //returns the number of items in the stack

    void PrintStack();      //prints the contents of the stack

};
```

Fig. 9-7a Stack.h.

The only private member variable in this example is the pointer to the top of the stack. The member functions in addition to the constructor are:

- push, or insert, an item onto the top of the stack
- pop, or remove, the top item
- look at the top item but leave it on the stack
- find the size
- print the stack

Push(Item x): It is important to note that in the push function, the only time the stack is full is if the computer's entire memory is used and the new() call returns a NULL. This can occasionally happen if a push function is in the body of an infinite loop. If the stack is not full, the Item x is placed at the top of the stack.

```
//Stack.cpp - dynamic version of stack

#include<iostream.h>
#include "Stack.h"

Stack::Stack() { stackTop=NULL; }        //initializes a new stack as empty

void Stack::Push(Item x)                 //pushes the item x onto the stack
{
    Node *p;
    p=new Node;
    if (p==NULL) cout<< "\n Stack::Push - entire memory is full \n";
    else
    {
        p->value=x;
        p->link=stackTop;
        stackTop=p;
    }
}

Item Stack::Pop()                        //pops and returns the top item from the stack
{
    Item x=0;                            //creates a null character
    Node *p;
    if (stackTop==NULL) cout<< "\n Stack::Pop - empty stack\n";
    else
    {
        p=stackTop;
        x=p->value;
        stackTop=p->link;
        delete p;                        //return location to available memory
    }
    return x;
}

Item Stack::Top()          //returns the top item from the stack without popping it
{

    Item x=0;              //creates a null character
    if (stackTop==NULL) cout<< "\n Stack::Top - empty stack \n";
    else x=stackTop->value;
    return x;
}

int Stack::Size()          //returns the number of items in the stack
{
    int j=0; Node *p;
    p=stackTop;
    while (p !=NULL)
    {
        p=p->link;
        j++;
    }
    return j;
}

void Stack::PrintStack() //prints the contents of the stack
{
    Node *p;
    p=stackTop;
    cout<<"\nThe STACK: \n";
    while (p !=NULL)
    {
        cout<<p->value<<endl;
        p=p->link;
    }
}
```

Fig. 9-7b Stack.cpp.

Pop(): The pop adjusts the *stackTop* pointer to remove the first item in the stack if the stack is not empty. The memory is returned to the operating system through the *delete p* command, and the Item is returned as the function value to the calling procedure.

Top(): This function returns the first item without actually removing it from the stack. In some implementations this is called *peek*.

Size() and PrintStack(): Both these functions traverse the entire stack, one counting the items and the other printing them. A separate pointer *p* must be used to traverse the stack rather than the *stackTop* so that the stack remains intact.

EXAMPLE 9.8 Write a short section of code to create and manipulate a simple character stack.
Here is a sample *main()* function along with the resultant output.

Consecutive Code Sections	Output

`Item x;`
`Stack myS;`
`myS.Push('c');`
`myS.Push('a');`
`myS.Push('t');`
`myS.PrintStack();`
	The STACK:
	t
	a
	c

`myS.Push('s');` `myS.PrintStack();`	The STACK: s t a c

`x=myS.Pop();`
`cout<<endl<<x<<" is popped\n";`
`myS.PrintStack();`
	s is popped
	The STACK:
	t
	a
	c

9.4 QUEUES

A ***queue*** is a particular type of linked list where the items are always added to the back and removed from the front. The queue is usually called a *first-in, first-out* (FIFO) structure. There can be a queue of people purchasing tickets, a queue of cars waiting at a car wash, or a queue of items on a conveyor belt. In each case, items are added at the back and leave from the front. Network operating systems use queues to process printing requests. Documents can be submitted to a printer, and the printer will process these documents in the order in which they were received.

EXAMPLE 9.9 Write the Java code to implement a Queue class.

A Java Queue class is shown below. The Node.java is in Fig. 9-8a and the Queue.java is in Fig. 9-8b. This queue implements dynamic memory with a queue of characters rather than the integers shown in the linked lists.

```
//Node.java for use in character Queue
public class Node
{
    char value;
    Node link; //pointer is implicit in Java
    //constructor to create a node with data of s
    Node (char x)     {this(x, null);}
    //constructor creates node with data of x and points to next in list
    Node(char x, Node next)
    {
      value=x;
      link=next;
    }
    //returns the value of the node
    char getValue() {return value;}
    //returns the next node in the list
    Node getLink() {return link;}
    //resets the value of link
    void setLink(Node newLink) {link=newLink;}
}
```

Fig. 9-8a Node.java.

Instance variables are pointers to the front and the rear of the queue. The methods implemented are similar to the ones needed for the Stack: the constructor, putting something onto the rear of the queue, removing a node from the front of the queue, looking at the front of the queue, finding the size, and returning the string value of the queue. Logic for these Queue functions is similar to the logic of the Stack functions.

```
//class definition (Queue.java file)
public class Queue
{
    //instance variables
    private Node front, rear;           //pointer to front and rear

    //methods
    public Queue()                      //default constructor
    { front=rear=null; }

    public void Enqueue(char x)         //inserts x at the end of the queue
    {
      Node p=new Node(x);               //create node with null link;
      if (rear==null)                   //if list is empty, item is first
      {
          front=p;
          rear=front;
      }
      else                              //insert at rear
      {
          rear.setLink(p);
          rear=p;
      }
    }

    public char Dequeue()               //removes from front of list
    {
      char ch=' ';
      if (front !=null)                 //if queue not empty
      {
        ch=front.getValue();
        front=front.getLink();          //unhook from front
      }
      return ch;
    }//end delete

    public char Front()                 //returns front of list
    {
      char ch=' ';
      if (front !=null)                 //if queue not empty
        ch=front.getValue();
      return ch;
    }//end delete
```

Fig. 9-8b Queue.java.

```
      int Size ()                          //returns size of queue
      {
        Node p;
        int j=0;
        p=front;
        while (p !=null)
        {
          j++;
          p=p.getLink();
        }
        return j;
      }
      public String toString()             //returns the current queue as a string
      {
        Node p;
        String message=" ";
        p=front;
        while (p !=null)
        {
          message=message+p.getValue()+" ";
          p=p.getLink();
        }
        return message;
      }
    }
```

Fig. 9-8b (*continued*)

EXAMPLE 9.10 Write a short Java function to test the Queue class.

Here is a sample *paint()* function to create and manipulate a simple character queue, along with the resultant output.

Consecutive Code Sections	Output

`myq=new Queue();`
`int yloc=0;`
`for (char ch='A'; ch<'D'; ch++) myq.Enqueue(ch);`
`g.drawString ("The queue is ",25, yloc+=15);`
`g.drawString (myq.toString(), 25,yloc+=15);`
	
	The queue is
	A B C

`char x=myq.Dequeue();`
`g.drawString`
`  (x+" was the character dequeued ",25, yloc += 25);`
`g.drawString ("The queue is ",25, yloc+=25);`
`g.drawString (myq.toString(), 25, yloc+=15);`
	
	A was the character dequeued
	The queue is
	B C

`for (char ch='x'; ch<='z'; ch++) myq.Enqueue(ch);`
`g.drawString`
`  ("The front of the q is "+myq.Front(),25, yloc+=25);`
`g.drawString ("The queue is ",25, yloc+=25);`
`g.drawString (myq.toString(), 25, yloc+=15);`
	
	The front of the q is B
	The queue is
	B C x y z

Many built-in structures are available for use both in C++ and Java. Other ADTs can be built by the programmer and adapted for any application. The linked lists, stacks, and queues explained in this chapter provide a starting-point. In each case, the Node contains the actual data. Those data could be an integer, a character, a string, or an object of any other class. Recall that one of the goals of object-oriented programming is the reuse of code. The sequential development of the structures in this chapter effectively illustrates this point. Several of the exercises at the end provide the reader a way to extend the use of these data structures.

Solved Problems

9.1 Which languages used in this book have built-in structures of the following types?

(*a*) string
(*b*) arrays
(*c*) classes
(*d*) linked lists

(*a*) Visual Basic and Java; C++ allows character arrays only
(*b*) Visual Basic, C++ and Java; most languages provide for arrays
(*c*) C++ and Java; Visual Basic does not allow classes in most early versions
(*d*) none; these must be created in most languages

9.2 Some ADTs which have been defined in this book are: arrays, linked lists, stacks, and queues. Which of these would be appropriate for the following applications?

(*a*) Grocery list
(*b*) Simulation of a grocery store checkout
(*c*) Company layoff policy where the people who had worked for the shortest period of time are laid off first
(*d*) University student records

Most appropriate ADT:

(*a*) Simple array or unordered linked list
(*b*) Queue
(*c*) Stack
(*d*) Ordered linked list or array

9.3 Add a function to the LinkedList class in Fig. 9-4 that would insert the item at the beginning of the list. The function heading would be:

void InsertBeginning(Item x);

Code:

```
void LinkedList::InsertBeginning(Item x)
//Inserts an item x in first available spot at the beginning of the list
{
```

```
    int p, current;
    //get the first spot
if (avail==END) cout<<"\n LinkedList::Insert -- list is full \n";
else
{
    p=avail;
    avail=space[avail].link;      //next available spot
    space[p].value=x;             //fill value

    //hook it at the beginning
    space[p].link=head;
    head=p;

    size++;
  }//end else list is full
}
```

This table demonstrates the use of the InsertBeginning(Item x) function:

Code	mylist.PrintList('o');	mylist.PrintList('a');

`LinkedList mylist(5);`
`Mylist.InsertBeginning(10);`
`Mylist.InsertBeginning(14);`
`Mylist.InsertBeginning(9);`
`Mylist.InsertBeginning(3);`
`Mylist.InsertBeginning(15);`
	The list:
	15
	3
	9
	14
	10
		The list: starts in spot 4
		The first available spot is −1
		[0] 10 −1
		[1] 14 0
		[2] 9 1
		[3] 3 2
		[4] 15 3
		[5] −1 6
		[6] −1 7
		[7] −1 −1

9.4 Draw the array for Fig. 9-5, before and after the deletion of 14.

Before	After deleting 14
[0] 10 1 head=0 [1] 12 2 avail=4 [2] 14 3 [3] 15 −1 [4] −1 −1 [5] −1 6 [6] −1 7 [7] −1 −1	[0] 10 1 head=0 [1] 12 3 avail=2 [2] 14 4 [3] 15 −1 [4] −1 −1 [5] −1 6 [6] −1 7 [7] −1 −1

Note: Following the links through the list begins at the head 0, and goes in this order: 0, 1, 3, −1(stop). Following the links through the available list begins at 2 and goes in this order: 2, 4, −1(stop).

9.5 What would be the output of the following sections of code for the unordered static C++ LinkedList class?

Code	mylist.PrintList('o');	mylist.PrintList('a');

LinkedList mylist(6);
 	
`//sets up empty list with:`
`//MAX of array=8 (see .h file)`
`//max size of this list=6`
	The list:
	Empty
		The list: starts in spot −1
		The first available spot is 0
		[0] −1 1
		[1] −1 2
		[2] −1 3
		[3] −1 4
		[4] −1 5
		[5] −1 −1
		[6] −1 7
		[7] −1 −1

`for (int i=0; i<3; i++)` `    mylist.Insert(50+(4*i));`	The list: 50 54 58	The list: starts in spot 0 The first available spot is 3 [0] 50 1 [1] 54 2 [2] 58 −1 [3] −1 4 [4] −1 5 [5] −1 −1 [6] −1 7 [7] −1 −1

`mylist.Insert(95);`
`mylist.Insert(54);`
`mylist.Delete(50);`
	The list:
	54
	58
	95
	54
		The list: starts in spot 1
		The first available spot is 0
		[0] 50 5
		[1] 54 2
		[2] 58 3
		[3] 95 4
		[4] 54 −1
		[5] −1 −1
		[6] −1 7
		[7] −1 −1

`mylist.Delete(95);`
`mylist.Delete(58);`
`mylist.Insert(25);`
	The list:
	54
	54
	25
		The list: starts in spot 1
		The first available spot is 3
		[0] 50 5
		[1] 54 4
		[2] 25 −1
		[3] 95 0
		[4] 54 2
		[5] −1 −1
		[6] −1 7
		[7] −1 −1

9.6 Write a Java function for an unordered dynamic LinkedList class to insert the node at the beginning of the list. The function heading would be ***void InsertBeginning(Item x);***

```
public void InsertBeginning(int x)  //inserts x and hooks to beginning of list
{
  if (head==null)                   //if list is empty, item is first
     head=new Node(x);
  else                              //insert in front
     head=new Node(x, head);
  size++;
}
```

9.7 What would be the output of the following consecutive sections of code using the Java ordered LinkedList class?

Consecutive Sections of Code	Output of paint()

`myList=new LinkedList();`
`int yloc=0;`
`for (int i=0; i<5; i++) myList.Insert((i+1)*3);`
`g.drawString ("The list is ",25, yloc+=15);`
`g.drawString (myList.toString(), 25,yloc+=15);`
	The list is
	3 6 9 12 15

`myList.Delete (9);`
`myList.Delete (15);`
`g.drawString ("The list is ",25, yloc+=15);`
`g.drawString (myList.toString(), 25, yloc+=15);`
	The list is
	3 6 12

`myList.Insert(2);`
`myList.Insert(34);`
`myList.Insert(23);`
`g.drawString ("The list is ",25, yloc+=15);`
`g.drawString (myList.toString(), 25, yloc+=15);`
	The list is
	2 3 6 12 23 34

9.8 One of the goals of object-oriented programming is to reuse as much code as possible. Which line(s) in Figs 9-7a and 9-7b would need to be changed to make the class a stack of integers instead of characters?

Answer: Only one line

typedef char Item; would change to typedef int Item;

All the rest of the code uses the generic Item rather than an explicit data type. Any other data type or class could be substituted for the *char* or *int.*

9.9 (*a*) Change the line in the C++ PrintStack() of Fig. 9-7b function to print the stack all on one line.

(*b*) What would be the output of this C++ code section if "Hello to you!" is entered by the user at the prompt?

Note: (1) Assume the #include <string.h> is at the beginning of the program.

(2) cin.get(str,num)=the input of an entire string of up to num characters

(*a*) `cout<<p->value<<endl;` would change to `cout<<p->value<<" ";`

(*b*)

Consecutive Sections of Code	Output

`int i;`
`Stack myS;`
`char message[80];`
`cout<<"Enter one line of text"<<endl;`
`cin.getline(message, 80);`
`for (i=0; i<strlen(message); i++)`
`   myS.Push(message[i]);`
`myS.PrintStack();`
`cout<<endl;`
	Enter one line of text
	Hello to you!
	
	The STACK:
	! u o y o t o l l e H

`char ch=myS.Pop();`
`cout<<ch<<" was popped"<<endl;`
`myS.PrintStack();`
	! was popped
	The STACK:
	u o y o t o l l e H

9.10 What would be the output of this Java code section?

Consecutive Code Section	Output

`myq=new Queue();`
`int yloc=0;`
`String message="Hello to you!";`
`for (int i=0; i<message.length(); i++)`
`   myq.Enqueue(message.charAt(i));`
`g.drawString ("The queue is ",25, yloc+=15);`
`g.drawString (myq.toString(), 25,yloc+=15);`
	The queue is
	H e l l o t o y o u !

`char x=myq.Dequeue();`	

`g.drawString`
`   (x+" was the character dequeued ",25, yloc+= 25);`
`g.drawString ("The queue is ",25, yloc+=25);`
`g.drawString (myq.toString(), 25, yloc+=15);`
	H was the character dequeued
	The queue is
	e l l o t o y o u !

9.11 Given the Java LinkedList class in Fig. 9-6, write a member function to add a given value to each element in the list.

Notes:

(1) For any traversal of the list, just go through the list from the beginning and get each value to add. Use the same algorithm of traversal anytime you want to go through the list to search for something or change each element.

(2) In the Node class, there is no function to set the value except the constructor. This problem requires a new function to be added to the Node class in addition to the function which is written for the LinkedList class.

Add to the Node class:

```
//sets the value of the node
void setValue(int x)    {value=x;}
```

Add to the Linked List class

```
public void Add(int num)         //adds num to each item in the list
{
    Node current;
    current=head;
    while (current !=null)
    {
        current.setValue(current.getValue()+ num); //add num to each value
        current=current.getLink();
    }
}
```

Supplementary Problems

9.12 What is the difference between **static** and **dynamic** data structures?

9.13 Which type of ADT would be appropriate for the following applications?

(*a*) Simulation of car wash
(*b*) Packing and unpacking a suitcase
(*c*) Parking lot that has one lane and only one way in or out
(*d*) Checking incoming string to see if it is a palindrome
(*e*) Simulation of a bank line
(*f*) Todo list where all jobs have the same priority
(*g*) Employee records

9.14 Add a function to the LinkedList class class in Fig. 9-4 that would insert the item in order and create an ordered list. The function heading would be ***void InsertInOrder(Item x);***

9.15 Draw the before and after array for Fig. 9-5 if the node 10 is deleted instead of the node 14.

9.16 What would be the output of the following sections of code for the unordered static C++ LinkedList class?

```
LinkedList mylist(7);
mylist.PrintList('o');
mylist.PrintList('a');
for (int i=2; i<6; i+=2)
    mylist.Insert(40-(3*i));
mylist.PrintList('o');
mylist.PrintList('a');
```

```
mylist.Insert(10);
mylist.Insert(20);
mylist.Insert(30);
mylist.Delete(34);
mylist.PrintList('o');
mylist.PrintList('a');

mylist.Delete(20);
mylist.Delete(30);
mylist.Insert(10);
mylist.PrintList('o');
mylist.PrintList('a');
```

9.17 Write a Java function for an unordered LinkedList class to insert the node at the end of the list. The function heading would be ***void InsertEnd(Item x);***

9.18 What would be the output of the following sections of code for the ordered dynamic Java LinkedList class?

```
myList=new LinkedList();
int yloc=0;
for (int i=2; i<7; i++) myList.Insert(i+5);
g.drawString ("The list is ",25, yloc+=15);
g.drawString (myList.toString(), 25,yloc+=15);

myList.Delete (9);
myList.Insert(2);
myList.Delete (11);
g.drawString ("The list is ",25, yloc+=15);
g.drawString (myList.toString(), 25, yloc+=15);

myList.Insert(34);
myList.Insert(7);
myList.Delete(8);
g.drawString ("The list is ",25, yloc+=15);
g.drawString (myList.toString(), 25, yloc+=15);
```

9.19 Using the PrintStack() from Solved Problem 9.9, what would be the output of this C++ code section?

```
int i;
Stack myS;
char word[30];
strcpy (word, "antidisestablishmentarianism");
for (i=0; i<strlen(word); i++)
   myS.Push(word[i]);
myS.PrintStack(); cout<<endl;

for (i=0; i<9; i++)
   myS.Pop();
myS.PrintStack(); cout<<endl;
```

9.20 What would be the output of this Java code section?

```
myq=new Queue();
int yloc=0;

String word="antidisestablishmentarianism";
for (int i=0; i<word.length(); i++)
   myq.Enqueue(word.charAt(i));
g.drawString ("The queue is ",25, yloc+=15);
g.drawString (myq.toString(), 25,yloc+=15);

for (int i=0; i<9; i++) myq.Dequeue();
g.drawString ("The queue is ",25, yloc+=25);
g.drawString (myq.toString(), 25, yloc+=15);
```

9.21 Given the Java LinkedList class in Fig. 9-6, write a member function which would find and return the number of times a given target item occurs in the list.

Answers to Supplementary Problems

9.12 **Static** data types use a fixed amount of memory even if not all locations are filled. **Dynamic** data types use pointer variables, and grow and shrink during the run of the program through the allocation and deallocation of memory.

9.13 ADTs:

(*a*) Queue
(*b*) Stack
(*c*) Stack
(*d*) Stack and queue together
(*e*) Queue
(*f*) Unordered linked list
(*g*) Ordered linked list

9.14 Code:

```
void LinkedList::InsertInOrder(Item x)
//Inserts an item x in first available spot and keep the list IN ORDER
{

   int p, prev, current;
   //get the first spot
   if (avail==END) cout<<"\n LinkedList::Insert -- list is full \n";
   else
   {
      p=avail;
      avail=space[avail].link; //next available spot
      space[p].value=x;        //fill values
```

```
      space[p].link=END;

      //find the correct spot to hook it up
      if (head==END)                  //hook it at the beginning
         head=p;
      else
      {
         current=head;
         prev=current;

         while (current!=END &&            //not the end
            space[current].value<x)        //in order
         {
            prev=current;
            current=space[current].link;
         }
         //now current points to item greater than x
         //OR points to first item in list
         if (current==prev)           //hook at beginning of list
         {
            space[p].link=head;
            head=p;
         }
         else                         //hook it up in proper sequence
         {
            space[p].link=space[prev].link;
            space[prev].link=p;
         }
     }//end else hook at end
     size++;
   }//end else list is full
  }
```

9.15 Before and after arrays

Before	After Deleting 10
[0] 10 1 head=0 [1] 12 2 avail=4 [2] 14 3 [3] 15 −1 [4] −1 −1 [5] −1 6 [6] −1 7 [7] −1 −1	[0] 10 4 head=1 [1] 12 2 avail=0 [2] 14 3 [3] 15 −1 [4] −1 −1 [5] −1 6 [6] −1 7 [7] −1 −1

9.16 Output:

<table>
<tr><th>Code</th><th>mylist.PrintList('o');</th><th>mylist.PrintList('a');</th></tr>
<tr><td><code>LinkedList mylist(7);</code></td><td>The list:
Empty</td><td>The list: starts in spot −1
The first available spot is 0
[0] −1 1
[1] −1 2
[2] −1 3
[3] −1 4
[4] −1 5
[5] −1 6
[6] −1 −1
[7] −1 −1</td></tr>
<tr><td><code>for (int i=2; i<6; i+=2)</code>
<code>   mylist.Insert(40-(3*i));</code></td><td>The list:
34
28</td><td>The list: starts in spot 0
The first available spot is 2
[0] 34 1
[1] 28 −1
[2] −1 3
[3] −1 4
[4] −1 5
[5] −1 6
[6] −1 −1
[7] −1 −1</td></tr>
<tr><td><code>mylist.Insert(10);</code>
<code>mylist.Insert(20);</code>
<code>mylist.Insert(30);</code>
<code>mylist.Delete(34);</code></td><td>The list:
28
10
20
30</td><td>The list: starts in spot 1
The first available spot is 0
[0] 34 5
[1] 28 2
[2] 10 3
[3] 20 4
[4] 30 −1
[5] −1 6
[6] −1 −1
[7] −1 −1</td></tr>
<tr><td><code>mylist.Delete(20);</code>
<code>mylist.Delete(30);</code>
<code>mylist.Insert(10);</code></td><td>The list:
28
10
10</td><td>The list: starts in spot 1
The first available spot is 3
[0] 34 5
[1] 28 2
[2] 10 4
[3] 20 0
[4] 10 −1
[5] −1 6
[6] −1 −1
[7] −1 −1</td></tr>
</table>

9.17 Code:

```
public void InsertEnd(int x)      //inserts x and hooks to end of list
{
  Node current, p;
  if (head==null)                 //if list is empty, item is first
      head=new Node(x);
  else                            //find end and insert
  {
      current=head;
      while (current.getLink() !=null)
          current=current.getLink();
      p=new Node(x);              //sets link null
      current.setLink(p);         //hooks to end
  }
  size++;
}
```

9.18 Output:

The list is
7 8 9 10 11
The list is
2 7 8 10
The list is
2 7 7 10 34

9.19 Output:

The STACK:
m s i n a i r a t n e m h s i l b a t s e s i d i t n a
The STACK:
n e m h s i l b a t s e s i d i t n a

9.20 Output:

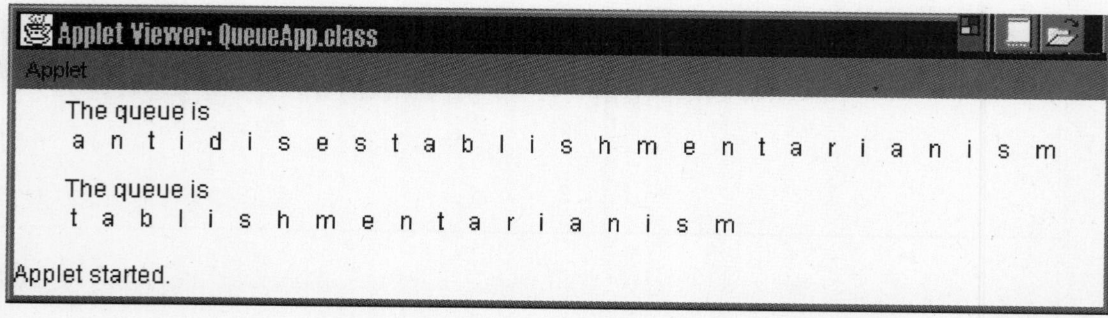

9.21 Code:

```
public int Count(int target) //counts the number of times target is in the list
{
   int counter=0;
   Node current;
   current=head;
   while (current !=null)
   {
      if (current.getValue()==target) counter++; //add one to counter if there
      current=current.getLink();
   }
   return counter;
}
```

The Translation Process

COMPILERS

As indicated in Chapter 1, the panorama inside any computer is comprised of sequences of 0's and 1's that can be easily understood by the computer but not by humans. On the other hand, whenever we write programs in high-level languages like C or Visual Basic, we are using a set of instructions or commands that can be understood by the programmers but not by the computer. To bridge the communication gap between the human and machine, it is necessary to carry out a translation process (see Fig. A-1). Since each computer can only understand its own native language (machine language), ultimately it is necessary to translate every program into an equivalent program written in machine language, so that the computer can understand it and execute the instructions specified in the program. The computer programs that carry out this translation process are called translators (see Fig. A-2). These translators usually work on specific languages. That is, the translator of C programs cannot translate Visual Basic programs and vice versa. There are two special types of translators to carry out the conversion process from high-level languages to machine language: compilers and interpreters.

The translation process itself consists of a series of transformations of the input language. Figure A-3 shows the general phases of a compiler. Although a general discussion of the activities comprised in each of these phases is beyond the scope of this book, we will consider some aspects of that translation process and how it relates to the programs that we write.

Before submitting the programs to any translator, the source program needs to be created using an **editor** or a word processor. Most translators require that the extensions of the files where the programs are saved be of a specific type. For example, the C compiler expects that the files that contain C programs have ".c" as their extensions. If a program submitted for translation does not have this particular extension, the compiler will not translate it.

Once the program has been created, it is submitted to a **preprocessor**. This program, as its name indicates, comes before the "processor" or compiler. This program may be a totally separate program from the compiler or it may be the same compiler acting with a "different hat." The preprocessor performs tasks such as merging the contents of one or more files into the program and replacing one string pattern with another throughout the program. The preprocessor scans the entire source code looking for "preprocessor directives." These directives begin with special characters or combination of characters. For example, the C compiler merges files when it encounters the #include directory. The same compiler performs string replacement when it encounters constant definitions such as the #define directive. Notice that, in C, these directives begin with #.

When the preprocessor has finished its tasks, the compiler starts executing. The first phase of the compiler – the lexical analysis phase – examines each one of the individual characters of the source program and groups them into logical units called *tokens* or *lexems*. For instance, when a C compiler

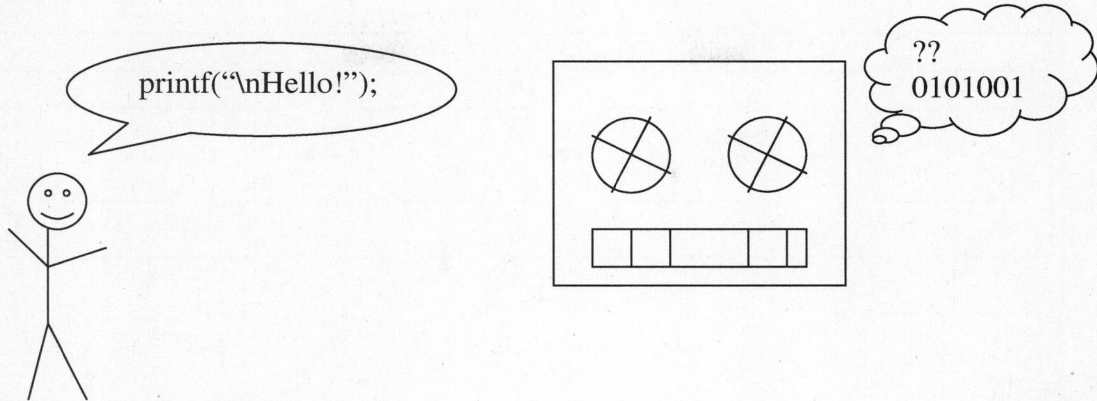

Fig. A-1 A communication gap between human and machine.

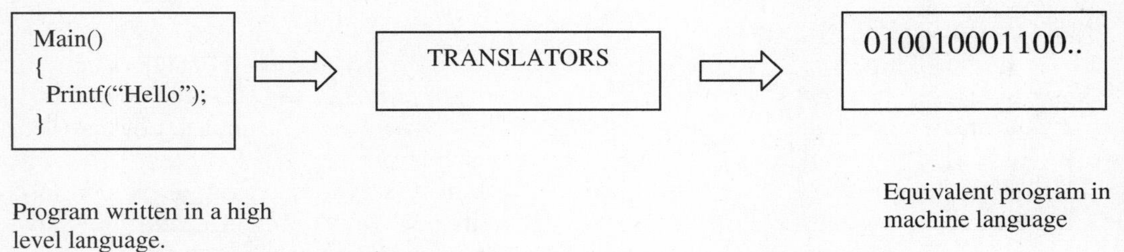

Fig. A-2 Basic role of the translators.

reads a sequence of characters like

```
if ( a > b)
  a++;
```

the compiler reads the sequence "i followed by an f" and recognizes it as a logical unit called "if" after it encounters the left parenthesis. This "if" and each one of the remaining characters comprising that sequence are recognized and translated into a predefined set of numerical code or tokens. The logic built into this phase allows the compiler to recognize every possible valid sequence of a C program. From the programmer's point of view, this phase is important because it is here that the compiler produces errors such as "unidentified characters." Consider, for example, that in a C program, the programmer types a character such as "ñ" that does not even belong to the English alphabet. When the compiler "sees" this character, it produces an error notifying the programmer that it has found an unidentifiable symbol. This type of error falls into the category of "fatal errors" because the compiler quits processing the program after it detects the error. Other errors produced by the compiler in this phase are: "program too big," and "unexpected end of file." The latter error is generally due to multiline comments not closed. For instance, the programmer may have opened a comment with "/*" but never closed it with "*/". When the lexical phase finishes its task, the entire source code has been transformed to a stream of integer numbers called tokens or lexems, as we indicated before.

The second phase of the compiler, carried out by the syntax analyzer, is also of interest from the programmer's point of view because it is here that the compiler looks for any syntax error in the C code. We can think of this phase as the counterpart of an English grammar checker. For example, assume that the programmer meant to type the assignment statement a = b; but instead he typed

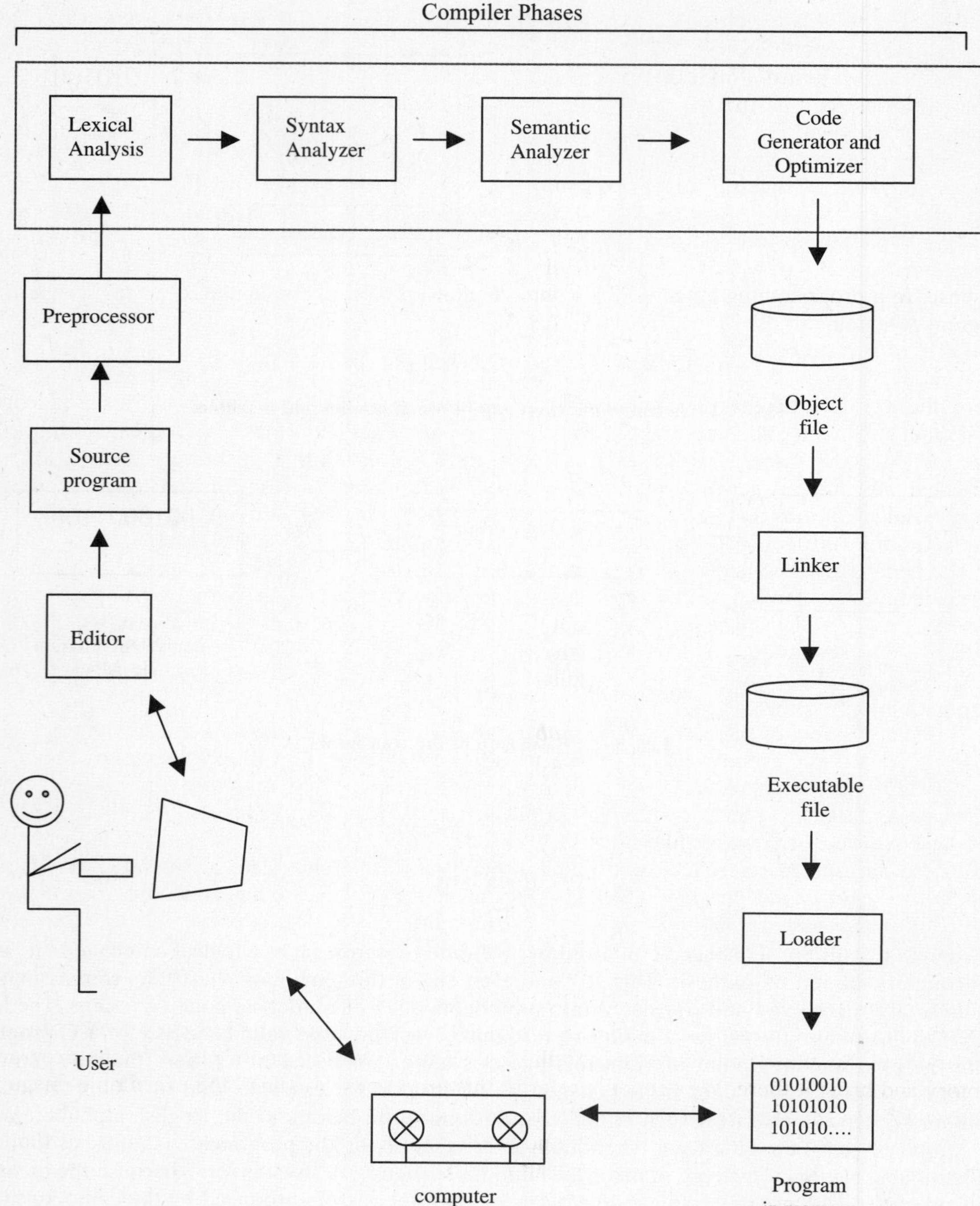

Fig. A-3 The compilation process and the linker and loader utilities.

a + + b;. The built-in logic of the syntax analyzer recognizes this as an "invalid expression" and produces the appropriate error. Other errors encountered in this phase are "missing ;", "unmatched number of parentheses," "missing function prototype," etc. In summary, we can think of this phase of the compiler as the one that checks that "every statement is grammatically correct and that all the punctuation marks are in their proper place."

The next phase of the compiler, or the semantic analysis phase, shown in Fig. A-3 as a separate phase, is sometimes combined with the syntax analysis phase. It is here that the compiler identifies statements that, although grammatically correct, make no sense in the language. Consider the equivalent situation in the English language. The sentence, "The green ideas slept furiously," from a grammatical point of view is correct. It has all the elements that a sentence may have and yet it makes no sense. In a programming language environment, consider, for example, the following Visual Basic assignment statement:

bIsTaskFinished = bIsTaskFinished + 2

where the variable bIsTaskFinished has been declared as a Boolean variable. This is a correct assignment statement and yet it makes no sense to add an integer constant to a Boolean variable. Not every compiler, the Visual Basic translator, for example, can detect this type of error. It is also in this phase that we generally get the "**warning messages**." What these messages mean is that the compiler has detected conditions that may cause some problems during the execution of the program. However, these conditions are not serious enough to stop the compilation of the program.

The **code generator** and **code optimizer** produce the final translation of the program into the corresponding machine language. According to the defaults or settings selected within the compiler environment, the code generated may be optimized for size (smaller possible code as measured by the number of bytes generated) or for speed (the fastest possible code). Most compilers favor speed over size. However, it is not unusual for a compiler to try to strike a balance between these two generally incompatible options.

The final product of the compiler is an ***object*** **file**. This file has the same name as the original file but has a ".obj" extension. This object file usually has references to library programs that reside somewhere in the system. At this point, the program is not ready to run since it has missing parts. In other words, the object file "knows" what parts are still missing but it does not know where to find them. It is the task of another system utility to resolve these references. This utility, called the **linker**, finds these unresolved references and replaces them with the appropriate addresses of the missing parts. If the linker cannot find the referenced programs, it will generate an error notifying the user of the problem and will treat this as a fatal error, stopping the linking process. If linking process is successful, the output of the linker is a file with the same name as the original file but with a ".exe" extension. This file is called an ***exe*****cutable image** or simply an ***exe*****cutable**. Using computer lingo, we can say that the program is ready "to run" or "ready to be **exe**cuted."

As indicated in Chapter 1, to execute a program both the program and its data need to reside in memory. It is the task of another system utility called the **loader** to find a place for the program in memory and bring it there. We generally refer to this process as "loading" the executable image into memory. Finally, the loader signals the CPU to start executing the program.

When the program is running we may encounter "**run time**" errors. These are some of the most difficult errors to find since they are, in general, the product of flaws in the logic of the program. Some of the most common errors of this type are addressing array locations past the last location of the array or dividing a quantity by zero. Depending on the support that the compiler provides, some of these errors may be easy or difficult to find. For example, the C compiler will not notify the user of errors that occur when addressing array elements past the last element of the array. Some other compilers like the Fortran compiler will notify the user of that type of error.

In the event of errors in the compiling, linking, or running of the program, the programmer needs to correct the problems causing the particular error. In computer lingo, we refer to this process as debugging. Once the programmer has located the errors, the source program is modified in the editor, and the compilation process starts all over again.

INTERPRETERS

In addition to compilers, there are other types of translators called **interpreters**. The main difference from an operational point of view is that the compiler translates the entire program before the program gets executed. An interpreter, on the other hand, translates and executes the program statements one at a time. As far as the internal processing that these two translators need to perform is concerned, their tasks are very similar. One advantage of interpreters over compilers is that interpreters provide immediate feedback to the user during the coding of the program. The main advantage of compilers over interpreters is that the compiled programs run faster since they need to be translated only once. To illustrate the major differences between these translators, consider the following loop written in a fictitious language:

```
While(a < 10000)
    c = a*b;
    d = a/b;
    a = a + 1
End While
```

A compiler for this language would translate each statement once and then execute it 10,000 times. An interpreter for the same language would translate, as well as execute, each statement 10,000 times. However, if the programmer makes a mistake when writing the instructions, the interpreter will produce an error message as soon as it detects the error. With a compiler, the programmer will not know about the error until much later, when the entire program is compiled.

INDEX

actual parameters, 120
address space, 2
ADT (Abstract Data Type), 229
algorithm 47
ALU (Arithmetic-Logic Unit), 4
AND, *see* logical operators
applets, 64, 241
applications in Java, 240
arguments, 117
arithmetic in number systems, 13–16
arithmetic operators, 69
arithmetic operators, order of precedence, 69
array, 155
array, declaring, 158, 164
array, two-dimensional, 157, 160, 166
ASCII (American Standard Code for Information Interchange), 24, 64
assignment statements, 67

BCD (Binary Coded Decimal), 22
binary code, 22
binary file, 195
binary search, 174
bit, 1
BOF (Beginning of File), 195
Boolean expressions, 89
bubble sort, 176
bus, 5
byte, 1

call by reference, *see* pass by reference
call by value, *see* pass by value
case structures, 97
`cerr`, 71
`cin`, 71
class, 230, 240
class interface, 229
class message, 229
closing files, 195, 197, 199
code generator, 293
comment statements, 70
compiler, 63, 290
computer, 1
`const`, 66
constant, 65
constructor, 235
`cout`, 71
CPU (Central Processing Unit), 4
CU (Control Unit), 4

data abstraction, 231
data structure, 261
data types, 65
`Dim`, 66
documentation, 70
dot operator (.), 237
dynamic data types, 269, 285

element, 156
EOF (End of File), 195, 198
equality operators, 90
event-driven programming, 232

fields, 194
file extension, 193
file streams, 199
file system, 193
`final`, 66
fixed repetition statements, 100
flowchart, 49
`for..` statements, 101
formal parameters, 120
function, 117

global scope, 126

Hamming code, 27
hardware, 1
header file, 235
heap space, 269
hierarchy charts, 50

IC (Instruction Counter), 6
`if..` statements, 95
`ifstream`, 199
implementation file, 238
`import`, 72
`include`, 71
inheritance, 231
input, C, 75
input, C++, 71
input, Java, 72
input, simple, 70
input, Visual Basic, 73
`InputBox`, 74
insertion sort, 179
instantiate, 230
interpreter, 63, 294
`iostream`, 71

IR (Instruction Register), 6

key field, 194

library of functions, 71
linked list, 261
linker, 293
local scope, 127
logical operators, 91

MAR (Memory Address Register), 6
MDR (Memory Data Register), 6
memory, 1
modular programming, 117
modulo arithmetic, 69
`MsgBox`, 74

`new`, 164, 243
node, 261
NOT, *see* logical operators
number systems, 8, 10

objects, 228
`ofstream`, 199
OOP (Object Oriented Programming), 228
opening files, 195, 196, 199
OR, *see* logical operators
output, C, 75
output, C++, 71
output, Java, 72
output, simple, 70
output, Visual Basic, 73
overloading, 235

parameter passing, 129–135
parameters, 117, 120
parity check, 24
pass by reference, 131
pass by value, 129
PC (Program Counter), 6
pointer, 132, 162, 272
positional systems, 8, 10
posttest repetition statements, 104
preprocessor, 290
pretest repetition statements, 102
`printf()`, 75
private, 127, 234
procedural programming, 228
program, 1
programmer, 1
programming, 46
programming process steps, 46
protected, 237
pseudocode, 48
public, 126, 234

queue, 274

RAM (Random Access Memory), 1
random file, 195
records, 194
relational operators, 90
repetition, 94, 100
`return`, 119

`scanf()`, 75
scope of identifiers, 123, 124
scope of procedures, 127
scope resolution operator (::), 235
searching, 171
`Select..` statements, 97
selection, 94
selection sort, 174
sequence, 94
sequential file, 195
sequential search, 171
sign magnitude, 17
software, 1
sorting, 174
stack, 271
static data types, 125, 263, 285
strings, 158, 161, 167, 169
subprogram, 117
subroutine, 117, 122
subscript, 156
`switch..` statements, 97
`System.in`, 72
`System.out`, 72

top-down design, 50
translator, 290
two's complement, 18

`until..` statements, 103–105

variable, 65

weighted codes, 22
`while..` statements, 103–105